JAZZ & BLUES MUSICIANS OF SOUTH CAROLINA

Left to right: Ron Free, Mose Allison, Lester Young, Mary Lou Williams, Charlie Rouse, and Oscar Pettiford. August 1958, 126th Street in Harlem. Photograph taken by Dizzy Gillespie immediately after Art Kane took the photograph known as "A Great Day in Harlem," for which Free and Allison were late. From the collection of Ron Free

JAZZ&BLUES
MUSICIANS OF SOUTH CAROLINA

Interviews with Jabbo, Dizzy, Drink, and Others

Benjamin Franklin V

The University of South Carolina Press

*Published in Cooperation with the South Caroliniana Library
with the Assistance of the Caroline McKissick Dial Publication
Fund and the University South Caroliniana Society*

© 2008 University of South Carolina

Published by the University of South Carolina Press
Columbia, South Carolina 29208

www.sc.edu/uscpress

Manufactured in the United States of America

17 16 15 14 13 12 11 10 09 08   10 9 8 7 6 5 4 3 2 1

Library of Congress Cataloging-in-Publication Data

Franklin, Benjamin V.
    Jazz and blues musicians of South Carolina : interviews with Jabbo, Dizzy, Drink, and others /
Benjamin V. Franklin.
        p. cm.
    Includes bibliographical references (p.   ), discography (p.   ), and index.
    ISBN 978-1-57003-743-6 (cloth : alk. paper)
    1. Jazz musicians—South Carolina—Interviews. 2. Blues musicians—South Carolina—Interviews.
I. Title.
    ML385.F86 2008
    781.65092'2757—dc22
    [B]

                                                                                        2007048831

Some of the interviews in this book were previously published:
        Tommy Benford, *Cadence* (September 1990): 13–16
        Nappy Brown, *Cadence* (April 1992): 11–14, 32
        Ron Free, *Cadence* (June 1994): 11–17, 105
        Dizzy Gillespie, *Cadence* (May 1991): 5–10
        Jack Howe, *Cadence* (July 1991): 10–14
        Etta Jones, *Cadence* (July 1991): 5–9
        Horace Ott, *Cadence* (May 1992): 14–18, 27
        Houston Person, *Cadence* (August 1990): 24–28
        Arthur Prysock, *Cadence* (December 1991): 11–14
        Johnny Williams, *Cadence* (October 1991): 9–14
        Webster Young, *Cadence* (June 1991): 9–17
All lyrics by Drink Small are used with the permission of Drink Small.
"Teardrops from My Eyes," by Rudolph Tombs, is used with the permission of Simon House,
        Len Freedman Music.

This book was printed on Glatfelter Natures, a recycled paper with 30 percent postconsumer waste
content.

To the memory of Ken Ewing

"He who leads the way saves his companion."
The Epic of Gilgamesh, translated by Robert Temple

To the memory of Kostas Yiannoulopoulos

A trustworthy Greek bearing gifts

To Michael Ullman

"Constancy is the complement of all other human virtues."
Giuseppe Mazzini, "On the Historical Drama"

CONTENTS

ILLUSTRATIONS

ACKNOWLEDGMENTS

I am grateful to the many people who helped me with this project. In the 1980s I could not have completed my work without the assistance of Thomas L. Johnson of the South Caroliniana Library. Edwin C. Breland, University of South Carolina, edited the tapes of the interviews for radio broadcast and added music to them. Robert D. Rusch published some of the interviews in *Cadence* and gave permission to publish them here in revised form. A grant from the South Carolina Committee for the Humanities (now known as the Humanities Council[SC]) permitted me to travel to interview musicians.

Allen H. Stokes, director of the South Caroliniana Library, supported my work from the beginning and was instrumental in securing funding from the Caroline McKissick Dial Fund, which enabled the publication of this book. With his encouragement, Nicholas G. Meriwether (my major associate beginning in 2005) and the Oral History Program at the South Caroliniana Library digitized old cassette tapes, recorded and transcribed new interviews, scanned images, and supported the research and writing of this book in every regard. Over a long period, Lorraine Gordon performed numerous kindnesses. I am grateful to Steven W. Lynn, former chair of the Department of English, University of South Carolina, for permitting this retired professor to retain an office in order to do my work, one example of which is this book. Kenneth Bryan and Mila Tasseva-Kurktchiev helped with computer problems. The reference and interlibrary loan departments at the Thomas Cooper Library, University of South Carolina, performed valuable service.

Individuals at this university and elsewhere who provided useful information include Kip Anderson, Dorothy Benford, Beth Bilderback, Marilee Birchfield, Daniel Brennan, Karen W. Brown, Beverly Bullock, Paul Cammarata, Karen A. Chandler, Roberta V. Copp, Gerri C. Corson, Jo Cottingham, Sara Crocker, Stanley W. Dubinsky, Joshua B. Garris, Mary W. George, Rebecca B. Gettys, Elmer Gibson, Winifred Goodwin, Jeffrey P. Green, Donald J. Greiner, Herbert J. Hartsook, Terri Hinte, Jackson Howe, Julia B. Hubbert, David Jellema, Doris E. Johnson, Jay Latham, Mary Lean, Thomas A. Marcil, Paula D. Matthews, Anthony McKissick, Natalie Mikysa, Dan

Morgenstern, Roger Mortimer, Hank O'Neal, Jennifer R. Ottervik, Scott Phinney, Aaron Pickett, Ellen Potter, Jean Prysock, Terry Sparks, John Steiner, Saddler Taylor, Michael A. Ullman, Tut Underwood, Sharon Verba, Virginia Weathers, Ann Wikoff, Crystal D. Williamson, Gregory J. Wilsbacher, Dave Withers, Deborah L. Yerkes, and Dorian Young.

INTRODUCTION

Before I moved to South Carolina from Michigan in 1976, the only jazz or blues musician I could identify as coming from the Palmetto State was Dizzy Gillespie. A decade later, supported by the South Caroliniana Library at the University of South Carolina and a grant from the South Carolina Committee for the Humanities, I attempted to document as many South Carolina jazz and blues musicians as possible. By "from the Palmetto State" I meant either born in or for a significant period a resident of South Carolina. Ultimately, I identified over a hundred of them. I interviewed a dozen of these musicians, published eleven of the interviews in *Cadence*, and broadcast the eleven, with music added, on the South Carolina Educational Radio Network. One of the programs was nominated for a Peabody Award. I wrote about my activities in "The Problem of Local Jazz History: The Example of South Carolina."[1]

Despite depositing the results of my work in the South Caroliniana Library for consultation by anybody, parts of my effort were ephemeral: people who read the interviews in *Cadence* probably disposed of the magazines in which they appeared; the radio programs were not re-broadcast. Believing in the value of the interviews, I decided to publish them as a book. As a group, they were too short to warrant book publication, so in late 2005 I began interviewing additional musicians, not only to generate enough text to interest a publisher but also because there were musicians I had overlooked earlier and because a new generation of musicians had emerged in the fifteen or so years since the time of the original interviews.

In selecting people to interview, I did not attempt to establish a theme or emphasize one aspect or style of music over another, though the disproportionate number of jazz musicians reflects my primary interest. While most of the musicians I invited to participate in this project accepted enthusiastically and often inconvenienced themselves to accommodate me, some elected not to become involved or placed unacceptable conditions on the interview.

I cannot say that the general South Carolina culture influenced some of its residents to become creative musicians or caused fledgling musicians to develop as they did; nor can I claim that there is an identifiable South Carolina sound or approach to music, as there is a "big sound," for example, with many tenor saxophonists from Texas.[2] Some South Carolinians were influenced by and probably became musicians because of local organizations, however.

If a South Carolina institution is famous for producing musicians, it is the Jenkins Orphanage, founded in Charleston in 1891 by the Reverend Daniel J. Jenkins. I was fortunate to interview two men who grew up there in the 1910s and 1920s. Both Tommy Benford and Jabbo Smith (Smith aided by Lorraine Gordon) made special efforts to speak with me. This was probably Smith's last interview, and possibly Benford's. Though diminished by time and therefore sketchy, these men's recollections are valuable because they offer first-hand impressions of the early years of the orphanage and because they are among the last—if not the last—recorded statements about it by men who were wards there before 1920. Despite having run away from the orphanage, as old men they remember it fondly, as they do Jenkins himself, who was, according to them, strict with the children, as he doubtless had to be. They mention the significance of music in the lives of the orphanage children, themselves included: upon arriving there, children were instructed on various instruments by good teachers, such as Eugene Mikell, Sr., and Alonzo Mills. Benford and Smith performed in orphanage bands that helped keep the institution afloat financially by generating income. So many of the children—including Cat Anderson, Peanuts Holland, and Ermitt V. Perry—became successful musicians that Englishman John Chilton wrote about the orphanage's musical organizations in *A Jazz Nursery: The Story of the Jenkins' Orphanage Bands of Charleston, South Carolina* (1980).[3]

South Carolina State University has also produced numerous musicians. Horace Ott, Houston Person, Ron Westray, and Johnny Williams all testify to the excellent training and support they received there. Until recently emphasizing classical music almost exclusively, its program prepared students for a career in music. One of its graduates, Ron Westray, not only succeeded as a professional musician, but he received a master's degree in music at another university (again, with a classical focus) and is, at this writing, a professor in the School of Music at the University of Texas, Austin.

The jazz program at the University of South Carolina has influenced numerous musicians, though none of its graduates is included in this book. Yet one of its retired professors is. Dick Goodwin taught students about jazz arranging, but he also demonstrated a high level of competence by performing frequently and widely, including internationally. Without being enrolled at this university, the young Chris Potter benefited from it through instruction by graduate student Bryson Borgstedt and professors John Emche and Doug Graham. Johnny Helms was graduated from this institution long before it had a jazz program.[4]

The interviewed musicians span the history of recorded jazz. Born before 1910, Tommy Benford, Jabbo Smith, and Jack Howe antedate the first jazz recording: a session by the Original Dixieland Jazz Band, a group of white musicians, in 1917, by which time Benford—and probably Smith—was already making music at the Jenkins Orphanage. During the 1920s, the Jazz Age, when Kid Ory led the first recording session by an all-black jazz group (1922), when Paul Whiteman became known as the King of Jazz, when Bix Beiderbecke appeared on and all but disappeared from the scene, and, when Louis Armstrong revolutionized jazz through recordings with his Hot Five and Hot Seven, Benford (1926), Smith (1927), and Howe (1928) recorded for the first time.[5]

Benford went on to record with such major figures as Benny Carter, Stephane Grappelli, Coleman Hawkins, Bubber Miley, Jelly Roll Morton, and Django Reinhardt; he also performed in Europe when jazz was becoming established there in the 1930s. Smith recorded with Duke Ellington, James P. Johnson, Fats Waller, and Clarence Williams and led his own group, the Rhythm Aces. The amateur Howe recorded with one of the first college jazz bands and later with Tommy Dorsey, Bobby Hackett, and Jimmy McPartland; he also participated in the Chicago jazz scene beginning in the late 1920s and knew Bix Beiderbecke.

Dizzy Gillespie (mainly with Cab Calloway), Etta Jones (with Buddy Johnson), and Arthur Prysock (also with Johnson) were full-time members of big bands; Johnny Williams has played with the Count Basie band since the early 1970s. Gillespie was an originator of the jazz movement known as bebop. Arthur Prysock had a substantial solo career and recorded with Count Basie, Bill Doggett, and Sy Oliver. Ron Free was involved with Lennie Tristano and musicians who absorbed his lessons, such as Lee Konitz and Warne Marsh. Webster Young played with Lester Young and recorded with Kenny Burrell, John Coltrane, and Jackie McLean.

In his long career, Houston Person performed and recorded frequently with Etta Jones and recorded with Gene Ammons, Ran Blake, and Horace Silver. In addition to her association with Houston Person, Etta Jones recorded with Gene Ammons, Earl Hines, and Pete Johnson and toured with Art Blakey. Horace Ott arranged music for Lou Donaldson, Nina Simone, and Joe Williams. Johnny Helms played with Bucky Pizzarelli, Red Rodney, and Clark Terry; Dick Goodwin, with Cab Calloway, Ray Charles, and Aretha Franklin. Ron Westray was a regular with Wynton Marsalis and recorded with him, Wycliffe Gordon, and Marcus Roberts; he also belonged to, recorded with, and wrote for the Lincoln Center Jazz Orchestra. Chris Potter leads his own group, is a member of groups led by Dave Holland, and has recorded with Marian McPartland, Red Rodney, and the Mingus Big Band. This abbreviated yet impressive list of associations covers many of the movements and major figures in jazz.

Of the blues musicians represented in this book, Drink Small, who began recording in the 1950s, is the one who devoted his life to music—blues and gospel—without interruption. Nappy Brown also began recording blues and gospel then, though there were, apparently, periods when he did not perform. Gary Erwin not only leads a group that performs regularly, but he has promoted the blues on radio programs, releases blues on his own label, and oversees much of the blues activity in South Carolina. Barry Walker operates a restaurant that serves as a venue for aspiring blues musicians and for his band to perform.

The musicians I interviewed speak engagingly about their lives in music and enliven their stories with anecdotes about such people as Squirrel Ashcraft, Tony Bennett, President Jimmy Carter, Miles Davis, Herman Lubinsky, Helen Merrill, Pharoah Sanders, and Sister Rosetta Tharpe. They express a dedication to their craft that usually began at an early age, though Ron Free, Jabbo Smith, and Webster Young withdrew from the big time while still in their twenties. As the interviews indicate, all the musicians with whom I spoke are significant, in one way or another.

In editing the interviews for publication, I attempted to present the musicians' words and thoughts as accurately as possible. At the same time, I was mindful of the requirements of readers, ease of reading paramount among them. As a result, in most instances I deleted "er"s, "uh"s, "you know"s, and other hesitation sounds some of the musicians use when speaking. When syntax was confusing, I clarified it.

All the musicians whose interviews appeared in *Cadence* authorized the texts that were published there, and all musicians living during the editorial work for this book had the opportunity to read and alter their interviews. Readers interested in hearing the interviews may do so at the South Caroliniana Library, where they are housed. The interviews from the 1980s were done on analog cassette tape; the more recent ones, digitally. In order to give some sense of evolving musical styles, I arranged the interviews chronologically, according to the musicians' birth dates.

Notes

1. One interview from the 1980s—the one with Jabbo Smith—was inadequate for broadcast or for separate publication. It is publishable here primarily because of the efforts of Lorraine Gordon. The essay is in *Jazz in Mind: Essays on the History and Meanings of Jazz*, ed. Reginald T. Buckner and Steven Weiland (Detroit: Wayne State University Press, 1991), 83–91.

2. Such South Carolina guitarists as Pink Anderson, Reverend Gary Davis, and Josh White played what is known as the Piedmont blues, though this manner of playing is not unique to South Carolina. Basically guitarists playing in this manner incorporated aspects of ragtime by using the thumb to play lines a pianist would play with the left hand, while using the fingers to play notes a pianist would play with the right hand.

3. Chilton's book was published in London by the Bloomsbury Book Shop. Two films exist of the Jenkins Orphanage band, both in the Fox Movietone News department of the Newsfilm Library, University of South Carolina. The first, shot on 22 May 1926, is silent; the second, made on 22 November 1928, has sound.

4. Serious musical instruction is available at other South Carolina colleges and universities, and the College of Charleston has a jazz program. I know of no state school with a curriculum in the blues.

5. In New York on 30 January 1917, the Original Dixieland Jazz (or Jass) Band recorded two takes each of "Darktown Strutters' Ball" and "Indiana." In Los Angeles, probably in June 1922, Spikes' Seven Pods of Pepper Orchestra (also known as Kid Ory's Sunshine Orchestra) recorded "Ory's Creole Trombone" and "Society Blues."

A Jenkins Orphanage band in St. Petersburg, Fla. Date, photographer, and personnel unknown. Courtesy of the South Caroliniana Library, University of South Carolina

JAZZ & BLUES MUSICIANS
OF SOUTH CAROLINA

Music is well said to be the speech of angels; in fact, nothing among the utterances allowed to man is felt to be so divine. It brings us near to the Infinite.

Thomas Carlyle, "The Opera"

TOMMY BENFORD

19 April 1905–24 March 1994

B.F. You were born in Charleston, West Virginia, and moved to the Jenkins Orphanage in Charleston, South Carolina. How did the orphanage attract talented children like you?

T.B. I never saw my mother; she died when I was young. My father and my aunt and uncle got messed up one of these years and called my brother and me to go to the Jenkins Orphanage, which was very good to us. Mr. Jenkins himself was a wonderful person, and the school was wonderful. They had kids in the school from all parts of the world—England, France, Germany—and from all parts of America. That's where I was brought up, and that's the school I love.

B.F. Did your family have to pay for you to live at the orphanage?

T.B. I don't know, but they put us there and the orphanage was lovely to us, especially Mr. Jenkins himself. I don't know of anybody who was any greater than this man because he treated the kids so wonderfully.

B.F. Was he difficult? Demanding?

T.B. He was a very nice, friendly person; but when he tells you to do something, please do it.

B.F. The reason most people today know of the orphanage is because of the great musicians who came out of there. You mentioned your brother, Bill Benford, who was a tuba player and was there with you. The Aiken brothers were there, Bud and Gus. Who were some of the other children who became musicians?

T.B. The Mikell brothers, Gene and his brother, Otto. Their father, a wonderful person, was one of the teachers at the orphanage.[1]

B.F. Was he the band leader?

T.B. He was one of them. We had three bands in the school.

B.F. Were any of them what we would now call a jazz band?

Tommy Benford. Date, location, and photographer unknown. From the collection of Dorothy Benford

T.B. We played all types of music. Any type of music you can mention, we played —from rags to marches to hymns; different songs, different types of music. Everyone you know who came out of that school was a wonderful musician.

B.F. When you played in these bands, did you just play for the children at the orphanage? Or did you play out in the Charleston community? What was your audience?

T.B. We played all over America and all over the world. Band number one got caught in London in the First World War. I was only five years old. The band director and I were the two youngest members of the band; the oldest, only seventeen. We had twenty-five kids in the band.[2]

B.F. How did they book the trip to England? Obviously it took a lot of money. Were you invited by the government? How was it set up?

T.B. Some person in England invited the band—I think it was the king and queen. We played before the queen just before the war.[3]

B.F. That must have been some band, ranging from you at age five to the oldest at seventeen. Was Mikell the leader of the group that went to England?

T.B. No. I can't remember his name, but the leader was only about fifteen years old.

B.F. Did you have adults with you?

T.B. Yes, we did, but not in the band. The matron and one of the chefs were the only two adults.[4]

B.F. How did you get there?

T.B. We took a train from Charleston to New York, and from there we took a boat to England.

B.F. Once you got to England, World War I broke out. What happened to the Jenkins Orphanage band?

T.B. They sent us back, but we couldn't come back right then. We had to wait. When we had a chance to come back, that's when we left England.

B.F. But you did play for the queen.

T.B. Yes. We played for the king and queen.

B.F. When you left the Jenkins Orphanage, you must have been around eighteen.

T.B. No. I must have been between sixteen and seventeen because I ran away, but only for a couple of weeks because they caught me. I finished my time when I was about sixteen. They didn't catch me the second time I ran away.

B.F. So what happened? This young fellow with some talent—even then a pretty good drummer—ran away from school. What did you do?

T.B. That's when I wanted to learn all types of music. I went all over Virginia, South Carolina, Florida, and Georgia.

B.F. With bands?

T.B. With bands and shows: minstrel shows and doctor shows and carnivals. I played all types of music. And that's where I am today.

B.F. Still playing the drums.

T.B. You'd better believe it. I love it.

B.F. Wasn't your first recording in 1926 with a piano player named Charlie Skeete?

T.B. That's right.

B.F. For the Edison Company in Brooklyn?

T.B. Right.

B.F. Was the music released on cylinders? On thick records?

T.B. On thick records.

B.F. Wasn't it in 1928 that you signed on with Jelly Roll Morton?

T.B. That's right. With my brother's band.

B.F. So Bill Benford and you went out as a pair? When you were doing the Carolinas and Virginia with the minstrel shows, was Bill with you?

T.B. Yes. That's why I left the orphanage—because my brother would look after me. He was leader of the band and leader of different things in the band.

B.F. After the band got to New York, how did Charley Skeete learn about you?

T.B. He learned about me through my brother. He heard my brother on tuba and liked the way he played. He wanted to know if my brother knew of a drummer, so my brother mentioned me. That's how we got together.

B.F. And the same thing happened with Jelly Roll Morton? He heard the Benford band?

T.B. That's right. That's how Jelly Roll Morton got the band, because he came here by himself and wanted a musician to finish his recordings. He heard about my brother, got in touch with him, and wanted to know if he could do any recordings with the band. He went around New York listening to different bands, and my brother's band was the band he liked. That's the band that did all of the recordings with Jelly Roll Morton.

B.F. Did he join you on the road? Or did you just record with him?

T.B. We just recorded with him. We never went on the road with him. We had only one session with him because we never went out of the city.[5] We stayed right here at home. We didn't want to travel with him.

B.F. But his regular drummer around that time was Zutty Singleton. You were just before Zutty?

T.B. No. I was with my brother's band, and that's the band he liked. And that's the band he wanted to do all of his recording with while he was here in New York. So he evidently let Zutty go and took my brother's band. In the band were myself and six other guys.

B.F. Soon after recording with Morton, you went back to Europe. You had already been there with the Jenkins Orphanage group. What took you to Europe the next time?

T.B. The next time I went to Europe was with Sy Devereaux.[6] He was a saxophonist who died shortly after that. He came to New York and got a job here playing saxophone, but he knew of my brother and of other musicians around New York at the time. He worked with different bands.

B.F. He had a gig in Paris?

T.B. Yes. He had a job in Paris and wanted me. He asked my brother if it was O.K. for him to have me. My brother said yes.

B.F. Did you record with Devereaux there?

T.B. No. I only worked one place with him, and that was the Chez France. We only worked there for a couple of months.

B.F. But soon you started recording in Paris.

T.B. Yes. Sy left, but I stayed in Paris.

B.F. You recorded with some French musicians.

T.B. Yes. With Django Reinhardt and Stephane Grappelli, with Bill Coleman, and also with some of the local musicians.

B.F. Perhaps the most famous session you had in Paris was one led by Coleman Hawkins, with Benny Carter, Django, and Grappelli. And Tommy Benford on drums. Great music.

T.B. It certainly was.

B.F. Did you ever again play with Hawkins?

T.B. Yes. In Amsterdam, Holland.

B.F. He played with a group called the Ramblers over there. Were you with them?

T.B. No.

B.F. Did you and Hawkins cross paths other than in Europe?

T.B. Yes. We did here in New York, right after he came back.

B.F. What kind of memories do you have of Django?

T.B. He was a wonderful person. He loved everybody.

B.F. So you were in France in the early '30s. You recorded in Paris a lot, but also in Hilversum and Zurich. You got around the continent a good bit. How did you do it? Did you go out with a group? Or did people call you from various places?

T.B. I went out with different groups from Paris. Just like New York here, Paris was the headquarters in Europe.

B.F. What brought you back to the United States?

T.B. I came back on account of the war.

B.F. Was getting back into the American scene easy for you?

T.B. It wasn't too bad. We ran into a storm coming back on the ship. It took us fifteen days from Lisbon to New York.

B.F. Did you have a home in New York?

T.B. No. I lived with my brother.

B.F. Who were some of the people you played with upon returning?

T.B. I played with all of them, all of my buddies. They knew that I was back in town, and they always tried to look after me and help me: Bob Greene and Benny Carter and different guys that I worked with in Europe who were here before I got back. I always try to be a nice person, and that has helped me quite a bit.

B.F. What did you think of the trombonist Jimmy Harrison?

T.B. He was a wonderful person.

B.F. You recorded with Harrison in France.

T.B. That's right.

B.F. What about Bubber Miley?

T.B. That's the guy that killed himself; he's another guy who drank so damn much.

B.F. You recorded with him early.

T.B. Yes, I did. We got together in New York. We were with different bands. He was a wonderful person and a wonderful musician. They were all such wonderful guys, too. I haven't played with a whole lot of heels; I've played with a lot of wonderful people. When you're nice, it makes you want to be with them. But when you're working with somebody that's a heel, you always think that he's greater than you are.

B.F. You mentioned Bob Greene. He's involved in what might be called the Jelly Roll Morton revival. You must get a kick out of doing that.

T.B. I do. And he's a nice guy, too. Now he's writing a book.[7]

B.F. Does he transcribe the Morton material for his band?

T.B. He does it.

B.F. They are faithful to the originals. They sound a good bit like Morton.

T.B. That's what he wanted to do.

B.F. Does the Bob Greene group still play?

T.B. Yes. But we haven't played together for four or five years because he's finishing a book. He calls me every once in awhile, and I call him.

B.F. You recorded with Noble Sissle in the early 1940s. What kind of group did he have? Was Eubie Blake with him then?

T.B. Sissle was all right, but he was not competitive with Mr. Blake. There was no comparison between Noble Sissle and Mr. Blake. Blake is the one who wrote all of the music. Sissle didn't do anything.

B.F. You played with George Lewis.

T.B. I played with him in Boston. Something happened to his drummer; his drummer's mother got very sick. I had just come off the road with Bob Wilber, and George Lewis had just opened at a place in Boston, the Savoy. The lady that ran the Savoy said, "I have a drummer for you. Mr. Benford—Tommy Benford—just came off the road with Bob Wilber. I'm pretty sure he'll help you out."

And so George told the lady to ask me to come to the Savoy. He wanted to know if I could fill this engagement for the drummer, and I said, "For how long?" He said, "For as long as I'm going to be here. I'm going to be here two weeks. Would you be able to do it?" I said, "Well, I haven't got anything else to do. It'll be a pleasure to help you." So he said, "When can you start?" I said, "When do you want me?" He said, "Can you open tonight?" I said yes. So I opened that night. And George took a liking to me. He said, "Mr. Benford, you have the job until I go back to New Orleans."

B.F. Let's return to the Jenkins Orphanage for a moment. There's a legendary figure, Herb Wright, a drummer. I think Roy Haynes, the drummer, was turned on to the drums because he heard Herb Wright play.

T.B. Both Herb Wright and Steve Wright, another drummer but no relation to Herb, were at the Jenkins Orphanage. Steve was there when I was, but not Herb. He was there before me.

B.F. But you got to know Herb Wright later.

T.B. Yes. He's the one that killed Jim Europe.[8]

B.F. What happened?

T.B. I don't know. They were in the army, in the Fifteenth Regiment out of New York. Steve Wright said that Jim Europe never liked Herb, that they were always arguing. He was always picking on Herb. Herb said once, "One of these days, I'm going to cut your throat." And the particular day came. Steve said that Herb killed Europe with a little penknife. He cut his throat.

B.F. What happened to Wright as a result of that?

T.B. They put him in prison. But he got out and died a natural death.

B.F. You continue to be active.

T.B. I do my damnedest. When you're doing something you like to do, that's it. I love to play my drums.

B.F. What drummers do you especially like?

T.B. Steve Wright was one of them. He's the one that taught me a lot. Steve and I used to hear Herb, but I heard Steve more because Herb was always up in Boston. Steve was something else. He was in the Fifteenth Regiment. Both of them were in the army together.

Mt. Vernon, N.Y., 14 March 1987

Notes

1. Eugene Mikell, Sr., was a noted music teacher.

2. The band left Charleston for England on 2 May 1914, two weeks after Benford's ninth birthday. Photographs of the band show no more than nineteen males in uniform. Two men without instruments, one mustachioed, appear significantly older than the others. Photographs may be seen at http://www.sc.edu/orphanfilm/orphanage/symposia/scholarship/hubbert/images/jazznursery1.gif and http://www.forachange.co.uk/browse/2142.html. Four other photographs of band members in England are known to exist. In addition to using the photograph available at the second link listed here, Howard Rye reproduces three other pictures in "Visiting Fireboys: The Jenkins' Orphanage Bands in Britain," *Storyville* 130 (1 June 1987): 137–43 (the photographs are on pages 139–41 of this British publication).

3. Benford refers to King George V and Queen Mary, for whom the band never played, though at least the king was scheduled to hear it. At the Anglo-American Exposition in London, however, it performed for Queen Alexandra (mother of King George V) and Empress Maria Feodorovna of Russia. British royalty did not invite the band to the exposition. Its appearance resulted from the interest of James Hurtig, a theater director and agent from Dayton, Ohio. For information about the band in England, see John Chilton, *A Jazz Nursery: The Story of the Jenkins' Orphanage Bands of Charleston, South Carolina* (London: Bloomsbury Book Shop, 1980), 15–21, and Jeffrey P. Green, *Edmund Thornton Jenkins: The Life and Times of an American Black Composer, 1894–1926* (Westport, Conn., and London: Greenwood Press, 1982), 37–42 (a photograph of the band, also present in Rye, appears on page 41).

Despite Bedford's recollections, evidence indicates that he did not accompany the band to England in 1914. From the official passenger lists, Howard Rye publishes the names of orphanage musicians who arrived in Liverpool aboard the *Campania* (Cunard Line) on 13 May 1914 and departed Liverpool aboard the *St. Louis* (American Line) on 5 September 1914. Although there are discrepancies between the two lists, the name of Tommy Benford appears on neither, while that of his brother, William, is present on both (Rye, "Visiting Fireboys," 138, 142). On 24 April 2007, I asked Benford's widow, Dorothy, about the discrepancy between her husband's recollections and Rye's findings. She said that Benford—an honorable man with a good memory—often spoke of having been with the band in England in 1914. They wed in 1951.

4. The conductor of the band was ten-year-old John Garlington. I cannot identify the adults to whom Benford refers.

5. Benford recorded at four Morton sessions. See discography.

6. Benford went to Europe in 1932, returning to the United States in 1941.

7. I cannot determine if Greene published the manuscript Benford mentions.

8. James Reese Europe led the band of the 15th National Guard Regiment of Harlem, though it was renamed the 369th Regiment in France during World War I. After the war Europe led the band in the United States until being stabbed to death by Herbert Wright in Boston on 9 May 1919.

JACK HOWE

22 February 1907–16 October 1992

J.H. I was born in Oak Park, Illinois, in 1907, and moved in 1917 to Chicago's North Side. I was very fortunate that jazz was at its height at that time in Chicago. There was the Austin High Gang which were playing all over the town, and I got to know them and play with them. So I had the good fortune of growing up with Benny Goodman, Bud Freeman, and Jimmy McPartland.

B.F. Did you just run around with them? Were they neighborhood chums?

J.H. No. I would go every place they played, so every once in awhile they'd ask me to sit in, and I got to know them. Later in life that became very useful because I got to play with them; and when they had sessions, I was invited.

B.F. That must have been in the 1920s.

J.H. Late '20s.

B.F. If they asked you to sit in, you must have had some musical proficiency. How did you get interested in music?

J.H. I got a saxophone for Christmas in about 1924, and my brother went over to the corner drug store to get some records; he came back and said, "I'm sorry, but these are the only ones they had." They were the Gennett records that the Wolverines made. So I learned by playing with the Wolverine records. It was a pretty good way to learn. If you play along with these records cut in Richmond, Indiana, you can't fail to absorb some of the fine ideas.

B.F. Was there a black jazz scene that you were part of or that you listened to—like Earl Hines, who was in Chicago around that time?

J.H. I'd go out to the Grand Terrace where Earl Hines was playing just because I loved his playing, but I wasn't particularly interested in that kind of music at that time.

B.F. You went off to college.

J.H. Right. I went off to college in 1926, to Princeton, where I found two or three fellows that had had the same introduction to jazz that I did. They were Wolverine

Jack Howe at his eightieth birthday celebration, F Street Club, Washington, D.C., 22 February 1987. Photographer unknown. From the collection of Jack Howe

fans, and Bix fans in particular.[1] Squirrel Ashcraft was really the father of getting that type of jazz started among the younger people in Chicago. He'd have sessions at his house and invite all the musicians that came to town to come out to them, and they became famous sessions. When the depression came along, musicians didn't have many jobs; they'd come out for those sessions every Monday night—and this went on every Monday night for about eight years.

B.F. This was after the Princeton career?

J.H. It was right after, in the 1930s. We had all left Princeton by that time.

B.F. So Squirrel was a little older than you?

J.H. He was one year ahead, as was Bill Priestley, the other member that continued to play with us up until the present time. And when Bill graduated in '29, he went to New York and played with some of the New York bands and got to know Bix. As a matter of fact, he had an apartment right underneath Bix, and he used to play seconds to Bix. That's how he learned to play the trumpet; he was a guitar player. When he heard Bix, he changed his mind.

B.F. Even now at Princeton we hear about the famous Triangle Club, and the Triangle Club had a band during your tenure there.[2]

J.H. That was our band, using the name of the Triangle Club, and we played the Triangle Club for two or three years, traveling all over the country. We were the stage jazz band, and of course in order to make it feasible we also played in the pit band, which was sort of odd because none of us could read music.

B.F. Were there many college bands at that time?

J.H. Very few. Those that were were playing dance music, sort of society music, as we used to call it. There were very few college bands playing what we call jazz.

B.F. You recorded with the Princeton Triangle Club Jazz Band. Was that the first college jazz recording?

J.H. It probably was the first, although shortly thereafter Dartmouth had a group that recorded.

B.F. It was 1928, I think, when this first session was held in New York, for Columbia. How did it come about?

J.H. We really weren't in the big time. We recorded these at the same time as we were recording the Triangle records. So we just had them—we talked with the people there and told them we were interested in jazz music, and they said, "Well, let's cut it." So we cut it for our own sake. It was never put out by Columbia as a commercial record.

B.F. But the music exists. What happened?

J.H. They later made some collective Princeton records. Columbia issued them under the auspices of Princeton, I presume. We got records of them for our own use.

B.F. At this same 1928 session, you also recorded as the Equinox Orchestra. What's the story?

J.H. The Equinox was a hotel in New Hampshire that the band used to play for during the summer. So they called themselves the Equinox Orchestra at Princeton. They weren't permitted to use the Princeton name when they played commercial jobs outside of Princeton.

B.F. So of the sides recorded that day in 1928, half were by the Princeton Triangle Club Jazz Band and half by the Equinox Orchestra, but featuring the same personnel. Another odd thing about the session has to do with Bix Beiderbecke himself. You tell a humorous story about collectors wanting these sides very badly because of their vague connection with Bix.

J.H. Squirrel had known Bix when he was at Lake Forest, in Chicago, so Bix had invited us to come over to a Paul Whiteman rehearsal one night. We went. When it was over, Bix said, "Come on, I want you to hear a band," and he took us to the Park Central, where Ben Pollack was playing.[3] This was like old times because Jimmy McPartland was playing, and Benny Goodman; Jack Teagarden was first trombone, and Glenn Miller was second trombone. It was a real all-star group—Ray Bauduc drumming—and it was just a wonderful evening for us. Later, Bix sat in with them. It was an evening we'll all remember forever.

Bix was feeling real good, so we said, "Bix, you gotta come and play a chorus on our record tomorrow." "Great, I'd love to. I'm staying right here in the hotel. If you'll wake me up, I'll come." So, unfortunately, we got there in time to wake him up, but the cold shower didn't. He couldn't make it. We couldn't get him in condition to come over and play, and we had to go because the time didn't permit our staying.[4] But it's always been strange because people seem to associate the fact that because Bix intended to be there, their collections wouldn't be complete unless they had that record. So much for collectors.

B.F. What was your involvement with music after Princeton?

J.H. When I got back to Chicago, I found that Squirrel, who had gotten back there a year earlier, had organized Monday night jam sessions. This was in 1930, and the depression was at its height then. All the musicians used to come out there—and particularly the ones from out of town who had heard about these sessions—and these became rather famous sessions. That's where I got to know all the musicians. It so happened that they needed a clarinet because their regular clarinet player was Pee Wee Russell who, for some reason which we won't go into, never was able to play after ten o'clock. And Rosy McHargue, who was then with Ted Weems—who, it being the depression, started booking his band on Monday nights, too—wasn't available. They were usually without a clarinet player, so they put up with me, which was fine for me. I guess music is a little like tennis: if you play with better players, some of it rubs off.

B.F. Were any of these sessions recorded?

J.H. Yes. They were all recorded on home recorders. They were discs—some of them were iron; some, aluminum—and later they were done on tape. These sessions went on for four or five years. The recordings were always very inferior, and they were made strictly for the players to listen to playbacks, which they enjoyed. It struck me as funny: seeing Jimmy McPartland and Bud Freeman listening to the playbacks, saying, "That's me. That's me." But they were enthusiastic about it because they were able to play for themselves. No audience was ever allowed; it was just for the players, so it was a real jam session. Jam sessions that are played to entertain people aren't really jam sessions, in our book. These recordings were later released in a series called Informal Sessions at Squirrel's by Hank O'Neal in New York. There are four albums released as More Informal Sessions (MIS), and these have become collectors' items.

B.F. These were the depression years, and you were working in Chicago. You were not a professional musician, getting paid for playing.

J.H. Exactly. I was never a professional. In fact I usually didn't even get expenses.

B.F. Nonetheless you were good enough to participate and they liked you well enough to bring you into the group. You were a major part of it because you were one of the Sons of Bix from the beginning.[5]

J.H. That's true. I knew them, and I gathered them all together when I was asked to get a group for the Princeton reunions.

B.F. When did the reunions start.

J.H. In 1975.

B.F. What happened to you, Squirrel Ashcraft, and the others during the war years?

J.H. The three of us that went to Princeton—Squirrel, Bill Priestley, and me—all went into the services, so we knew that this was going to be our last get-together. Squirrel arranged to have a recording made at World Broadcasting Company. We cut a record there called *Monday Nights* that was mainly for ourselves. Later, Decca, which was the company that actually made them, put them out as a regular release.

B.F. This was just before you went into the service?

J.H. Right.

B.F. When did you go in?

J.H. I think it was '41.

B.F. Apparently you were able to keep up connections during the war.

J.H. That's true. And with Spencer Clark, an integral part of the Sons of Bix. He learned to play bass sax by sitting outside the window where Adrian Rollini was playing, and became friends; when Rollini left, Spence took his place in the California Ramblers and has since been established as probably the best bass sax player in the country. He played for four or five years abroad—in Germany, mainly—and then came back to New York and played with all the New York bands.

B.F. During the war, when you and Ashcraft were there and the guys would pass through, what would you do, get together and have sessions?

J.H. Correct.

B.F. Is that music available? Where the sessions recorded?

J.H. Yes. Everything was recorded—poorly, but recorded.

B.F. Somebody—Ashcraft, you, or somebody else—must have thought that the music you were playing for your own enjoyment had value or else the recordings would not have been made. Recording instruments in the '30s and '40s were rather primitive. Who was in charge of the recordings? Did you have just one microphone? What were the technical aspects?

J.H. Usually just one microphone. They turned out remarkably well for the conditions, but the conditions were bad.

B.F. Whose idea was it to record these sessions?

J.H. Mainly Joe Rushton, the bass saxophone player who was with Red Nichols for ten years.[6] He was the enthusiastic one about this. He managed to swipe most of them and hide them, but he finally coughed them up. We collected them and had records made. It started out being on discs, and they were very primitive. Some of them were aluminum and some were iron. And then it went to tape, and the tapes weren't very good. In fact, we started out with something that seemed to be paper tapes, but we later got into better tapes. They were good enough for us; we were just using them for ourselves. We didn't intend to ever have them published. But Rushton was in charge of all of that, and he took charge of the tapes. That material has surfaced.

B.F. What happened to you after the war, and how did you keep up your musical interests?

J.H. Squirrel and I both went back to Evanston, as did Bill Priestley, who had been overseas with the army most of the time but had passed through Washington several times, and we had sessions then. The three of us wound up back in Chicago. We thought we ought to have a reunion, so we started having a Bix festival, which went on for four years. They were called First Squirrel, Second Squirrel, Third Squirrel, and Fourth Squirrel. These were reunions of the people that had played at the Squirrel sessions.

B.F. Squirrel Ashcraft is an elusive figure to me. He played the accordion, the piano. Was he the nominal leader of all of this from the beginning?

J.H. Yes. He was really the catalyst that brought these all together. First of all, he knew all the professional musicians, and he helped them out in many ways. When they came to Chicago, particularly during the depression when things were tough, he had a big home and also a cottage next to it, which was really a home, and they could stay there for weeks at a time, if necessary. So he became the musicians' friend. All the musicians loved Squirrel. When he said there was going to be a session, it was amazing how many people wanted to be there. He had a good sense of humor, but I think jazz musicians of this era all had a good sense of humor; that was one of the things that brought them together. The sessions were always fun.

B.F. Presumably Benny Goodman did not have. Did you know him well enough to judge his sense of humor?

J.H. No. As a matter of fact, Benny never attended any of the sessions. Maybe that was one of the reasons. Whereas I knew him slightly, I didn't know him like I knew the other fellows.

B.F. What about the 1950s.

J.H. This was a time when Squirrel went off to Washington with the CIA and left Evanston. However, he didn't know whether he was going to like it there, so he had us live in his house. We lived in the House of Jazz, as it is known in that area. So all of the musicians continued to come. We had sessions for the next ten years. Any time a musician from out of town came in, he'd call up—"Could we get together some musicians?"—and we'd have sessions. We had wonderful sessions; at least we thought they were wonderful—the neighbors didn't.

B.F. Did Squirrel return for some of the sessions?

J.H. He'd return about once a year. We'd have them whenever musicians came to town, so we'd have five or six of them during a year. Jam sessions is what they were.

B.F. Was Jimmy McPartland still on the Chicago scene?

J.H. He was in New York, mainly, but he came to Chicago frequently because his family was there. His sister was there. She had married Jim Lanigan, who was the bass player with the original Austin High Gang and was also with the Chicago Symphony. So he was there, and Jimmy's brother, earlier.[7] Jimmy was very popular in Chicago, so he frequently came out with a band.

B.F. What happened after you moved out and Squirrel moved back in?

J.H. He didn't return. He stayed in Washington the rest of his life, so we lived in the house for nineteen years. We had nineteen years of jazz.

B.F. Did you buy the house from him?

J.H. No. We just lived there. Oddly enough, something rather interesting happened in the '60s at that house. In the early 1960s, Jimmy McPartland was staying out at the house, and our son, who was thirteen years old, was playing the ukulele then, which pleased me very much. And so before Jimmy left, I said, "I wish we could get Jackson interested in playing cornet." Jimmy said, "I'll take care of that." He got hold of Jackson and said, "Get your ukulele"; and he played with him. So when they got through, Jackson came to me and said, "I gotta have a cornet." So I said, "All right.

There's only one way to learn to play jazz"—which is what he wanted to play, oddly enough—"and that is to get a group together."

Squirrel had left his record collection—and this is a famous record collection—at his house. I said, "If you get all of the kids you think might be interested in music and bring them over to the house, we'll introduce them to this and see if they want to form a band." Which is exactly what happened. He brought about twenty kids over, without their instruments, and I said, "We're just going to listen to this music." I watched them. When they got through, I said to those that could tap their feet in time and seemed interested, "You, you, you . . . ,"—I picked seven of them—"we're going to start a band." They were all in the seventh and eighth grades. I said, "When you go into high school next year, you're going to be the best band in the school." Well, they said, "My goodness. Evanston has four thousand students, and they have wonderful bands. But we'd like to do it anyway." They liked that music.

This was quite a band. We had two drummers, two guitar players, a piano, and a clarinet player. So I had one of the guitar players change to bass and one of the drummers to trombone—got the proper combination—and we started. I said, "You're going to learn the way these other fellows did that you're listening to, and that is you're not going to see a note of music for a year. You're going to play the way they did; you're going to learn by playing with records." They loved this idea because it was fun. Practicing isn't very much fun if you have to try to read music, particularly when you don't know how, or if you have to do it for school. They were doing it for fun. So they formed this band. Within a year, when they went into high school, there was a contest for the best band in Chicago. Thirty-seven schools entered it, and these kids—who were called the Windjammers—won first prize of a thousand dollars, and there wasn't anyone close.

The reason I mention this is that two of these players are now members of the Sons of Bix; and all of them turned out to be fine musicians. Two of them are in symphony orchestras now, and they learned by starting with jazz. People say that jazz would ruin you for classical music, but the reverse was true. They are two of the finest clarinet players in the country: Ron Hockett and Billy Rappaport. Billy Rappaport is with the Atlanta Symphony, and Ron Hockett is with the Marine Band in Washington, D.C., the one Sousa once conducted, and plays at the White House all the time. He's the featured soloist in the Marine Band, which is known as the top band in the country, and you have to have symphony status to play in it. He majored in music at Princeton and earned his master's degree at Northwestern University.

B.F. Obviously you have kept your Princeton connections. You're famous for playing reunions there.

J.H. Well, 1975 was the forty-fifth reunion of my class, and they asked me to get a band together for it, so I did. This was like a dream band. I had always dreamt of being able to pick the people I wanted in this band. Of course, most of them were ones I had known at the sessions at Squirrel's, though some were younger. Two of them were ex-Windjammers.

One of them—and the main one, and why we called it the Sons of Bix—was Tom Pletcher. As a matter of fact, his father was at Yale the same time Squirrel, Bill, and I were at Princeton. We knew him, and he went with Red Norvo for years.[8] But Tom has become the outstanding Bix-type player in the country, so he was our first choice. And then we rounded up some of the others, including Bud Wilson. Bob Haggart later wanted to play with the group because we had known him and told him about it, so he said he'd play. So we founded a group. However, every one of the seven was from a different state, so we'd all fly into Princeton every year, which was fine. We weren't in it for the money; we just wanted to go to the reunions.

We arrived an hour before we were going to play, and it just went off. It was very successful the first two years, and after that just automatically every class for the fiftieth reunion—which is the big reunion—had us for twelve years. In fact, this band had so much fun playing at reunions that we said we ought to do it again. Bob Haggart at that time was living in Mexico, so he drove from New York to Mexico every year. We said, "Bob, when you drive to Mexico, can you come via the Carolinas? Two of us—Spencer Clark and I—live there, and we'll get the other guys to fly in and we'll have a band reunion every year."[9] He said, "Fine." We arranged it so that when Bob drove to Mexico, on the way back we'd have a session, and then on his way back the next year we'd have another session. We started to play every year in the Carolinas, and we did recordings then. These recordings were done in the studio, so the recording quality is much better.

B.F. Do you play other than at the reunions and the sessions in the Carolinas?

J.H. I only play when the Sons of Bix play; I don't play with any other band. We play every year in Vero Beach, Florida, at a private party. We've played the last three years in Hartford, Connecticut. And we played twice in Chicago. We've flown all over the country to play, mainly because of our reputation from the records we made at Princeton. It's a band that has a great following, although it only plays four or five times a year.

B.F. All of this began in 1928 when, as a Princeton student, you had that New York session with the Princeton Triangle Club Jazz Band and the Equinox Orchestra—fully sixty years ago. So you, one of the real jazz veterans, are carrying on the tradition of Bix Beiderbecke.

J.H. Ron Hockett planned a surprise eightieth birthday party for me in Washington, where he lives. He invited me to come up there on the pretense that we'd just have a little session with him and a couple of friends. When I arrived, everything was fine; we went for dinner at the F Street Club. When I walked in, here were all the Windjammers, and all the Sons of Bix. They came from fourteen different states at their own expense to attend this party. So that was quite a tribute. That's where I got the title of the only saxophone player they know who peaked at age eighty.

Chapin, S.C., 11 November 1987

Notes

1. Howe refers to cornetist Bix Beiderbecke, a member of the Wolverines.

2. The Princeton Triangle Club produces musical productions by undergraduates and takes the shows on tour.

3. The Park Central is a New York hotel. Beiderbecke was then a member of the Paul Whiteman band.

4. Another version of this episode appears in an appendix to *Bix: Man & Legend*, by Richard M. Sudhalater and Philip R. Evans, with William Dean-Myatt (New Rochelle, N.Y.: Arlington House, 1974). On Friday, 30 March 1928, in New York City, "Bix, Bill Priestley and Squirrel Ashcraft make the rounds of places featuring jazz bands, including a visit to the Little Club on 44th Street to hear Ben Pollack's orchestra. Priestley persuades Bix to sit in on Princeton Triangle Club band's record date the following afternoon and Bix consents. At the last moment, Whiteman calls an afternoon rehearsal and Bix has to miss the Princeton date" (367).

5. The Sons of Bix were musicians, headed by Squirrel Ashcraft, who played in the manner of Bix Beiderbecke.

6. Joe Rushton played with Red Nichols from 1947 until 1963.

7. Jimmy McPartland's sister was Ethel; his brother, Dick, was a jazz guitarist.

8. Trumpeter Stew Pletcher played with Red Norvo in the 1930s.

9. Spencer Clark lived in Webster, N.C., from 1971 until his death in 1998.

JABBO SMITH

24 December 1908–16 January 1991

With Lorraine Gordon

Because Smith was suffering the effects of a stroke when I spoke with him in 1987, communication was difficult. At the Greenwich Village home of Lorraine Gordon, owner of the Village Vanguard, we conversed for perhaps forty-five minutes.[1] Smith was as forthcoming as possible, though his speech was so slurred that I had difficulty understanding it and later could not easily transcribe the recording of the interview. Working separately, Gordon and I were able to establish the following dialogue. Despite its brevity and occasional lack of clarity, I include it in this book because of Smith's significance and because it is probably his last interview. Toward the end of our conversation, Gordon offered firsthand observations about Smith's performances during the last years of his life. I include her comments because of their historical importance and because they flowed naturally from the discussion between Smith and me, which occurred in her presence and with her assistance. His silence while Gordon spoke implied agreement with all she said.

B.F. When were you at the Jenkins Orphanage? What was life like there?

J.S. I went there in 1914; I came out in '25. I spent a long time there—about ten years—just traveling with the band. That's the way they had to make money to support the orphanage. We went down to Florida in the winter and come up here in the summer.[2] I did a lot of traveling with the band.

B.F. A lot of good musicians came out of there. Did you know Eugene Mikell, one of the music teachers and band leaders?

J.S. No, he was before my time. I came there in 1914 and he just came back from Europe. That's when I got there, when the band just got back from England.[3]

Jabbo Smith at the home of Lorraine Gordon, New York City, 14 March 1987. Photograph by Benjamin Franklin V

B.F. Why did the orphanage band tour?

J.S. That's the way he had to make money 'cause the state didn't offer nothin'. For the city of Charleston during that time to give an institution $250 was a lot of money. So the city give him $250.[4]

B.F. Could you describe the orphanage—the building, the grounds?[5]

J.S. The orphanage building was once the old marine building, and that building took care of sick seamen. The orphanage got the building after the marines left it. There were tombstones in the back from where it was used by the marine building. The kids who played there thought the place was haunted, and naturally—with tombstones and kids running around playing tag—they always felt that it was a spooky place. And then the city jail was right next to it, which also filled the kids' heads with stories of kidnappings.

B.F. Can you remember what happened when you reported to the orphanage? What did you do?

J.S. I was six years old when I went there. The first thing they do is send you out on the farm for two years. I was working on the farm and taken in the store. In Ladson, the people willed Mr. Jenkins this land—two hundred sixty acres out of Ladson.[6] So the young kids, they send them out to the farm. So you get a farm life out there, then you come on back to town and get back to people. I guess because I was living out of town I got a chance to see people. Like they put you in the band because the band had grown.

B.F. What was it like going to the city of Charleston after having lived on a farm?

J.S. Well, they call you a yard boy when you come back from the farm to come to the city in Charleston. The farm is in Ladson. But when you come to Charleston you come there as a yard boy. You didn't do nothin' until the guy calls you and they tell you what you're goin' to do—shoemaker or baker or anything. They tell you, "You come here. You come here." So they was pickin' for the band. I guess that was Mr. Jenkins's way of doing it, because people lived down town so he got us so all could play all the instruments—all the brass instruments. And so anyway, I learned the trombone and things like that.

B.F. Who taught you to play?

J.S. Alonzo Mills taught me. Yes sir; he was the teacher I knew. He showed all the musicians I know during my time. I stayed in there from 1914 to 1925.

B.F. Some of the good musicians from the orphanage were trumpeters. Did any of the children there with you become professional musicians?

J.S. Gus Aiken and his brother, Gene.

B.F. Any others?

J.S. The Benford brothers and Peanuts Holland.

B.F. How did you end up leaving the orphanage?

J.S. I came out and went to. . . . They sent me to Georgia, but no sooner than I got in there I messed up. I shot myself in the leg. They sent me back home from Georgia.[7] Mr. Jenkins said, "What did you do?" He did the best he could for me. "So, too bad," he said. He took my body around there and told me these things—"I'll let you go," because I ran away all the time. He let me go from there and he gave me nine dollars. That's what the kids take to survive.

B.F. Where did you go from the orphanage?

J.S. I went to Philadelphia because I wanted to come up North, 'cause I didn't like the South at that time. So I went out to Philadelphia and got a job. I used to run away all the time. When I would run away to Jacksonville, people would hear me there. Little bands would pick me up. When I got to Philadelphia, I went back to the place where I was working at. Harry Marsh, he heard me, and he wanted me to come down and make an audition with him. I went down there and I went to work for him.

B.F. Was your first recording in 1926 with Thomas Morris?

J.S. I can't remember, but that's what everybody seems to remember. I don't remember. At that time, my first recording was with Clarence Williams. Charlie Irvis, he was playing trombone with Clarence Williams. So he got me the date. In any event, I made that thing with Eva Taylor, "If I Could Be with You One Hour Tonight." That was a big hit for her at that time.[8]

B.F. In 1927, not long after your first recordings, you made a great record with Duke Ellington. How did you become affiliated with him?

J.S. Bubber Miley, he was with Duke Ellington. He was on those tunes like da-da-da-da-da—jungle tunes. He did that kind of mess. I guess he must 'a got sick, or something happened.

B.F. Did you know Miley?

J.S. No, I didn't know him. I heard him on the records with Duke. That was his popular record—what's the name of it, that popular record he made? I recorded it with Ellington. Oh, "Black and Tan Fantasy."

B.F. Why did you replace him for that recording of "Black and Tan Fantasy"?

J.S. This is what happened. Something happened to Bubber 'cause Harry Carney, he used to come down to Small's all the time.[9] Whatever happened to him, he must have told Duke about me. And so they got me to fill in there.

B.F. Did you tour with Ellington? Or did you just appear at that one session?

J.S. I just recorded with him, including "What Can a Poor Fellow Do?"

B.F. How did the Louisiana Sugar Babes get together?

J.S. What's his name? You'll pick it up. He was playing oboe with the show that he was with, *Keep Shufflin'*. That's the show he was with. We just took the oboe player—I forget his name—and me and Fats and Jimmy.[10] They were working all the time. I used to save my money. Fats spent a lot of money and they borrowed money. I run into them that way. They played in concerts and took me along, just three of us, two pianos and a trumpet. I was just tagging along.

B.F. Did the group tour?

J.S. No. Louisiana Sugar Babes was just the name for recording. Fats Waller's numbers and Jimmy's—I guess because they were together.[11]

B.F. Then how did you put together your group, the Rhythm Aces?

J.S. I just used them to record the date—Omer Simeon, Buford. 'Course they belonged to other bands. Omer Simeon, he was with the Earl Hines band. Lawson Buford, he was staying in New York, but we went to Chicago together. I stayed there at his house. Therefore, I got jobs they'd taken along with me. I had him and Omer Simeon—bass player, no drums; four pieces.[12]

B.F. Did your records sell well?

J.S. No. They didn't sell too much 'cause Louie had it all locked up. His recording company, Okeh, had better advertising.[13] He had that all locked up. But the people said they liked him better, which was all right.

B.F. After the Rhythm Aces, you essentially disappeared from the scene. What happened next, during the depression?

J.S. I was in Milwaukee and worked for the Flame Club. I messed around with them for about six years. Wasn't nothin' else to do.

B.F. And you stayed in Milwaukee? Did you make your living from music?

J.S. Yeah, I was there. We worked every night at the Roof—biggest place there.[14]

B.F. But why did you soon give up playing?

J.S. Nothin' happened. I just put everything down. I went to work with Avis Rent-a-Car. That's what happened during that time.

B.F. Seemingly out of the blue, two albums of your recordings from 1961 recently appeared. Lorraine Gordon released them on Jazz Art Productions. What's the story?

J.S. There's a guy named Steiner, John Steiner. What he did, he come and get me. He had an idea. He recorded a lot of musicians, and his idea was to do the same as a lot of other people do. But she heard this thing and bought these things from John Steiner.[15]

L.G. [Lorraine Gordon]. John Steiner is a jazz collector of importance in Milwaukee. He loves jazz. He's always followed Jabbo's career. He made these recordings when Jabbo had not been playing. He took him out to the University of Chicago with Marty Grosz and others and put it down, but didn't do anything with it. Maybe he didn't think they were good enough. He left them on the shelf for twenty years. When I visited John with Jabbo in Milwaukee—he has an enormous record collection—he just played a little snatch of this. I said, "Is this Jabbo?" I'd never heard these. He said yes. So he sent me a cassette of more of it. For two years I asked what he was going to do with them. He was going to sell them to someone else. I said, "Look, I'm willing to buy them." It took two years to get him to sell me the tapes, which I then put out as records, even though they may be rough and not thoroughly rehearsed. To me, it was the most valuable legacy I'd ever heard of Jabbo in those years.

There was nothing of Jabbo in '61. I didn't care if Jabbo just played two notes on it—it's so important. Perfect they're not: I left everything on the records—all the takes, starts, starting again, bloopers. I just thought it was an historic document to have.

B.F. So it's Jabbo Smith, many years since his last recording. Is that the last Jabbo recording we have to this point?

L.G. There's a wonderful session he had in Holland with Ralph Sutton on piano and a Dutch bassist and drummer. The drummer has a big band in Holland. He got Jabbo into a recording studio there when he was still playing good trumpet. I was there with him. I offered to buy those tapes. Here's a man who has shelves full of tapes of musicians who came through Holland, and he does nothing about them. I almost got him to agree to sell them to me, but he backed off. So I haven't got those tapes.

B.F. So they've not been released?

L.G. Never—and they're beautiful: Jabbo sings on them, and plays trumpet. Ralph Sutton's on piano.

B.F. When was that?

L.G. Around 1981—early '80s. I'm determined someday to get those things.

B.F. This past February, I was surprised to learn that the legendary Jabbo Smith remains active. Thumbing through the *Village Voice*, I saw an advertisement for Don Cherry at the Village Vanguard. The ad said, "Featuring Jabbo Smith." As far as I know, there's only one Jabbo Smith. I didn't know what had happened to him. What knocked me over was that this was the real Jabbo—and there he was on the same bill as Don Cherry, generations removed from Jabbo. I assume that Cherry backed Jabbo's singing. Who were the other musicians?

L.G. Jim Pepper on sax, the wonderful tuba player Bob Stewart, Kirk Lightsey on piano, and Ed Blackwell on drums. A first-rate group.

B.F. So Jabbo remains active. Lorraine, you were recently in Berlin with Jabbo, who knocked out that audience with his singing.

L.G. Yes. That was Philharmonia Hall—two thousand people in this beautiful concert hall in the round. Very elegant. Modern. Don Cherry's group played, like, three numbers at the beginning, and they're pretty far out, but not as far out as some of the other groups there. Then, Jabbo came out at the end of their three numbers. He just sat down in the front of the stage and opened up his mouth and sang—and the audience just was stunned because this was the last thing in the world they thought they were going to hear. The first thing they really loved was that, Jabbo. It struck a chord. He got encores and encores. It was beautiful.

B.F. Last year, 1986, Charleston, South Carolina, welcomed back its own—those native sons who had made a name in music. The most famous of them all and the highlight of that gathering was Jabbo. Jabbo, you've been so active; are you planning more gigs?

J.S. No.

L.G. It's all my fault. He suffered a couple of strokes. Three days before he went on with Don Cherry at the Vanguard, during rehearsal he suffered a minor stroke and went totally blind. We had him in and out of many hospitals. But come the night of the opening, Jabbo was there and he sang. He performed six nights, and he could barely see. Nobody really knows that. So I say he's a real showman. I don't know what I have planned for you next, Jabbo.

B.F. Is there anything you'd like to add.

J.S. I can't think of anything.

L.G. This has nothing to do directly with Jabbo, but the Reverend Jenkins's daughter, Olive, is a friend.[16] She's alive and well and living up here in Westchester. We see her occasionally. She's a good friend of Jabbo.

B.F. Do you know what happened to the Jenkins Orphanage records?

L.G. I would hope that the city of Charleston has them. I don't know. I would think they should have. They certainly preserved the building that was the original orphanage. If they have the records, it would be fantastic.

B.F. John Chilton wrote about the orphanage. Wouldn't you know it: an Englishman documents an important aspect of American culture.

L.G. Generally Europeans are more interested in American culture than the Americans are.

B.F. All the discographies come out of Europe, for example.

L.G. Charles Delaunay. Brian Rust.[17] We don't really know what our culture is. We need other people to tell us.

B.F. Alas.

L.G. Alas.

New York City, 14 March 1987

Notes

1. For the nature of the friendship between Smith and Gordon, see Lorraine Gordon (as told to Barry Singer), *Alive at the Village Vanguard: My Life in and out of Jazz Time* (Milwaukee: Hal Leonard, 2006), 36–38, 179–86.

2. Smith means that he and the band returned to Charleston in the summer.

3. A letter (dated 25 July 1914) from Jenkins in London to Eugene Mikell in Jacksonville, Florida, indicates that Mikell did not accompany the band to London. The letter is reproduced in Jeffrey P. Green, *Edmund Thornton Jenkins: The Life and Times of an American Black Composer, 1894–1926* (Westport, Conn., and London: Greenwood Press, 1982), 39. The band left Liverpool on 5 September 1914 and returned to Charleston by the end of October. See Green, 42, and Howard Rye, "Visiting Fireboys: The Jenkins' Orphanage Bands in Britain," *Storyville* 130 (1 June 1987): 138.

4. In this response, "he" and "him" refer to the Reverend Daniel J. Jenkins, who ran the orphanage.

5. Smith's response to the question was so garbled that Lorraine Gordon summarized it as best as possible.

6. Ladson is approximately twenty miles northwest of Charleston.

7. By "home" Smith means the orphanage.

8. Smith first recorded with Thomas Morris in 1926. In 1927 he recorded with Clarence Williams on a session led by Eva Taylor. See discography.

9. Smith refers to Small's Paradise, a Harlem club where in 1926 he played with the Charlie Johnson band. Harry Carney was the baritone saxophonist with the Duke Ellington band.

10. Smith refers to Garvin Bushell. In 1928 Smith, Bushell, James P. Johnson, and Fats Waller were in the pit band of *Keep Shufflin'*, an all-black musical financed by Arnold Rothstein, who apparently fixed the 1919 World Series. When Rothstein was murdered, funding ceased, and the touring show, including Smith, became stranded in Chicago. Smith, Bushell, Johnson, and Waller recorded as the Louisiana Sugar Babes. Smith misremembers the details about the group. See discography.

11. Among the tunes in *Keep Shufflin'* are "'Sippi," by James P. Johnson, Clarence Todd, and Henry Creamer and "Willow Tree," by Fats Waller and Andy Razaf.

12. The musicians on the first Rhythm Aces recording (January 1929) are Smith, Omer Simeon, Cassino Simpson, and Ikey Robinson. Tuba player Lawson Buford recorded with the group in August 1929. See discography.

13. Smith refers to Louis Armstrong. Smith recorded for Brunswick.

14. Smith refers to the Wisconsin Roof Ballroom.

15. Smith means that Steiner recorded the material released on Jazz Art.

16. Gordon refers to Olive Aston Harleston.

17. Gordon refers to Frenchman Charles Delaunay's *Hot Discography* and Englishman Brian Rust's *Jazz Records*.

DIZZY GILLESPIE

21 October 1917–6 January 1993

B.F. What was the scene in Cheraw when you were young? What led you to music?

D.G. Maybe it was my father having all those instruments around the house. Or that the school I was going to, Robert Smalls, came into some instruments when I was in the fifth or sixth grade. The principal of the school was a cornet player named Mr. Lynch.[1] He organized a band, and of course they didn't have too many instruments.

When they got down to me, the only instrument they had left was a trombone. I said, "I'll take it." I was so small that I could only reach to about the fourth position. But I took it anyway and learned how to play the scale. I learned how to play the chromatic scale. Eventually my next-door neighbor came into a trumpet—his father bought him one—and I fell in love with it. I asked him if I could practice on it, and he said yes. He was just like my brother. In fact, I called him Brother Harrington.[2] I used to practice on his horn and go to school and play the school's horn.

After that, my third grade teacher, Miss Alice Wilson, formed a group—which was a band with three singers and some dancers—for a performance called a minstrel show at the school. She taught two of my cousins and another boy to sing; she taught me to play the trumpet, although she never knew how to play it herself and could only play in B-flat. She taught Bill McNeil how to play the trombone; she played the piano herself, only in B-flat. We had two drummers. At that time, in the early 1930s, they didn't have one drummer: one drummer played the bass drum, and one drummer played the snare drum. We did the minstrel show, and that developed into us playing together outside at dances. So we started playing for dances—for the white high school, for rent parties. We got famous, and we started playing out of town a little bit, like in Darlington or Florence.

I was around twelve or thirteen or fourteen years old. We became very famous in our hometown as Wes Buchanan and his Dixie Stompers. Wes Buchanan was a bass drummer. The reason it was his band was that he was a good dancer. He got out in

Dizzy Gillespie at the University of South Carolina. Date and photographer unknown. Courtesy of the South Caroliniana Library, University of South Carolina

front of the band and danced. His mother had a little money—not much—but she had a stipend from the government: two of her sons were in the army. It seemed like a lot of money in those days. For example, my mother did a family's laundry for a dollar and a half, and that took care of our four children.

 B.F. Your father had died by then, so the burden was on your mother?

 D.G. Yes, he died; and then the bank closed up with the money.

 B.F. When you were with Wes Buchanan, did you play jazz? Stock arrangements?

 D.G. No. We didn't know how to read, so we played halfway sanctified and halfway jazz.

B.F. Did you solo on trumpet?

D.G. Somewhat.

B.F. You stayed in Cheraw for a while.

D.G. Only through ninth grade. I finished high school at Laurinburg, North Caro-lina.[3] There was another school there—Coulter Memorial Academy—that had a very expansive program. They had a guy who only taught music. My friend Norman Powe wasn't in Miss Alice Wilson's band; but he decided he wanted to be a musician, so he took up the trombone.[4]

He was taking lessons from another guy named Ralph Powe. Ralph Powe was a genius. He didn't go into music because he got a scholarship to Tuskegee, and he later moved to Brooklyn and became a lawyer for all these left-wing organizations. If a communist got in jail, Ralph Powe was the lawyer. He was a very fine lawyer. He was a fine musician; he taught Norman how to read for the trombone. Norman taught me, but he taught me the bass clef. So I could read it before I could read the treble clef. Norman and I finally wound up going to Laurinburg together. We were room-mates, and we were in the band together.

Laurinburg is very famous for sports, and for basketball particularly. Some of its alumni are Sam Jones, Wes Covington, Charlie Scott, and Jimmy Walker. But it so happened that the principal's son was a trombone player and the dean's son was a trumpet player. They graduated at the same time, so they didn't have a trumpet player or a trombone player. A girl from my hometown who was studying to be a nurse there told Mr. McDuffy that there were two musicians she knew on her street that could play pretty good and would be interested in a scholarship to come to Laurin-burg. So they got in touch with us, and we accepted.[5]

B.F. So they recruited you to come there?

D.G. Yes.

B.F. I imagine that the music scene at Laurinburg was good.

D.G. Yes. They had a Mr. Barnes, who was an alto saxophonist. After him, they had a very fine teacher named Shorty Hall, Sylvester Hall from Tuskegee. He was a master. He played solo trumpet at the 1919 World's Fair. He was there only for my last year.

B.F. At Laurinburg, did you feel your life going toward music?

D.G. Definitely.

B.F. How did you make the transition from student to performer?

D.G. I was pretty good. I could read very well; I could read stock arrangements, such as "Casa Loma Stomp" and "King Porter's Stomp" and "Mule Face Blues." All of the stock arrangements used to come out of the bands: Casa Loma, Chick Webb. We used to play them, and they were pretty hard. So when I left Laurinburg, I could read very well. I went to Philadelphia, and it didn't take me one week to get a job, and I didn't even have a horn. My brother-in-law went to the pawn shop and bought me one.[6] I went to work at a place called the Green Gate Inn.

B.F. Did you go to Philadelphia because of your brother-in-law?

D.G. My mother moved to Philadelphia while I was in school, and I was ready to move then. They decided that I should stay there until the end of the term. Within five or six weeks, I had four different gigs—steady jobs—and each one paid a little more money.

Then, I went with Frankie Fairfax. I stayed around Philadelphia for two years. In the interim, Frankie Fairfax's whole band quit him, and that's when I went into the band. Tiny Bradshaw came through and took Frankie Fairfax's whole band down to Charlotte, North Carolina. I also had a chance to play with Charlie Shavers and Bama, and that gave me another breadth of experience.[7] Then, they cruised me over to New York to go with Lucky Millinder. I stayed there for a while, but Lucky decided—even before he heard me play; he was taking me on the recommendation of Charlie Shavers and Bama—to keep Harry Edison. I don't blame him, because Harry Edison was really a good trumpet player. But then, Harry Edison left and went with Count Basie. By that time, I went with Teddy Hill to Europe.

B.F. Following that, though, weren't you with Cab Calloway for a long time?

D.G. I was with Cab from '39 to '41. That's the longest I stayed with one band.

B.F. How was it playing with him? We all know the spitball episode.[8]

D.G. It was purely a professional band. It was the best band in our profession.

B.F. Was Chu Berry still with Calloway when you were there?

D.G. Yes. And Hilton Jefferson was the lead alto player. He was some musician. Cab could get any musician he wanted, because he paid the money.

B.F. Around the time you left him, the scene uptown at Minton's started to develop.

D.G. I never worked at Minton's. I was just a jammer. But Monk and I were close, and Kenny Clarke and I were close—and Nick Fenton and Joe Guy and Scotty.[9] In the daytime, we'd call up one another. We'd learn something and show it to the other one.

I remember one time I brought up "How High the Moon." I was playing down on Fifty-second Street, and the Nat "King" Cole trio was also at the club. I heard them play this tune, and I didn't know what it was. I was enthralled with it. It changes keys so many times. I came up and taught it to Monk. We started playing it up at Minton's, and that guy started writing tunes based on "How High the Moon"—Benny Harris did. That was some era in music. I don't think there will ever be another era just like that. There will be greater eras in our music, I'm sure, because we are traveling forward all the while in music, but they will remember that era.

B.F. Wasn't it Jerry Newman who recorded those sessions at Minton's?

D.G. Yes, with his wire recorder.

B.F. Were you aware that he was doing it?

D.G. No, but it didn't make any difference.

B.F. When that music was released, one of the tunes was called "Kerouac." Was Jack Kerouac hanging around there then?

D.G. Later.

B.F. Did Bird ever hang out there?[10]

D.G. He was still in Kansas City then. But all the modern musicians hung out there. Bird came to New York eventually.

B.F. You left Cab Calloway in '41.

D.G. I then went with Ella Fitzgerald's band. Chick Webb had just died. I was only with her for two or three weeks. Teddy McRae was the straw boss.[11] I think they fired him, and Taft Jordan became the new straw boss. He kept the guys that he wanted. Then, I went with Charlie Barnet for a couple of months. I was lonesome in that band; I was the only black guy in it. I said we should get some more blacks, and he asked who I would suggest. I said, "Get Joe Guy." So he got Joe Guy, and we hung out together.

B.F. You played with Coleman Hawkins on Fifty-second Street. Isn't it supposed to have been the first truly bebop group? Wasn't Oscar Pettiford in it?

D.G. No. The first real bebop group was mine with Oscar Pettiford. We were coleaders. We had Max Roach and George Wallington. And then Don Byas came to work at the Onyx Club, and he played with us. Officially he wasn't a member of the group, but he was a musical member. Then, we broke up, and Budd Johnson and I got a group together across the street at the Downbeat. A little after that, I finally located Charlie Parker after trying to get him by telegram. I formed a group with Charlie Parker, Ray Brown, Stan Levey, and Al Haig at the Three Deuces. Then we went to California.

B.F. I'd like to talk about "Night in Tunisia."

D.G. I wrote it when I was with Benny Carter, around 1941.

B.F. I'm interested in the title. Originally it was called "Interlude," wasn't it?

D.G. No. It was "Night in Tunisia" at first. Lyrics became a problem; Sarah Vaughan couldn't find them. I don't even know where I got the name Tunisia. No one knows about Tunisia. I know I didn't.

B.F. You didn't write it as a dedication to that country?

D.G. No.

B.F. So Sarah Vaughan had a problem with the lyrics at her recording session.

D.G. Yes. So we changed it to "Interlude."

B.F. You took your group to Billy Berg's club in Los Angeles, which was the first time bop went west. The jazz histories say the gig wasn't terribly successful.

D.G. It was successful monetarily, but it was too fast for the people out there. They couldn't get with it. The guys out there were trying, too. There were guys in California from the East: the Candoli brothers.[12] The younger guys were beboppers. They were copying all of our records. We went to California, and they were making records right and left out there. Charlie Parker was going that way, and I was going this way. Even Slim Gaillard.

B.F. You and Bird first got together in Earl Hines's band?

D.G. I met him when I was with Cab Calloway, but we got together with Earl Hines in '42.

B.F. Did you two really hit it off immediately?

D.G. Very well. Unprecedentedly so.

B.F. What kind of leader was Hines?

D.G. He was a great leader. He gave us a free rein.

B.F. So he encouraged the new music?

D.G. That's right. We had to play his arrangements, naturally.

B.F. In 1946–47 you signed on with RCA records and made some great recordings with them. Also at that time, you formed your first big band. You brought in Chano Pozo. How did you get in touch with him?

D.G. Through Mario Bauza.[13]

B.F. You found a young composer, George Russell, who wrote "Cubana Be" and "Cubana Bop."

D.G. It was a collaboration of three of us. George Russell wrote and arranged the introduction, I wrote and arranged the middle part, and Chano Pozo—who couldn't write—composed the part after mine. And then George Russell took what I had done in the front and meshed it into an ending. I think that was the greatest collaboration of any three musicians in the history of the world. Even in classical music there hasn't been anything to equal that.

B.F. A few years after you left RCA, you went into the record business yourself. You had Dee Gee Records in Detroit.

D.G. My friend Dave Usher and I were partners. He ran it.

B.F. You were the first jazz musician the State Department sent overseas, in 1956. How did that come about?

D.G. I was working in Washington, D.C., and got a call from Adam Powell, the congressman, who was a fan and who was close to jazz because of his wife, Hazel Scott.[14] I went down to the House office building and was confronted with all of these newspapermen. Then, the Reverend Powell stood up to make a speech. He said, "I want to propose that the United States send its only exportable item overseas to represent us in cultural circles. And that is jazz. And I propose that we build a big band for Dizzy Gillespie to take." I almost fainted. It came to pass. But Adam Powell was the one who thought that up.

B.F. About your duet with Max Roach at the White House on "Salt Peanuts," with President Carter sitting in on vocal—was it impromptu?[15]

D.G. At the concert that afternoon, I brought President Carter a book called *Bahá'í Administration*. He was sitting on the grass. I started over to give him the book, and Willis Conover said, "Hey, where are you going, man?"[16] I said, "I'm going over here to speak with Jimmy Carter." He said, "Did you get permission?" I said, "Permission? I know the dude." So I walked on over with the book under my arm, and nobody stopped me. I said, "Mr. President, I have a present for you." He said, "Thank you very much." He didn't recognize me, though, with my jaws down.[17] So he took the book with a smile—he's a nice guy—and I went on. When I got up on the stand and started playing, that's when he recognized me. All the time I was on the stage, he was waving at me.

Afterwards, we were standing in the back, and I saw some Secret Service men go toward the toilets, where the president had gone. I was talking to Benny Carter, Hazel Scott, and Mary Lou Williams when I felt something grab my hand. I thought it was another musician, but I saw the people I was talking with looking strangely; so finally I turned around and almost fainted—it was the president holding my hand.

He told me how much he enjoyed the performance. So I told Max, "Max, after everybody is finished, you and I are going to do a duet, so keep your sock cymbal out."[18] I had played the White House for President Carter and for the Shah of Iran and his wife, and I played "Salt Peanuts" then. He remembered it and wanted me to play it. So I said to myself, "If he wants 'Salt Peanuts,' he's going to have to work for it." I said, "Ladies and gentlemen, our president has asked for 'Salt Peanuts.' I will play it if he will come up here and sing it with us." He was embarrassed; he got all red in the face. I said, "Come on; we'll teach it to you." I went down to the edge of the stand and put out my hand; he grabbed it, and I pulled him up. We practiced on the stage. He did it out of time, but he meant well. But we did it, and it went all over the world.

B.F. That was also one of Charles Mingus's last outings.

D.G. I almost cried. I'll show you what a man Jimmy Carter is. Somebody told him that Mingus was there in a wheelchair and couldn't walk. Jimmy Carter got up and went over to where Mingus was, put his arms around him, and said, "We're happy that you are here," and hugged him. Mingus was crying.[19] President Carter was the warmest president we've had. He felt humanity in his heart. He's my favorite president.

Englewood, N.J., 21 March 1987

Notes

1. Lynch's given name is Leonard.

2. Brother Harrington's given name is James.

3. Gillespie attended the Laurinburg Technical Institute from 1933 to 1935, but he was not graduated until many years later.

4. Norman Powe became a professional musician, recording with Louis Armstrong and Doc Wheeler in the 1940s.

5. Catherine McKay told Frank McDuffy, the principal of the school, about Gillespie and Powe.

6. This man, named Bill, was married to Gillespie's sister, Mattie Laura Gillespie.

7. "Bama" is Carl Warwick.

8. During a 1941 engagement in Hartford, Conn., trumpeter Jonah Jones threw spitballs at drummer Cozy Cole. After Cab Calloway, the leader, blamed Gillespie for the incident, and he and Gillespie fought, he fired Gillespie. For accounts of this event by Gillespie, bassist Milt Hinton, and Calloway, see Gillespie's *To Be or Not to Bop: Memoirs* (Garden City, N.Y.: Doubleday, 1979), 128–33.

9. Gillespie refers to Thelonious Monk and Kermit Scott.

10. "Bird" is Charlie Parker.

11. Ella Fitzgerald sang in the Chick Webb band. When he died in 1939, she assumed its leadership. A straw boss manages a band for its leader. Often the straw boss is a musician, a member of the band.

12. Gillespie refers to trumpeters Conte Candoli and Pete Candoli.

13. Trumpeter Mario Bauza played with Gillespie in the Cab Calloway band.

14. Hazel Scott was a jazz pianist.

15. The event was the White House Jazz Festival, 18 June 1978.

16. Willis Conover hosted the influential "Voice of America Jazz Hour."

17. Gillespie refers to the unorthodox technique of puffing out his cheeks when playing the trumpet. He means that President Carter would recognize him if he, Gillespie, were playing because the president had seen him perform and would remember Gillespie from his cheeks, if not his playing.

18. A sock cymbal, also called hi-hat, consists of two cymbals that the drummer closes by depressing a pedal with the left foot. Their touching creates a "ching" sound.

19. Charles Mingus died on 5 January 1979.

ETTA JONES

25 November 1928–16 October 2001

B.F. Weren't you born in Aiken, South Carolina?

E.J. I was born in Aiken, but never lived there. We moved to Detroit, where I stayed until I was about three, and then I stayed in New York for the rest of my life.

B.F. So you are really a New Yorker. You were on the road with Buddy Johnson at age sixteen. He's a South Carolinian. How did you two meet?

E.J. I was on the amateur hour at the Apollo in 1944. I happened to go there on a Wednesday night, and I left with him on Friday. His sister was expecting a baby, and in those days you didn't appear on stage expecting.[1] That was a no-no. The Buddy Johnson band was appearing that week. Every Wednesday night was the amateur hour, and I happened to be there that Wednesday. I went the previous Wednesday, but didn't get on. There were too many, so they said to come back next week.

B.F. Were you off on your own then?

E.J. No. I was living with my parents, with my mother.

B.F. And you were only about sixteen.

E.J. Yes. After everyone left the Apollo, I stayed. Joe Medlin, who was the vocalist with the band, told me to stay because Buddy Johnson was looking for a vocalist. Buddy and I sat at the piano, on the empty stage, and he played "Please, Mr. Johnson." Another young lady was there, but she didn't know the songs; but because I listened to the juke boxes, I knew everything, word for word, note for note. So when I started singing "Please, Mr. Johnson," he said, "That's Ella. That's Ella."[2] Of course, you sing like what you hear. That was the beginning.

B.F. He signed you up and your mother didn't object?

E.J. I went to my mother and begged her—it was in the summer, so I was out of school—and she said, "Yes." I never went back to school. I left on Friday with Buddy Johnson.

B.F. Did you win the talent show?

Etta Jones. Date, place, and photographer unknown. Used with the permission of HighNote Records

E.J. No. I almost got booed off the stage. I started in the wrong key. They used to have a hook there to pull people off the stage, and a man would shoot a gun and dance all over the stage. Puerto Rico, they called him. But he didn't get me.

B.F. You became a professional right then and did not finish high school.

E.J. Yes. They taught me the arrangements right there on the bus. Our first stop out of New York was a dance in Delaware. We toured the South and went to Chicago and Baltimore.

B.F. When you went south, did you get a lot of the hassles everyone always talks about?

E.J. No. I didn't run into any. The fellows would get off and get my food. Because I was so young, they would look after me like I was a little girl, which I was. I didn't think so then, but now I know that I was.

B.F. Your schooling must have been finished in the bus. They taught you.

E.J. They taught me, and I learned everything from them.

B.F. Did you stay with Buddy Johnson when Ella came back?

E.J. She couldn't leave the baby immediately, so I stayed about a year. Then, she went back with the band.

B.F. Was Arthur Prysock with the band then?

E.J. No. I was before Arthur Prysock. Joe Medlin was the male vocalist then. Arthur came after I left.

B.F. Did you record with Buddy Johnson?

E.J. No.

B.F. Didn't you first record with yourself as leader, with Barney Bigard?

E.J. Right. Georgie Auld was on it, and Leonard Feather. Leonard Feather instigated it. He was on piano because the pianist didn't show up. He wrote "Blow Top Blues," and maybe "Evil Gal Blues" and "Salty Papa Blues." In '45 or '46—after I left Buddy—I went to the Onyx Club, and Leonard Feather used to frequent the Onyx Club. He heard me singing there and got me my first record date, so I sang his songs.

B.F. With whom were you at the Onyx Club?

E.J. I was a single, but Stuff Smith was there with Jimmy Jones on piano, Stan Levey on drums, and John Levy on bass.

B.F. Did your mother say anything when you left the band and went out on your own?

E.J. No. I would have died if she hadn't agreed to let me go. When I went with Buddy, he was like my guardian, and he would fine the fellows if they would curse. They were all wonderful men. It was a really wonderful learning experience.

B.F. How did you get together with Floyd "Horsecollar" Williams, which was just after the session with Barney Bigard?

E.J. He's a sweetheart. He was with the Savoy Sultans, and I used to go to the Savoy. We got to be friends. I recorded something with him, with Pete Johnson. Horsecollar and I became friends from that.

B.F. This was just after the war. Didn't you record around that time with RCA under your own name?

E.J. Yes, I was with them for three years.

B.F. You weren't yet twenty.

E.J. No. The sides were released, but nothing ever happened with them.

B.F. The ones with Horsecollar Williams have been released on Savoy, though they were originally on National.

E.J. One time, I think I made a big mistake. Victor wanted me, and National wanted me. National was a small company; RCA was a big company. Billy Eckstine went with National. All you could hear was Billy Eckstine. I went with Victor, and you couldn't find me. National was a company that pushed whoever was on their label. In other words, sometimes you should take a small slice of pie instead of a large one. It might be more beneficial.

B.F. Was it primarily a black label?

E.J. I don't think so, but it might have been. They really pushed Billy Eckstine: "Cottage for Sale," "I'm in the Mood for Love," "Prisoner of Love." They were every-where. I don't know if they were cross-country, but in New York that's all you could hear.

B.F. How did Earl Hines become interested in you?

E.J. I was working at a small club on 145th Street in Harlem, between 7th and 8th, and he was getting ready to take out a small group of all-stars: Art Blakey, Bennie Green, Jonah Jones, Tommy Potter. Earl wanted a female vocalist. He had a male vocalist. This fellow, Dave Turner, came back to see me and told me he'd take me to see Earl. I auditioned for Earl, and he took me instead of Dave. He told Dave that he'd send for him later, but never did. I stayed with the group, and I felt so bad for a long time. But Earl Hines had great taste in vocalists. After all, Billy Eckstine was with him, as was Sarah Vaughan. I stayed with Earl for two and a half years.

B.F. Didn't he also have Helen Merrill?

E.J. Aaron Sachs was with the band, so Helen, his wife, would join him out in Cali-fornia.

B.F. So she wasn't on the road with the band, but you were?

E.J. Yes. We were working in Los Angeles and stayed there about six months. When Helen came—Earl was a wonderful guy—Earl said, "Are you a vocalist, too? I'll use you while we're out here." So he started using both of us. He would make a produc-tion thing, and Helen would sing four bars, and I would sing four bars. Helen is a mess. She's my buddy. She'd say, "Etta, the harmony is so corny." So we would go out onstage and laugh. Earl would get angry with us.

We had a song which went, "It's so nice to have a man around the house," and at the end we would go into barbershop harmony. Helen would say, "Etta, the harmony is no good," and so when we got to the end, we would start laughing. We could not sing it. Earl threatened us. People would come out of the restrooms, bartenders would listen—people wanted to see if we were going to sing this part. We would start laughing uncontrollably. I told Helen that we were going to get fired. Earl gave us a reprimand and said, "Listen. This is no joke. This is your job."

Helen would always frighten me before we went on. She'd say, "Etta, don't look at me, and I won't look at you." We agreed that when we got to that part we'd turn our backs. But when we did that, we could feel each other's vibrations, and both of us would start laughing again. It was terrible. And so one night, Osie Jonson and Ben-nie Green pushed us out of the way, and they sang the end. The people used to just die laughing. She stayed with the band when we were in L.A. She recorded with us. I had a solo on "Charlie, My Boy"; she liked real hip tunes, like "'Round Midnight." She liked modern, out changes. We had a ball.

B.F. There was also a male singer with Earl Hines then, Lonnie Satin.

E.J. Earl started the amateur hour at the Oasis in L.A., and Lonnie Satin won three or four weeks in a row. He just recorded with Earl; he didn't go on the road. He wanted to go into acting. I just wanted to stand in front of the band and sing. I'm just a flat-footed singer. I never aspired to be in the movies. I have accomplished exactly what I wanted to do. I always wanted one hit record, which I had in '59 with "Don't Go to Strangers," and the Grammy nomination was icing on the cake.[3] I never dreamt that would ever fall my way. I'm grateful for it. The other stuff I don't want, although I would like to sing a sound track. I would just want to be so good; I wouldn't want to be mediocre. I would want to be exceptional; I would want it to be so real.

B.F. There's a story about you with Earl Hines, and it has to do with Bennie Green and the trombone.

E.J. He was teaching me to play the trombone. I've forgotten it now because I haven't picked up the trombone in years. I played a few notes. I was learning how to read. He'd write something out, and he'd show me the positions on the horn. I would take his horn home. I sounded pretty good, but maybe it was because it was Bennie's horn.

B.F. Was Earl Hines a good leader?

E.J. Oh, yes. And he paid his men well. I remember one time we were working in Chicago, but they didn't have a cabaret license or something and I couldn't work. They stayed there about six weeks, and I went back to New York. He paid me for the whole time. He didn't have to do that. He could have paid half.

B.F. When you recorded with him, it was for the obscure D'Oro label, reissued on Xanadu. Earl Hines himself sang around that time.

E.J. We had a duo together. Earl wanted all of us to introduce a song, or each one had a specialty in the show. We all knew Art Blakey's speech. Everyone used to mouth it with him. Art Blakey would say, "Just to show you that the African rhythms are no different from our very own. . . ."[4]

B.F. One of the great losses in jazz history is when Earl Hines had Bird and Diz—no recordings of that band exist.[5]

E.J. I worked with Charlie Parker after I was with Earl. We worked a club together. I sang a song then that he had recorded with Earl Coleman, "This Is Always." I sang it, and Bird backed me.

B.F. Who else was in that group?

E.J. Walter Bishop was on piano; Kenny Dorham or Red Rodney on trumpet.

B.F. It must have been soon after that that you had a session for King.

E.J. Yes.

B.F. Around that time, you seem really to have started making it as a singer.

E.J. Yes.

B.F. Then, soon after that to Prestige?

E.J. Right.

B.F. And that's when you had "Don't Go to Strangers." Who was your producer there?

E.J. Esmond Edwards. Esmond produced my first album and a number of them after that. Then, he left.

B.F. Did you get royalties for "Don't Go to Strangers"?

E.J. I saw some, but mainly what I reaped was the work I got from it. I'm still working from it.

B.F. After "Don't Go to Strangers," how many albums of yours sold?

E.J. I don't know. All of them would sell if you could find them. A lot of companies only put out what you ask for. Like Diana Ross: you can go into any store and buy her albums, but you can't go into any store and buy mine. So there's no telling how they would sell unless they're in the stores to be sold.

B.F. You've had a long affiliation with Houston Person. Did that start when you were with Prestige?

E.J. No. We've been working together for about eighteen years. We were booked on the same job. He was booked in Washington at this club, and so was I. We had passed each other briefly during the years—a passing acquaintance—but without really knowing each other. We worked together, and it worked well. When we first started working together, we would both do other things. After awhile, we said that we worked well together and decided to make it a real twosome. I went to Japan with Art Blakey, and when I got back, I did things with Billy Taylor and with Cedar Walton. Then, I just started working with Houston solely. I didn't take any jobs without him. When they asked, I said, "We work together." He did the same thing.

B.F. Things come full circle. You worked with Cedar Walton, who was a great piano player with Art Blakey, who played with Billy Eckstine, who was with Earl Hines. And Houston Person is from South Carolina.

E.J. I used to work with Art a lot. He would call me for gigs. The musicians kept me working. As Dizzy said, "Old Cadillacs never die, they just fade away." That's what Art Blakey is going to do.[6]

B.F. You went from Prestige to Muse. You've done a lot of albums for Muse.

E.J. I don't know the number, exactly, but it is at least seven or eight, or ten, maybe.

B.F. Have you always selected your own material and sidemen? Or do you have an A&R man set it up?[7]

E.J. Houston sets it up with the musicians. We talk about it, but most of the time he chooses the musicians unless there is someone especially that I want. I choose my own songs.

B.F. Everyone who listens to you hears Billie Holiday. I hear some Dinah Washington in you.

E.J. I love Billie; Dinah and I were friends. Billie Holiday was my inspiration. After hearing her "Fine and Mellow"—that song just did something to me.

B.F. Did you know her?

E.J. No. I met her maybe twice, and I saw her many times on stage. Just to watch her was a treat, whether she opened her mouth or not. There was some kind of air about her.

B.F. You mentioned Diana Ross. I did not like the movie *Lady Sings the Blues*.

E.J. I won't comment on that. I'll stay in neutral there; I won't say a word. Reach your own conclusion.

B.F. We have talked about Billie Holiday and Dinah Washington, vocalists out of the past. What singers do you listen to these days?

E.J. I like Lorez Alexandria, Betty Carter, Carmen McRae, Sarah Vaughan. Of the newer singers, Gladys Knight—I think she's wonderful. I don't like all the music that the singers sing today. That's not my type of music. I like standards. Most of the songs I sing are standards. Every now and then, I'll sing an original, but I haven't found an original that's outstanding.

B.F. Where are the young singers who are more or less in your vein?

E.J. I don't know. I ask them what songs they'll have to remember. Their music advocates free love—not that I'm holier-than-thou or that I'm all that wholesome—but I like a good lyric that's not jumping into bed in the next line. I like a lyric that means something, one that can be around two hundred years from today. And folks will be glad that the lyrics are around.

I don't sound like Etta James, who can sound like the real blues singers. And Aretha Franklin's sound is mixed with the church and the blues—that feeling is all in there. I never sang in a choir; I never sang in church. Maybe that's why I don't have that certain thing that they have. I like the blues, and Aretha is wonderful. At age nine she sang "There's a Land Where We'll Never Grow Old"—which is wonderful.[8] I like Maxine Weldon, but I don't hear too many standards from her. She does a lot of originals, but I heard her do "But Beautiful," and that was but beautiful.

B.F. Do you listen to instrumentalists as well as singers?

E.J. Yes. That's how I usually learn my songs, by listening to the horns. Sometimes, people say that I sound like a horn. I used to listen to Sonny Stitt and Gene Ammons and Houston. I get a lot of licks from them. I would learn the song from the way they were playing it. Maybe that's where my style comes from.

B.F. You've been with Houston Person for a good while now. What's it like working with someone that good for so long?

E.J. Houston and I sort of jelled. It was like bacon and eggs, macaroni and cheese. He knows how to play with me, and I know how to sing with him. And he's such a fine person and such an easy guy to work with. Sometimes I want to kill him. We have our spats and our ups and downs, but we smooth them out, and no one could turn us around or change our minds about working together. We'll go out that way. He's a wonderful guy. My career will end working with Houston. When something works, why knock it? If it's not broken, don't fix it.

Secaucus, N.J., 13 March 1987

Notes

1. Ella Johnson sang with the band of her brother, Buddy Johnson.
2. Ella Johnson recorded "Please, Mr. Johnson" with her brother's band in 1940.
3. Jones's album *Don't Go to Strangers* was nominated for a Grammy in 1960.
4. The joke hinges on knowing that drummer Art Blakey is black.

5. "Bird" is Charlie Parker; "Diz" is Dizzy Gillespie. Because of a recording ban imposed by the American Federation of Musicians, the Hines band with Parker and Gillespie did not record.

6. Jones paraphrases a famous line from Gillespie's recording of "Swing Low, Sweet Cadillac." Blakey died in 1990.

7. A&R is the abbreviation for artists and repertoire.

8. Aretha Franklin was fourteen when she recorded "Never Grow Old" at her father's church in Detroit. The performance is on the CD *Aretha Gospel* (MCA).

ARTHUR PRYSOCK

2 January 1929–7 June 1997

B.F. You were born in Spartanburg on January 2, 1929. How was it growing up there?

A.P. I was born there, and my family moved to North Carolina; but we'd go back every summer to help my grandfather on the farm—cotton and the crops. We went to school in North Carolina, in Greensboro; but we were always back in South Carolina.

B.F. So South Carolina was your grandparents' home?

A.P. Yes. I was about three when my family moved to North Carolina. Every year we would go back. I went back to Spartanburg to stay for a while, and I lived with my uncle, who still lives there. He's about eighty-eight and more active than I am. In fact, I have to ask him to slow down. His name is Shafter Mills. Then I left to try to go out and sing, and I ended up in Hartford, Connecticut, at the age of sixteen.

B.F. Did you leave home and try to make it on your own?

A.P. Yes.

B.F. Had you sung?

A.P. Not much. Only in church. I didn't have any idea that I could sing, really. The people I got a room with, their son played piano. I sang in the bathroom. You know what they say: a singer in the bathroom sounds good. He was listening to me, and one day after a month or two he asked me to come into his part of the house, where he had a piano. He asked if I could sing in tune, and I said, "I guess so." He hit a note, and I hit the note. He asked what songs I knew. One I knew was Nat "King" Cole's "That Ain't Right." It's a blues thing. He played it and I sang it. He said he'd teach me a lot of songs. He took me to the club and introduced me as his little brother and had me come up there to sing. I almost fainted.

B.F. This was 1943?

A.P. Yes. I sang one song, and the girls screamed. The man who owned the place came out and asked where I'd come from. He hired me for three dollars a night,

Arthur Prysock. Date, place, and photographer unknown. From the collection of Jean Prysock

which was a lot of money. I was working at Pratt and Whitney Aircraft, until they found that I was sixteen, and they fired me. So I stayed around there for about a year and became the biggest singer there.

Buddy Johnson came through, and I asked if I could sing a song. His singer was sick. He said, "Well, if you know any of my songs, yes." I said, "I know them all. I do them nightly." I sang three or four songs, and when it was over, he asked if I'd like to sing with his band. I said, "I'd love it." He said, "You'll hear from me in a couple of weeks." He gave me twenty-five dollars for singing that night with him.

B.F. Who was the singer who was ill?

A.P. Joe Medlin.

B.F. If someone were to look at your career and see that you began with Buddy Johnson, one would think—as I did—that you got together in South Carolina. Buddy Johnson is from Darlington.

A.P. No. We got together in Hartford. Then, I wrote a letter home telling everybody that I was singing with Buddy Johnson's band. The girl I was going with down there before I left said I was the biggest liar and that I should not write to her anymore. When we got down there—we played Greensboro, Spartanburg, Darlington: the cornbread circuit—everyone knew then that I was singing with Buddy Johnson.

B.F. You were only sixteen then?

A.P. Yes. In fact, when the tour was over, I was seventeen. He was known as the king of the one-nighters. I was too young to go into the clubs.

B.F. Being on the road with the band must have been a maturing experience for you.

A.P. Yes. I wouldn't give it up for anything because Buddy Johnson was like a teacher. He would write the songs, and he would teach them to you the way they should be sung. Today, when I sing one of Buddy's songs, I always think about how he brought me up, teaching me how to present myself to the audience, lyric-wise. He couldn't sing too good, but he was a heck of a teacher.

We got back after three months—all the way to California—and opened at the Apollo Theater. That was the biggest thing in my life. The fellows kidded me: "If they don't like you in the Apollo Theater, they'll throw tomatoes at you, and they're still in the can." I was scared to death. When I walked out on stage, the girls screamed. I went backstage for about five minutes; they couldn't get me out there. I was scared to death. Buddy was a quiet man. He said, "Come on, Arthur, they love you." They brought me back on stage. I started singing, and they started screaming again. Buddy said, "They love you."

He was right. I became the number-one singer with Buddy. My first record was a million seller—"They All Say I'm the Biggest Fool." I stayed with the band for about eight years as a singer, and when I left, I went out as a single. Of course, it wasn't too good for me then. Then, rock and roll came in, and it almost killed me, almost knocked me out of the business. But I stuck to it, and I'm very happy I did.

B.F. When you were beginning, did you listen to other singers? The most obvious comparison is with Billy Eckstine.

A.P. Eckstine was my idol. I loved his singing. We had similar voices. Mine is a bass-baritone; I imagine he's a baritone. I still like him, and we're good friends. Whenever we're around, we see each other. We almost spend the night together, just talking. He's much older than I am.

B.F. Did you listen to people like Johnny Hartman, who is roughly your age?

A.P. No. I think I was up there before Johnny. But he and I were very good friends.

B.F. Earl Coleman is another one in that vein.

A.P. All of them. Yes, I admired all of them; I still do. But B. was like the boss of all the black singers.[1] And Johnny Hartman—a beautiful voice. Earl Coleman has a beautiful voice, but you don't hear too much about him right now. I heard a record by him not too long ago, and I said, "I hope he's coming back." There were a lot of singers out there then: Al Hibbler, Herb Jeffries.

B.F. Did you consciously pattern yourself after any of them? Or did you develop your own style?

A.P. Now it's identified as Arthur Prysock, not as a copy of Billy Eckstine. Of course, I don't mind being called a copy of the great ones. I went into my own. I had to sit up and think of the things Buddy taught me and put myself into the things that he taught me to remember.

B.F. When you left Buddy Johnson, you were still young. How did you make the step from band singer to being on your own as a soloist?

A.P. I told Milt Gabler, who was the president of Decca Records, that this would be my last record date with Buddy, that I was going out on my own. He said, "Well, you're going to sign up with us." I said, "Gladly." I wasn't thinking about asking him. We started recording, and the records that I did on my own sold good, but not like the ones with Buddy. He had a name.

After a couple of years, my first child was born. That's when I knew I had to leave Buddy because I wasn't making enough money to support my family. I had to try to make more money or stop and go into some other profession. I was lucky. I bought a little house in Jamaica, New York, and my note was sixty-four dollars a month. A lot of times I'd be two months behind—I wasn't making any money—and so I would pick up little odd things to do. I'm a cook by trade; I could get a job cooking tomorrow. This is the way I survived.

B.F. Do you mean by making records?

A.P. Yes, by making records and getting my name out there. They only knew me as Buddy Johnson's singer. When I made my first record with Buddy, they wanted to change my name because Prysock was a hard name for people to remember. My daddy said, "No, your name is Arthur Prysock, and that's what it's going to stay. My name is Arthur Prysock; your name is Arthur Prysock." I was the first boy. And he said, "You're a junior; you can add that on it if you want." After they got used to pronouncing the name, it came easy to people.

B.F. At this time, was your brother Red Prysock playing?[2] Did you two perform together?

A.P. No. I started out before he did. He came out of service and ended up in Hartford, where I was. Then I left. My sister moved up to New York, so he went there to stay with her. In school down South he played, but he didn't really play until he went in service. He came out of service and was a pretty good horn player.

B.F. When did you get together professionally?

A.P. Not until about ten years ago.

B.F. You left Buddy Johnson to go out on your own. It must have been tough at the beginning.

A.P. It was tough. My wife also worked to help the family and to help me. She said, "As long as you want to try it. . . . " After about a year, she said, "Are you sure you don't want to get a job?" I said, "No, I gotta stick it out." She went along with it. It's good when you got a good woman, because you can have a bad one and that's the end of it. They don't care whether you make it or not. The first thing they want is the lawyer.

B.F. I first became aware of you in the mid 1950s, when you recorded for Old Town.

A.P. Hy Weiss owned it. He still owns it, but he's not recording anybody. Since I signed with another company, he said that he'll wait for me. But he and I are still friends.

B.F. When did you sign with Old Town?

A.P. Mid-'50s. I stayed with him until the '70s, I think.[3] It was a long time.

B.F. On some of those Old Town recordings, the backing musicians are not identified; but I think I hear the Basie band on *Coast to Coast*.

A.P. No. That was my brother's band. *Count Basie/Arthur Prysock* was another one.

B.F. On Verve.

A.P. Yes. There's another we did together. He and I were good friends. I was a friend to a lot of the old band leaders. Duke Ellington was a very sweet fellow. I did concerts with most of these people. They liked me as a singer. Basie offered me a job with his band. I said, "No, I've got to make it as a single." It was after Jimmy Rushing left.

B.F. On one of the Old Town recordings is an arranger named Herb Gordy. He also played bass.

A.P. He was traveling with my brother's band as the arranger and bassist. Then he met a girl out there who trained animals, and he married her. He's still playing, at Disneyland.

B.F. I've seen you live only once, and that was at the 502 Club in Columbus, Ohio.

A.P. It cost about a dollar to get in. There were some beautiful girls there. They support you. Without the women, you can't make it. That's the greatest hand you can get—from a woman.

B.F. You really gained acclaim from the Lowenbrau beer commercial. On it, you are not identified, but anyone who knows your voice knows it's you. How did it come about?

A.P. I was in the studio at the time making Miller commercials. When I finished, the producer asked, "Arthur, would you like to try out for a new beer, Lowenbrau?" I said that I had never heard of it, but I'd be glad to do it. He said, "Next week, maybe." I said, "OK." He called and asked if I had a key on the Lowenbrau commercial. I said, "Sure." (I can't remember what key it's in.) He said, "That's mighty low." I said, "Don't worry about it." So I went into the studio and did it; and he said, "Damn, I didn't think you were going to make it. I almost put it a half tone higher." They loved the commercial because of the depth of it. I was contracted to them for about eight years.

B.F. Did they provide you with beer?

A.P. They used to give me quite a bit of beer, but I buy it, too.

B.F. You also cashed in on that by releasing an album called *Here's to Good Friends*, which is part of the lyrics to the tune.

A.P. And the residuals were lovely. A lot of people didn't know that it was me. When I started doing it in nightclubs, they would always say, "Oh, that's you."

B.F. You've not exactly gone into obscurity since then. You've been nominated for a Grammy, you've released an album, and you've had another singer on an album.

A.P. Betty Joplin. I met her in Michigan. In fact, she booked the group up in Lansing. That's how I met her; she was singing on the show. She opened the show, and I said, "My God, listen to the girl sing." I asked her if she was on a recording contract. She said, "No, I've never seen a studio. I work for the governor." I had a choice of other women, but I chose her. I'm glad I did, because the record turned out to be nominated for a Grammy.[4] She's on the next album called *This Guy's in Love with You*.

B.F. Now, you're with the Fantasy group.[5] How did you get to them?

A.P. A producer named Bob Porter approached me and said, "I haven't heard any records from you in a long time." I said, "No; I'm going with so-and-so." He said, "He didn't record you; did you sign up yet?" I said, "No." Well, he said, "I want to record you." I said, "With who?" He said, "With Fantasy." I said, "OK." That's how I started. I have a contract with them for no more than two albums a year. I haven't been with them a year yet, and already we have another one out. That means the other one was selling like hell. I let Bob select a lot of songs—like about fifty—-and I choose from them. I don't have time to go looking for and listening to hundreds of songs a day, so I just have him select some. Usually they are old songs. Occasionally I put one of my songs in, or somebody else's that's good. Good writers. It turned out to be a very successful album, and I'm happy with it—and with the girl, too.

B.F. Years ago musicians went into the studio, the band was right there, and they did a take.

A.P. I do that with my band.

B.F. There are now so many tracks. The guys lay down a track a month before the singer comes in.

A.P. That's no good. You can't get that feeling. I make an album in four to six hours. I'm finished. I won't be going back the next day. If there's something wrong with it— that first Betty Joplin album had a couple of mistakes—I'd go back into the studio and correct it in about ten minutes. But these people that record and take days and months, sometimes. . . . The studio loves these people. It destroys the spirit, the *spontaneousness* of it: the closeness, the feeling. When the music is written, the arranger's there. If he's not there when I'm recording, he can't tell me how he would like for me to phrase. All these things are necessary.

Earlier, when I was recording, they used a big disc, with a needle cutting into the record. The band was right there with me. When the band would mess up, I'd wait for them to start over again. It's better that way; I like it that way. In fact, the studio doesn't like it because we're in and out of there. They want the discos in there, playing one song for four hours.

B.F. What now?

A.P. We are going to continue to record and stay on the road, because I can't stay around home too long. I have two grandkids, two daughters, and a wife; and they love it when I'm gone.

B.F. Is there anything you'd like to add?

A.P. Thank God for giving me the power to select things that all people like. You can hurt yourself sometimes by not knowing how to pick songs that will fit anybody. In fact, we get as many young people in to see me as the older folks. One album in particular that I think caused all this is one I recited from the book *This Is My Beloved*. In fact, if it was re-released, it would sell just as many now as it did then. Verve owns all the tapes I had with Old Town.

Searingtown, N.Y., 15 March 1987

Notes

1. Billy Eckstine was known as "Mr. B.," or "B."

2. Wilbur "Red" Prysock played the tenor saxophone.

3. After recording with Old Town from the late 1950s until approximately 1964, Prysock recorded with Verve, King, and Bethlehem before returning to Old Town for two sessions, one around 1977 and another in 1980. His final recording contract was with Milestone, with which he first recorded in 1985.

4. Prysock and Betty Joplin's "Teach Me Tonight," from the album *A Rockin' Good Way*, was nominated for a Grammy in 1987.

5. Fantasy was then the parent company of Milestone.

NAPPY BROWN

12 October 1929–

B.F. Nappy, you were born in Charlotte, North Carolina, in October 1929. But what is your name? Some people say Napoleon Brown, while others say Napoleon Culp.

N.B. My real name—my birth name—is Napoleon Brown Culp. My stage name is Nappy Brown. Back in '55, when I recorded, that name was too long to go on the record, so Herman Lubinsky of Savoy Records suggested Nappy Brown because it's short.[1] Culp is my last name; Brown is my middle name.

B.F. You were born and reared in Charlotte, and your father was important in the church there. Who were your parents?

N.B. Maggie and Fred Culp. They were from around Fort Mill and Rock Hill, South Carolina—between Pinesville, North Carolina, and Rock Hill, South Carolina.

B.F. Did you complete school?

N.B. No. I was more interested in my gift and my talent. Most of the way I got through was by singing. My voice was so high that I used to sound like a girl. Singing is all I would do. I was so carried away about my talent that I didn't go further than the eleventh grade.

B.F. Did you listen to live music around Charlotte that might have inspired you to go into the blues, or rhythm and blues?

N.B. No. What inspired me to go into it was Savoy. I left Charlotte and went to New Jersey.

B.F. But before you left Charlotte you had sung with gospel groups, hadn't you?

N.B. Yes. I was raised in the church. About 1941, I started in a local gospel group, the Traveling Sons of Harmony. I then moved on up to a large gospel group that was famous at the time, the Golden Bells. They had a talent show out at the army auditorium, and I won first place with them. They hired me. I was about fifteen years old.

Nappy Brown. Date, place, and photographer unknown. From the collection of Nappy Brown

B.F. Had your voice changed?

N.B. No. It was still high. From then on we started to broadcast on CBS, which was WBT, Charlotte. Then, Grady Cole kept putting us on our feet.[2] But my mother didn't know that I could sing the blues. A lady named Miss Clayton had a nightclub where I was washing dishes with my cousin on a New Year's night. She saw us in the back of the kitchen where, after finishing the dishes, we were tap dancing. She said, "How would you like to put on a show for us at the club, the Pinehurst Club?" We said, "Yes, ma'am, we'll try." So we went out to the club that night and started tap dancing, and from tap dancing we started singing the blues. It all started there.

Then I got to standing around clubs or standing by the piccolo, and people would pay me to sing along with the piccolo.[3] That's where "Lemon Squeezin' Daddy" comes in. I wrote it years ago, but at the time they wouldn't let you record anything like that because everything had to be clean and polished. It wasn't like it is today: anything you want to say, you can. So I kept "Lemon Squeezin' Daddy" in the bag.

I used it at a talent show in Newark. Roy Hamilton and I were on the same show. We started off at the same time. He had "You'll Never Walk Alone." They had a discussion about it. They wanted me to take "You'll Never Walk Alone," but it wasn't in my range. So I sang "Lemon Squeezin' Daddy" that night and won second place in the blues. Roy won first place. I'd also written "Don't Be Angry," but I didn't do it at the talent show. I just did the blues, because Newark likes the blues.

B.F. Before you went up there, you sang with the Sela Jubilee Singers, didn't you?

N.B. Yes. They were out of Raleigh. I recorded with them at Bell Tone studios in New York. I was the lead singer on "Why Not Today?" Then we split up, and I came back to Charlotte. Then I went to Newark again, and that's where "Don't Be Angry" comes in.

B.F. What about the group called the Heavenly Lights? Weren't they after the Sela Jubilee Singers and before you went to Newark again?

N.B. That's right. That's where Herman Lubinsky got me. We were recording a spiritual called "Jesus Said It," and Lubinsky called me off to the side and asked if I could sing the blues. I told him that I could. He said that he hadn't had a hit in years. I had "Don't Be Angry" with me. He went on and recorded the group, so I had to go back there. He had an old pasteboard box for him, Bruce Milson, and me, and he started beating on the box. I started singing. He said something like, "This is my lucky day. This is it, right here." It all started then.

B.F. You were not the only one to do "Don't Be Angry." The Crew Cuts covered it with some success. Aren't there legal difficulties with that tune? Didn't you have a problem with Savoy?

N.B. Yes. I never got the money off of "Don't Be Angry."

B.F. Do you mean from the Crew Cuts' recording of it?

N.B. That's right. I didn't get what I was supposed to have gotten. Just like "Night Time Is the Right Time," which I wrote and was a hit for me. Ray Charles also recorded it, but I didn't get any money from it. We're working on it now.

B.F. How does it happen? You write the tunes and record them; other people hear them and cover them, but these other artists need some kind of permission or must pay a fee to use your music. Did Lubinsky sell the rights out from under you?

N.B. Right. They have to get permission from him in order to do it.

B.F. But what authority did he have to sell or lease your music?

N.B. I wrote "Don't Be Angry." If you look on the record, you will see three people on there: me, Rose Marie McCoy, and Herman Lubinsky. At that time no artist knew what was going on. I didn't know. You didn't have people then like different lawyers to look out for you. You did it on your own. So that's where they got advantage of you. A lot of blues singers got caught in that net. We just didn't know. I didn't find out until later years. I've been getting some money. Two white boys have been writing me hundreds of letters. They came down here and spent two weeks with me, digging up all this stuff.

B.F. You had a long relationship with Lubinsky and Savoy—from roughly 1954 to 1961. So you must have been on pretty good terms with him.

N.B. I was the only one who could handle him. The reason I could handle him was that when I first went there—I call it giving each other respect—I said, "Yes, sir" and "No, sir, Mr. Lubinsky." Everybody else called him Herman. He said, "Well, gee whiz. I've never been called Mr. Lubinsky." He'd never been given that recognition, but that's the way we're raised in the South. From then on, we always got along.

B.F. Was he the one responsible for getting good musicians to back you? Or was it Fred Mendelsohn?

N.B. Lubinsky was the one; Fred Mendelsohn was the A&R man.[4] Fred should have been at the Savoy, because if it hadn't been for him, Lubinsky wouldn't have any artists. Freddie was the one that kept the thing together. He's the one who gave me my first coat—to have my picture taken in when I went up there—because I didn't have any clothes.

B.F. You had people like Mickey Baker, Sam Taylor, Panama Francis, Budd Johnson—all kinds of really wonderful musicians.

N.B. He had the best. And when I went into the studio to record—they have a union—he'd tell them he didn't care if it took a whole week staying in the studio. He wanted it done right.

B.F. What was the most successful or most popular of your tunes?

N.B. "Don't Be Angry," which went pop. Then, "Night Time Is the Right Time," which was blues. After that was "Well, Well, Well, Baby-La."

B.F. How did you come to use the "l" sound, as at the beginning of "Don't Be Angry"?

N.B. I used to listen to foreign music late at night, and I've been doing it ever since. I also liked to go to the movies, and some of my songs sound like Tarzan in them. I don't know the meaning of the "l" sound; it was just a gimmick. But I liked it, and I picked it up. I didn't know what "Well, Well, Well, Baby-La" was until Lubinsky told me. Some places it means "diapers" or "baby." At that time I was supposed to go to France, but Lubinsky blocked it. I had a great offer, but Lubinsky thought the French would want to make me white; he wanted me to stay black. But he thought that because things were going good for him.

B.F. Did you make any money from the Savoy recordings?

N.B. On the road.

B.F. Did you get royalties?

N.B. Just a few. But if I needed something, I'd just tell Fred and I'd go downtown and get it. That's one way of getting your money. I saw there was no money coming in, so I always was in need.

B.F. But you did go on tour.

N.B. Yes. Me, Jackie Wilson, Sarah Vaughan, Al Hibbler, Muddy Waters, Little Walter—just a whole host of them. The promoters put together the package shows. I worked them 365 days a year. I never was off, unless I wanted to take off. That's where my money was coming from. I was making $3,100 a night. When we came off the road, we always had a club to go to, our stomping ground. Then I went out as a sin-gle. I went to Sweden in '83, I believe, and that was also my first time to England. It was my first time playing across the water.

B.F. By the end of your stay with Savoy, the rhythm-and-blues market had essen-tially dried up. There was no longer a great demand for the music you sang.

N.B. That's right. I went out of the picture; I came in off the road and went back into gospel. I went on the Jewel label and recorded a big hit, "Do You Know the Man from Galilee?" That was with the Bell Jubilees. We went on the road and started working. Then I decided to get back in it because there was another big demand for it. What was here in the '50s is over across the pond now. They don't want pop or Beatles songs: they want nothing but the blues. It's a strange thing. Most of the blues acts are overseas.

B.F. But in the '60s you were by and large out of the blues business.

N.B. Right.

B.F. When did you come to South Carolina?

N.B. It was '77 when I came to South Carolina. I got tired of the city and came here. I like that quiet out-life.

B.F. How did you choose Pomaria?

N.B. By meeting a young lady here.

B.F. The next time you're really heard of as a blues singer is on an album you recorded for Elephant V.

N.B. When I recorded it, I wasn't trusting anybody. I just recorded it and sold it outright for ten thousand dollars. If it hit, it hit; if it didn't, it didn't. It did pretty well.

B.F. Savoy released an album of gospel tunes by someone called Brother Napoleon Brown. Is that you?

N.B. That's me. It was Brother Napoleon Brown and the Southern Sisters. We're still together every now and then. When I'm in and they have a concert, I'll be with them. To me, the blues is a job, but I believe in making people happy. The blues will make you happy, and they'll make you sad. Spirituals will make you happy, and spir-ituals will make you sad.

One thing concerns me a little bit. Wherever I play, you see only one, two, or three blacks. We all got concerned about that. One person asked me what I thought about it. I said, "The whites have done gone black, and the blacks have done gone white." All of this is our support. That's our audience now. They are into it. They are *into* it. Oh, Jesus.

I came across this when playing in Savannah. On a radio station, I asked, "Where are the soul brothers? Where are the roots of this?" That night on the Savannah lake-front, you couldn't get in there for all the blacks. They were lining up. Some of them didn't even know where the place was. The owner of the club said that I had done something nobody else ever did. He said he'd been trying, and I told him that I got on the radio and talked to blacks about it. It's just amazing to see all over the world how everybody's into this thing. Over here, the whites are deep into it. They're the ones keeping it alive. They have these blues societies, and hospitality. It's just nice all the way.

B.F. There are some pretty good white blues singers, such as John Hammond.

N.B. I met John. He sings stuff by himself. I played the festival in Sacramento, California, where I met him. John's a peculiar guy. He does it because he likes it; there doesn't have to be money involved.

B.F. You've also had an association with Mr. R&B Records in Sweden.

N.B. It's a company over there that had all of my recordings. Here's what happened. I was playing a club in New York and Screamin' Jay Hawkins came in. He acts crazy anyhow. He said, "Nappy, I've got a message for you. Here." He stopped me on the stage. The message was, "Plenty of money." So I said, "I'll take it." He said to put on a note, "Please send money." I did, and sent the note in a letter to Mr. R&B in Sweden: "Please send money." I said, "This is just one of Screamin' Jay's tricks. He's always acting crazy." But then, here comes a check for six thousand dollars from Jonas Bernholm's Mr. R&B Records in Sweden. And that's how it came about. And then he called me.

B.F. What was the six thousand dollars for?

N.B. That was for my royalties. They've got all my records over there, and I didn't know it. Then he called me on the phone; he had heard that I was dead. Then he heard that I was in prison for murder. I said, "Yes, this is Nappy." He asked my real name. I said, "Napoleon Brown Culp." He said, "Well, this must be Nappy." He said that he'd been trying to track me down to pay me my royalties, but he heard that I was dead or in prison for life. I told him that I've never been in prison, that I've never been in trouble, that I've never killed anybody.

He said, "How would you like to come over here?" I told him, "Fine." He said he'd line up something for me. In about a month, I got a contract to sign. They treat you good: a round-trip ticket and all expenses. He called me back and said, "For two weeks, how would twelve thousand dollars sound to you?" I said, "It would be wonderful." He said, "OK. You sign the contract and send it back." So that's the way it all began.[5] So I went over there, and I didn't play anywhere but Scandinavia, Sweden. The next time I looked around they were contacting me about England. And I always have wanted to go to England. Then I started over there, and now they're keeping me over there most of the time.

B.F. I'd think you would have found the correspondence from Sweden strange. Blues is American and primarily black.

N.B. Right. I thought that at first. I was kind of skeptical of it. But when I got there, there's no difference. They've got it down, just like the blacks have. They got it down, music-wise, plus singing-wise. When you go there, you've got to sing the blues, because the guy that's got his band together can sing the blues. In fact, they've studied us. Everything is tight. All I had to do was go there and sit; I didn't have to rehearse. We had to get the timing, and what time I had to come on the stage. They are great. There are some great people over there. They definitely want nothing but the blues.

B.F. These are young guys?

N.B. Yes. Twenty-five, nineteen. They're into it. They're more deeply into it than we are. It's hard for me to figure out. Everything we did here in the '50s is there. The dances we did in the '50s are there. It carried me back to the days of the jitterbug. Even the clothes they wear to the dances are fifties. It's a miracle. Just like Japan has gone blues.

B.F. How did American trumpeter Willie Cook come to record with you in Stockholm in 1983?

N.B. They needed a horn player, and he lives over there. He does different gigs, and he's the best, so he went on the tour with us.

B.F. Things started picking up for you around that time. In 1984 a group in Atlanta had you record an album for them and their label. What is your connection with the Atlanta group?

N.B. Mike Rothschild called me about recording with them.[6] They needed a blues singer. He said he didn't consider me a blues singer. I told him that I'm a variety singer. I sing pop and ballads, but I love them blues. I told him, "All right." We had a long discussion about it, and I met Tinsley Ellis and his band.

B.F. These are white guys.

N.B. Yes. And we recorded. Tinsley loves the blues. My first start, when I came back from Europe, was around Atlanta. A lot of people think that Atlanta's my home, but it's not. One of my albums has that, but it's a mistake. I started playing at the Fox Theatre. Then I played the Moonshadow with the Allman Brothers. It all started out from there.

B.F. At the 1984 session in Atlanta you recorded "Lemon Squeezin' Daddy" for the first time.

N.B. I wrote that tune when I was about fourteen years old, but I kept it from my mother. That is the number-one hit everywhere I've played. That's what they want, especially the ladies. They call for the "Lemon Squeezin' Daddy." That's all they want. I can't leave until I've done it.

B.F. Have you recorded since the '84 Atlanta session?

N.B. Now, I'm on the Black Top label, which is connected with Rounder. That's with Anson Funderburgh and the Thunderbirds and Room Full of Blues, a white band; but I call them black because it's from the heart. Some people ask how they can feel it, but they do feel it. They play from the soul. The name of that album is *Something Gonna Jump Out the Bushes!* I wrote the title tune, which is kind of like "Lemon Squeezin' Daddy."

B.F. When you're on the road now, is it mostly in the Southeast?

N.B. Any place in the world. Wherever they'll book me, that's where I'll go.

B.F. Is there anything you'd like to add about your life and career?

N.B. The only thing I would like to add is that I appreciate what they're doing in sticking with the blues. The blacks need to get into it more because the whites are already into it. That is our roots. I hope they'll come back to the roots. I'm hoping for greater success. In fact, things are going real great for me so far, and this is the second time around for me. Everybody really appreciates me being back, and I'm doing a lot of traveling. And sometimes I do a few spirituals.

B.F. When you do spirituals, are you still Nappy Brown? Or are you Brother Napoleon Brown?

N.B. Napoleon Brown, but the people in the spirituals still call me Nappy, Brother Nappy.

Pomaria, S.C., 6 June 1987

Notes

1. Herman Lubinsky owned Savoy Records.
2. Grady Cole was a popular announcer on WBT.
3. A piccolo is a jukebox.
4. A&R stands for artist and repertoire.
5. In 1979 Mr. R&B Records released seventeen of Nappy Brown's Savoy recordings on Brown's *That Man* (R&B-100). A statement on the back cover confirms, in broad outline, Brown's story about his dealings with Jonas Bernholm, owner of Mr. R&B records: "Mr. R&B Records reissues forgotten but essential recordings from the 50-s of Rhythm and Blues, Doo Wop and Black Rock and Roll. Mr. R&B Records supports the artists with royalties (0,40 $/lp) and promotional tours. Money will be forwarded to Nappy Brown when his present address is known." Bernholm writes about Brown in the liner notes to Brown's 1985 release on Stockholm Records, *I Done Got Over*. Stockholm Records is a division of Mr. R&B Records.
6. Michael Rothschild founded and was president of Landslide Records.

WEBSTER YOUNG

3 December 1932–13 December 2003

B.F. You were born in Columbia, South Carolina, weren't you?

W.Y. I was born in Lexington County, which is Columbia. It was the third of December 1932, a Saturday.

B.F. Did your family live there?

W.Y. My mom and her family were from there. My aunt moved to Washington, D.C., but she came back. Then she took her brothers and sisters back to Washington with her because it was supposed to have been *the* place. My earliest recollection is of Washington. I was about three, I think.

B.F. Have you always lived in Washington?

W.Y. No. I lived in New York; in New Haven, Connecticut.

B.F. But you grew up and went to school in Washington.

W.Y. Yes. I don't know anything about Columbia. I was there briefly on several occasions, once when I was in the service. On a weekend, I went home with a friend of mine from Columbia. When I came out of the service in '55, I joined Lloyd Price's rock-and-roll band, or rhythm-and-blues, as we called it.

B.F. When did it begin to dawn on you that you wanted to be an improvising musician?

W.Y. I always had a good musical ear; I used to sing. I had an aunt who used to sing, and she used to teach me all of the words to tunes. So I had a good musical awareness. But as far as playing an instrument was concerned, my mother took me to see the picture *Cabin in the Sky*. The Duke Ellington band was in it, but the cat I dug was Louis Armstrong. My mom had been asking me what instrument I wanted. So when I saw Louis Armstrong with the trumpet, just to shut her up I said, "That's what I want." I took lessons from a music teacher named Mr. Edward Minor. He was good, but he was an old man.

B.F. This was all legit, I take it; all technique.

Webster Young, mid-1990s.
Place and photographer
unknown. From the collection
of Gretchen Young and Dorian
Young

W.Y. Yes. I couldn't play the horn; I didn't even have a horn. My mom sent me to this guy to take a lesson, and she went with me. He had an old, beat-up cornet, but to me it looked good because it was a horn. The teacher told me to try getting a sound out of it, so I took it to the corner of the room for the whole lesson and tried it. I became familiar with it. That was that.

He told my mother to get me a horn. She asked where to go, and he said to go to a good music store, Kitt's, which at that time was the best music store in Washington. It still exists. My mom bought me a Vincent Bach; I'm still playing a Vincent Bach. She paid, I think, $105 for it, and I thought it was a new horn. Years later, I found out it was a reconditioned horn. It looked brand new, and I loved it. So I had music lessons that cost seventy-five cents. I'd have two sessions a week, on Tuesday and Thursday. I studied with him for about a year.

B.F. How old were you then?

W.Y. About ten. When you're young like that, everything you learn you retain. I hadn't gotten into chicks yet. I just listened to Louis Armstrong and I dug him. Also, I listened to Harry James, who was hot then; he's what the media played, and Charlie Spivak.

This cat I heard with Gene Krupa, Roy Eldridge: there was something about the way he played that I could feel. I knew that Louis was the cat, and I was hip to that. If you couldn't play "Stardust" then like Louis Armstrong, then you couldn't play. I dug Louis, but I was partial to Roy Eldridge. He had made some sides of his own. I remember his "Twilight Time." These are the things I was listening to. He also played with Artie Shaw. He recorded "Rockin' Chair," and I was listening to it on the radio when my mom told me to do something. But I was listening to Roy. She came over and turned off the radio. Whew. It messed me up. Roy was my first influence.

B.F. What happened next?

W.Y. I used to live at 1825 Sixth Street, right around the corner from the Howard Theater. In those days, it was *the* place. Every week, it would have a different band. They'd have Duke Ellington, Count Basie, Jimmie Lunceford, everybody. Even Billy Eckstine.

My thing was this. I had heard Roy, and then on the street you hear everything. One day, when I was around thirteen, a cat named Tim Paulin had a hot dog shop and had the baddest juke box. If it was happening, it was on his box. I was listening, and he was playing a riff, "Salt Peanuts." It was Dizzy.[1] At that time, listening to Roy was beautiful, Louis was solid. I had met Louis at the Howard, and Roy, also. Dizzy was talking about something else, and those tempos that he was playing—whew. The speed and facility this guy had from top to bottom—uncanny. I said I got to meet this dude, because he has everything.

I waited. Before that, Billy Eckstine came to the Howard Theater. I asked Illinois Jacquet if he knew Dizzy, and he said, "Yes." Illinois had this record, "Robbins' Nest." I went to see him; I went to see Billy Eckstine. As a matter of fact, Billy Eckstine would come out and grab a couple of us who were standing outside and take us in so we could see the show. At the time, Dizzy had just left the band, and Fats Navarro had taken over. John Malachi was in the band. After the show, I went into the pit, where someone said, "Hey, Fat Girl, here's a trumpet player." Fats was really fat then. He told me about Dizzy. He was talking to someone and said, "What's this kid's age?" So Fats told me some things. He said, "Kid, playing this horn is very serious. It's not easy." He was very gracious. When Dizzy was with the band, he was also musical director. Bird was in the band.[2] But when Diz left, that's when he recommended Fat Girl. Diz, Fats, and Miles Davis were never there together.

I remember Dizzy coming to the Howard Theater, and I used to cut school. I waited a couple of days, but I never saw him. I had a book by him, one I had bought in the '40s. I bought it again, and he recently autographed it for me. It's titled *Dizzy Gillespie Jazz Master* now, but then it was *The Dizzy Gillespie Trumpet Style*. I took this book to school with me and to music lessons. My teacher dug it. I got a chance to meet Dizzy on a Sunday backstage. Ella Fitzgerald walked out with James Moody and said, "Oh, James, here's a young trumpet player." He asked if I wanted to meet Dizzy, so he took me back to Dizzy's dressing room. Dizzy told me to take my horn out. I did and played "Groovin' High," one of the tunes in his book. He showed me how to play the music. Students play the way it is written, but you need to be told how to do it. Dizzy was the man. At that time, all the cats called me Little Diz, and it stuck. He was a very positive influence. Personally he was very firm and stern. He wouldn't tell you anything that was wrong. He was very strict.

I heard cats talking—I had heard Bird, but I didn't know that he was a brother. One day, I was looking in Waxie Maxie's record shop, and there was a picture of Charlie Parker. He needed a shave. That was the next thing. Yard came to a club on Fourteenth Street, the Club Bali, Fourteenth and T.[3] This was the cat. So I thought he'd have Miles Davis with him—at that time I didn't dig Miles as much as Diz. Diz was the man.

When Yard came, he had Benny Harris, a beautiful cat. He was extroverted, outgoing. He used to try to help me. He's the one who introduced me to Charlie Parker. One night on Fourteenth Street, I saw Benny during intermission, and he introduced me to Bird. Yard talked to me. Whew. He's another cat. That whole week, every chance I had I hung out with him. I went to his room at the Dunbar Hotel, just to be near him. He was also a beautiful cat—very encouraging. He didn't have a lot to say, but what he said made a lot of sense. He said I had a beautiful sound. I went to his rehearsal, and I wanted to play. He let me. We weren't playing anything, so he sat me down.

Those were my two influences: Diz and Bird. Bird had Max Roach, Duke Jordan, Tommy Potter, and Benny Harris. Sometimes he'd come to Washington by himself as a soloist. The last time I saw Yard, he came to the Uline Arena, which was used as a setting for the Ice Capades and such. During the summer, they used it for concerts. I remember going to one when Duke Ellington's band was there, and Charlie Parker was there with strings. It must have been 1949. I went with Leo Parker. Leo amazed me. There was a cat named Carrington Visor, a tenor player who went to Howard University. They had a club called Little Harlem, on Seventh and T, where Visor and Benny Golson played. For my money, I dug Benny, but Visor seemed to have the edge. He sounded like Don Byas. Visor was one of my influences. One night, Leo told me to get my horn.

B.F. Was he a professional then, and you weren't?

W.Y. Right. I was just learning. Leo liked what I was trying to do, so he asked me to play with him. I played a gig with him, and he paid me. I was learning the music and trying to play. Dizzy told me to learn to play the piano, and that is something I didn't have. Most people in my block did. In those days, cats wouldn't tell you anything. If it hadn't been for the Howard Theater, I would have been in trouble. We didn't have the aids—such as books—that cats have today. We used to have books called Black's chord books. They had changes—"I Got Rhythm," "Sweet Georgia Brown," "How High the Moon," et cetera.[4]

Cats were listening to Diz's and Bird's records. It was either Dizzy or Yard. I'd also listen to Fats Navarro. He didn't get the ink that Dizzy did. The first time I heard Miles Davis playing with Charlie Parker, he was playing "Night in Tunisia." I like the tune. I used to prefer Bird's rendition to Dizzy's. I really loved Miles's solo. I still play it note for note today. Later, I heard Dizzy do it on record with Don Byas and Milt

Jackson, and they did "Ol' Man Rebop" and "Anthropology." Dizzy's solo on this version of "Tunisia" is in his book. I still can't play it. I listened to Diz and Bird, and this was what was happening in Washington.

Today, thank God, David Baker and Jerry Coker do jazz improvisation books. Those are good aids, if you do what they tell you to do. We didn't have that then. You had to listen to the records, and had to emulate what Diz, Miles, Fats, Howard McGhee, and Benny Harris do. Benny used to come to town with Dizzy's band and Boyd Raeburn's band. He'd come out, and I'd be peeking in the pit. He'd be down there teaching. They were good readers. Benny showed them how to do things. He was a great teacher. He was with Bird a lot. I gave up lessons; I couldn't afford them. I was on my own.

B.F. How did you become a professional musician?

W.Y. I don't consider myself to have been a professional in Washington. I was a local. You're always looking to New York. I was too young—about seventeen. I did a very foolish thing and got married at seventeen. So I went to New York and got stranded.

I first met Miles Davis there in 1951. He had left Bird and had already done *Birth of the Cool*. In those days, they were on 78s. I loved a couple of them: "Godchild" and "Israel." Fats had died; there was Miles. He didn't have the range that Diz had—Diz was something—but there was something about Miles. He was so slick. He really was playing like himself. Red Rodney made a comment in *Down Beat* that Miles had impressed him because Miles played like himself. He wasn't anything like Diz and Fats. He was developing his own thing. What really knocked me out was when he went with Prestige with Sonny Rollins and Jackie McLean. He did the ballad "My Old Flame," a classic that I still listen to.

After I went to New York—I met Miles briefly in 1951—I came back to Washington and thought it was going to be a drag since nothing was happening here. I was tired. I had to do something. It was during the Korean conflict, and I was about eighteen or nineteen. If you weren't cool, they'd draft you. I had to get my act together, so I volunteered for the air force. They told me I'd be able to go into the band. But when I got in, I wound up being in supply.

I tried to make the best of it. I was stationed in Geneva, New York, at Sampson Air Force Base. Then, they flew me to Cheyenne, Wyoming. I went to supply school for a couple of months. They gave me some leave, and I came to Washington. When I had time off, I could never go back. If they gave me ten days, I'd take twenty. When I fucked up, I fucked up. When I went to Greenville Air Force Base in South Carolina, I went home when I had a chance.

One day I looked in the day room and saw that I was scheduled to be sent to Japan, to Ashiya Air Base in southern Japan, not far from Korea. They gave us about twenty days of leave, and I took forty. I forgot about the service. I knew I had to go back and turn myself in after I had some fun. I went to the Far East, to Japan. When I got there, it wasn't Tokyo. Japan wasn't what it is today. Where I went, it was something else. I tried every way I could to get discharged. It was the end of the world. Very

sad. Bad racism. We had a commander who wouldn't let qualified blacks get promoted. One cat told us that over there they did things their way. You're in this; do
your time, and you'll go home. You can do it that way, you can die, or you can go to
jail. So that was it. I couldn't wait to get back to the States.

In 1955 I came back to Washington. I'd been away from music, so I didn't know
what was happening. I stopped in California on my way home, and that's the first
time I heard Miles playing with Jackie McLean. Miles recorded "CTA" with Jimmy
Heath. Miles made two records with Blue Note, and that was it, as far as I know.

I also met Hampton Hawes in Japan. He was a positive influence on me. He was
playing with Shorty Rogers. Hamp heard me play and said I played good. At that time,
I could play and I could hear changes; but if you asked what I was playing, I didn't
know. I didn't know about chord changes. Hamp used to show me every day about
chord changes. It was hip; it knocked me out. Every day, he'd show me something
new. Cats were writing out there.

I had a chance to get with a band. I used to play marches every day and do
concert-band work. We had a jazz ensemble, combos. As a result of the lessons I'd
taken in Washington, I thought I was a good trumpet player. But these cats were a
bitch. Gregory Dykes, a trumpet player, could play and read.

The bandmaster would call a rehearsal and I'd hide. He caught on to it, so he
locked the toilets. At concerts, we'd be playing concertos. It's not that I didn't want to
do it; I was just sensitive. I didn't want people laughing at me while I was reading.
One day, I thought I was going to make a mistake. I tensed up and fucked up. I made
a mistake. I thought the cats would laugh. Everyone was so intense doing his thing
that no one noticed. I then made up my mind to get my shit together. The lead trumpet player was going to be gone. He told me that I was it, and I became a good trumpet player because I had to do it. I had responsibility. It was a new world.

Then things began to open up to me—like changes. I learned to write. When my
time was up, I returned to Washington. I'd been away for four years. In 1955 a lot was
happening. Bird died in '55. Dizzy came to Washington to Olivia Davis's Patio
Lounge. When I saw Diz, he had Walter Davis, Jr., on piano. Diz was still playing; he
was still a monster. He asked me to come up and play. If you did that, he'd bury you.

At this time, a rumor was going around that Miles was in the army. Someone said
that he was coming to town, to Olivia Davis's Patio Lounge. So Miles came, but he
came as a soloist. I went to see him; he remembered me. He was staying at the Dunbar Hotel. He had Philly Joe Jones with him. He came back again and played with
Rick Henderson, a local alto player. He's a great alto player. I used to look up to him.
I used to play with his band. Rick is a great arranger; he played with Duke Ellington
and Dizzy. He made some records with Clark Terry, and with Dinah Washington on
"Blue Skies." He had a big band. At the Howard Theater, they had a band called the
Washingtonians. He became the leader.

During this time when Miles would come to Washington, and Bird had died, I was
beginning to be influenced more by Miles than Diz. Diz was up in the stratosphere,
and he doubles up.[5] You have to be a freak to play like that. So I started to play like

someone I could play like. When Miles would come to town, I'd talk to him. At the time, he was telling me what I wanted to hear. In '55, there was nothing happening for me in D.C. People started talking about rock and roll. I had a gig downtown at Fourteenth and was playing rock. I quit. I went to Philadelphia for a brief moment, but I came back. This cat Lloyd Price was coming out of the army, and he was starting a band. He was traveling. I liked to travel, so I said I'd go with him. I was musical director, but it was no challenge because no one in the band could read.

B.F. Was this before he became famous with "Personality"?

W.Y. Yes. There was a piano player who couldn't read, but he was musical. I had to show the cat how to play the tunes we played. But he got it all together on the road. He was amazing, even at that time. We would go on one-nighters and into theaters like the Howard and the Apollo. Lloyd Price would have to augment the band with cats who could read. The other cats would just sit there and hold their horns. I was sick of that. I was making a little bit of money, but I was playing my horn.

On the days we had off, we'd try to play some bebop. At the Apollo, the cat had an act where he was doing "Lawdy Miss Clawdy." He had a drummer who was an idiot— Lloyd's "yes man." During "Lawdy Miss Clawdy," Lloyd would get down on his knees and wanted everyone else to get down. The cat messed with the money, and I was really mad. He wanted us to wear plaid suits that made us look like Louis Jordan's band. The pianist was John Patton. He got tired of the shit, quit, and went to New York where he learned to play the organ. He used to pick me up. I finally told Lloyd that I quit. I talked with Rick Henderson, who told me that Miles was coming to play with him. He asked if I knew any tunes that Miles played. I gave him "Ray's Idea" and some other tunes he played on the Blue Note albums. Miles came, and I was in heaven.

B.F. Did you record with Lloyd Price?

W.Y. No. I hadn't recorded with anybody. I was trying to keep away from the day jobs. They would have really put me out of it. After Miles left, Rick Henderson asked me to sit in the section of his band; but I had to try to go to New York. Ben Dixon, a very hip drummer, and I went to New York. We were very brave and dumb. Now you can't do it. The subway scene is bad.

B.F. This was 1956?

W.Y. Yes. We'd taken a saxophone player with us, a good alto player. At one point, Dizzy had built a band around him. His name was Leo Williams. He had some problems. When we got to New York, we ran out of money quickly. There were three of us in a room. The drummer and I decided to try to stay together, but Leo had some other shit on his mind. He really didn't care. When we found this out, we had to get away from him. He was out to hurt himself, and us, too. We let him have the room.

We went to Brooklyn, and this is where we really started paying dues. We were strangers in Brooklyn. We slept in trains and cars until we made some friends. I was determined not to go back to Washington. We managed to hold out. When you're young, you can do it. At the end of six months, we made friends with the cats, and they got to like us. Eventually I got a job in the garment center, and we met a broad named Mildred Jenkins. Everyone called her Millie.

B.F. Millie's pad.

W.Y. Yes. She was a South Carolina girl. She was a nurse. Not only was she of great assistance to us, but also to Freddie Hubbard. Millie had an apartment in Brooklyn, in Bedford-Stuyvesant. This little pad in Brooklyn I used to call Millie's pad. We met Millie when we were out playing gigs. She said she had a big apartment, and she let Ben and me crib there. Eventually we got our act together. At Millie's pad, after hours, anybody who was anybody—except maybe Miles and the other big cats—would be there. All the cats loved Millie.

Just before this time, I formed a band made up of Brooklyn cats. I did my gig thing at night. We'd rehearse two nights a week, on Wednesdays and Fridays, if cats weren't working. I was happy with it; I hadn't met any cats in New York. I ran into Miles Davis, and I would go to see him. He'd let me sit in. That did wonders for me. I would be scared to death on the stand with John Coltrane, and Miles would tell the band to play some blues. With him and Red Garland, it was impossible. Paul Chambers was cool. You had to get to know Red, and he had to get to know you. Trane was cool; Philly was cool. That was a hell of a rhythm section. I'd go up there to play, and there was Miles looking at me—and Howard McGhee and Thelonious Monk and Milt Jackson, et cetera. But man, you do it. Maybe you don't feel good about it then, but when you go back to Brooklyn, you feel good.

Every chance I could, I'd be up at Miles's crib. He'd show me certain things and would encourage me. He'd keep you in check. If you wanted to show off, Miles would say, "You got a Cadillac outside?" In other words, "What's wrong with you?" I dug it. I needed that. I kept doing my thing in Brooklyn.

One time, I looked around at my rehearsal and saw a little guy who came over from New York and had a tuba. The cats said it was Ray Draper. I didn't know who he was. He'd been playing some sessions in New York and at some competitions at Birdland. He had been going to the High School of Performing Arts in New York. He was a nice cat—seventeen years old. He was full of himself. I was a little bit older, and I helped him to be serious. We were playing some of Horace Silver's compositions. I didn't know that it was hip. Ray came with a proposal. If he could play with us, he'd get us to the New York competitions. I said, "No." And I didn't want a tuba player. But the other cats said that if we did it, we'd be doing something. So I thought that if we didn't do it, I'd lose the band. We let Ray play with us, and we had the competitions. Nat Hentoff was at that time new to us, and he was one of the judges. We played three competitions. We won them all—my band. In the other band was George Braithwaite, who was one of Ray's schoolmates; Pete LaRoca, the drummer; and a little cat who played the piano named Jon Mayer.

Someone had started talking with Bob Weinstock over at Prestige Records and the liner-note writer Ira Gitler. Miles had spoken highly of me to Bob. I wasn't concerned with the competitions; I tried to forget about it. About a month later, Ray called me and said he was making his first record date that day with Jackie McLean. He said to come over to Jackie's house, but I didn't have any money. I told him I'd make it if I could. The fare was about fifteen cents. Within an hour, the postman came with a box from my mother with food and also a money order for ten dollars or fifteen dollars. So I took the A train to lower Manhattan. I didn't know Jackie McLean, although I knew of him. I heard cats talking about him. I got to the address that Ray had given me, and I went up to meet Jackie. The door was open. There were Ray Draper, Doug Watkins, and Bill Hardman and his lady. They said they were waiting for Jackie, who had gone uptown to sign a contract for a gig later that night.

Finally someone suggested that we go over to Prestige. I asked what we were going to do with the cat's crib. They had good neighbors, so we left the door open. The kids didn't have keys. René McLean was just tiny then, and also Vernone; and little Melonae was with Dollie.[6] So we went to Prestige. Arthur Taylor was the drummer, and Mal Waldron was the piano player. Finally, when Jackie McLean showed up, Ray and I were at a sandwich shop next to Prestige. Jackie came in, and Ray introduced us. Jackie said that he had a date in Hackensack, New Jersey, and that I was welcome to come if there was enough room. They had just enough room for me and Bill Hardman's lady. We got out there, and I got to see what was happening. It was a record date called *Jackie McLean and Co.* It was Ray's first date. I watched the session.

B.F. Did Rudy Van Gelder record it?

W.Y. Yes, the doctor. In those days, you had to be on time. During intermission, when they listened to the playback, Bob Weinstock came over to Ray and said that he was going to record him and Webster. He didn't even know me. He gave us a date. Jackie was supposed to be on the date, but it was really Ray's date. Being that Jackie McLean had more experience than either one of us, he was the cat. Mal Waldron, Spanky DeBrest, and Ben Dixon rounded out the date.

What happened with this date was that I was to write two tunes and Ray was to write two. I wrote a tune called "Terry Ann," for my daughter, and one for Miles called "The House of Davis." Ray wrote "Jackie's Dolly" and "Mimi's Interlude." I requested that we play "You're My Thrill," because of Billie Holiday; it's a tune she did. Mal Waldron wrote "Pivot." There's a record with Jackie, Donald Byrd, Jimmy Raney, and Mal Waldron—they also did this tune.

B.F. Nineteen fifty-seven was a big year for you. Most of the recordings you made that year were with Jackie McLean.

W.Y. After that date, I felt good. There was something about that record. It was nice. When I left Washington, I left with the drummer Ben Dixon. I told Ray that I'd make the date as long as we had Ben Dixon on drums. About two weeks later, Mal Waldron called me and said, "I have a record date." I asked who was on it, and he told me himself, John Coltrane—my knees began to sink; its bad enough playing with Jackie—Idrees Sulieman, Kenny Burrell, Paul Chambers, and Arthur Taylor. These were heavyweights. Bobby Jaspar was there on tenor. I said, "OK."

On the morning of the date, I went over to see Miles, and he convinced me that I could do it. I said, "Shit. I'm scared to death." I asked him to play a record he did with Jackie McLean, Milt Jackson, Ray Bryant, Percy Heath, and Arthur Taylor. The tune was "Minor March." He showed me a few licks. He was living around Tenth Avenue, and I had to get to Prestige on Fiftieth Street.

I walked out to make the date. I was with Idrees Sulieman; I didn't know him. Another cat, a photographer, was with us. The only one on the date I knew was John Coltrane. I got to the date after a Coltrane date had been held there. Me, Bobby Jaspar, and Idrees Sulieman went out together. The other cats were already there. Red Garland was there with his wife; Trane was there with his wife, Naima. It was Mal's date. He had written four tunes: "Interplay," which was "I Got Rhythm"; "Anatomy," which was "All the Things You Are"; "Light Blue," which was a blues; and the tune that made the album, "Soul Eyes." I was nervous as hell, but I was determined. Everything that we did was one take. Between John Coltrane and Bobby Jaspar, that was something. Bobby Jaspar was a good player, very good. He was tight with Idrees; he was a nice cat. I liked him and Trane. It was a hell of a date.

So then I'm living in Brooklyn. I was working at the Arlington Inn in Brooklyn with a local organ player. I needed these kinds of gigs to help me pay the rent. I was hanging out with some broad; I had taken her on this gig, and I'm playing this modern Martin trumpet. I'm looking down, and this chick had had too much to drink. During intermission, I went down and tried to revive her. Junkies were running through the club, and they took anything they saw. My horn was one of the things they took. They left me with a brown trumpet bag and a mouthpiece that Miles had just given me. So I called my mom, who said, "No way. I'm sorry, but I have no money for shit like that."

Someone told Miles about my bad luck, so Miles told him to tell me that if I need a horn to come over to his house and he'd give me one. So the cat came to my crib— I was to play a gig with him—and I told him that I couldn't make the gig because I didn't have an axe.[7] He told me what Miles had said. Gil Coggins was one of my heroes because he had played and recorded with Miles. He was at my house, and he drove me over to Miles's. I went to see Bob Weinstock. I told Bob about my bad luck. We talked about my making another album, and I told him I wanted to make a tribute to Billie Holiday. He asked who I wanted to use. I thought immediately of Lester Young. Bob called me and said that we were going to use Paul Quinichette, Joe Puma, Mal Waldron. Mal was playing for Lady Day then.[8] I wanted Philly Joe Jones and Paul Chambers. That would be it.

But the day of the date—I had a cornet Miles had given me—we found out that Paul Chambers couldn't make the date and neither could Philly Joe because Miles was going to play in Ohio.[9] So we used Earl May and Ed Thigpen, two-thirds of Billy Taylor's trio. I'd never met Paul Quinichette. I'd written a tune called "The Lady." We played it, Mal's arrangement of "God Bless the Child," and another tune that Billie did with Teddy Wilson, "Moanin' Low." On the other side, we did "Good Morning, Heartache," "Don't Explain," and Mal's arrangement of "Strange Fruit." This album was rereleased in a limited edition in 1986.

After we made the Lady album, I went back in the studio with Jackie McLean and Ray Draper. We recorded two tunes from the album *Strange Blues*. I recorded again with Jackie, Curtis Fuller, Gil Coggins, Louis Hayes, and Paul Chambers. When the session came out, it was on two records. The first was *Makin' the Changes*. This had parts of things that Jackie had done and some things that we had done: "What's New" and "Jackie's Ghost"—which is my tune, but they credited it to Ray Draper—and "Chasin' the Bird." Then, they came out with another album called *A Long Drink of the Blues*.

B.F. There's a false start on "A Long Drink of the Blues." What happened?

W.Y. Bob had some funny feelings about that date. He was mad at everybody. There was some misunderstanding. We were supposed to have money for transportation, and Jackie was supposed to handle it. He told Gil Coggins to deal with it. So Gil did the best he could. Gil had a friend who had a truck. That's what we had for transportation. It was OK with me, but Paul Chambers was on the date, and he was playing with Miles Davis. He rode in limousines with Miles, so Paul was burning. That was the problem. I was laughing. Curtis Fuller and I were cracking up. The drama and the theatrics that you hear are between Jackie McLean and Paul Chambers because Paul is warm.

The next thing that came out was under Jackie McLean's name. They were some of the things that Ray and Jackie and I had done. I told Ray to get a better piano player, but he wanted to use one of his friends. We used Larry Ritchie on the date. I told Ray that I liked the cats. One of the cats was Jon Mayer and another was Bill Salter. He wrote the tune "Where Is the Love," which Roberta Flack recorded. He turned out to be a composer, but he was a bass player then. That's the way Ray was acting; he was under peer pressure, and it was his date. It came out as *Strange Blues* on Prestige.

B.F. *Fat Jazz* was on Jubilee.

W.Y. Right. Charlie Mack was the producer. We had Gil Coggins and Ray Draper. This was our band, our sound. We didn't work much with this band, although we worked at the Continental. Then, we went to Newark to Sugar Hill—me, Ray, Jackie, Gil Coggins; and when we made the record, we had George Tucker and Larry Ritchie. Other times, we had a Brooklyn bass player named Tommy Williams.

"What Good Am I without You" is a tune I heard a chick named Jerri Southern do a long time ago. I liked it so much that I had to do it. Jackie walked in while Gil and I were playing this ballad, and he said that we had to do that tune. I was talking with Jackie later, and he said that tune is worth the price of the album.

B.F. That was your last recording in 1957, a big year for you. Then you disappeared. What happened?

W.Y. New York began to be like Washington. I began to worry about my mom, and I wasn't doing what I wanted. I decided to come home and stay for a while. In '58, Miles came to Washington, and his manager asked when I was coming to New York. I said I was going to see a broad there, and he said to look him up because Prez needed a trumpet player.[10] He said to bring a copy of *For Lady*.

When I got to New York, I went to a store and got a copy of the record. The next thing I knew, I was playing with Prez. We played Birdland and around Brooklyn. But it was more than that to me because it was Lester Young. When I came home from playing with Prez, my mom really got fearful of my going back to New York. What made matters worse, when Lester got back to New York, he was staying at the Alvin Hotel across the street from Birdland, on Fifty-second Street. Mom became very skeptical. When Prez came back from Europe, he died. He was an epileptic, which I didn't know. His lady didn't know that he was coming back, so when he came in, there was nobody there to care for him. He had one of his seizures, and that was it. This is what I heard.

B.F. So you never recorded with Lester Young?

W.Y. No.

B.F. How long were you with him? How many dates did you have?

W.Y. Maybe about nine months.

B.F. Were you his last trumpet player?

W.Y. Right. We didn't get any ink or anything like that because everyone knew Prez and loved him. It was one of those things. Everyone was talking about Trane. When we played Birdland, I saw Gerry Mulligan there. Everyone who loved Prez was there. Symphony Sid was in control of all of this, and he was emcee that night. It was something. It was an education for me.

B.F. So you played with him right up until he died?

W.Y. Right. But when he went to Europe, I came home. When he came back, I didn't know it.

B.F. What happened to you?

W.Y. Jackie McLean asked me to come back to the Apple and do our thing again. I went back, and we formed a band. This was when he left Prestige and went with Blue Note. He had made an album with Donald Byrd, Walter Davis, Jr.—*New Soil*—and they played "Minor March," which they called "Minor Apprehension." We had a good band. We had Walter Davis, Jr., Reggie Workman, and I can't recall the drummer. Jackie couldn't work in New York because he didn't have a cabaret card. He could work on Long Island and out of state, so we came to Washington and Philly. I had a card. I was getting tired of New York; it was becoming like Washington: you go uptown and see cats falling all around. I was really sick of that. I needed to get away from New York.

I went to New Haven for a year or two. After that I didn't want to go back to New York. It was like a rat race. I went from New Haven to Boston for a minute. I met a piano player who had a lot of talent—John Hicks—who was going to Berklee.[11] He told me that he was from St. Louis, Miles's town. I wasn't thinking about St. Louis, but John Hicks said he was going home, so I decided to go to St. Louis—not to stay, but to see what it was like. I stayed there for a while and moved on to Kansas City.

B.F. In St. Louis, you played at Jorgies. Someone had a tape recorder going, and the only other recordings I know by you are three records on VGM recorded there. Were you aware that you were being recorded?

W.Y. No. Those are all bootleg. They're not really legitimate.

B.F. You sing on "What's New."

W.Y. I just did that one night when I was feeling good.

B.F. Have you recorded since then?

W.Y. No. I'm in no hurry to record.

B.F. But it's been a quarter century.

W.Y. It's gotten to the point where there's so much corruption.

B.F. I think that on the liner notes to the VGM records, your Washington friend Andrew White is quoted as saying that in 1960 he couldn't find you, that you had disappeared.

W.Y. No. Let me tell you something. A couple of years ago, Julius Hemphill came to Washington. We have an organization in Washington called D.C. Curators. So this cat writes an opera.[12] It's actually a work he did for saxophones. Julius Hemphill is known for playing with the World Saxophone Quartet, with Hamiet Bluiett, Oliver Lake, and David Murray. So when he came here by himself to do a workshop, he wrote a beautiful ballad called "For Billie."

Carl Grubbs was the leader of the band called the D.C. Workshop Orchestra, and he had a singer named Larita Gaskins. She's in New York now. She's a great vocalist; but being in Washington, she couldn't get into anything. No one would help her, so I got John Malachi to help her. Early this year we did this opera. They had a pit band with Malachi Thompson and me on trumpet, plus some other fine musicians living in this area. They had a cat conducting. Andrew White was one of the saxophone players. Julius Hemphill is a great writer, but when it comes to writing for brass, he's not clear. He should at least give cats time to breathe and get their chops together. He writes good for saxophones. But I don't even know Andrew White, and he doesn't know me. So that's bullshit, pardon my French.

B.F. But the point is that some people thought you had disappeared. I had difficulty finding you. You're a hard man to find.

W.Y. I look at it like this. I don't want to be exploited. I took a long view of it. It doesn't work to be second best; you have to have the stomach to deal with that shit. It got to be real ugly. It's not the music; I love the music. It's the business.

After I left St. Louis and Kansas City, I found out that Kansas City, the town Charlie Parker came from, didn't even have a picture of Charlie Parker. I was hurt. Black people didn't seem to support their music. So I went to L.A., and it was corrupt. I left there for San Francisco. There was very little music there. When I was there, you had a little cat who called himself Little Rock. When he came to New York, his name was Farrell Sanders. He became Pharoah Sanders. I remember him in Frisco. The only major club we had there was the Blackhawk. Miles would play there. Everyone else played the Jazz Workshop. I couldn't stand Frisco, maybe because it's ruled by Gemini.

I went to Portland, Oregon, and met my wife. We went back to New York in '63, a week before John Kennedy was assassinated. New York was changing. I hadn't been home in a long time, so I decided to return to Washington and see my relatives. My mom died in '59, the same year as Billie Holiday. So I really didn't have anything to come back here for.

Washington, D.C., 30 July 1987

Notes

1. Young refers to Dizzy Gillespie.

2. "Bird" is Charlie Parker.

3. Young refers to Waxie Maxie Quality Music Shop. Waxie Maxie was Max Silverman. "Yard" (short for "Yard Bird," or "Yardbird") is Charlie Parker.

4. By "changes" Young means chord changes.

5. Young means that Dizzy Gillespie would double the tempo.

6. Young refers to Jackie McLean's wife, Dollie, and their children, René, Vernone, and Melonae.

7. To jazz musicians, an axe is a musical instrument.

8. "Lady Day" (or "Lady") is Billie Holiday.

9. Paul Chambers and Philly Joe Jones were part of the Miles Davis rhythm section.

10. "Prez" is Lester Young.

11. Young refers to Berklee College of Music.

12. Young refers to Julius Hemphill's *Long Tongues: A Saxophone Opera.*

DRINK SMALL

28 January 1933–

B.F. You are one of the legends of South Carolina music, widely known as the Blues Doctor. Weren't you born in Bishopville in 1933?

D.S. That's correct.

B.F. What was the date?

D.S. I was born January 28th, 1933. Bishopville is located in Lee County. That's in the Piedmont, the Pee Dee area of South Carolina.

B.F. Were you born in the town itself?

D.S. I was born out in the county there, about ten miles out in Lee County. There's a Hickory Hill district that's right across from the Browntown area. But the Browntown area, that's where the Lizard Man was.[1] Lizard Man was down there in that area where I'm talking about.

B.F. I assume you grew up in Bishopville.

D.S. Yes, I grew up there. I had all my schooling there. I was reared in a musical family. An uncle used to play guitar, but he went away to World War II. I had another uncle in Columbia who played guitar and pump organ, and another one who could blow the harmonica. All of them could play a little music and sing. My aunt said that my mama could sing. My mama never got married, but my daddy, I learned later, could play accordion a little bit, dance, and cut up; so he had music in him. My daddy never was married, but he got children four different places. I guess I take after him because I didn't get married.

When my uncle went into the service, he left the old guitar around the house. I fooled around with that on one string. We had an old pump organ there, and I learned to play "Coon Shine Baby" on it. That's a song people in the country who had an old pump organ or piano learned to play. Another guy, a friend of the family, had a guitar. I borrowed it and learned to play a little bit. When my uncle came back out of the service and got another guitar, I fooled around with that. Then, my uncle that

Drink Small at the University of South Carolina, 1986. Photograph by Benjamin Franklin V

lived in Columbia brought down a steel guitar and we played on it real good, so he was ashamed to take it back. So all during the elementary school, I was playing the guitar. I just played; I didn't sing.

A lot of the guys around could play. One old guy named Green back in the neighborhood could play. In fact, every neighborhood had a guitar player. That's the reason why I'm going to write a book, just write about guitar players. There's so many of them I could name, but if I do that I'd take all my time off myself and put it in other guitar players. But you're trying to get my history, so it's too heavy for me to call all of their names. I learned to play pretty well in elementary school, and I played in high school—and sang in the glee club and played piano and guitar at my church. I started singing later on because I was playing at house parties. The first group I organized was a little gospel group called the Six Stars. They broke up, but they were pretty good.

B.F. How old were you then?

D.S. In my teens when I organized that group. I'll never forget that group, the Six Stars. It was kind of funny. Our first program was on a Monday night. We'd go to visit the St. Mark Baptist Church down there in a little section called Manville. We raised one dollar. One dollar. We thought that was money. Some of the guys in the group moved to Michigan, and so I got some more guys to fill their place. When the group broke up, I got with a group down there called the Golden Five, and they still sing.

B.F. This was still in Bishopville?

D.S. Yes. So I'm a big fella now, a teenager, and so I'm singing bass in the glee club and Friday and Saturday nights playing house parties by myself. That's the reason people would never tell my story right. They say a blues-gospel player turned to blues. What happened, I was playing both of them to start with. It wasn't no blues player or no gospel; I was just playing both of them to start with. And at that time, I used to listen at a lot of radio. We had an old battery radio. I used to listen at WLAC in Nashville, Tennessee. I used to listen at WCKY in Cincinnati. And I used to listen at Tennessee Ernie Ford and Merle Travis and John Lee Hooker. So I came up listening to everybody—Fats Domino and a lot of them. So I came up listening to all the music.

B.F. When you listened, did you pick up licks from them?

D.S. I had it all. I didn't need to pick it up. I'm godsent. They learned licks from me. And so my intention was to be the best guitar in my hometown by the time I got twenty-one. But by the time I got sixteen, I was kind of killing everybody. I listened to quartets, too. I listened to the Fairfield Four, the Sensational Nightingales, and all that kind of group. I was a teenager with the Golden Five. That was the best group down there at that time, still is. And we used to bring the top gospel groups—the Nightingales, Harmonizing Four. I was singing bass and playing guitar in the quartet and still playing at house parties, too.

Our group, we'd listen to WOIC in Columbia. At that time Charles Derrick, a radio announcer in Columbia, had a group called the Spiritualaires, and they were a top group here in Columbia on the Bowman label.[2] So our group, we got them to come down to our church, to our program. They came down, man, and they could beat us singing a little bit, but not much; but we were *bad*.[3] And so I was singing bass and playing the guitar. So now the Spiritualaires, they want me to join them because they were living over here; and also at that time I was singing bass in the junior choir at my church with the young people. We would go to places where young-people choirs were singing on a program, and I'd be there. And so I was doing that, and I was doing so many things; and so after high school in '53, I went off to Denmark to take up barbering. They used to call it South Carolina Trade School, but now they call it Denmark Tech.[4] I went there and took up barbering, but I didn't want to cut no hair.

I wanted to cut up. As you can tell by my talk, I ended up cutting up. I wasn't going to pick no cotton. And so I finished the barber training in '54, but it was a one-year course. You finished in September; you had to go back that June to march in commencement. I finished in '54, but I marched in '55.

So now I'm still playing with the quartet group when I come home, and the weekend parties, still doing both. But after I joined the group—Charles Derrick and the group that was on the Bowman label—they finally got on Vee-Jay; and so on the Vee-Jay label, you're big time. When the Golden Five used to book all the professional groups down to Bishopville, when those guys went back on the road, they'd be telling one another, "Boy, the guy down there in Bishopville, he's bad. Somebody's got to get him." They were talking about me. So when I got on the road with the Spiritualaires, a lot of people knew about me. When I got out there, we were ready to go.

So our group, we were real good, too good to be true. We sang on the floor with Suwanee Quintet, Sam Cooke, all of them—Lou Rawls—big-time singers; but we were big time, too. But our group broke up. Our group was rated number two at that time, and I was at that time rated number one gospel quartet guitarist. Ain't many guitar players would walk out there and make them sisters shout. I could make them shout. We were at the Apollo Theater when it was the real Apollo, I mean the real one.[5] And we toured a lot of states with the Swan Silvertones, a lot of groups.

B.F. When was this, around 1954 or so?

D.S. No, '55 is when I came with them—'56, '57. What happened, a group called the Chosen Gospel Singers had a song out, "When the Saints Go Marching In," and we had it out, too. This guy singing with them got his own group now in New York.[6] He was one of the leaders at that time, and we all had the same songs. They had the gold cup; the group that sang the best won the gold cup.

In Norfolk, Virginia, Mark Richards had the Dixie Hummingbirds's twenty-fifth anniversary and had the singers out there; we won it, but they gave it to the Dixie Hummingbirds. And we also recorded another song, "Pressing On." The Nightingales, they recorded it, and all of us recorded it at the same time, too.[7] So they had gold cup singers out there in New Jersey. Used to have a program there at the Laurel Gardens, but they tore that down, and now they use the new Newark Armory. We had a sing-out there. We won it, but they gave cups to all the groups. And they'd have bets on the guitar players, on who could play the best.

B.F. So there were gospel competitions up and down the coast?

D.S. Well, no. Two of us recorded the same song, and there'd be a battle to see which one the people would like the best—just a battle on the song. See, we recorded "When the Saints Go Marching In," and the Chosen Gospel Singers, they recorded the same song. So we got in front of the audience and let the people select which one they liked the best. We always come out on top, but they give it to the other group who had been singing longer. And I won a lot of trophies.

At that time, Sister Rosetta Tharpe, she was a popular guitar player. A lot of people know about her. She was out there, a lady playing the guitar, so everybody loved her. So what happened, they rated her the number one lady gospel guitar, and they labeled me as the number one male gospel guitar. And at that time, Les Paul and Mary Ford, they were the pop duo. They made "The World Is Waiting for the Sunrise," "How High the Moon." They were the pop duo. Now this black group called Mickey and Sylvia. Mickey was a blues and jazz guitarist.

B.F. Mickey Baker.

D.S. Yeah, Mickey and Sylvia; they had a duo called "Love Is Strange." So what Rosetta wanted me to do—she and I were the number one gospel guitar players—we could have been the gospel duo, while Mickey and Sylvia was the blues, and Les Paul and Mary Ford were the pop. But I guess me being a country boy, I ain't going to take that up. So I didn't do it. I didn't do it. I mean, we could have done it because she was beating all the lady players, and we could have got together as a duo, lady guitar player and me a guitar player. People go wild if we had done it, but I was from the country: get me out of the country, but they can't get the country out of me.

But I grew up. A couple of the Spiritualaires wanted to stay in New York, and some wanted to come back here. So what happened, two of them stayed up there. Matter of fact, some of my original guys had already quit. But we carried the group on, so we had the best guys when we broke up: me, Louis Johnson, Norris Turner, Fred Davis, and Bernard Codwell.[8] Only two of the originals stayed from the start, so we couldn't get the sound back together. Louis Johnson got with the Swan Silvertones. While we were there, we toured with the Staple Singers, Five Blind Boys, and recorded for Vee-Jay.

After we broke up, then I started fooling around here, in Columbia. I stayed here. I already could play the blues. During that time, wasn't anybody much playing Jimmy Reed and all that kind of stuff. So I started playing around here and made a little thing called "I Love You Alberta" on Savoy Records, but it came out on the Sharp label, which is a subsidiary label for Savoy. Kip Anderson at that time made "Oh, My Linda," and we did that then. Mine was "I Love You, Alberta" and "Cold, Cold Rain" on the Sharp label.

B.F. When you recorded for Vee-Jay, did you go to them in Chicago? Or did they come to you?

D.S. Well, what happened, a lot of people didn't know our group. Our manager was Charles Derrick at WOIC; but the Spiritualaires, we called him. We'd never been in Vee-Jay studio. Matter of fact, I've never seen it. All our stuff was recorded at WOIC on the board by Derrick.[9] Being the deejay, he got the mix down and knew where to send it off. One song got drums on there, and a lot of people don't know what it was. That was Derrick beating the trash can. The trash can was the drums. The Spiritualaires never been in the Vee-Jay studio. All our stuff was recorded at WOIC.

B.F. Were you doing a demonstration record?

D.S. No. Derrick was the deejay and he knew how to get it mastered, and so he knew how to make it right when it got to Vee-Jay. All they had to do was do it.

B.F. But when it came time for the Spiritualaires to record for Sharp, did you go to Newark?

D.S. No. Sharp ain't got nothing to do with the Spiritualaires.

B.F. So it recorded you, Drink Small?

D.S. Yeah, the blues. We went to the studio in Newark, New Jersey. Herman Lubinsky owned the Savoy label, but Sharp was a subsidiary. After that, I've only been in his studio once. He recorded gospel singers, but not the Spiritualaires. Vee-Jay did our gospel.

B.F. How was it working with Lubinsky? He has a reputation for being tough.

D.S. Yeah, any millionaire is tough. He's tough as he want to be. So what happened, he had Savoy. A lot of your jazz artists recorded for Savoy, a lot of gospel. I think some people are still on Savoy label. I think somebody bought the catalogue. Savoy still goes on.

B.F. When was that Sharp recording?

D.S. '59 or '60. I'm in the neighborhood, and, like, I know my blues. They're on the CD that George Buck put out on the Southland label.[10] Lot of noise. Later on, in New York, I recorded "I'm Gonna Shag My Blues Away" and "I'm in Love with a Grandma." And then I did *Drink Small Does It All*. Before that, I did two for Ichiban around '91, '92: *Drink Small: The Blues Doctor* and *Round Two*.

B.F. You also recorded for Bishopville, which I assume is your label.

D.S. I did "I'm in Love with a Grandma" and "I'm Gonna Shag My Blues Away." I got tied up with the Arts Commission, and I've been dealing with them for a good many years. That led me to the Foothills Festival.[11] I ended up playing at Wolf Trap in Vienna, Virginia, and out at the colleges and for a lot of prisons. I've played in a lot of festivals, you know.

B.F. You've been to New Orleans.

D.S. Oh, yeah. I've been there three or four times. Last year, we played the Three Rivers Festival in Columbia. Koko Taylor was after me, and then Buddy Guy. On the first of May last year, I played down there in New Orleans.[12] We knocked them out. I had them hollering down there. And so we've done that and recorded *Blues Doctor: Live & Outrageous!* for Gary Erwin in '88. He reissued that one just this year. Hope it does something.

B.F. All along, did you make your living entirely from music? Or did you have another job?

D.S. Well, about ninety percent music. I won't say living. I make my existence—not living, but existence. When you're living below poverty, what do you call that? Poverty, you're down to start with; but when you get below poverty, what do you call that? Wouldn't that be existence?

B.F. Maybe.

D.S. Just like, if you were supposed to eat three meals a day and you eat two, what you call that?

B.F. Hunger.

D.S. If you cut it down below that, what you call that?

B.F. More hunger.

D.S. So wouldn't you say existence would be the same?

B.F. That might be.

D.S. It ain't good to say it, but, when I say it exactly the way it is, it makes people start crying. Say, "How are you today?," and he says "Existing." He ain't dead; he's alive. So when you live in poverty, you're just getting by by the standards. You'd be surprised: I been lower than those who were supposed to be living by the standards.

For instance, a truck driver, a guy that drives trucks, he has a per diem. He's supposed to eat three meals a day. Let's say, well, ten dollars a meal. Mathematics speaks that's thirty dollars. He's supposed to eat three meals. That's the standard for a bus driver, truck driver. But if you stop by a little neighborhood store and buy some sardines, some crackers, and some pork 'n' beans, and loaf of bread, he can live on that. He takes ten dollars and live two days. Am I right? He got twenty dollars in his pants. He's supposed to eat three, but he can't eat but one. They can't take the money from him for it. That's the per diem. He might have a thousand dollars in his pocket extra by just eating sardines.

Things like that will keep you living. You won't die. You eat pork 'n' beans, honeybuns, sodas every day, you will live.[13] You won't die. So that's the way it is. So I still make existence, and that's my world; but I feel just as good as you. That's just like a car. A man got a Mercedes, one got a Rolls Royce, and one got a Toyota, and one got a moped going to Charlotte. All of them will get to Charlotte. The moped might take five dollars worth of gas, big car might cost twenty, but all of them will get you to Charlotte. Does it make sense?

B.F. Perfect.

D.S. So what's poor to somebody else, it might be rich to somebody else. And what proves that, you got enough people that got money where nobody supposed to be hungry. You know that. For all the wealth America has, nobody supposed to be hungry, but they are. I know you've heard that before. I'm pretty sure you heard it. But they are, and that's a sin. But like I tell people, I had me a lady almost cry. I said, "Lady, nobody going to heaven but me." I looked dead at her: "Nobody going to heaven but me." She said, "Why do you say that?" "Because I tell the truth. Nobody going to heaven." What you got to say about that?

B.F. I don't know, Drink.

D.S. Plenty going, but they might not get in. They going, you might not get in. You going, but you will not get in. When it come down to money and sex, people lie about that. Money, sex, and religion rule the world.

A lot of people are just Bible toting—I can't say what I want to say—bull jivers, Bible-toting bull jivers. I'll tell you why. When it comes to sex, the Bible plainly says man marries, have all the sex he wants. Man marries, cuts out; that's adultery. Sell sex in the streets, prostitution. Not married and have it, it's fornication. Now if that's the case, ain't nobody going to heaven. That's what the Bible says now. I don't write Bibles. But I say if the Bible right. . . . What can you say about that?

B.F. I'd say you're probably right.

D.S. If you read the Bible, that's supposed to be the best book in the world. Now, I didn't wrote it. I can't back it up. But from what I was told and what I hear the preachers say and what I hear Bible scholars say, that's all I can depend on. I don't call myself a Christian. I'm a believer. You know why? Would you like to know?

B.F. I would.

D.S. I'm going to take you back to the root word. I'm more than a blues player. I'm a philosopher, too. The Lord give me a big head, and I'm loaded, about to explode. The word, the root word, is Christ. That's the root word. Okay, now it leads into Christian. After it gets to Christian, it leads to Christianity. But the basic word is Christ. So I can't call myself a Christian, because I don't act like Christ. I do some things that Christ never did. So cut that Christ word off me. If I'd act like Christ, I could call myself a Christian. And if I get to be a Christian, that will stretch me into Christianity; and I'm going to take it further. I'm going to throw a word you never heard this way. Christ, Christians, Christianity will lead you into Christianity-lism, and will lead you into Christianity-lismization. You never heard that before, have you?

B.F. No.

D.S.: Christianity-lismization. So start off from Christian, but I'm a believer; I believe, but I'm not a Christian because I ain't doing things in a Christlike way. You can't be a singer unless you can sing. Cannot be a Christian unless you have Christ. You cannot beat a man unless you can fight. So if you ain't got the basics, the rest ain't going to come. What the tree look like without a root? What it going to stand on? Huh?

B.F. Nothing.

D.S. So got to have the basics. So I don't act like a Christian, but I believe; I'm a believer.

B.F. Back to music: when you were growing up, I know you picked up instruments around the house, but were there any musicians in the area? Was there a small-town Carolina blues scene? Did you know Josh White or Pink Anderson or Baby Tate—any of them?

D.S. No.

B.F. Did you hear people talk about them?

D.S. No. See, wasn't nobody down that way thinking about nothing like that. The way I learned about Josh White was in high school, reading history about Josh White, but they called him a folk singer from Greenville. I never heard about Pearly Brown 'til later on because at a time like that. . . .[14]

I'll tell you another thing. The blacks had one book and the whites had one book, and then the blacks started using the white books. A lot of kids down there didn't know who Mary McCloud Bethune was, and she was from down that way. You got a lot of kids down there now: "Who is Mary McCloud Bethune? I don't know her." And out from Bishopville, there you got a road called Mary McCloud Bethune Road. Out there at the school where she went to, they made a little park, the Mary McCloud Bethune Park.[15] And see, when it come to black history, it wasn't being taught because the blacks had one book and the whites had another book.

I learned about the Bill of Rights when I got to high school. Now, kids learn about the Bill of Rights almost from the second or third grade. And see, the school I went to, we had two rooms. One school down there had one room, one teacher; that's all. And some part of the school went six months a year, some of them four months. The school I went to, there were two teachers. Some had to walk four and five miles to school.

B.F. Are you talking about grade school or high school—or all of it?

D.S. My elementary school right by my church. That school went through the seventh grade, and the teacher there she taught us the eighth grade. It was me and two girls there, and we couldn't get to high school. She taught us the eighth grade on her own. And so when you come to Pink Anderson, a lot of people down there don't know who that is now. See what happened, that wasn't even mentioned.

B.F. What was the name of your high school?

D.S. Dennis High, but it's a middle school now, and they got Bishopville High. The high school I really went to, they tore it down and built another one after I left. And then after they built the other Dennis High, then they changed that one to a middle school—and the whites they already had Bishopville High. So what they did, after they rebuilt Dennis High, then they changed it to a middle school and took the elementary school and made a community center, and everybody went to one high school, Bishopville High.

Yeah, so what I'm trying to say, blues and things like that, they don't know who that is now. A lot of them don't know me, and I'm from there. See, what happened, in the black race one time, some churches wouldn't let a guitar player come in the church. Called it the devil's instrument because a lot of the guys used to drink moonshine liquor, pick guitar at house parties, and they figured they'd be drunk when they come to church. You take some churches now; they don't want the music too loud. Some churches got some strict rules, and all the churches ain't up on it yet. Some churches don't allow modern-day quartets because they stomp the floor out and they sing too loud. And some churches got some pretty rough policies, you know; and that's that. That's why a lot of people don't deal with blues, because, like I tell them, what the black need to do, have more black history in the schools and demand that the students study these things; but the people in the curriculum are doing nothing about it.

As I was standing on my porch, four black kids came by, two boys and two girls. One of the girls was about fourteen, and the other one about twelve. One of the boys, he seemed to be about ten, the other one about eight. The one about eight said, "You play jazz, don't you? You play blues?" I said, "Yes." So the little boy told the girls, "That's the Blues Doctor." She said, "So?" He said, "That's the Blues Doctor." She said, "So?" What she was saying: "Shut up."

Right now, I hate to say it, you got more whites know about me than blacks do. I hate to say that because they consider blues as low-down music and nobody never taken the time with it. You take now Benedict and Allen: they will never bring B. B. King there, or Bobby Bland.[16] They'll never do it. Ain't going to have no blues in that church school. Here's the man, "The King of the Blues." But, see, people who are in the church don't want them blues; that's low-down dirty.

Well, you got millions of people think that way. A lot of people go to church and a few of them say, "Well, he blues. He ought to try serving the Lord, now the Lord done blessed him." See, they put Jesus in there. Just like Elvis Presley or Arthur Crudup. Elvis Presley, he came by and made a million off a black man's song. Black man couldn't make enough to buy peanuts. It's a black man's song.[17] Just like the guy overseas, Eric Clapton, in England. Now, a poor blues player got to go overseas to make some money, and this is home. That just really makes me mad. I'm born in America, hundred percent American, and got to go to another country to make money, and this is home. That's why some jazz and blues players go overseas, and they don't come back. People abroad treat you better than your homeplace. If people don't like you at home, what's wrong?

B.F. Have you performed abroad? Have you been to Europe?

D.S. Yeah, I've been there; but I'm still saying, why I got to go over there? If you live in a million-dollar place and not happy, another man living in a storefront, the one that's happy, that's home. Am I right?

B.F. Yes, indeed.

D.S. If your home people don't like you, what's wrong? Huh?

B.F. What do you think is the answer to that question?

D.S. Well, I'm doing the best I can. I'm playing. I can't do no more. I'm getting mad. See, if you're being good, trying to do the right thing, what's wrong with doing the right thing? I'm not going to change that. I love it. I say, "God bless America." You got to go overseas to get my blessing, but God bless America. Tell God to come back and bless me where I'm at. Doesn't that make sense?

B.F. Yes.

D.S. All right, then. I'm not getting "amen."

B.F. Amen.

D.S. I get mad, you know. I get mad, and I'm right.

B.F. But you have a lot of engagements, don't you? I mean you play a good bit?

D.S. No, it ain't no good because people ain't doing much. When the last you heard me play?

B.F. I go to bed early.

D.S. There's your answer.

B.F. I said that about your engagements because I looked at your Web site before coming over here. It looked to me as though you have ten or so engagements for August.

D.S. But that ain't much. You think I'd be living here if I was making money? Come on now. I ain't mad. I'm kind of sick. I'm kind of under the weather, but I ain't finished yet. I got a lot of bills. See my medicine there?

B.F. Yes.

D.S. I ain't out of the woods, but I'm glad to be here. The Lord blessed me. People say they like you. They don't care nothing about you. They don't care nothing about you. Don't let them fool you.

B.F. In your playing, were you influenced by anybody?

D.S. Well, I tell you. I listen to a lot of people but always figured if somebody else could do it, I could do it. I never was an imitator. I'm an originator. That's why I tell people, "Come hear me play. When you leave, you'll never forget because nobody sounds like me, and I'm going to keep it like that. When you hear my voice, you say that got to be Drink. I don't imitate nobody. I see another man get in his britches, I can get in mine. What's wrong with mine? Does that made sense?

B.F. Yes.

D.S. I tell them, "Shame me in my game, ain't going to never see my service."

B.F. So when you were growing up and listening to WLAC or WCKY, you might have liked the music but didn't try to play like any of the musicians.

D.S. Well, let me tell you something about me, okay? My people sang. I listened to Tennessee Ernie Ford and a man they called Buddy Johnson.

B.F. From Darlington.

D.S. Yeah, his sister named Ella died year before last. He's been dead some time back before then.[18] Okay, my tenth-grade teacher in high school was Mrs. White. She was from Darlington, so she and Buddy Johnson were classmates. So what happened, Buddy had this guy from Spartanburg called Arthur Prysock was the male vocalist, and Ella was the female vocalist. Like I said, when they come to me, I was a jack of all trades. I used to say to Arthur, "I saw you." Mrs. White said at lunchtime to sing Arthur's songs. I would go the other way because she'd be worrying me to sing Arthur's songs. Now, I've been playing the boogie-woogie piano in school, but, see, that's another instrument and another style music. That's a big difference from Arthur Prysock's songs. And then I'm singing gospel, and then on Friday and Saturday night playing the blues with the guitar. So what I was saying, I came up doing a lot of things. That's why my story is hard to write because I kept on doing too many things, and it would take a lot of time.

Here's a song I used to sing in the choir, "You'd Better Mind":
[Drink Small plays and sings.]

> You'd better mind
> You'd better mind
> You'd better mind, brother
> You'd better mind
> How you're walking across
> Right foot slip and you all be lost
> You'd better mind.[19]

That's Sunday morning. That's a style, so I kept on doing a lot of things, you know. [Drink Small plays and sings.]

> C. C. Rider
> See what you done done

. . . .
And your man done come.[20]

Going down to the river
Jump overboard and drown
. . . .[21]

That good old Piedmont jazz. A lot of people sing it. Yeah, this kind of music is fun. You can see people dancing by it, it would be fun. Probably need to teach somebody how to do that dance, country dance. It would be fun. Some young people learn it. Some old people still know it. They know how to do it. Young ones, you'd have to teach them. We can talk some more. This is one I got recorded, but you know it.
[Drink Small plays and sings.]

There is too
Too much water
Too much water
You don't have to be funky
Going, going around here
Going around here
Smelling like a monkey
Now you oughta be
You oughta be
. . . .[22]

B.F. Drink, you do a lot of things.
D.S. That's what makes me mad. How much can you do? Do everything in the book.
B.F. But is your point that people like Les Paul and Mary Ford did the pop thing and Mickey and Sylvia did rhythm and blues; but because you do it all, you're not identified as one certain thing? Is that your point?
D.S. Yeah, that's why I want to be a legend.
[Drink Small plays and sings.]

I'm a funky old man
I'm a funky old man
When I walk up
On the bandstand
With this guitar
In my hand
. . . .[23]

B.F. Did you write that, too?
D.S. Yeah.
B.F. You're a real talent.
D.S. I was here in the '50s.

B.F. Have you always lived in South Carolina?

D.S. Uh-huh.

B.F. Either Bishopville or Columbia?

D.S. I been here fifty-one years.

B.F. In Columbia?

D.S. Yeah, I came here about twenty-two years old.

B.F. You've done a lot of things at the University of South Carolina, like parties.

D.S. Oh, yeah; oh, yeah. If everybody I know give me a dime apiece, I'd be all right. Ten cents.

B.F. Are most of your gigs away from Columbia?

D.S. Anywhere I can get them. They're scattered about. But I don't play too regular now, you know. Here's a song about Bishopville. I plan to record this one.

[Drink Small plays and sings.]

> Bishopville
> Is my hometown
>
> That is my
> Old stomping ground
> That old house where I used to live
> It's torn down[24]

. . . .

B.F. When you write these tunes and record them, do you publish them with ASCAP or BMI?[25]

D.S. Yeah, me and Gary Erwin are working with BMI.

B.F. Have other people recorded your tunes?

D.S. No. A lot of money and large legalization got to go with things like that.

B.F. You have a lot to offer.

D.S. But I ain't getting nothing for it. I'm retired and ain't retired. I need to be hired. I might as well retire; I ain't being hired.

B.F. You've told a good story about your life.

D.S. If people would stop crying and see it. People start crying when they hear it. I don't want to hear it because I feel bad. I done live it. I don't want to hear it after I live it. But I live it. Hear it again, that sounds like going back through it.

I don't know what the problem is; I can't make no money. If I'm worth some money, where the money is? I don't see none. Somebody must be lying. Like I say, I tell the truth. That's why my story is hard to write; I tell the truth. A lot of people know I'm catching hell. Oh, man, I can't believe it. Just couldn't believe it. Maybe I ain't doing what the Lord wants me to do. If you do what the Lord wants you to do, He ain't going to kill you, but He will beat your butt and make you suffer. And that's just as sure as a martin will go to a gourd, and I know it. You play music any?

B.F. No, I love it but don't play it.

D.S. You done put Dizzy's story together?[26]

B.F. Yes. Did you know him at all?

D.S. I met him. Last I saw him, I stepped on his foot. I tell you what happened. Me and my band, we were playing in Poughkeepsie, New York, and he was in town, too. And so what happened, we stayed at the same hotel. Well, I ain't never seen that much country people. Kenny Rogers had a one-nighter at the Civic Center there. Man, I bet you I saw five thousand boots like cowboys. I ain't never been to a hotel that fine.

So what happened, Dizzy was playing at a theater for a week; and at the theater they turn out at ten o'clock at night.[27] Where I was, a jazz and blues club, they didn't start 'til ten. From the theater where Dizzy was playing, they walked to where we were playing. Everything was close together like. So Dizzy said he wanted to meet me because, see, I'm from Bishopville and he's from Cheraw. Someone said, "Yeah, man, Dizzy wants to meet you; he's your homeboy." And so we started playing at ten and Dizzy ended playing. So the guy said, "Dizzy Gillespie's band's in the house."

So after we finished playing at the club, we all got together. The club owner and his wife and some more people were there. We all sitting there. We took pictures with Dizzy. I had a manager along with me. So it was cold. Ice was on the ground. It gets cold up there. Snow was on the ground, but everybody up there was used to it.

And so what happened, we all took pictures together, and I got the picture here somewhere. We took a picture together, and it was cold; so my man said, "All right," and so they got ready to leave. He said, "Let's take a picture out in front of the club." Went out there—you know, playing and got sweaty—so I went outside with no coat on. I had my suit coat on, but I didn't have my overcoat on. So went on the outside, the porch—boy, the wind was cutting out there—with my regular suit on. And so I go like this [makes a stepping motion]. "I didn't mean to step on your foot, Dizzy." I said, "Excuse me, man." "That's all right." He had a raggedy voice. "That's all right, brother." I tell a lot of people about that, and they took the picture. I got the picture with me and him standing in front of the club, and we took one inside the club. But I took a picture with him in front of the club. We were out and it was cold, and I was trying to duck the wind, you know, and stepped on his foot.

B.F. I found him a nice man, and very funny.

D.S. Yeah, I went down to the coliseum one night and saw him down there.[28] He was down there. The mayor from Cheraw was visiting, and he was playing at the coliseum. He started doing this special song, I believe "Wade in the Water," an old Negro spiritual, and he started singing it. He said, "Y'all sound damn good!"

Now you know when he blows his horn how his cheeks would swell up and fall right back in playing. Nobody in the world could do that but him. He had a technique that nobody learned yet, and they won't learn it—can't. Ain't nobody can do that. You know somebody was going to try it. Got to give him that.

You know, a trumpet ain't got but three valves, and you could hear a hundred notes come out of there. That means that one valve probably got about thirty notes. You know it ain't but certain way to do it. The more wind you get, the more notes you can make, I think. And, see, with him, the more pressure the wind got, I think more notes you can blow. When his jaws get full of air, he got a lot of air to blow out. And where one guy might get ten notes off one of those things, he might could get thirty. He's got so much air to blow out and ain't nobody can do that. Nobody can do that. He's got some of the air stored up there in a tank just to push it out.

You know why his horn was bent? What happened in his band, somebody sat on his horn and mashed it. So what he did, he tried it out, and by the thing going up, it sound different. It sounded different, you know. So he kept it up, and he started getting it made like that. So he got them all made up.

And Wes Montgomery, he start playing a guitar with his thumb. What happened, he used to play with picks, and his wife used to be aggravating him about it trying to practice with the guitar. So he started playing with his thumb and got good at it. Since he got good at it, he just started doing it. And his wife was the one caused him to start playing with his thumb. He started playing too loud so he started playing with his thumb real soft. Kept doing that right, got pretty good. See, the pick got a different touch rather than meat. The meat has a softer tone. He started playing with his thumb and the thing sounded good. That's why he started playing with his thumb. His wife caused that, sure did. Like Dizzy, somebody sat on his trumpet and bent it, and he tried it and it sounded different. It sounded good. He just started getting them made like that.

B.F. You mentioned Arthur Prysock. Did you meet him?

D.S. No, but I know how he sounds.

B.F. He'll be in this book. I tried to speak with Ella Johnson, but she was ill when I contacted her.

D.S. She died year before last.

B.F. But she was ill for a long time. She lived in New York, I think.

D.S. I went to a buddy of mine's funeral down there, went to the hospital to see him. He was in Carolina Pines.[29] That was the last time I saw him because he died the next day. I was sitting up there at the hospital at Carolina Pines, and they said Ella Johnson died. Buddy got a brother in Darlington, if he hadn't left. I can't think of his name, but he lives in Darlington. He's a nice fella; used to play drums. Buddy had a smooth band. Sister used to sing. And Ruth Brown still sings.

[Drink Small plays and sings.]

> Every time it rains
> Teardrops from my eyes
> Remember the night you told me
> Love would always be
> I won't be sad and lonely
> If you come back to me
> Every single cloud
> Would disappear
> I'd be happy
> If you were near.[30]

That was Ruth Brown. Yeah, boy. Those were the good old days; good songs.

Columbia, S.C., 11 August 2006

Notes

1. Small was born in the Hickory Hill district. In June 1988 a large creature resembling a lizard was reported as having attacked a parked car with the driver in it. Although the resulting furor lasted for several months, the creature was never found.

2. In order to distinguish the group from another group called the Spiritualaires, Derrick's singers were known as the Spiritualaires of Columbia, S.C., although the label on their first Vee-Jay release identifies them as the Spiritual Airs of Columbia, S.C.

3. By "bad" Small means good.

4. In 1948 Denmark Technical College—in Denmark, S.C.—opened as a branch of the South Carolina Trade School System.

5. In June 1957 the Spiritualaires performed at the Apollo Theater in New York.

6. In 1955 the Chosen Gospel Singers recorded "When the Saints Go Marching In" for Nashboro; the Spiritualaires recorded it for Vee-Jay the next year. Small refers to Tommy Ellison as being active in New York in mid-2006.

7. In 1957 the Spiritualaires recorded "Pressing On" for Vee-Jay. The Sensational Nightingales recorded this song for Peacock, also in 1957.

8. According to Small, when he joined the Spiritualaires, the personnel consisted of Bernard Codwell, Charles Derrick, Jimmy Foster, Joseph Hollis, Louis Johnson, and Sonny Boy Johnson. When Foster and Sonny Boy Johnson left, A. J. Thompson and Norris Turner replaced them. When Hollis and Thompson quit, Fred Davis replaced them. The final personnel consisted of Bernard Codwell, Fred Davis, Louis Johnson, Drink Small, and Norris Turner. I cannot determine when Charles Derrick left the group.

9. Small refers to the studio mixing board.

10. Small refers to his blues recordings for Southland, not to the songs he recorded for Sharp.

11. The South Carolina Arts Commission helped underwrite—or underwrote—the production of "I'm Gonna Shag My Blues Away," "I'm in Love with a Grandma," *Blues Doctor: Live & Outrageous!*, and *Drink Small Does It All*. The Foothills Festival is held in Easley, S.C.

12. Small appeared at the 2005 Three Rivers Festival on 24 April. According to the schedule for the 2005 New Orleans Jazz and Heritage Festival, Small played there on 30 April and 1 May.

13. A honeybun is "a flat yeast-raised bread roll glazed with honey before baking," according to *International Dictionary of Food & Cooking*, comp. C. G. Sinclair (Chicago: Fitzroy Dearborn, 1998), 262.

14. The Reverend Pearly Brown was a blind street singer and guitarist from Americus, Georgia.

15. On 10 July 1875 educator and activist Mary McCloud Bethune was born in Mayesville, S.C., approximately twenty miles south of Bishopville. She attended the Mayesville Presbyterian Mission School.

16. Benedict College and Allen University are predominately black schools in Columbia, S.C.

17. Small refers to "That's All Right, Mama," recorded by its composer, Arthur "Big Boy" Crudup, in 1946. Elvis Presley's 1954 recording of the tune was the first single released by this singer. Crudup, who died poor, apparently received no royalties for his song.

18. Ella Johnson died on 16 February 2004, and Buddy Johnson on 9 February 1977.

19. "You'd Better Mind" is an old Negro spiritual.

20. Ma Rainey recorded her "C. C. Rider" (or "See See Rider") in 1924.

21. "Going Down to the River" is an old blues song.

22. Small recorded his own "You Don't Have to Be Funky" on the 2003 CD *Drink Small Does It All*.

23. Small has not recorded his "Funky Old Man."

24. Small has not recorded his "Bishopville Is My Home Town."

25. The American Society of Composers, Authors and Publishers (ASCAP) and Broadcast Music, Inc. (BMI) license members' creations and distribute royalties.

26. Small refers to Dizzy Gillespie.

27. Small means that the theater's performances conclude at ten o'clock.

28. Small refers to the coliseum at the University of South Carolina.

29. Carolina Pines is a hospital in Hartsville, S.C.

30. Ruth Brown recorded "Teardrops from My Eyes" in 1950.

HORACE OTT

15 April 1933–

B.F. You are from St. Matthews. When were you born?

H.O. I was born in 1933 and went to school for the first ten years in St. Matthews. At that time there were people who had gotten interested in me and suggested to my mother that maybe she could get me into Wilkinson High School in Orangeburg so I could be better in touch with things that might help me later in life. My last two years were at Wilkinson. There, I joined the band, and we had a jazz combo on the side. The combo played all over the state.

B.F. What kind of music did you play?

H.O. Jazz: "All the Things You Are," "Perdido," "How High the Moon," and so forth.

B.F. Were you encouraged to improvise? Or was it all charts?

H.O. It was charts, but there were places to improvise. At that time, in addition to the school band, a bunch of us formed a jazz band to play on the side. There were five of us. We got fifty cents per person in Orangeburg. We then contacted a place to play, and one of the fellows had an uncle who gave us a piano to use at the place. The piano was on the back of a pickup truck. The driver cut a corner too sharply, and the piano fell off. So by that time rubber bands were holding it together. Rubber bands are often used on saxophones. When I was in college, a fantastic alto player named Aaron Harvey, who became a judge in Charleston, used rubber bands on his saxophone.

B.F. When I listen to musicians coming out of jazz schools, they have great technique, but generally don't solo particularly well.

H.O. That was not the case with us. When I began arranging in the eleventh grade, my brother, who is four years older than I am, bought me a lead sheet of "Satin Doll."[1] That was my first arrangement. South Carolina State College was next door to the high school, so I went there and spoke to Professor Reginald Thomasson, who was head of the marching band and orchestra. He took a great interest in it and told me to bring him whatever I wrote. Had it not been for that, my interest would probably

Horace Ott. Date, place, and photographer unknown. From the collection of Horace Ott

not have been sustained. This was two years before I went to college. Even though I was classically trained and gave concerts, I had this thing of wanting to write music and be in jazz. When I went to college, he took me under his wing, and I started writing for the seventeen-piece band we had. If I didn't have that atmosphere, I wouldn't have stayed with writing, although the interest was always there. I can't think of an arrangement I've ever written that hasn't been played. Why write if no one plays it?

B.F. How did you get into writing?

H.O. When I was sixteen or seventeen, I dreamed that I'd be writing. It was a drive in me. There were many great players, but they didn't think about arranging. One musician, Shelly Thomas, who was a year ahead of me at Wilkinson, also wrote. He also wrote in college.

B.F. What about your composing?

H.O. I tried to write songs, lyrics. In high school, I wrote and self-copyrighted them by mailing them to myself. I knew nothing about formal copyrighting. My writing wasn't then terribly sophisticated.

B.F. Did you have a music scholarship?

H.O. They knew me because the high school was right next to the college. When I started taking piano lessons at age ten and a half in St. Matthews, I had two teachers. When I got to the second teacher, she said to extend myself. Everyone was trying to get me to another level. She suggested another teacher in Orangeburg. Several other kids in St. Matthews also went to that teacher in Orangeburg. So I quit taking lessons in St. Matthews. At the same time, I was trying to improvise.

One time the teacher left the room, and I started playing something. When the teacher returned, I thought I'd get in trouble. She told me later that she thought I should move on to the next level. She said she'd introduce me to Professor F. P. Abraham at the college. She did, and I started taking piano lessons there. This was before I started going to Wilkinson. Professor Abraham's background was classical, and he didn't want to hear about playing jazz. He didn't want to hear "Blue Moon" or "Stardust." My original interest was classical. He became the person at the college to oversee me and my development. With this and Professor Thomasson in the orchestra, I was surrounded by the best.

When I finished Wilkinson and enrolled in South Carolina State, there was no scholarship, but there was an easy transition. I majored in music. The years at South Carolina State were great because I played tympani in the concert orchestra and glockenspiel in the marching band. These were things to make sure I was always in music. And of course we had the jazz band on the side, and another little jazz group, just like in high school. We'd find gigs and make a little money on the side. Most of the dances were at the Dukes Gymnasium. Kids today don't get too much of that. One night we were playing there—and I had several arrangements in the orchestra—and the pop-blues singer Chuck Jackson came there and sat in with us. He sang "Ebb Tide" and some of Roy Hamilton's tunes. I played piano for him. Years later in New York, I recorded with Chuck Jackson. I love things like that.

When I was still a teenager and playing song sheets—at that same time I was playing the classics and taking lessons—I wanted to play the popular songs of the day. In St. Matthews, I'd go uptown to the drugstore and look at the song sheets, go to the store's piano and play them through, and pay for the sheets. Actually there wasn't too much money then, but I didn't know I was poor. My mother gave me money to pay for one song sheet. I'd look at the song sheets and wanted them all. I'd play nine or ten of them—everyone was trying to help me out—and put them all back on the rack except for the one I bought; I'd go right home and play the others before I forgot them. I learned them that way. The necessity was there: I wanted more but could have only one. At the college, it was one long, sustaining experience in music. From the formative years until now, I can't remember not being in music: in high school playing the piano, in college playing the piano and writing music. When I graduated, Professor Abraham told me I could go any place and teach.

B.F. What was your degree?

H.O. Music education. I told him that I didn't want to teach, and he almost fell off his seat. He was like a guardian to me. I told him that I wanted to go to New York and play music. He got angry with me.

B.F. Had you then ever been out of South Carolina?

H.O. Sometimes during the summer I would go to New York and stay with an aunt in the Bronx, but there was no playing involved. One other time, when I was a junior or senior at Wilkinson, there was a saxophonist who had played with bands, and he wanted a piano player to go to Charlevoix, Michigan. I went since I was the pianist then. That was my first real gig. I worked as a bellhop and played the piano.

Someone suggested that in order to get into the mainstream and get acquainted with some of the kids in Orangeburg, I go to swimming lessons at South Carolina State. I took the lessons and met some kids who became friends for life. One was Paul Weber, who is a judge in Washington, D.C. Earlier, I met Dr. William Hixon, a dentist in Orangeburg. I made the transition from St. Matthews into Wilkinson very easily. By the time I started school, everyone knew me and knew that I could play the piano. Paul was playing saxophone in the band. So I didn't enter cold; I was accepted. We all played in the band for the next two years, and several of us were at South Carolina State together, including Paul.

B.F. So you majored in music and played both classical music and jazz. You played piano, glockenspiel, and tympani.

H.O. I also took organ lessons. As a pianist at State, I would be chosen to accompany the student who was graduating. I accompanied the senior recitals. That was classical, but on Saturday night I'd be down at Dukes Gymnasium playing jazz. These were invaluable experiences because they fortified whatever talents I had.

B.F. Did you find many students there who played improvised music?

H.O. Several, but not a lot. In four years there, players came and went.

B.F. Did any of them go on to become professional musicians?

H.O. Yes. Shelly Thomas played in the Ray Charles orchestra. He played saxophones, woodwinds. He now teaches and has a music school in Los Angeles. John Williams, a year or two behind me, is now the baritone player with Count Basie. When I conducted the Basie band for Joe Williams in 1970, John Williams was the baritone player.

There were other good players, but people have different drives. Aaron Harvey could have played with anybody. Another saxophonist, Lonnie Hamilton, could have played with anybody. He became a councilman in Charleston, South Carolina. Robert Ephriam, a trumpet player, was fantastic. He could have been a Clifford Brown. He went into the army.

B.F. So there was a good atmosphere?

H.O. Yes. They used to have state band competitions there. I remember once meeting Rufus Jones, who played drums with Basie. Another musician who came to South Carolina State was a blind musician who played well: he could do Erroll Garner and George Shearing. I used all of that music as inspiration. It was like being in a sea of music.

B.F. What year did you take your degree?

H.O. I graduated in 1955.

B.F. What does a talented guy like you do then? It's a big step from Orangeburg to New York.

H.O. Here's what happened. I told my mentor, Professor Abraham, that I wanted to go to New York and play. He was upset. All of this happened very fast at the end of my senior year. Lonnie Hamilton had opted for a teaching job at Sims High School in Union, South Carolina. Later, he got an offer to teach in Charleston. Professor Abraham asked if I would take Lonnie's job in Union so he could move to Charleston. Agreed. I was there for one year, and that is the only year I taught. This was 1955–1956. I was to be the band director and biology teacher. I wrote some of the arrangements for the music for football halftimes.

In the spring, there was a statewide competition for instrumentalists and singers. Some of the girls wanted to sing, so I formed a trio and taught them songs and harmonies. Six weeks later, they competed and came in first. The key was my experience: reading, writing, musical background. I gave them intricate harmonies, suspended fourths and seconds. It was beautiful stuff. The other groups weren't so sophisticated. That one year of teaching was a great experience. I was relegated to that area, so I didn't do much playing.

I had a military obligation. I'd been deferred during college, and I had another deferment to teach school. When I went to New York to live with my aunt, I registered with the local draft board, which took me into the army in the fall of 1956. I went in for two years. There was no letdown of musical activity. I went to Fort Dix, New Jersey. I started playing the piano, even in basic training.

I went to the band training unit, but there was no need in a marching band for a pianist. I told them that I played the trombone. In college, I had maybe ten lessons on the trombone with Professor Thomasson. I picked it up in the army and played it for the next eighteen months in the army's marching band. I remember being the only trombonist on some of those gigs, and the trombone is the background for a lot of marching music.

You do what is necessary. I wanted to be in the band and not in the regular army. I was sent to Fort Leonard Wood, Missouri. I got there on a Friday afternoon. As soon as I walked into the band barracks and asked if there's a jazz band, the guys said that there is a guy named Frank Hooks who has a band that was playing that night at a local high school. I went there, and everything fell into place. There was Frank Hooks playing trombone, a drummer, a bass player, and a piano with nobody at it. I asked to sit in, and they sat me down. I was a lock. After awhile Frank dropped out, and I formed a combo called the Men of Note. We played that area—colleges, on post, a club called the Strip. We played some Horace Silver, and I kept the writing going by playing some of his tapes and learning "Sister Sadie."

Another thing that helped me at Fort Leonard Wood was the all-army talent shows. The winners would appear on the *Ed Sullivan Show*. This was the Fifth Army area that I was in. I got the gig of forming the orchestra, and I wrote the arrangements. An invaluable experience. The army asked the Men of Note to go to St. Louis to perform on radio and television. We were among the first to wear the new dress blues.

From the army—I got out in 1958—I went to New York and had to find my way. I did what I had to do. I got a job in a plastics factory and in a factory where they made caps for fountain pens. In the meantime, I practiced.

Then, you could go places and sit in. Tuesday was sit-in night. A guy in the army told me that he knew Slide Hampton, who lived behind the Apollo Theater on 126th Street. I looked him up, and he helped me. He let me practice with him. One of the other guys practicing with us was young Freddie Hubbard. Another guy named Rocky, a tenor saxophonist, was also there.[2] Slide was with Maynard Ferguson, but Freddie was still local. Slide told me that Maynard was auditioning pianists at Birdland. I auditioned, but Lalo Schifrin got the job. It was a great experience.

Maurice Waller, Fats's son, had a rehearsal band on Long Island. He asked me to write arrangements, and every Tuesday I would bring him two. These weren't money-paying gigs, but the experience was great. I got some pressure from my mother and brother, but I asked them to give me more time. They backed off. I ran into a girl from St. Matthews named Lillie Pearl Woods. She wrote tunes, including some for Etta James. She told me to go to Tin Pan Alley and get myself known. I ran into the singer Dean Barlow, who asked me to play piano for him at the Town Hill club on Bedford and Eastern Parkway in Brooklyn. I played two or three places with him.

In the meantime, I ran into Pearl again, and again she encouraged me to come downtown. Eight months had gone by, and I went downtown. Within three days, I'd made over three hundred dollars playing demos. Barney Richmond asked me to do them.[3] Other people started calling me, and it began building up that way. The musicians used to go to a bar on Fiftieth Street between sessions. I ran into a singer from one of my demo sessions there, and she told me to see Luther Dixon, a songwriter who needed a pianist. I auditioned and got the job. Within a month, he got an assignment to produce the Shirelles. He knew I could write arrangements. I wrote the arrangement for "Tonight's the Night," which I think sold 750,000 copies. The phone started jumping off the hook. That was it. It also convinced my mother and brother. I took my mother to one of the Shirelles's sessions. One night listening to the radio back in South Carolina, she heard one of the songs she'd heard at the recording session. Then I was OK, as far as she was concerned.

B.F. Did that arrangement give you financial security?

H.O. A little bit. I had given up my factory jobs. I got out of the army around September 1958 and was fumbling. I met this young lady I had known in South Carolina when I was eight and she was six. Her family moved up here. We started dating. In 1960 we got married, and I didn't have a job. Within a month of being married, we did the Shirelles's session. Then, it was a whole sequence of recordings.

B.F. Your first jazz or blues recording was with Nina Simone, wasn't it?

H.O. Yes. But I had other hits. I had recorded Gladys Knight and the Pips with "Letter Full of Tears." I did some things with Hank Ballard, including "The Continental Walk." We went to the studio to record, and the engineer was getting his levels. We counted off, did a take, and that was it. We didn't even rehearse. I think the tune went to number twenty-one on the national charts. Don Covay wrote it.

I did "Years from Now" and "I'm Coming on Back to You" with Jackie Wilson and "Just One Look" for Doris Troy. "Just One Look" turned out to be a landmark for her because the off-Broadway play *Mama, I Want to Sing* is about the life of Doris Troy. Her biggest hit was "Just One Look," which I arranged.

There was a group called the Jive Five that had a hit called "I'm a Happy Man." Don Covay and I wrote and I arranged "You're Good for Me" for Solomon Burke. For Don Covay, I arranged "Checkin' In and Checkin' Out" and "It's Better to Have and Not Need Than to Need and not Have." For Nina Simone, I arranged "Don't Let Me Be Misunderstood" and "Do What You Gotta Do." Joe Cocker subsequently recorded "Don't Let Me Be Misunderstood," and of course the Animals recorded it right after Nina Simone.

I did Helena Ferguson's "Where Is the Party?," and "Send Me Some Lovin'" for Sam Cooke. For Aretha Franklin, I wrote "Prove It," which was on the flipside of "Chain of Fools." For Johnny Taylor, I arranged "Love Is Better in the A.M." When the disco thing started, I did "That Old Black Magic" for the Softones.

B.F. How did you get together with Aretha Franklin?

H.O. The cowriter was a girl named Randy Evrett, and she knew Aretha. A guy in Philadelphia asked me to arrange some songs. For one of them, all I had was the lyric Randi Everett had given me. As I was writing the melody, all done in one stroke, we recorded it with a young lady, and Randi submitted it to Aretha. She loved it and recorded it. Another arrangement was "You Don't Have to Be a Star," by Marilyn McCoo and Billy Davis.

I met up with two guys from France, Henri Belolo and Jacques Morali, who had been recording in Philadelphia and wanted to move to New York. They called me for strong disco arrangements. They asked five people who should arrange for them, and all five said me. We met, got our lawyers, and started recording. Out of this association came all of the Village People hits: "Macho Man," "Y.M.C.A.," "In the Navy," "San Francisco/Hollywood," which were all multimillion sellers. There was another artist we recorded at the same time, Patrick Juvet. I arranged "I Love America" for him, and it was a tremendous hit.

B.F. You've also done musicals.

H.O. I was the arranger for the all-black *Guys and Dolls*. Out of that show came Robert Guillaume, who later had his show.[4] Ken Page was in it. We did a fantastic arrangement of "Sit Down, You're Rockin' the Boat," which stopped the show. The critics liked it, but it didn't really make it. Clive Barnes himself stated something like, "Those arrangements are fantastic. Horace Ott put sounds in the Broadway theater that have never been there before, but should always be there."[5] As arranger, I had carte blanche for going there; I had two seats every night.

I also arranged *Inner City*, where I did an arrangement for Linda Hopkins, who got a Tony award for that. In the movies, I arranged the music for *Gordon's War*, which starred Paul Winfield. It's considered a black-exploitation film. The Village People did a movie that bombed, but we got reviews that the music was great.

Around this time we did an international tour, so I went to Japan and Australia, where the movie premiered. Complete wonderment. The record went gold in three days in Australia. Here, the critics panned it. Jacques Morali wanted an orchestra of 120 musicians for the recording. I called the studio, which said they couldn't accommodate that many. So we used a 95-piece orchestra for the score of *Can't Stop the Music*. They had booked me to stay in the Beverly Hilton for three months. It didn't take all that time to record, but because we were doing some other recordings I stayed there for three months. I pinched myself quite often.

In 1980 I went to Africa, where I had gone two years before. My neighbor in Montclair, New Jersey, is from the Ivory Coast, and we became good friends. I had him to my house to watch the Super Bowl. He was unassuming. A few months later he asked me to go to Africa. They had just gotten a new jet for the Ivory Coast president. A few days later, my neighbor asked me to meet him in Savannah, Georgia. I went there, boarded the private jet, and flew to Martinique for gas; to Recife, Brazil; to Abidjan, on the west coast of the Ivory Coast. That was an experience. The guy who invited me headed a company over there that discovered oil. I stayed there seven days; it was carte blanche treatment.

One day I went to the presidential village, Yamoussoukro, and as I was going in I saw the neatly made stone buildings. We went into the President Hotel, which impressed me as much as any hotel in New York. At the desk I asked for a driver to take me sightseeing. The driver spoke no English; I spoke no French. For five and a half hours he drove me around thirty villages. Downstairs at the hotel they played jazz and disco, and they asked me to come down. I went down and talked with the deejay. For the next two hours he played nothing but the music of Horace Ott. In Africa. I went to one African village that had a juke box with "Macho Man" by the Village People. That knocked me out.

B.F. You've recorded with South Carolinians Houston Person and Arthur Prysock.

H.O. I went to school with Houston; he was a year or two behind me. He was recognized as a great player. One night as we rehearsed for something in a girls' dormitory, on the first floor, we got locked in. Rather than create a fuss, we just cooled it and stayed for the night, playing and studying.

We've maintained a relationship. In New York, we hooked up again. I did about four albums with him. One album with him took me to Georgia. He had a gospel album for Fred Mendelsohn on Prestige, and he did it down there. I had done a commercial for Standard Oil of New Jersey, and I always had an agreement that if I wanted to expand it into a song, the publishing would revert to me. I took one of the songs, "Enjoy," and recorded it with Houston on *Clouds of Joy*. We did it with the Atlanta Tabernacle Choir backing us. Beautiful sounds.

B.F. Is Etta Jones on any of those albums?

H.O. We used them both on a commercial. Maybe she was on one we did at Rudy Van Gelder's recording studio.

B.F. Do you go way back with Arthur Prysock?

H.O. No. I was a fan. The guys who used to manage him—Hy Weiss and his brother—called me to produce an album.[6] I wrote "The Love I Need to Survive" for him. I love being a fan of someone and later get the chance to work with him.

When I was young, I used to see the name Bennie Benjamin on a lot of the songs I learned: "Jet, My Love," "Can Anyone Explain?," "Rumors Are Flying," "Oh, What It Seemed to Be," "When the Lights Go on All Over the World," "I Don't Want to Set the World on Fire." His name was on all of them. After I got into the music business, I wrote the biggest tune of my career with him: "Don't Let Me Be Misunderstood," which we did with Nina Simone. The Animals did it; Joe Cocker did it; Esmeralda did it. It was in Joe Cocker's album that stayed on the charts for a year and a half.

B.F. You've had a lot of hit recordings. How is the composer paid? Do you get royalties? A flat fee?

H.O. At the beginning of my career, I was an arranger, and I got paid whatever I could get. How big was your last record was what mattered. It got more sophisticated later on when they discovered that I was an integral part to a hit record. When I got with the Village People, they threw figures at me. I preferred a piece of the action.

B.F. Did you get cash up front plus a piece of the action?

H.O. Yes. If it becomes a hit, it's a bonus. It's an incentive, although I don't need incentive. I don't write music at the drop of a hat. But it is business incentive. Songwriting is a locked-in situation. You get so many cents per copy. You're paid by ASCAP or BMI.[7] If you publish a song, you get paid by the recording company that pays you as publisher, and you pay yourself.

B.F. There's a lot of soul in your music. You've written for organ players Jimmy McGriff and Richard "Groove" Holmes.

H.O. Sonny Lester was the guy at Groove Merchant. I don't know why I got the calls. On *Electric Funk*, by Jimmy McGriff, I wrote five tunes. I wrote "Criss Cross" for my son Chris; "Miss Poopie" for my daughter. That was my pet name for her.

B.F. What about Richard "Groove" Holmes? Can you discern a difference between him and McGriff?

H.O. Groove was up for a recording, and Sonny Lester asked me to arrange. I also wrote a couple of tunes. Jimmy McGriff and Groove Holmes also recorded together for Groove Merchant.

B.F. You also did a session with Dakota Staton for Groove Merchant.

H.O. Yes. We got together a little bit before the recording. We decided on the songs, tempos, and keys. After that, we met in the studio.

B.F. Also in the 1970s you worked for Blue Note, including a date with Joe Williams.

H.O. The connection there was Dr. George Butler, who was then at Blue Note. I'd done some sessions with him when he first came into the business. He called me to record; we were friends, and the calls kept coming. We did Lea Roberts from Dayton, Ohio, for Untied Artists. George asked me to do some things for Little Anthony and the Imperials. The Blue Note things were jazz, and I got them through George. We recorded Bobbi Humphrey and Lou Donaldson's *Sweet Lou*. I wrote "Sassy Soul Strut" for that album.

B.F. What about Bobbi Humphrey? How was it writing for the flute? She was young then. Did that present a problem?

H.O. No. I've had so much experience that I had no trouble. I knew that she needed a certain lightness, and good rhythm and freedom.

B.F. Who are your favorite arrangers?

H.O. In my formative years, I didn't have the financial means to buy the records to dissect. I listened to the radio. I listened to Mr. B. and Sarah Vaughan and wanted to write like their arrangers.[8] Now I can tell a Neal Hefti or a Nelson Riddle arrangement and know what I like. I like lightness. How you encase it and end it are important.

New York City, 1987

Notes

1. A lead sheet is a musical score containing only the melody, chord symbols, and lyrics, if any.

2. Ott possibly refers to the saxophonist Rocky Boyd.

3. Barney Richmond was a recording contractor and jazz bassist.

4. Ott probably refers to *Benson*, a television program starring Robert Guillaume that aired from 1979 to 1986.

5. Ott shares arranging credit for *Guys and Dolls* with Danny Holgate. In a review titled "New 'Guys and Dolls' Comes Seven Again," Clive Barnes writes of Frank Loesser's compositions, "Mr. Loesser's score has a bounce that jumps off the stage. Song after song emerges with a sort of pungent charm, and the words and the music are beautifully matched" (*New York Times*, 22 July 1976, p. 26).

6. The brother of Hy Weiss is Sam Weiss.

7. ASCAP and BMI license members' creations and distribute royalties.

8. Billy Eckstine was known as "Mr. B.," or "B."

HOUSTON PERSON

10 November 1934–

B.F. When you were growing up in Florence, South Carolina, what kind of music did you listen to that might have caused you to go into jazz, and where did you hear it?

H.P. Radio, mostly. My mother and father required that I listen to all types of music. I listened to everything from Sammy Kaye to *Piano Playhouse* to the Metropolitan Opera broadcasts on Saturdays to Symphony Sid from New York. I also caught the broadcasts from New Orleans, from the Roosevelt Hotel. I listened to everything.

B.F. Are your parents musical?

H.P. My mother played piano. There was a piano in the house. She just played for her own enjoyment. But I wasn't interested in music; I was interested in sports. I didn't start music until late, but I was still required to listen to music.

B.F. When did you come to music?

H.P. Almost my senior year in high school. My father gave me a saxophone one Christmas, and I just took it up. It was just one of my Christmas presents.

B.F. Was it a tenor?

H.P. Yes. And then I got involved with it and joined the band. I was still involved with sports—and the band.

B.F. What sports did you play?

H.P. Football and basketball.

B.F. You were in high school in Florence, and then went to college at South Carolina State. Did you have a scholarship, either music or athletic?

H.P. No, but I did have a goal of getting on the band that I heard from South Carolina State, which was a good band. They played our senior prom.

B.F. Did any of the people in that band turn out to be professional musicians?

H.P. Yes. Horace Ott is a big arranger now. He writes for Broadway shows. We still do things together. In fact, we just did an album together. And Danny Wright, who

Houston Person. Photograph by Gene Martin. Date and place unknown. Used with the permission of HighNote Records

has done some arranging. Most of the other fellows went into teaching. Aaron Harvey, the student director of the band, had already been on the road with Tiny Bradshaw. He's a judge now, in Charleston.

B.F. Everyone associated with South Carolina State mentions Aaron Harvey.

H.P. Yes. He was a big influence on me. He was the director of the dance band. He was studying at the time. After being on the road, he decided to return to school and study law.

B.F. What charts did they use?

H.P. Everybody in the band was writing good arrangements. They didn't use a lot of stock arrangements.

B.F. As a freshman at South Carolina State, you wanted to go into the band. How did you take that step?

H.P. Bobby Ephriam—a great trumpet player from Charleston and a colonel in the air force now—and I played together on a talent show. They invited both of us to join the band. I couldn't believe that I made it my first year, but I did. They carried me along because I wasn't really that great. They just carried me along. I've always been grateful for that. I stayed there, and then I went into the service. That's where I met Eddie Harris and Cedar Walton.

B.F. You went into the service after four years at South Carolina State?

H.P. I stayed there three years, and then I went in the service. They sent me to Germany. I didn't get in the band, so I just played around with Cedar and Eddie and Leo Wright and Don Menza, Lanny Morgan, Lex Humphries. And they carried me along. I was just lucky; people were tolerant of me.

B.F. I've listened to a good many college jazz bands, and they all have a lot of energy. They fail, ultimately, when it comes to solos. Was that the case at South Carolina State?

H.P. No. They had good soloists, and all the bands I came into contact with had good soloists. One year, Florida A&M's dance band came up to play for us, and they had Cannonball and Nat Adderley. Alabama State had a good band. North Carolina A&T had a good band with Lou Donaldson.

B.F. When did the band tell you to get out there and take a solo?

H.P. From the moment I joined the band. I was just lucky. I always had a knack for that; I don't know what it was. Some people have a knack for soloing, and some have a knack for section work. I was glad I was put in the role of getting the experience of playing in the section and getting ensemble work. I soloed more than anyone else.

B.F. You must have been awfully good, then.

H.P. No, I really wasn't. I guess to be a soloist you have to take chances and be uninhibited to get out front. Like Freddie Green: his job with Count Basie is to keep things together.[1] The other guy who's wild and uninhibited can take the solos. The first alto player holds the saxophones together; the first trumpeter holds the trumpet players together. They don't take many solos. In a way, they're much more important than the soloists. It's just role playing, I guess. That's the way I've always looked at it. You've got to have that thing of taking chances. My friend Johnny Williams, who plays in the Basie saxophone section and never solos, is more important than the soloists because you can always get somebody to solo. You can't always find somebody to play in the section.

When you're forming a group, it takes both ingredients. One without the other, it's lost. You look at groups like Clifford Brown and Max Roach. When they had that group, I always thought the most important guy was Richie Powell because he wrote the arrangements and kept everyone together. All those different personalities; somebody's got to keep them together. Look at groups like the Modern Jazz Quartet. Everybody talks about Milt Jackson, but it's John Lewis who really holds things together.

B.F. So from the beginning, Aaron Harvey, who was leading the band, said, "OK, Houston, take the solo on 'Body and Soul,'" or whatever it might be. You did, and from then on you were the major soloist in the band. Is this how it happened?

H.P. Yes. But there was another guy, Orlando White, who played alto. I thought he had the prettiest alto sound I'd ever heard. He's from Charleston. I used to think that all the greatest musicians came from Charleston. Charleston musicians are respected all over the world. He's in the school system in Charleston.

B.F. Were you drafted into the army?

H.P. No. I volunteered during the Korean War, almost at the end of it. It enabled me to get the G.I. Bill so I could continue my education up at Hartt College of Music.

B.F. So after South Carolina State, you went to Germany. You mentioned Cedar Walton, Lex Humphries, Eddie Harris, and others. Did you feel that you were in over your head?

H.P. Yes. Cedar Walton was a giant then. All these guys were. Don Ellis was tremendous; Eddie Harris was unbelievable.

B.F. Were you in the army band?

H.P. I was in the air force; the other guys were in the army. They were in the Seventh Army jazz band, which toured Europe, spreading public relations for the armed forces.

B.F. How did you connect with them?

H.P. We used to meet in Heidelberg at the jazz club Cave 54. All the service men would meet there on the weekend and jam. We'd play Friday night and Saturday night and then head back to the base. I never played with their group. On the weekends, everyone was free.

B.F. You came back after two and a half years in Germany?

H.P. I had the G.I. Bill, so I went to school in Hartford, Connecticut, at Hartt College of Music. There, I started over again. It's a good classical school. I just wanted to learn music. What I had learned at South Carolina State really helped me get accepted at Hartt.

B.F. How long were you there?

H.P. About two and a half years. I was there one day and got a job working in a band, and I worked behind a lot of people. I worked behind Arthur Prysock in Hartford. That's where I first met him. The bass player Ron McClure was at Hartt, and Dionne Warwick was there at the same time. We went to school together. So we were the few jazz people on the campus. It was mostly a classical school.

B.F. I assume you tried to make it as a professional musician when you left there.

H.P. Yes. You just start. There's no formula. It's all in making contacts, in meeting people. I went to New Haven for a while, and I went to New York. I didn't like New York, so I moved back to New Haven; and then I moved to Boston. Boston is a seaport town, so there were a lot of clubs that you could work.

B.F. Is that where you met Ran Blake?

H.P. No. I met Ran Blake at Hartt. He was at Bard College and would come down on weekends. We met and hung around together. We just had a certain empathy with each other.

B.F. *Suffield Gothic*—the duet with you and Ran Blake—really came off. Whose idea was it?

H.P. Ran's. We always said back in those days that we'd record together. We were the only ones who had any faith in it. Every review, every magazine, every jazz periodical in the world reviewed that album. It made some ten-best lists. Every review we read started with the statement that nobody could even conceive of us playing together.

B.F. So you settled in Boston after Hartford?

H.P. There was a lot of work in Boston. I needed a place where I could work. There were bars, strip joints, and jazz clubs where I played. There were a lot of after-hours places; there were a lot of things there. I figured that it was the place for me at that particular time. I stayed there for about six years. I worked a lot in New Bedford. I had my own group.

B.F. Did you ever encounter Madame Chaloff? She's such a famous teacher. Do you know of her?

H.P. I knew of her. A lot of guys studied with her; I knew Serge Chaloff's music, but I didn't know him.[2] I knew Alan Dawson. I was with my own groups. Lennie's on the Turnpike was there, and Paul's Mall. So there was a lot of work.

B.F. Who was with you in some of those early groups?

H.P. My drummer for a long time, Frankie Jones, was in that group. He and I, mostly. We'd bring in guys for the rest of the rhythm section, but we were basically the group.

B.F. You must have been able to make a living.

H.P. Yes. I got married up there. Then I started spreading out a little, and I had been going to Newark for some time. With all the negative images of Newark, I didn't particularly like it; but then I started getting around the city and saw that there was more to Newark than I had seen. So I moved there, and that's where I've been. That's where I live. There's a lot of jazz in Newark. There used to be much more, but there used to be much more everywhere.

B.F. When did you move to Newark?

H.P. In 1967.

B.F. How did you get together with Horace Silver?

H.P. I was recommended to him by an organist that I had been playing with, Gloria Coleman. I met him, and he asked me to do that album, which I was very proud of. I learned a lot from doing it. He is precise, and a perfectionist.

B.F. I imagine it also gave you a lot of exposure.

H.P. It gave quite a boost to my career. I just made the recording; it was just a session. I still had my group together.

B.F. Did that exposure with Silver lead to a lot more gigs?

H.P. Yes. And it helped my record sales, also.

B.F. At that time, weren't you recording for Prestige?

H.P. Yes. Cal Lampley was responsible for bringing me to Prestige. Then, I worked with Don Schlitten, and next with Bob Porter.

B.F. I've heard from several musicians about Prestige, that it was pretty tight with a buck. Was that your experience?

H.P. I look at it two ways. All jazz companies are pretty strapped financially. I'm not defending them, but as I went along in my recording career, I learned to use what exposure I got from records to help my personal appearances. And then I'd try to make up for any economical deficiencies through my personal appearances. You learn a lot from musicians as you go along in life. A lot of people operate to get as much as they can up front and let the chips fall where they may. But the records do serve a purpose: they expose you to the public. In the media society we live in, you need the exposure to get employment or get in different settings. Records have helped me immensely; without them, I wouldn't be anywhere.

B.F. I take it that you really don't have trouble working, that you work pretty much as you like.

H.P. Yes. And records are responsible for it, too. You don't just do it alone. But yes, as for the musicians saying that the record companies are tight with a buck; yes, they are. But they are very important, too.

B.F. You've been teamed up professionally with Etta Jones for fifteen years or so.

H.P. Yes. When I formed a group, I always wanted a vocalist in the band. So I got a band with a vocalist—and I'm recording, she's recording, and I try to get everyone in the group recorded. It keeps more records out. And so we try to alternate the releases so we'll always have something out. That helps the bookings. That's the way I use records. They have a purpose, and an important purpose. The other way you can look at the record companies being tight with a buck is that if they were not patient and tolerant, the musicians would not be recording at all. If it was just based on a fact sheet—on accountants telling you who to record—a lot of musicians wouldn't be recording.

B.F. You've been a sideman with quite a few musicians—with Bernard Purdie on his recording of "Shaft," with a lot of different people for Prestige, such as Sonny Phillips.

H.P. Yes. Sonny Phillips worked for me for almost ten years. I recorded with Tiny Grimes and Johnny "Hammond" Smith, who originally brought me to Prestige.

B.F. How did you get together with Gene Ammons?

H.P. I just did that one session with him, one song. I was just sitting there. I came to the session because my drummer was playing on it. They asked me to play on one tune. That was just fun.

B.F. How did you come to be featured on "Shaft"?

H.P. Bernard Purdie called me and wanted me to do the solo. I didn't have to play any parts or anything. Just that one solo.

B.F. You went from Prestige to Muse, Joe Fields's company.

H.P. I went first to Eastbound Records from Prestige. I had a nice stay there. In fact, that's where I did my live recording, in Detroit. I used a lot of musicians; they had a lot of musicians in Detroit. I just talked to myself one night: it would be wonderful to get all of these guys together and do a live, party-type date.

B.F. Who were some of them?

H.P. Donald Townes, Wild Bill Moore, Marcus Belgrave, Spanky Wilson, Etta Jones, Hank Brown, Jack McDuff, Sonny Phillips, Idris Muhammad.

B.F. They were hanging around Detroit at that time?

H.P. Some of them. I brought Idris in from New York—we were working at the club—but the rest of the guys were there.

B.F. Whose company was Eastbound?

H.P. Armen Boladian was the owner. He owned Westbound Records, which was the rhythm-and-blues label that had the Ohio Players, the Detroit Emeralds, and those guys.

B.F. How long were you with Eastbound?

H.P. I was there for about two or three years. From there I went to Mercury. That was run by another guy I met during the Ran Blake era up at Hartt, Robin McBride. I did three albums over there.

B.F. I have a question about *Harmony*. What is the blue water pictured on the cover?

H.P. Everybody wants to ask me about that cover. I don't know what it means, but it's eye catching.

B.F. There's a picture of a woman on a bathroom floor.

H.P. That's my daughter. Can you believe that album has been out about ten years? People still ask me about it. It did what it was supposed to do. I never understood it.

B.F. Did it sell?

H.P. It sold. I have people now ask me about it.

B.F. After your affiliation with Mercury, you went to Muse.

H.P. At Muse, I got more involved in straight-ahead jazz. Just straight jazz, as opposed to Eastbound and Mercury, where I had been doing more commercially oriented music. We have a good relationship. A lot of people don't understand Joe Fields, but we get along well. It was an opportunity, too, to get Etta on a label that respected her talents, that respected her for what she is and didn't try to remake her. It's been a good arrangement.

B.F. Some Muse albums have sexy covers. Obviously it's a marketing ploy, but do you have any say about how your music is packaged? Do they ever consult with you about it?

H.P. I consult with them. When I can, I tell Joe I don't want that. Sometimes he'll describe it to me over the phone because I'm on the road. A couple of times he smuggled a few good ones on me. His secretary usually tries to hold it back a little bit. I do have a say when I'm around. Now, after one cover I didn't like, I tell him beforehand to watch it.

B.F. What about the cover of *Stolen Sweets*?

H.P. When I look back on it now—comparing it with one of the other covers—it was nothing. Surprisingly he gave me one cover I couldn't stop because it was already made, but I did check around. I went to people and asked their opinion. I went to my bank and asked the women what they thought about the cover, and they weren't offended. I couldn't believe it. I went to the church and asked, and they weren't offended. But when I asked people on the street, they were offended. The people I thought would be up in arms about it didn't think anything of it. They thought it was cute.

B.F. What album is it?

H.P. The *Wild Flower* cover. After that, I didn't bother Muse too much. As far as I was concerned, I didn't care too much for the covers; but after I did my survey, I felt that they knew more about marketing than I did. That particular cover created a lot of interest. People always ask about my covers. It's surprising when you're involved with music that you don't consider the marketing aspects of it. But evidently everybody else does. I started reading about marketing. Companies spend just as much money on packaging their soap powder as they do on the actual product—or more—just to attract the eye.

B.F. When you have a session for Muse, are you in control? Do you go in with various tunes you want to do, and do you choose the musicians?

H.P. Yes. Joe Fields doesn't bother me about anything.

B.F. So you don't have an A&R man.[3]

H.P. No. I'm my own A&R man. I do consult with Joe about what I'm going to do, and we talk it over. If we have some point of disagreement, we resolve it. We both feel about the same thing at the same time, so it's worked pretty well. That's why I'm still around.

Florence, S.C., 17 March 1987

Notes

1. For decades Freddie Green played rhythm guitar with the Count Basie band.
2. Baritone saxophonist Serge Chaloff was the son of Madame Chaloff.
3. A&R means artists and repertoire.

JOHNNY HELMS

10 February 1935–

B.F. You were born in 1935 in Columbia, grew up here, and went to public school. Music was and is a big part of your life. You're a professional musician; you're a music teacher. How did the bug bite you? What did you hear? There couldn't have been much of an improvising scene.

J.H. My brother was a very good trumpet player. At about age seven, I decided to play the trumpet like he does, so I got a trumpet and started playing it. A lot of it was just God-given talent, just kind of something you don't actually learn. It's something that's given to you as a gift, and you have to develop it. So I started at seven, and when I was ten I played on a radio show in Columbia. When I was twelve, I was playing around town with the big musicians.

B.F. How did you get on a radio program? You must have had some reputation. Did they invite you? Were you part of a group?

J.H. It was kind of an all-star kiddie show, a local talent thing. An ice cream company sponsored it, and it was at the Palmetto Theater in Columbia. That was the first public thing, and I did a lot of things for the troops, played a lot of Veterans Hospital things.

B.F. Locally, like out at Fort Jackson?

J.H. Yes. The hospitals and anything like that—USO—anything that was entertaining the troops, and it was giving me experience, too. So I did a lot of that.

B.F. So the war was still going on then, and you were nine or ten.

J.H. Yes. My brother, Eddie, was a prominent trumpet player in town, and he would take me on gigs. I would sit over in the corner and listen. Occasionally he would let me play. But we didn't realize that my brain was sucking up all of these tunes. The songs I heard then, I can play today. If I've heard a tune once, I can play it. And that's a gift.

B.F. Was Eddie playing jazz?

Johnny Helms at the South Caroliniana Library, University of South Carolina, 19 March 2007.
Used with the permission of the photographer, Nicholas G. Meriwether

J.H. Yes. At that time, the thing was swing and dixieland, which were the forerunners of modern jazz, or mainstream, as it is called.

B.F. How did you become proficient on the trumpet? Did you have lessons?

J.H. Yes, I had lessons, but not really trumpet lessons. I had a cellist trying to teach me, and I had a tenor saxophone teacher. They were wonderful people, but they didn't know anything about trumpets. So I didn't really get any sort of formal teaching until Pat Garnett in high school. High school band is where I was taught how to play the trumpet. Everything else was by ear.

B.F. But before that, you were able to put a trumpet to your mouth, blow, get a sound, and work the valves?

J.H. Actually I could play songs.

B.F. Where did you attend high school?

J.H. Columbia High School. In fact, I played at Columbia High School, but I also played with the bands at Dreher and Brookland-Cayce high schools. The Dreher band was going on a tour, and they wanted me to come along and play. I was probably the only one to ever play in all three high school bands.

B.F. You must have been considered *the* young trumpet player in town if you played with three different high school bands.

J.H. Yes, I guess so. Not too many kids were playing in clubs at eleven or twelve years old, as I was.

B.F. In high school, did you basically learn technique?

J.H. I was in the Columbia High School band when I was in the seventh grade. When I was in the ninth grade, I was in the University of South Carolina band.

B.F. Did they recruit you?

J.H. My brother was in the USC band, and I don't know whether he put the bug in their ear. I was a pretty good player for my age, so I started rehearsing and playing with the band. Actually I went to St. Peter's parochial school, and in the seventh grade I was playing in the Columbia High School band. A lot of this didn't require any work. In fact, I'm ashamed of what little work I've done to develop my talent. But it's a God-given talent.

B.F. When you were with the USC band, did you play at football games? Is that basically what you did?

J.H. I did everything the band did: parades, football games, whatever. I was just like one of the guys. In fact, my high school band director was in the Carolina band at the time, so we would go out on weekends to Carolina football games and on Monday morning I'm saying, "Yes, sir, Mr. Moore." You know, strictly business.

B.F. What was his name?

J.H. Heyward Moore. In fact, in West Columbia they named a theater for him: Heyward Moore Theater. He was a great musician and great person.

B.F. But at about age seventeen or eighteen, your high school career came to an end. Here's this hot trumpet player who's in demand. What did you do? What happened after that?

J.H. While I was in high school, I was working as a musician. I had a band working six nights a week when I was in tenth grade. I started when I was about twelve, so by the time I got to high school, I was playing with everybody in town.

B.F. Where did your band play? You were too young for clubs, weren't you? Or were there clubs then?

J.H. There were plenty of clubs. When I was in the seventh and eighth grades, I played at the VFW Club, which is a bar. There were a couple of clubs on Main Street. I played the DAV clubs. I played the Elks Club. I played high school formals. Whatever was around, I played it. In fact, I was too young to be in the union, so the local union secretary wrote the national in New York to get me special permission to play. You had to be in the union to play. They gave me special dispensation, I guess, so I could do it.

B.F. Did they go to local 802 in New York?

J.H. Yes, local 802. Actually 802 is a New York local, but this was the national local. Later, I was in 802, the Jersey local, the Atlanta local, the Columbia local. When I was in the seventh and eighth grades, I was playing at local clubs, just like a big person.

B.F. Did you play jazz? Charts?

J.H. It was mostly combo work. We played the hits of the time. I could do that because I had followed my brother around and learned enough tunes to go out on my own and play gigs.

B.F. Was he a professional?

J.H. Yes, he was and is a very good trumpet player. He could do anything he wanted but gave up the trumpet when he got married. He just recently reorganized a nice ten-piece band. They're doing dates around town for fun, but he's a very good trumpet player.

B.F. Did any of your chums have a career in music?

J.H. Not that I recall. I was given a special gift, there's no doubt about it. It's nothing I could have done on my own.

B.F. Those years were before integration. Were there integrated groups? Was race an issue?

J.H. Oh, absolutely. I was probably the first local white kid to play with a black band. It was frowned on, but I did it because they were great players and they were my friends. One Sunday afternoon, we were playing at a club that the sheriff shut down because it had an integrated audience. I didn't let that bother me. We still played. The black guys were the ones that really progressed jazz-wise because they were the better players. They were very influential in what I did musically. Everybody wanted to hear Harry James and Billy Butterfield. They, Chet Baker, Clifford Brown, and Clark Terry were my influences.

B.F. You were listening to them when you were so young?

J.H. Yes, though I didn't really hear Clifford until I was eighteen. Of course, Clifford was young, too. Before that, in my early high school years—say, ninth grade—I was listening to Chet Baker, but I admired a lot of the things that were being done by these other gentlemen. I took whatever I liked from this one or that one and put it together.

B.F. Did you know Clark Terry's music then? When did you become aware of his unmistakable tone and style?

J.H. I'd heard him on records. He was a prominent soloist with Basie and Ellington, but he didn't have the reputation he has today. He was just a very good trumpet player. As years went on, he became more popular. In summer, when I wasn't teaching, I would hang out and play with buddies in New Jersey and New York. About 1962, I heard Clark in Clifton, New Jersey, at the Clifton Tap Room. I'd never met him and really never heard him play to any great extent, but I asked to sit in. He was gracious enough to let me, and I played the rest of the night. He didn't throw me off the stand.

When we finished the gig around two o'clock or three o'clock in the morning, I thanked him for letting me play and offered to buy him breakfast. We went to a diner where we ate and talked. When I got back home a few days later, I called to thank him again for being so gracious and letting me play. Since then, we've been very good friends. He's one of my dearest friends. He's a great person.

B.F. After high school did you go to college?

J.H. Yes. I started at the University of South Carolina, where I was in the band. While there, I got a scholarship offer from the University of Miami band. It was for a full scholarship, so I transferred there because Carolina wasn't giving scholarships.

B.F. How did Miami know about you? Did you apply for the scholarship?

J.H. I was in the Military Police National Guard, which went to summer camp each year. Once, we went where the Florida National Guard band was stationed. After hearing me play, one of the officers in the Florida band told Fred McCall, director of the University of Miami band, about me. He asked if I would go to his university, and I said yes. They gave me a scholarship and I went. That's how it happened: no audition or anything, just on the word of the Florida National Guard band director. This was around 1954. From 1958 to 1960 I played in the New Jersey National Guard band.

B.F. Before going to Miami, did you spend a full year at USC?

J.H. Only a semester. I was in the band and pitched on the baseball team.

B.F. Were the USC and Miami bands of comparable quality?

J.H. No, they weren't. To begin with, Miami had a hundred-piece band and everybody in it was on full scholarship, so naturally they had better players. Plus, the location didn't hurt them. It's a prominent private school. While I was there, I performed in the Florida National Guard band.

B.F. This was the group that heard you at summer camp?

J.H. Yes. That was one of the reasons they wanted to get me to Miami: so I could play in their National Guard band.

B.F. I assume that your experience with the Miami band was good.

J.H. Yes. A marching band is a marching band; it's just what it is. It was a good band with good players, but they played the marches that other bands played. There used to be the Cities Service Band of America, with Paul Lavalle. He came down to Miami to conduct a concert with the University of Miami band for his national radio show.

B.F. Was there a scene there in those days?

J.H. Yes, but I didn't know where it was. I didn't know anybody and didn't know where to go. One night, I got my horn and just started walking around Miami, looking for a place to play. I ran into a guy at a club in a Mexican restaurant. He was a tenor saxophone player, and a good one. He told me what he was doing and where he was playing, so I went there and sat in. They hired me. I stayed with them as long as I was in Miami.

We would do a lot of Sunday jazz concerts, and I met some good players there. A prominent one was Billy Usselton, who for many years was a tenor soloist for Les Brown. I was in the Miami band with Gene Goe, who became lead trumpet for Si Zentner and played with Maynard Ferguson. In fact, he ended up playing lead for Basie for many years. I think he was the best lead player Basie ever had. When he was back in the area, we'd hang out. Once, the Basie band was to play at the naval base in Charleston, and my friend Mitch Santiago and I went. The guard at the gate wouldn't let us in. I asked him to call where the band was. The band manager told him that if I didn't get in, the band would not play.

B.F. The Adderley brothers—Cannonball and Nat—were from Florida. Did you run into them?

J.H. I was playing at this one place with some pretty good players, and someone told me about an alto player at Porky's in Ft. Lauderdale, Cannonball Adderley. I was looking for a place to play. I didn't know much about him, so I went in one night and asked if I could sit in. Nat was there, of course. When he took a break, I'd play.[1]

It became almost a regular thing. Cannonball didn't take it easy on me. He tested me; he didn't play around. He called Clifford Brown tunes that a lot of people can't play. We had a lot of fun. That was only a few months before he became famous.[2] I think at the time he was with Florida A&M. Later on when we did the Main Street Jazz Festival in Columbia, I got Nat to come. Cannonball had already died. Whenever Cannonball was in the area, we'd hang out. We were very good friends.

B.F. Did you finish your degree at Miami?

J.H. No. I stayed a year. I was about nineteen years old, so I decided to come on back to Columbia. A friend told me that high schools at Irmo, Chapin, and Dutch Fork wanted to start band programs and asked if I would take the job. I had less than two years of college, but I had a background; and I'd had good teachers in the marching bands.

B.F. Didn't you need to be accredited to teach school?

J.H. You were supposed to be, but they let me slide, and eventually I worked part time on the degree and got it at the University of South Carolina. I was nineteen or twenty when I took the high school job—only a little bit older than the students. We had good bands from the beginning. In 1958 I moved to New Jersey, where I sought Bucky Pizzarelli.

B.F. Why did you go to New Jersey?

J.H. Because that's where my friends were.

B.F. Your musical friends?

J.H. Yes.

B.F. Who were some of them?

J.H. Bucky was the biggest of them. This was before Clark Terry.

B.F. How and when did you get to know Bucky?

J.H. He was playing with the Three Suns in Columbia at the Lester Bates Supper Club, also called Laurel Hill Supper Club. They had different bands each week. The Three Suns were a popular commercial group. I was playing at the Web with a black group and was really getting involved with the jazz thing seriously. They were good players; we had a good band.

One night Bucky came in. Someone said the Three Suns's guitar player was there and wanted to sit in. Here we were, playing these ridiculous bebop tunes—and a commercial guitarist wanted to sit in! I thought it was a joke, but toward the end of the night, I felt guilty and asked him to sit in for a couple of tunes. He played quite well. The next night I went to the supper club to see Bucky with the Three Suns. He was playing a white guitar and smiling—as commercial as you can get. He was here for a few weeks. It was summer and I wasn't teaching, so we played golf just about every day and kept in touch.

B.F. When was this?

J.H. About 1956.

B.F. So as a result of that chance meeting you became friends?

J.H. Yes. But we wanted to play some, and the only drummer at the time that could play was a black cat at Fort Jackson. Bucky stayed at a motel across the street from the Laurel Hill Supper Club. I'd drive to Fort Jackson, get the drummer, and sneak him into Bucky's room so we could play. That's ridiculous, but it's what we had to do.

B.F. Who was the drummer?

J.H. Paul Drummond, who was good. After leaving Fort Jackson, he went to Kentucky as a warrant officer to fly helicopters.

B.F. If you played in a motel room, I assume he played brushes.

J.H. Yes. Or light sticks. But Bucky and I became very close, and we've stayed in touch all these years. He's one of my oldest, dearest friends.

B.F. So on the basis of that friendship, you moved to New Jersey to be close to him? Does New Jersey mean the greater New York area?

J.H. Yes. In Paterson. Bucky was born there, though at the time he was living in Clifton, New Jersey. Bucky was one of the first-call guitar players in New York, and there were a lot of jingles being made there. Playing jingles was the hot thing to do in New York. Because he played guitar, banjo, ukulele—any stringed instrument—he would do several jingles a day. Also, when Tony Martin was in town, Bucky would be the guitar player.

He was really the top. He started playing with the Vaughn Monroe band right out of high school. From there he went to the Three Suns, but left them to go to New York because that's where the money was. Jingles paid well, but musicians also got residuals. He made a million dollars just off of jingles. Of course, he was with the *Tonight Show* band for fifteen years. That kind of band is great because it gives you a fixed income. But when the show moved to Los Angeles, Bucky stayed in New Jersey. He invested his money wisely. He's been a true friend.

B.F. So you got to New Jersey largely because of your friendship with Bucky Pizzarelli. How did you make a living? From teaching music? From playing?

J.H. I did some substitute teaching there, and I played. I was doing pretty well. I was fortunate because Bucky knew everybody. At one point in Newark, I was working Friday and Saturday nights in a polka band. It's funny.

Later on I found out about a Newark bar called the Circus Room. They had Vinnie Burke's trio and on Sundays had featured soloists like Al Cohn, Sam Most, and me. Sam Most played tenor and flute. He was the best flute player I ever heard, especially at that time. He and I were doing things together.

Once, during a break, he asked what else I was doing. When I told him that I was playing with a polka band on Fridays and Saturdays, he told me that he was playing piano in a rock-and-roll band. When I heard that someone of his quality had to play rock and roll to survive, I decided that I'd better leave the fast life of New Jersey and return to South Carolina where the weather is warm. I'm a Southern boy, and I like to slow things down. I got a lot of good out of living in New Jersey because I played with a lot of good players in the New York area and we've maintained a relationship all these years. Most of the cats I played with up there later played in Columbia at the Main Street Jazz Festival.

B.F. How long were you in New Jersey and New York?

J.H. It was about eighteen months.

B.F. Did you have any straight jazz gigs?

J.H. Yes. I was doing a lot of the New Jersey jazz things.

B.F. Did you record?

J.H. Yes, but not under my name. Just with other groups. Bucky brought Savoy Records to hear me, and they promised my own date. Bucky, Vinnie Burke, and I started rehearsing. I was to do dates with Urbie Green. Then I threw in the towel. I didn't want to make the sacrifices to be a "star." I just wanted to be accepted by the good players.

B.F. When you returned to Columbia, what did you do? Teach?

J.H. Yes. Each summer I would run up to Jersey and renew all my acquaintances, play with the guys, and sit in wherever they were. Bucky was playing. He had several duos: with George Barnes, Les Paul, Zoot Sims, Stephane Grappelli. Bucky is a band within himself. He plays that seven-string guitar, and he's great. But I would go back up there and hang out, especially with Clark and Bucky. Some summers, Clark would have a string of dates, and I would do them with him.

B.F. Two trumpets playing at the same time?

J.H. It was a sixteen-piece band. Its first album was *Clark Terry and the Big Bad Band*. It was a great band, with Phil Woods, Curtis Fuller, Jimmy Heath, Ed Soph, Jimmy Nottingham, Victor Sproles—a bunch of New York players. Most of the book was written by Ernie Wilkins, who did a lot of writing for Basie and others. So I would do things like that in the summer with Clark. On other occasions I went on the jazz cruise ship *Norway*. It had good musicians like Mel Tormé and George Shearing, Bucky Pizzarelli and Clark Terry. I did it twice.

B.F. As a player?

J.H. Yes. And I've done other things. For instance, Clark asked me to come up and play the JVC Jazz Festival with him at Town Hall. It was billed as Clark Terry and Friends, and I was one of the four or five friends included. I was on the same program as Oscar Peterson, Louis Bellson, and Kenny Burrell. So this country boy flew in for a few days, played with the stars, and went back home. A lot of guys would give their right arm to do that.

B.F. When was that?

J.H. It was the late 1970s or early 1980s. In fact, I took my friend Veron Melonas with me. I said, "Let's go to the big town." We did, and it was fun.

B.F. But there's a big block of time between when you returned south from New Jersey and the time of this JVC engagement. In the interim, you had a life, a career. What was the local scene in those years?

J.H. When I got back, I was playing with the local guys; most of them were good friends and competent musicians. I started booking my own quartet, and I would play supper clubs like six nights a week for extended periods of time. In 1967 the Pirate's Cove opened in the Capital Cabana Motor Inn. I was its music director. They booked people who had been on the *Tonight Show*. On Sunday, they'd be here for rehearsal and stay for a week or two. My house band was a quartet.

B.F. Just you and a rhythm section?

J.H. Yes. But quite often they would need a larger band, so I would just get the local guys that could play and do it. The local guys did a good job. But we did that from 1967 to 1971, six nights a week.

B.F. Was the local scene rewarding enough for you? You'd been on the New York scene and then returned to Columbia, which is not known as a jazz haven. You were just one of the guys in New York, I assume, but you were the big guy locally. Was it fulfilling enough for you musically?

J.H. It was fulfilling because in the summers I'd return to New Jersey and New York to play. Another thing I did was at the New School in New York. I played with Clark's big band in a memorial for Duke Ellington. Everybody was there: Count Basie, Marian McPartland, Dizzy Gillespie, Waymon Reed, Phil Woods, Jimmy Heath, Ernie Wilkins. Being there was some experience.

B.F. But is your point that you essentially created a scene at the Pirate's Cove in Columbia but each summer got recharged by playing again on the New York scene, as at the Ellington memorial?

J.H. I'll tell you an interesting story. The band director locally at A. C. Flora High School was a friend of mine, Mitch Santiago. He had a student who wanted to be a trumpet player. Mitch told me that the kid was going up to New York and wondered if I could arrange for him to listen to the *Tonight Show* rehearsal. I told him I'd try, so I called Clark, who was in the band. Clark agreed to help. When the kid got to New York, Clark had a limousine waiting for him. Clark didn't know him from anybody, yet he had a limousine take him to the *Tonight Show* rehearsal, sat him down there, and treated him royally. That's the kind of person and friend Clark Terry is.

Also, when Bucky found out I was coming in to do the JVC festival for Clark, Bucky insisted on picking up Veron and me. He took us to the hotel, dropped us off, and went home. I didn't want him to do it, but I couldn't talk him out of it. That's just the kind of people they are. They're not only great musicians, but as far as people are concerned, they're unbeatable. They really are.

B.F. You mentioned Veron Melonas, who I believe helped you create a local scene. Tell about him.

J.H. Veron and I were in high school together. In fact, we were in the high school band together and were friends ever after. He owned the Elite Restaurant on Main Street that was there seemingly forever. We always talked about putting on a jazz festival. One day, he said, "Let's do it." That's how the Main Street Jazz Festival got started. I made some phone calls and found that the musicians wanted to do it.

Veron was a genius when it came to having a festival because he provided a great atmosphere and gourmet food. How do you prepare gourmet food when you don't know the number of people who will be there—anywhere from three hundred to five hundred? In fact we were lucky. The only hitch was the year we were rained out. I was amazed that nobody asked for a refund. Instead of packing up and going home, the musicians went to a hall in the Greek Orthodox Church, set up, and played as though it never rained. This was the first year that John Pizzarelli's trio was here. He'd come before with his dad, Bucky, but this was when he just started his trio, and John was supposed to perform. What does he do when it rains? He sets up and plays inside the Elite, after which everybody went to the church as though nothing happened.

It's just amazing the spirit the musicians had when they came to Columbia to play. They had fire in their eyes when they came here. I couldn't get over it. The stage was in the middle of the street at an intersection, and there were tables extending up the block. The music lasted for about five hours. Because Veron owned the restaurant, he prepared scrumptious food and had an open bar—all you could eat and drink—for one hundred dollars, music included.

B.F. Who was the first musician you called for the first festival? Bucky?

J.H. Yes. So many great musicians played here, like Milt Hinton, Louis Bellson, Eddie Daniels, and Mundell Lowe, and they were great people. We had no problems. We set up a table for the musicians right out there by the paying customers so the people could come over and talk with them, get autographs, and so forth. The musicians—all gracious—loved it.

At most festivals, the musicians are behind the stage so they don't get to mingle with the crowd. Every player we had was a great musician. That's the true essence of jazz: having guys play together for the first time. I would make up a roster of who would play when, and that was it. They were there; they were ready to play. They did it. The cooperation and the love these guys had for this festival was unbelievable. Bernard Purdie was almost in tears when he heard about it. The festival's demise was a sad day for a lot of musicians because this was their favorite venue.

B.F. As proven by the fact that most of them came back year after year.

J.H. Yes. And it was such a warm group of good players. I was very careful not to mess with the chemistry too much. I would always bring in a featured singer or somebody. There would always be changes, but the nucleus of the festival pretty much remained the same because the guys I had couldn't be surpassed. Most of them were from the *Tonight Show* band and played with everybody. It was just really a who's who of great jazz musicians. Zoot Sims and Cannonball Adderley would have been here.

B.F. Which ones constituted the nucleus? Bucky, Red Rodney, Urbie Green, and Bill Watrous, for sure.

J.H. Yes, and Jim Ferguson and all the rhythm players, like Ed Soph and Bernard Purdie. The rhythm section is where it all begins.

B.F. Like Derek Smith?

J.H. Derek Smith and Ross Tompkins were both with the *Tonight Show* band; Ed Soph played with Clark, Woody Herman, and a whole bunch of bands; and Bernard

Purdie. The chemistry was so good. If you go back and look at the tapes of the festival, everybody on the stage is smiling. You don't get that often. Someone interviewed Tommy Newsom from the *Tonight Show* band. He said he loved it here.

It's like kids in a pickup game in that you don't know who you're going to play with, but you know they're going to be good. Even though we might have had the same people every year, I was constantly trying make sure everybody got to play with everybody else. I had the hard-driving people with Red Rodney, and opposite them I had the more mellow cats. They played bebop; but it was the swing version, and I didn't mix them. You wouldn't put a violin player with Bernard Purdie or with Red Rodney. You put the fire-eaters with Red Rodney: Chris Potter, Ed Soph, and Brian Torff.

And then other cats like Urbie Green are sweet players. I had them separate because even though as great as someone like Urbie is—he's one of the greatest—he didn't have that burning style of these other younger guys. So there was a lot of thought going into what we did, a lot of soul-searching.

I'm proud that only one time in the eleven years of the festival did a musician complain about the personnel. One year we had Dorothy Donegan backed by Bernard Purdie on drums and Brian Torff on bass. Another year, we had Brian, but also Cleveland Eaton, a monster bass player who is black. I decided to put a solid-black group up there: Dorothy Donegan, Bernard Purdie, and Cleveland Eaton. When Bernard got to his hotel and read the schedule, he noticed that I had replaced Brian with Cleveland. He said he wanted to talk. He said, "Last year, Brian did this show, and he's familiar with it. Don't you think it would be better to leave him there?" I said, "You got it." That's the only question I received. I appreciated it because I was trying to do a good thing, but if I could do better, I would. So we switched it back so that Brian did the show.

Brian was a duo with George Shearing for years, as was another of our bass players, Don Thompson. So these are top-of-the-line musicians. I also tried to use multi-instrumentalists because they gave me more to work with. Eddie Daniels played clarinet, flute, and saxophone; Ira Sullivan played everything. Don Thompson played vibes, bass, and piano. I loved it. The musicians never argued; they never gave me any grief.

B.F. You mentioned that in programming each year you tried to separate the fire-eaters from the smoother ones. But then at the end of the evening, at the end of the festivities, they all got together on stage and played together in a mammoth jam session on a tune such as "One O'Clock Jump." So it wasn't exclusively divided that way. They all ultimately came together.

J.H. Anybody could play with anybody. I was just trying to stylize it because I didn't want everybody burning. I think you're better off breaking it up, like having a good vocalist relieving the monotony of the horns. So I used everything I could think of to break the monotony for the people and the players. The multi-instrumentalists played all their horns, further breaking it up.

We were unfairly criticized by the newspaper for having the same people every year. Well, we did get the same people. Who would not want to hear some of these people once a year? In New York, you can't get in to hear them; here, you can practically live with them. I mean, the ballet does the *Nutcracker* every year, and nobody complains. The symphony orchestra plays a lot of the same tunes. We weren't treated fairly. This isn't to cast aspersions on the arts in Columbia. They do a great job.

B.F. You mentioned playing on a stage in the street and at the Greek Orthodox church, but didn't Sarah Vaughan perform at the Koger Center?

J.H. That's the only time Veron got into booking. We both wanted to get Sarah Vaughan, and I told him I would look into it. In the meantime, he contacted her agent. I wouldn't go through an agent. But he did, and we ended up paying through the nose. Vernon signed the contract and sent a check back, a deposit, and the manager was supposed to return it. He didn't. He dragged his feet until about two weeks before the engagement, which didn't give us much time to advertise. And he really had us over a barrel. I think he was holding out for a better deal. If he got more money from somebody else, he'd cut us out. As a result, we didn't have the crowd we should have had. Ordinarily Sarah Vaughan sold out, no matter where she performed. Veron paid twenty-five thousand dollars, just for Sarah.

B.F. When you say we lost a lot of money, I assume we is Veron.

J.H. Yes.

B.F. I mean, this was his financial deal.

J.H. Yes, absolutely.

B.F. How did he do over the life of the festival?

J.H. He lost about $150,000.

B.F. Because he kept putting on the festival, I assume he didn't complain.

J.H. That's right. But we could have done it differently. We wanted some money. The city would offer money but back out; they were screwing us around. In fact, we told them we weren't going to do it one year, and the mayor came over all upset about it. He said, "Well, I'll give you twenty-five thousand dollars," but he wouldn't give all the details.

So Veron, being a man of his word, took his licks. He didn't complain, but he lost a lot of money. He put on the festival for the music and the city. We even had bleachers outside the food area where people could sit and hear the music for *free*. There was so much good there for the city and the state that wasn't taken advantage of because officials lacked foresight: they couldn't anticipate that the festival would continue being broadcast all over the world. What city wouldn't pay, say, $25,000 to have a yearly show of the best players in the world shown all over the world? That's peanuts. You can't afford not to buy that. But they didn't do it.

B.F. What year was the first one?

J.H. The first was in 1987; the last, 1997.

B.F. That's a pretty good run, though.

J.H. Yes, it was. And a lot of people really loved it. In fact Veron paid ETV to tape it every year. I know of people in Rock Hill who planned a dinner party around the broadcast so they could experience the festival. We once had a guy come to the festival from India; others came from other countries. All of them were exposed to it on television.

It was just a shame that Veron had to bite the bullet. He wanted to help the city; it wasn't for his benefit. When we began, I said, "Let's call it the Elite Jazz Festival." He wouldn't do it. I played for free the first couple of years to save money. But then I didn't want to play because I didn't want it to look like I was taking advantage of my position with the festival.

B.F. Which musicians played at every festival? Bucky Pizzarelli? Red Rodney?

J.H. Red missed one when he died. Bucky missed one. Urbie Green missed one. My problem was booking all the musicians who wanted to come here. All those who were here once wanted to return. So I was caught between the veterans and musicians who had not been here but wanted to participate. I just did what I had to do to keep it successful. It was all designed for the city, but the city didn't know how to take it. They just didn't know what they were doing. It's a shame.

B.F. Did you have to turn down many musicians who wanted to be here?

J.H. There were a lot of people that heard about it and wanted to come. Here's an example. One of the greatest players you've ever heard came here twice. The first year there were no problems, so I brought him back the next year. When I paid him, I gave him what he got the previous year. He looked at it and said, "It's not right." I said, "What do you mean? That's what I paid you last year." He said, "But that's not right." I said, "If I get the canceled check and show it to you, will you believe me then?" He said, "Yes, but I want more money than this." We paid him what he wanted. Every year after that, somebody would come with a message from him, saying that he wants to come to the festival. I said, "Good luck." So I replaced him with another great musician, who loved being here, Bill Watrous. He said, "You got to practice to come to Columbia." That's the truth. And he's a great player.

B.F. But you mentioned how civic-minded Veron was in wanting to do right by his city, Columbia. He also established a scholarship fund for young musicians. Ron Westray is one who benefited from it. Did Chris Potter also receive funds?

J.H. Yes.

B.F. Those are two of the really outstanding musicians to come out of Columbia.

J.H. Yes. There is also Joe Hinson, a very good alto player, who was at USC and wanted to go to North Texas State. We helped him. But these are things nobody knew anything about. We didn't publicize them. One of the great things I enjoyed was on Saturday when we had ten or twelve high school stage bands from across the state come in for their own festival. After one band finished playing, another band followed it. It was great for the kids. Mitch Santiago handled these bands for me. Everything we did was for the community, for the kids, and we got no appreciation for it. Veron didn't get anything out of it, though he really didn't want anything. We did everything we could to get the state and local kids involved in this thing. At every intersection of Main Street, we had a band playing. The same festival in Charleston or Charlotte would have blossomed. But it was done in Columbia, and Veron lost $150,000 promoting his city.

We did it the way we did because we didn't want some screwball coming in and playing something that wasn't jazz. You'd have had rock and roll and all kind of crap in there, and we didn't want that. Everything played at that festival was mainstream jazz, nothing else. I'm not putting other stuff down, but I don't mix it with this. This was probably the only pure jazz festival in America, if not the world, because others have rock-and-roll groups. So, yes, we wanted to keep it pure. That's what we did. We got a lot of good help from the board of directors and others, but we pretty much wanted to control the talent that came in here.

B.F. What has happened to you since the end of the festival? Obviously you were a big part of the Main Street Jazz Festival; but primarily you're a player.

J.H. I just did most of the booking. I've continued to play around and go out from time to time to do certain things. If somebody calls me, I go out. But I just stick around here and play some. Pug's had a band going a couple of nights a week, and that was strictly jazz, too. That's where Chris Potter started, at Pug's. And early there was the Coal Company. There was always some kind of good jazz scene in Columbia. But since Pug's left, there is not much going on. I think the jazz talent has dropped off considerably.

One good element to the Columbia jazz scene has been the influence of Roger Pemberton and Dick Goodwin and his guys from Texas. They're all very good players and very good people. They're a plus for the music scene in Columbia. Before they arrived, Columbia had some good musicians, but not enough to do much of anything. And then Dick came in from Texas and brought all of his buddies with him— Doug Graham, Jim Mings, Jim Hall. There are so many of the guys because of Dick, and that's a good thing. Whenever I could use them at the festival, I would.

I wanted to have a big band every year, and we did for three or four years. We'd get Clark Terry to send us his big-band book. Dick would put the band together and rehearse it, and Clark would front it and play with it, so it was the Clark Terry band. It sounded the way his regular band sounded. Terry Gibbs did it the same way. I tried to utilize the local guys as much as I could. For instance, one time we had three locations in the Town House Hotel. At each were two alternating bands, so there were six bands working. Where are you going to find anything like that, six bands? And people were probably let in for free. They would move all around, go anywhere they wanted. It was a great festival, it really was.

B.F. But in the last decade or so, have you had a regular group?

J.H. Not so much. I've had a lot of problems with my back, and so I'm kind of semi-retired right now. But there are good players around, such as Dick Goodwin and his guys.

B.F. When you get a call, do you put together a combo?

J.H. I do wedding receptions and things like that.

B.F. Do you call Dick Goodwin's people to be your rhythm section?

J.H. In some cases. Ted Linder is one of my guys that's been here for a long time. Jim Mings. Terry Rosen was in the group, too, until he passed away. We had a quartet or quintet of players. Chris Potter and Terry Rosen were gifted musicians. Stars would come in and really be amazed at the level of talent in a little place like Columbia.

B.F. What do you consider the highlights of your career?

J.H. One would be the Duke Ellington memorial at the New School. Others would be playing at the JVC festival at Town Hall and on the *Norway* cruise with great players. These things keep me going sometimes. I did a couple of things in my legitimate trumpet days. I did the Haydn trumpet concerto with the USC Symphony Orchestra. I'll tell you, a jazz musician can play classical music better than classical musicians can play jazz. Most good jazz players, like Bucky Pizzarelli, have studied classically and have a legitimate foundation. They don't just pick up a horn and start blowing it. Jazz players couldn't play great jazz if they didn't have the facility to execute. That's why it's so important to have that legit foundation.

B.F. Wynton Marsalis is a good example. He's a fantastic classical player.

J.H. He's a great trumpet player. But I've had great relationships with great musicians. Back in the 1960s, the Columbia Jazz Club—a dixieland club—had concerts. One summer I got Clark to bring in his quartet. I got Marian McPartland to come in with Helen Merrill. I got Duke Pearson to come in and back me. Little things like that go by the wayside, and I forget about them until I think about my career.

B.F. Was Ambrose Hampton involved with the Columbia Jazz Club?

J.H. Yes. Ambrose was a great supporter of jazz. The party he gave on Saturday before the Main Street Jazz Festival on Sunday was for the musicians. Ira Sullivan came to the party for the first time and said that he forgot his horn. Ambrose said, "You don't need a horn, baby; you're a guest." Ira couldn't get over that. Some musical guests played there, but nobody expected it of them. They were the guests of honor. They should be. Ambrose did that every year and did a terrific job.

B.F. You mentioned Marian McPartland.

J.H. Back in the 1960s, I got Marian to come in with Helen Merrill, who was quite a singer at the time. Marian and I became good friends and kept in touch, and her husband was Jimmy McPartland, the great dixieland cornet player. When Marian came to town, she would call me, inviting me to play at a party.

Once, I got a good rhythm section and took them because she was at the mercy of whatever they put there, and she was so gracious that she wouldn't turn up her nose about who was there. But I brought my rhythm section one time to a party where Marian and Jimmy were playing. Jimmy and I got along great right away. Later, Jimmy and I spoke frequently on the telephone, but Marian and I have been friends for a long time. She's a great player, too, and she played at the Main Street Jazz Festival. Jimmy is the only dixieland player to ever play at the festival. He played a tune with Marian.

B.F. Any other highlights?

J.H. Did I tell you about the art museum? Jack Craft was the director of the museum at the time, and my dear friend J. Bardin was there. They decided for the first time that they wanted to have a Sunday jazz concert in the museum. So I called Bucky and asked if he'd come. He said, "Sure." I asked how much he wanted. He said, "I don't want anything. I'll be there." So he showed up. The same weekend, Clark Terry was doing a clinic at Lexington High School and was staying with me. We were getting ready to meet Bucky. I said, "C.T., get your horn and let's go play." So Bucky, Clark, and I played together at the museum.

B.F. Anything else?

J.H. I didn't tell you about Woody Herman.

B.F. No, you didn't.

J.H. In Miami, I met Al Porcino, the great lead trumpet player. He was with Woody's band in Texas. Al had been asked to go to Rochester, New York, to record with Chuck Mangione. Al wanted to get off of Woody's band, so he called me from Texas and asked if I would sub for him on the band while he did the Mangione sessions. I said I would. So I did some dates with Woody's band. When I was preparing to leave the band, the manager said how much they all enjoyed having me and asked if I would consider staying. I appreciated the offer, but I had a teaching gig to return to.

B.F. How long were you with the band?

J.H. Just a couple of weeks in the late 1970s. It was fun.

Columbia, S.C., 19 March 2007

Notes

1. Nat Adderley played cornet.
2. Cannonball Adderley became famous shortly after moving to New York in 1955.

RON FREE

15 January 1936–

B.F. You were especially active in New York in the late 1950s. You recorded with some of the heavyweights of the time. What is your history? What led you to music? What got you from Charleston to New York?

R.F. My father was instrumental in getting me into the music business. He was a frustrated jazz fan; he'd never played an instrument, although I think he had some latent talent that he never developed. So he took it out on me. He arranged for me to get drum lessons, and used to stand over me and make me practice. I was fortunate in that regard, I guess, because I probably wouldn't have had the discipline to do it on my own. It kind of paid off in the long run. I grew up in Charleston playing with different bands around town.

B.F. When was that?

R.F. I was born in 1936—January 15th, which happens also to be Gene Krupa's birthday. When I discovered it, it was quite a thrill. I knew it was in the stars then that this was my destiny. This was back when I was ten or twelve years old hearing the Jenkins Orphanage bands playing on the street corners, which was an early source of inspiration.

My daddy would buy records for us to listen to. Anytime a band would come to town, he would be sure and take me there, and he would arrange to meet some of the musicians. He usually got me a front-row seat—or sometimes got me backstage—where I could see the drummer's hands and feet. When I was about twelve years old, I went to County Hall where the Krupa band was appearing. I got to meet Gene. He even let me sit in and play two or three numbers with the band, which was really a great thrill. He was quite a nice guy.

B.F. The Jenkins Orphanage bands are certainly legendary. Did they play regularly on the street corners? Was it on weekends? Were they scheduled? Or did you just happen upon them?

Ron Free. Date, place, and photographer unknown. From the collection of Ron Free

R.F. I just happened upon them. I didn't know when they were going to be there. Sometimes from my house I could hear them off in the distance, and I'd go running to listen to them. It was kind of periodic. I don't know that there was any regular schedule to it. They did it to raise funds; they would pass the hat around. They had some good bands. A lot of good musicians came out of there. It wasn't exactly jazz that they were playing. It was more marching music, like the Dirty Dozen band from New Orleans now. But a lot of good jazz players came out of the organization.

B.F. So you sat in with Krupa.

R.F. I dropped out of high school in the tenth grade to go on the road with Tommy Weeks and His Merry Madcaps. That was my first road gig, for ninety dollars a week, and I thought I was in the big time. We used to do record pantomimes and comedy skits; music was the least of our concerns.

B.F. You were only about sixteen then. Did you have your parents' blessing?

R.F. Yes. They approved of it. They figured it was good experience for me. I did get to hear a lot of good bands and musicians while traveling.

B.F. I don't know of that band.

R.F. Few people do. It was just a little trio—trumpet player, piano, and drums—and it was musically very poor. The comedy was pretty good. Tommy Weeks was a pretty competent comedian. So we played all through the southern states, mostly, and some in the Midwest. We were in Illinois, Ohio, and so forth. We spent a lot of time in Miami, so I got to hear a lot of good musicians there. We stayed about a solid year in Miami.

I left Tommy Weeks and joined Royal American Shows, which was billed as the world's largest carnival. I was playing drums for the girlie show. I was about seventeen years old and had a great time. It was quite an education. It was a show, a musical review. They had singers and dancers and comedians and girls. We did a couple of musical numbers where I did a drum solo. These little high school girls used to come to the matinees, and they would be screeching like they used to do for Frank Sinatra in his young days, so I was in high heaven then. I thought I had found my calling.

B.F. So you were on the road with Weeks for about a year?

R.F. Off and on for probably two or three years. I came home every now and then, and then he'd call and I'd go back out with him for a few months.

B.F. Then after him, off to the carnival.

R.F. Yes. I was working with him in Minnesota—in Minneapolis, actually—and that's where I hooked up with the carnival. I joined it there and did the rest of the circuit until they got to their winter quarters in Tampa. And then I came back to Charleston. I was working in a club here with a local band.

A friend of the family visited from New York—he used to live in Charleston—and invited me up to New York to stay with him on Staten Island while I was getting my union card, because that's where the action was, musically speaking. That's where all the famous players were, and so everybody I talked to said if you really want to make it in the music business, you've got to go to New York sooner or later. I was about eighteen then. So I took him up on that and lived with him on Staten Island when I moved to New York. I started out working at a supermarket in the daytime to make a few dollars. I wasn't doing that very long before I managed to get a weekend job at a club on Staten Island.

It takes six months, I think, to get your union card. That's before you can do any recording or can do any six-nights-a-week jobs. Meanwhile, you can work one-nighters, so I booked a weekend job on South Beach, on Staten Island, at a place called Crocitto's. They used to have a weekend review of Italian singers. I don't know if you saw the Woody Allen movie called *Broadway Danny Rose*, but that was typical of the kind of scene they had going there: singers, comedians, dancers, and so forth. I made as much money playing weekends there as I did working all week at the supermarket.

Needless to say, I quit the supermarket. At some point in there I started taking drum lessons from a fellow named Moe Goldenberg, one of the staff percussionists at NBC; he was also a faculty member at the Juilliard School of Music. I had gone to New York with every intention of furthering my education and learning. It was such a learning opportunity because that's where all the good players were. I could hear people like Max Roach and Art Blakey and Buddy Rich.

I didn't really have a lot of self-confidence at that point. I was a very shy, timid kid. Moe was so impressed with my reading and my hands that he got me an audition with an off-Broadway show that was starting up called *Shoestring '57*. I got the job. The pit band consisted of two pianos and drums. But there were a couple of dance numbers in the show that had nothing but drums accompaniment. I had a chance to stretch out a little bit.

Opening night, I went into Charlie's Bar, where all the musicians hung out at that time, and passed out some complimentary tickets. One of the people who showed up was Oscar Pettiford. He was very impressed with what he heard, so he called me the next day for a record date. That was my first record date, with Mat Mathews. And then he called me shortly after that for another record date with Chris Connor, and he recommended me to Woody Herman. He got me on Woody Herman's band.

B.F. Was the Mat Mathews recording released?

R.F. I don't believe it ever was released. I don't know what happened to it. We didn't do a complete album; we just did one three-hour session, and I think they had some technical difficulties, or something. I don't think they were satisfied with the fidelity, but there were some good players on it, including Oscar Pettiford and Barry Galbraith. It must have been 1956 or 1957 because the show was *Shoestring '57*. Carol Burnett was originally scheduled to do the leading part in that show, incidentally, that wound up being Dody Goodman. It was a pretty good show; I got a lot of exposure through it that led to some other things. But Oscar was really my mentor, so to speak. He gave me my first break. That's the way it all started.

B.F. Did you hang out with Pettiford?

R.F. Not exactly. I'd run into him in Charlie's every now and then, or at another place called Junior's, and we would hang out a little bit. One night we were both in Junior's Bar, and Woody Herman happened to come in. We all wound up at Oscar's house, and me and Oscar—we called him O.P.—wound up playing a little duet thing. His son had a set of drums there, so Oscar got his bass out, and we just played a little bit together.

About a week or so after that, Woody Herman's manager called and asked if I could join the band. Roy Burns was with the band at the time, and he was leaving to join Benny Goodman. I wasn't with the band that long; I just filled in toward the end of their road trip. It was the very first big band I ever played with, and it scared the hell out of me.

B.F. Did you record with Herman?

R.F. No. We did several broadcasts from different towns, but I don't know if they were recorded.

B.F. You mentioned that your next recording session after Mat Mathews was with Chris Connor. Was that before you went out with Herman?

R.F. Before.

B.F. How did you get from Mat Mathews to Chris Connor?

R.F. Oscar Pettiford. He did a lot of recording—he was one of those studio musicians who was on call and went from one recording session to another. They had very full days like that. Oscar was very prominent among the studio men, so any time they needed an extra musician, they would always ask one of the players to recommend somebody. Fortunately he kept me in mind.

B.F. What happens at a recording date like that? Do you remember how you were paid?

R.F. In those days, it was just a straight fee for the sidemen. It was probably $100–$150 for a three-hour session, and that was it. I understand that nowadays they get residuals and royalties and so forth, but at that time royalties only went to the songwriters and the leader of the date.

B.F. How did you like working with Chris Connor?

R.F. I really didn't have much contact with her. The studio is a strange scene. She was in a little booth back behind us, and while we were recording I couldn't even hear her. It was kind of awkward for me. I hadn't done any recording—it was all a very strange scene to me, and I was nervous, needless to say. Fortunately it was all kind of easy stuff—brushwork—and I didn't have a real prominent part to play, so I guess it was all right. I don't even think we were introduced, to tell you the truth.

B.F. You then went with Oscar Pettiford on the road with Woody Herman?

R.F. No. Oscar wasn't on Woody's band. He'd played with Woody Herman years before, but at that point Oscar was just doing record dates. He had his own band, too. I played some things with his band. He had about a twelve- or thirteen-piece band.

B.F. Was Lucky Thompson with him then?

R.F. No, not at that time. Julius Watkins was with him. I can't even remember all the bands I played with. If you're around New York for any length of time and you've got anything at all going as far as your talent is concerned, you end up playing with just about everybody, at one time or another—particularly rhythm section workers —because there's always people who can't find a drummer or bass player. You get a lot of opportunities that way.

B.F. How did you link up with Mose Allison?

R.F. There was a loft on East Thirty-fourth Street that a couple of Southerners lived in—a couple of Mississippi fellows—and of course I'm a Southern boy myself. We had jam sessions there because they could board up the windows and play all hours of the day and night. That's where I met Mose. We had a pretty good chemistry, so it wasn't long before he called me for a record date. I was totally shocked; I didn't expect it. Of course, I was thrilled. That was for Prestige. We recorded in a little studio over in New Jersey.

B.F. Was that at Rudy Van Gelder's?

R.F. Yes. Then I worked with Mose quite a bit, and he was instrumental in getting me other jobs because he'd worked with Stan Getz, for example. I played a couple of one-nighters with Getz when he was in town. Mose had also worked with Zoot Sims and Al Cohn quite a bit, so I eventually worked quite a few jobs with them, also. Mose was established as far as the musicians were concerned, but he hadn't yet gotten fully established on his own as a recording artist. He had done one or two albums. I think

Back Country Suite was his first album, and that got, I think, five stars in *Down Beat*. So he was well on his way, but he was still young and upcoming at that time. I was upcoming with him.

B.F. How did you get to Lee Konitz?

R.F. I don't remember. I think maybe at a jam session. There were a lot of lofts around town at that time—musicians would live in them; I lived in two or three different ones—and you never knew who was liable to show up at those things. I think that's probably where I met Lee. First, I met Lennie Tristano, who was one of Lee's mentors, and there was a whole little clique of Tristanoans: Lee Konitz, Warne Marsh, Peter Ind, Sal Mosca. So maybe I met them through Lennie. As a matter of fact, I was working some gigs with Lennie and Lee and Warne. Lennie had a loft where he had some sessions, and Peter Ind introduced me to Lennie. It was just a word-of-mouth thing; word gets around.

A lot of it is very vague because I used to do a lot of drugs. There are whole blocks of my memory that are blank. I don't remember all of the details, but I worked quite a bit with Lennie Tristano and Lee Konitz and Warne Marsh, individually and together, as a group. We did a package tour one time where I was traveling with Lennie—Lennie had a band with Lee and Warne and a bass player named Sonny Dallas—and we did mostly one-nighters. The package had a couple of bands from England, and I think Thelonious Monk had his quartet there; George Shearing. Later on, we did a little recording. Obviously the recording is Tristano influenced. Lee Konitz is the leader, and Warne Marsh and Ted Brown are both along on saxophone. All of them were disciples of Lennie Tristano.

B.F. It must have been a pretty heady experience being with Tristano.

R.F. He was pretty cerebral. We would talk sometimes, but I was pretty intimidated by that whole crowd. I felt like I was in over my head because I was still like nineteen or twenty years old, a kid from the sticks who went to the city to learn how to play. Lennie was also a kind of Freudian psychologist, so he was always psychoanalyzing us, and God knows I needed it. I was a neurotic mess at that point. I don't remember any specific discussions, but he was always quick to point out any little neurotic tendencies that we had, and we all had a bunch of them.

B.F. Did Tristano talk much about Bird?[1] He recorded with him.

R.F. Tristano's music was very much Charlie Parker influenced. I don't know exactly how he got to where he did from Charlie Parker, but he was really a Parker fan. He thought that Bird was the greatest thing that ever happened, as do many others, of course. Tristano's playing took on a whole different flavor, but Bird's music was cerebral in its own right. It also had a lot of fire in it, whereas Lennie's was notably cooler. He talked about Bird quite a bit. He worshipped him.

B.F. There's another musician you were involved with in New York, guitar player Sal Salvador. You recorded with him for Bethlehem. How did you get together?

R.F. Somebody introduced me to him in Junior's Bar. It was another guitar player named Park Hill, who had never even heard me play. He'd had a few drinks, and Sal came in. Park introduced me to him. Park said, "Boy, if you ever need a drummer, this guy is really great." Next thing you know, Sal was calling me for record dates. It's crazy the way things happen sometime. A lot of it is luck.

B.F. These recordings we've talked about were made in the 1956–1958 period. After that, you disappeared. What happened?

R.F. I came back to Charleston with every intention of going back to New York posthaste—I left my drums there, and a lot of my other belongings—but I wound up getting involved with a lady that I'd known from many years back, but we'd kind of lost contact. She was having some marital problems. I felt responsible for having broken up her marriage, so I jumped on my white charger, and the hero came to rescue her from this bad situation. I ended up getting married and inheriting two stepchildren, and I was certainly in no condition to be married to anybody. My stepchildren were probably more mature than I was at that particular point. But there I was, in that situation, so I never did make it back to New York.

I wound up staying here in Charleston. I played a little music for a while, but ended up getting some day jobs because the music scene wasn't all that great around Charleston. I needed to get my head screwed on right anyway; I'd been through a lot of drug addiction and a lot of pretty severe depressions and all. It took me awhile to really get my bearings and grow up, which is what it amounted to. After all those years you spend doing drugs, you turn out to be a kind of retard; you don't really grow emotionally, and you don't do much maturing until you come out from behind the bushes and face things head-on. So I wound up staying here in Charleston, and the marriage, of course, was a disaster from the very beginning. I stayed in it for fourteen years before I finally got a divorce.

Then, I moved out to the West Coast. Meanwhile, I'd quit playing for close to fifteen years. I'd play an occasional commercial job which I could almost do in my sleep. But as far as any serious jazz or anything artistically challenging, I'd quit. I had some friends on the coast, and through a series of circumstances—more luck—I was driving a cab out in San Diego. Some guy got into the cab—he was a bartender at the Elks Club—who happened to be a jazz fan. Somehow or other, we got on the subject of jazz, and he'd heard of me. He said, "I've got *The Encyclopedia of Jazz* at home. Aren't you in Leonard Feather's book?"[2] I said, "Yeah."

And so he went home and found some Mose Allison records that I was on. I was like his discovery. He introduced me to some jazz players that he knew, and they had me sit in. I hadn't done any playing in years; it's not exactly like riding a bicycle. But evidently I did all right, so I started getting calls for a few jobs. I didn't even have any drums. A vibraphone player named Jim West had a makeshift set of drums in his garage, so I put it together and started playing a few jobs around town. There are some pretty good musicians in San Diego. Charles McPherson, who lives in La Jolla now, heard me and started calling me for gigs. The next thing you know, I was back in it. This was about seven or eight years ago, so I've only been back in it about that long.

B.F. How long were you in San Diego?

R.F. Close to ten years. I've been back here about three years, and I had been play-ing again for about two years before I left San Diego, so I guess I've been playing again for about five years, although it's gone downhill again since I've been back in Charles-ton because there's not that much opportunity here. My chops are down. I quit my day job. I was doing a little teaching at a music store where I had some private drum students. I stayed pretty busy musically. There was a little club in La Jolla called the Blue Parrot where they used to bring a lot of L. A. players. I played with quite a few of them. Jack Sheldon came down occasionally, and Ross Tompkins.

B.F. Why did you return to Charleston?

R.F. Family circumstances. I still have some relatives around here. I never really expected to come back, but I always seem to wind up back here, much to my surprise. Actually a friend of mine who had extended some help to me when I really needed it. . . . I came to provide whatever help I could. Turnabout is fair play. I had every inten-tion of going back to New York, now that I was back playing again. I was antsy to get back into the fire, so to speak. That's where the action is. I thought I'd give it another try now that I was a little more mature. But this is as far as I've gotten. I've gotten into playing volleyball over on the Isle of Palms, and I'm enjoying that more than I enjoy music these days. I don't know if I'll ever get back to New York. We'll see.

B.F. How is the music scene in Charleston?

R.F. It's real good for about two weeks every year during Spoleto in the spring. I stay pretty busy for those two weeks. Then, there's the post-Spoleto depression that sets in, and the scene really slows down for quite awhile. I imagine I could probably go out and drum up some jobs if I was really motivated, but there are so few musi-cians around of any competence. There are a few, but they tend to be scattered out. It's hard to get them all together. So I just play volleyball and don't worry about it. If the phone rings for a music job, I'll take it. But it's so spread apart that you don't have a chance to do enough playing to stay in shape.

B.F. Would you reflect on some musicians you've either played with or come across? What about Marian McPartland?

R.F. A very nice lady. I like Marian; she's a very good musician, too. She's well versed in many branches or styles of jazz. I just worked with her briefly. I did another pack-age tour. I was playing with Zoot Sims and Mose; I was playing with two or three dif-ferent groups, and Marian had her trio. That's where we first met. Then, I worked with her at the Hickory House in New York. This was after Joe Morello had gone with Brubeck.

B.F. Bill Evans?

R.F. A really beautiful person. I really loved him, and I worked with him quite a bit. He was on the record date I did with Lee Konitz. He also worked a few dates with Sal Salvador. I played a few jobs with Bill before he went with Miles Davis and before he got so well known with his own trio. I ran into Bill on the street one time in New York after he had joined Miles Davis and stopped to talk with him for a while. He seemed sad. I thought that this must be the pinnacle of his career, playing with Miles Davis and Cannonball Adderley. There was really something deeply sad about him. I got depressed after that.

B.F. Was he strung out?

R.F. He may have been. That may have been the problem, because I understand he did get pretty seriously strung out. But we had kind of lost contact, so I didn't really know that at the time. That may have been what the problem was, but of course that's not a problem; it's just a symptom of something much deeper. That was a whole different era back then. Back in the '50s, the racial situation was really intense—not that that's changed a whole lot, though I guess it's improved somewhat. It was kind of a dark era in many ways.

B.F. Do you mean that the racial scene with musicians was not very good?

R.F. No. Not with musicians. I don't know that it ever was a big problem with musicians, because if you can make music with somebody, it's like making love with somebody. It was not a problem among the musicians particularly, but just the racial situation in the world.

To give an example, I grew up in Charleston. My father wanted me to be a jazz musician, and yet he was one of the biggest rednecks in the world. Talk about contradictory input into a child's head. Here I am supposed to be a jazz drummer, and yet I'm not supposed to associate with the black people, and this is basically their music, to a very large extent. Jazz musicians—it didn't matter what color you were— encountered a lot of the same kinds of prejudice that black people encounter, I guess, just from being associated with the music. You were like a second-class citizen in many ways. I hate to sound like Rodney Dangerfield, but we got no respect.

B.F. Did you get any heat for rooming with Ben Tucker?

R.F. No. There was no problem with that sort of thing in New York. It was all kind of a vibrational thing more than anything else. I remember one incident with Miles Davis. He was standing out in front of Birdland during intermission, and some policeman came along and wound up clubbing him. I don't know what that was all about, but that was just one of many similar situations. As a matter of fact, I used to say that if you had a lot of real bad karma in a previous lifetime, you came back in this one as a jazz musician. Fortunately a lot of that is changing now; it's a new world we're in, and there are some sweeping changes taking place. There's a new consciousness in people, and the old order is on the way out, thank God.

B.F. What drummers do you listen to?

R.F. Jack DeJohnnette is right at the top of the list, as far as something really fresh and different. And of course Steve Gadd brought in a lot of new things. I love a lot of the stuff he does. There's a whole bunch of them that I haven't really given a fair listening to. There's Peter Erskine and a lot of the fusion-type drummers that are just doing some incredible things. I listen to all drummers. I learn something from everybody.

B.F. Did you listen to Elvin Jones?

R.F. Yes. You bet. Elvin used to room with Ben and me in a loft. I used to hang out with Elvin a lot. I was on the scene when Coltrane was at his peak, working down at the Half Note. So that was quite an experience.

B.F. Did you know Coltrane?

R.F. I never really met him, but I certainly heard him play quite a bit. He was really something.

B.F. Did you know Miles?

R.F. I never met him. That was one of my unfulfilled goals. I always wanted to play with Miles Davis

B.F. Do you miss the jazz life?

R.F. I don't particularly miss it. I'm still in it to a large extent, although not so much here in Charleston where there are not that many jazz musicians. But I don't miss the lifestyle; I enjoy my present lifestyle a lot more. Fortunately I think musicians' lifestyles are changing somewhat. They're a little more health conscious. There was a lot of self-destructive behavior that kind of went along with being in the jazz field. It's a crazy life. You're playing one-nighters and you have to appear before large audiences that are paying a lot of money to hear you play, so they expect top performances. And you haven't had any sleep, maybe, and you're tired and not feeling up to snuff, so the next thing you know you start taking pills or a few drinks to make yourself feel better. The next thing you know, you've got a serious problem.

It's kind of a crazy, unnatural way of life. Jazz was born in smoke-filled night spots, and that's been part of the ambience. Finally it's moving into concert halls, and, hopefully, that can lead to a little more healthy lifestyle. Maybe someday jazz musicians will have the kind of recognition where they can make a living with their art without having to play in clubs. Don't get me wrong. A lot of musicians like the nightclubs. They'd rather play in the clubs because there's a certain freedom there that you might lose in the concert hall because jazz is above all things, as far as I'm concerned, spontaneous.

It's the improvisation that I really like. When it works, there's nothing quite like it. There's nothing worse than bad jazz. It doesn't always work. You've got to have the right chemistry. Art Blakey once said that it comes straight from the creator through the musician to the audience. It doesn't always come from the creator; it sometimes comes from other things. But when it comes from that point of creativity within us, there is nothing more exciting and nothing more magical than good jazz.

Charleston, S.C., 29 August 1987

Notes

1. "Bird" is Charlie Parker.

2. Leonard Feather published several editions of *The Encyclopedia of Jazz*. Free probably refers to *The New Edition of the Encyclopedia of Jazz* (New York: Horizon, 1960).

JOHNNY WILLIAMS

31 October 1936–

B.F. Would you tell a little about yourself?

J.W. I was born October 31, 1936, in Orangeburg, South Carolina. My family was musical, but not professionally. My dad played fiddle; my mother, piano. My grandmother was the church organist in Georgetown for maybe fifty-five years, and her father was a cornet player. My dad would often play the fiddle around the house, most often on holidays and Sundays. Sometimes we'd play trios, with my mother, after I started playing alto saxophone. I must have been about twelve or thirteen at the time.

Prior to that, I started on piano when I was three and a half or four years old. A lady across the street, a family friend, started me on piano. I gave a recital when I was less than five. Later, at Claflin College, which neighbors South Carolina State, the president's wife taught piano. I was with her for a few years. I was no prodigy; I had average talent. I didn't enjoy the lessons. Emotionally, I was terrified. I enjoyed playing with my friends when they taught me boogie-woogie.

B.F. Could you improvise then?

J.W. No, not then. My friends could. They would teach me by rote. I remember a blind pianist in the neighborhood who only showed up on Saturdays. The children would gather round him, and he would play the blues, spirituals, a little jazz. He was the first musician I heard improvise, and I loved it. I was not yet eight. I remember being barefooted; I recall standing around the piano with five or six other children listening to him play. I don't remember his name; he just passed through. South Carolina State had a concert and a marching band, and the bandmaster let me play the bass drum on some of the marches. It was a huge, old-fashioned, concert bass drum, probably twice as tall as I was.

We were always interested in hearing any music that was going on in the community. When I was eleven or twelve, I began to notice the musicians there. There was a dormitory named Lowman Hall, which is still there. There was a trumpeter there

Johnny Williams soloing with Count Basie's band. Date, place, and photographer unknown.
From the collection of Johnny Williams

named Eddie Williams, who recently died, who later played with Lionel Hampton. He'd invite me to his room; I'd sit on his bunk and he'd play jazz standards like "Body and Soul." There was a guy from Beaufort named Robert Earl Thompson who had a beautiful alto saxophone tone. I remember him playing jazz. He was killed in the Korean conflict.

It must have been around 1948 that I listened to the jazz musicians playing around South Carolina State. There were some local guys, too. Most of them were blues musicians who were not associated with the college but who were playing dances around Orangeburg. I started to Wilkinson High School at the age of twelve—as a mater of fact, a month before my twelfth birthday in 1948. I joined the band and began playing alto sax.

B.F. Did they play stock arrangements?

J.W. The bandmaster was very versatile and had to be. He's still in Orangeburg; his name is J. B. Hunt. He played all the instruments and had to do most of the arranging. We played stock arrangements of Basie tunes, Stan Kenton, "Early Autumn" by Woody Herman—all the standards of the time. Everything we could afford to get we played. We started playing gigs right away. He must have formed the dance band about a year before I got there. After I was there about a year, I was part of the dance band. We started playing gigs and dances around South Carolina and were paid fifty cents apiece.

B.F. How did you make the transition from piano to alto?

J.W. I must have stopped playing piano a couple of years before I started playing alto. Between the ages of nine and eleven, I didn't play music at all. I wanted to be a baseball player. I had a friend who played saxophone and who encouraged me to start on clarinet. He told me that if I wanted to be a good saxophone player, I had to start on clarinet.

B.F. Did you know you wanted to play the saxophone?

J.W. At that time, my heroes were local. They were the guys who were in college in Orangeburg and the better-playing high school guys. From the beginning, I wanted to play alto. I didn't take my friend's advice, and I asked my father to buy an alto sax for me. He did. A local bandmaster, whose name was Gentry, happened to have a used silver Cavalier saxophone that he sold to my father. I remember my father coming home one night with that saxophone and saying, "Johnny, this saxophone cost one hundred dollars. I want you to take care of it." He showed me how to assemble it, and he gave me his violin book. I started trying to learn how to read music again by the use of that violin tutor.

My dad was setting a standard, giving me directions, trying to help me along. Mr. Hunt, at Wilkinson, started teaching me the fingerings. The first couple of weeks, I couldn't get a sound out of the instrument. I was very concerned, so I went to my buddies. Finally I passed it on to Mr. Hunt, who told me that the reed was too stiff. After getting a softer reed, I could begin to play.

B.F. And for all of the high school years you were playing with the dance band?

J.W. Yes, and the marching band and the concert band. All the bands. After high school, I went to South Carolina State College, right next door. I had known for some years Reggie Thomasson, the bandmaster there. He and Mr. Hunt had been good friends, and they had started the South Carolina All-State Band Association. By then —1952–1953—I was fortunate to have won an alto chair in that band.

B.F. By this time, though, I imagine that you had begun listening seriously to music and your influences were other than strictly local.

J.W. Yes. I was buying records every week—old 78s.

B.F. Did you focus on alto players? Did you listen to Johnny Hodges? To Bird?[1]

J.W. No. I didn't hear Charlie Parker until later. I recall hearing Art Pepper with Stan Kenton and being excited about the solos he played. I have an uncle, John Collins, who married my mother's sister. He was a guitarist with Nat "King" Cole. They came through Columbia with the *Big Show of 1951:* Nat Cole, Sarah Vaughan, and Duke Ellington. He told me that Art Pepper was a fine saxophonist, but he wanted me to listen to Charlie Parker. That inspired me to start buying Charlie Parker records.

B.F. Were there other name alto players you listened to, such as Benny Carter?

J.W. I didn't listen to Benny Carter until later. I heard Willie Smith with Duke Ellington in Columbia in 1951. He had replaced Johnny Hodges. The sax section was Willie Smith, Harry Carney, Paul Gonsalves, Jimmy Hamilton, and Hilton Jefferson. It was one of the greatest bands I've ever heard. I didn't hear Willie Smith again until years later with Harry James. I didn't even know that he had played with Jimmie Lunceford. I was young then, and there was a lot of the historical part of it I had missed.

B.F. Is there a South Carolina connection: you, Jimmy Hamilton, Willie Smith, all from South Carolina?

J.W. These men were superb musicians, and I never knew them as peers. I never really met Willie Smith. There were great musicians who came through Orangeburg. There was Lonnie Hamilton from Charleston, who didn't record. Aaron Harvey, who played with Tiny Bradshaw, returned to South Carolina State after years on the road as a professional musician and became an attorney in Charleston.

There were younger players: Oscar Rivers from Charleston, who is back there now after living in Chicago. I don't know if he recorded. They were excellent musicians who were capable of writing as well as playing. Everything you read about happening in New Orleans was happening in Charleston. Most of the pure musicians at South Carolina State came from Charleston. They were well equipped. Someone at the Jenkins Orphanage or at Burke High School gave them the mechanics they needed to play jazz, such as how to play chord changes.

B.F. Which musicians do you have in mind?

J.W. George Kenny was one. Lucius Weathers, from Columbia, died about seven years ago.

B.F. Were you at school on a music scholarship?

J.W. Not for the first couple of years. But I lived in Orangeburg, and it cost only about two hundred dollars a year to go to South Carolina State. When I got a scholarship, it was for $13.50 a month, which was plenty. We played gigs. Professor Thomasson had been to Oklahoma City, where he met Thad Jones. Thad had done some small-band arrangements that Professor Thomasson rearranged for our big band. We had about sixteen pieces: five saxes, three trombones, four trumpets, and three rhythm, plus a vocalist. The arrangements were difficult, but we mastered them. We also played some stocks, but we had some guys who were arrangers. We had Bobby Ephriam, an outstanding trumpet player from Charleston who is now assistant principal at a school there.

B.F. Were there good improvisers then?

J.W. Yes. And there were some who were not in the big band who decided they wanted to play solos on every tune, and they didn't want to be restricted. There was Houston Person. He just enjoyed being the only horn in the group. He would use the rhythm section and play his own jobs.

I fell more in line with the recreative group. I learned early that my forte was ensemble playing. I heard Marshal Royal playing with the Count Basie band at the Township Auditorium in Columbia and decided right then, even though Charlie Parker was my great hero, that I wanted to be a lead alto player. That was all I thought about. Marshal Royal was my hero in that regard. By then, I had heard Lionel Hampton at Township; I had heard another Basie band, a Stan Kenton band, Buddy Johnson, and many small groups. There was something about the Marshal Royal tone and command—the authority with which he played—that enthralled me.

B.F. Did that inspire you to go in the direction of Basie?

J.W. It was such an awesome organization that I never dreamt that I could play with him. I heard Marshal in 1951, right after the septet.[2] Marshal replaced Buddy DeFranco with the septet. Buddy told me that he came to New York as an alto player but decided that he'd better concentrate on his clarinet after hearing Bird. About that same time, he got the job with Basie, who also had Wardell Gray, Clark Terry, Freddie Green. After Marshal replaced Buddy, Basie reformed his big band. My predecessor, Charlie Fowlkes, was instrumental in helping Basie get together the horn men for the band. This was 1951.

B.F. Over the years, Basie really only had two baritone players until you got there: Jack Washington and Charlie Fowlkes.

J.W. That's right. Jack Washington was drafted, and during the war Rudy Rutherford came in. He wasn't really a baritone player; he came in as an alto player and was handcuffed into going to baritone. Preston Love played lead alto in Earle Warren's place. Upon being released from the military, Jack Washington came back in on baritone.

B.F. Charlie Fowlkes followed Jack Washington, and you followed Fowlkes.

J.W. Charlie Fowlkes was there from '51 until '69. He was decorating his home for Christmas when he had an accident and broke both of his kneecaps. At the same time, Marshal Royal was leaving the band to settle down in Los Angeles after eighteen or nineteen years in the band. They left about the same time, 1969. Cecil Payne was Charlie Fowlkes's immediate replacement. Just before that time Eddie "Lockjaw" Davis had heard me playing with Billy Daniels in Los Angeles and encouraged me to stay on top of it because if Basie made a change on baritone, he'd recommend me.

B.F. Did you know Davis then?

J.W. There was a good arranger named John Anderson who had played with Basie. He had a big band in Los Angeles. Eddie "Lockjaw" Davis was sitting in with the rehearsal band, and I was the regular baritone player with it. That was our first meeting. Later, he came back to Los Angeles when Basie came there and heard me at a club called the Baby Grand West, playing with Billy Daniels. I said hello to him at the bar, and he said he'd contact me later. I took it as a compliment, but didn't take it seriously. I didn't think I would ever play with Basie.

B.F. When did you come on board?

J.W. When I heard that Cecil Payne had replaced Charlie Fowlkes, I decided that Davis wasn't able to keep his promise, and he was known as a man of his word. But Basie had the last say. Often, he would accept men recommended to him, but it was his decision as to who would stay in the band.

Sure enough, about five months after Cecil Payne joined the band, I got a call early one morning from Eddie Davis, telling me to come to New York to join the band in mid-June. They were going on a three-month tour with Tom Jones, the British singer. It must have been late May or early June 1970. I had played with Ray Charles and was living right around the corner from his studio in Los Angeles. I borrowed fifty-five dollars from John Collins, bought a new suit with shirt and tie to match, and went to New York to meet the Basie band. The first job was in Boston backing Tom Jones, Gladys Knight and the Pips, and Norm Crosby. We opened with a set of our own.

B.F. Once you signed on with Basie and toured with Tom Jones, when was your first recording with him?

J.W. I left the band after six months and decided to go back to Los Angeles. It wasn't a very good decision, but that's part of life. I didn't give Basie much notice, so he hired Cecil Payne. This time Cecil Payne replaced me. The first time he had spent six months there as Charlie Fowlkes's replacement, and this time he spent five months until he decided to get married and leave the road. Fortunately Basie called me to come back. Then, we did *Have a Nice Day*, which is all Sammy Nestico arrangements, on a label called Daybreak. I thought it was a pretty good album. It must have been the summer of 1971. That was my recording debut with Basie.

B.F. Let's back up. You were playing alto at South Carolina State when you took your degree.

J.W. Yes. In music education.

B.F. When you were there, did you begin to double on baritone?

J.W. Yes, I did. As a matter of fact, that's where I first became attracted to baritone. By then, the college dance band had been reduced to an octet. Oscar Rivers, who was an outstanding alto saxophonist, came to South Carolina State as a freshman. I had known him for a couple of years; we had met at the All-State Band Association meetings. I asked George Kenny, the leader of the dance band, to let Oscar Rivers play alto and for me to play baritone. We had a baritone player who was leaving the band: his name was Leroy Shannon. I saw it as a wonderful opportunity to play baritone and to have Oscar Rivers on the team. He was a wonderful jazz player.

B.F. But what inspired you to change from alto to baritone?

J.W. At that time, I had no particular love of baritone. I just felt, in reference to the team, that we needed Oscar Rivers. It worked out just fine because I doubled on alto, played baritone, and kept my little features on alto. I had some solo space. I had the great thrill of playing with Oscar Rivers.

B.F. Did any of those college groups ever record?

J.W. No. Sometimes one of the guys would hook up a reel-to-reel recorder in the band room, and we'd get our kicks listening to it. But nothing was released.

B.F. You got a degree, so if all else failed, you could get a job teaching music.

J.W. I may have been trained to do so, but I'm not sure I was equipped to do it.

B.F. You were set on becoming a professional?

J.W. All the way.

B.F. How did you make the transition from amateur to professional?

J.W. The transition wasn't immediate because I stayed in school. I went to Indiana University as a clarinet major, supposedly to pursue a master's degree. I lived with the clarinet. I met a wonderful man there who just retired this year: Henry Gulick. He was a master—and still is a master—clarinetist. He also had played baritone in the army band. We had a lot in common. While he was a classical player, he had great admiration for the great jazz players. Whenever he had time to spare, he'd talk about people like Ben Webster that he had heard.

By that time—during my four semesters at Indiana—I practically stopped playing saxophone. I played gigs at fraternity parties on weekends, but during the week I never touched the saxophone. It was all clarinet. I had been playing clarinet in the latter years at South Carolina State, partly self-taught. There was a great clarinetist, Eddie Pazant, who came through South Carolina State for one semester, but left to join Lionel Hampton. By the time he left, I had a pretty good idea of how the clarinet was supposed to sound.

So when I got to Indiana, I didn't intend to major in clarinet, but I had it with me. I found out that they wouldn't let me audition on alto, and that was a great shock. I had my clarinet. I had learned how to play the Mozart clarinet concerto, and they let me play it as my audition. For four semesters, I was a clarinet major there with Henry Gulick. I did not complete the program, though I completed the course work. I decided to go to California. John Collins was living there, as well as another friend from Orangeburg. That begins a new phase of my life.

B.F. The Montgomery brothers and Freddie Hubbard are from Indiana. Did you ever encounter them?

J.W. Freddie Hubbard had just left to make his first road trip with J. J. Johnson. Virgil Jones, the trumpet player, replaced him in David Baker's band. Wes Montgomery was still working at a club called the Missile in Indianapolis. I only saw Wes once. I went with David to Indianapolis to one of Wes's concerts with a trombonist named Bill Hanna, from North Carolina. Wes sat in with David Baker's band and turned the auditorium upside down. Everyone thought that Wes was a student at Indiana. David just went along with it. The clarinetist from New Orleans, George Lewis, opened with the first set, and David followed with the second set. Of course, Wes was already a legend. This was Thanksgiving 1958.

B.F. From Indiana, you went to Los Angeles. What about Los Angeles, other than the John Collins connection, appealed to you? Was there something in the music scene?

J.W. Was there ever something! All of a sudden, I was in the environment that I had craved. Los Angeles was the ultimate, although New York was the Mecca. I thought that things would move along a little quicker; I had a lot to learn. John Collins was then taking me to Nat Cole's recording sessions at Capitol. There was a multi-reed player, Bill Green, who was the professor of clarinet at the Los Angeles Conservatory. John Collins suggested that I study with Bill Green. I started going to him on Saturday afternoons at the Conservatory on Sunset Strip; the Whiskey A Go Go is now there. Bill Green has remained my teacher from that day in 1960 until this day. He is a fantastic instrumentalist and teacher.

I worked as a bus boy, took courses at Cal State, and finished my course work toward the master's all over again. I played some gigs. I got tired of school; I wanted to play. After completing the course work, I decided to drop out and do a master's thesis later, which was a mistake. I was drafted, which was a blessing because I got three years of solid performing experience in the military. I was first sent to the Navy School of Music, in a suburb of Washington, D.C.

I was there for four or five months and was then sent to the Seventy-second Army band in San Pedro, California. There, I played first alto in the dance band and first clarinet in the concert band. It was the Sleepy Hollow of the army, but that would soon change. I was sent to the Twenty-fourth Division band in Augsburg, West Germany, which was an even better musical experience. I was, in addition to being solo clarinetist, the rehearsal conductor and leader of the dance band.

B.F. In your time in the army band, did you encounter any musicians who went on to make names for themselves?

J.W. Hamiet Bluiett and I were friends at the Navy School. Thurman Green, an excellent trombonist who lives in Los Angeles, was also in the Navy School and became one of my closest friends.

B.F. Upon being discharged after three years, what happened?

J.W. I had a friend, Gabe Flemming, a trumpet player in the Twenty-fourth Division band, who came to Los Angeles with the blues singer Joe Tex. He called me one evening and said that Ike and Tina Turner needed a baritone player and a trumpet player. He wanted to know if I'd meet Ike Turner, who had come up from Texas to fill the two chairs. Ike hired us that night, and the next day we left for San Antonio with Ike and Tina. That was the beginning of civilian road life for me as a professional musician.

B.F. Did you record with them?

J.W. We did some live things, but I don't think they were released. I was with them for six months. I returned to Los Angeles, where I worked with a lot of the Motown acts: Stevie Wonder, Gladys Knight and the Pips, the Four Tops, the Temptations, and Marvin Gaye.

B.F. How did you get into that scene?

J.W. Preston Love, first alto player with Basie during the war years, was the West Coast contractor for Motown. During those years, the Motown acts would bring their rhythm sections, but would need a horn section. Preston Love would contact the horn players. He kept two Motown bands working, and usually I was in one or the other. The Motown connection lasted off and on for a couple of years.

By then—and going back a little—I had become a full-time baritone player in the Twenty-fourth Division band in Germany. So I had begun to establish myself as a baritone player exclusively. My last gig on alto was with Claude Gordon, a trumpet player who led a dance band. After that, I tried to establish myself as a full-time baritone player. I did a lot of recording work in Los Angeles around 1966–1967. I worked with Ray Charles in 1968; I was on the road with him twice, for a few months each time.

B.F. Did you record with Ray Charles?

J.W. No.

B.F. Didn't you record with T-Bone Walker around this time?

J.W. Yes, among many other blues singers. Working with him was a wonderful experience; he was a wonderful person, low key. He always had a straw boss, and the one then was a friend of mine, Clifford Solomon.[3] Clifford Solomon would run these blues dates. If we got stuck without something to play, he would help get the head arrangement together.[4] I recorded a lot for Bob Thiele. I recorded with Joe Turner.

B.F. When did you get into what might strictly be called jazz?

J.W. I've never referred to myself as a jazz musician. I've heard too many great players. But my experience with Basie was my first real experience touring with a jazz band. Ray Charles's band played jazz, but it was also there to accompany his vocals.

B.F. Who did most of the Basie arrangements when you were there?

J.W. Sammy Nestico. By the way, Sammy Nestico was writing for the band at the Navy School of Music when I was there. Grover Mitchell recommended him to Basie; they are both from Pittsburgh. When I came to Basie's band, Sammy had contributed a lot to the book, but we were playing arrangements by Frank Foster, Thad Jones, Ernie Wilkins, Neal Hefti, and others. The book was so big we could play for days without repeating. Sammy was the outstanding arranger of that period. Then came *Have a Nice Day* in 1971.

B.F. When Thad Jones took over the band, did he bring a lot of his own music into the book?

J.W. No. He wanted to stay within the Basie tradition and merely to embellish the book. He did "One to Another"; a blues for his boy called "Blues for the Wee One"; a vocal arrangement of "Stormy Weather"; an arrangement of "To You," which Basie and Ellington recorded together. Many people thought that he would make the Basie band the Thad Jones band. He didn't want that; he wanted to keep the Basie tradition alive. So for that reason, he didn't contribute many new arrangements to the book. He was a very considerate, great man. Eric Dixon led the band before Thad and Frank Foster.

B.F. What effect did Thad's death have on the band?

J.W. Frank Foster joined us in June 1986. In mid-May 1986, Thad did a European tour with us and Catarina Valente; this was his last work with us. He was ailing at the time, but, miraculously, he conducted beautifully and wrote some beautiful arrangements for Catarina Valente. He didn't play on that tour at all. He played through the last exclusively band jobs, in March. He had been a member of the Basie family since the early '50s, so he wasn't like someone who had just come on to lead the band. He was a complete musician.

B.F. Thad Jones did the original solo on "April in Paris," the famous "Pop Goes the Weasel" solo.

J.W. Thad told me a story about that. Norman Granz, who is not often a perfectionist when it comes to big band jazz—he likes the spontaneous small-group jam session dates—kept asking Basie to repeat the number. They had done so many takes that Thad, in jest, put the "Pop, Goes the Weasel" into his solo.

B.F. Isn't that a Wild Bill Davis arrangement?

J.W. Yes.

B.F. Neal Hefti once told me that at the atomic Basie session for Roulette, "Li'l Darlin'" was done in one take at the end of the session. Hefti conceived it originally as something of a jump tune, but Basie told him it would be better at a slower tempo.

J.W. I've been told that Wendell Culley's trumpet solo was written—that Neal Hefti wrote it out.

B.F. My theory about that recording's success is that it's the last piece on that dynamite album. It's like a whisper following all the wailing and Eddie "Lockjaw" Davis's great solos.

J.W. It's perfect. It's contemporary classical music. Basie hired Eddie Davis just to solo; there were already five saxophonists: Frank Foster, Frank Wess, and the others. Basie asked Eddie Davis for that one date. Things were just right for that album.

B.F. The last few times I saw Basie, he was ill. I always thought the best way to get an encore was to give him an ovation that wouldn't stop. He seemed so uneasy speaking that he'd strike up the band again to avoid speaking.

J.W. He was not a great public speaker. He could speak if he had to; he could be eloquent. For years, he had the reputation of giving a lot of music and little talk. He wanted to be thought of as just a guy in the band. Of course, we all knew, without any doubt, he was the boss.

B.F. How was it recording with Basie?

J.W. If I ever disagreed with anything Basie did, it would be the way he conducted recording sessions. My first recording with him—*Have a Nice Day*—was a happy session. It was relaxed. We were at the Tropicana Hotel with Joe Williams just prior to the date. Sammy Nestico came to Las Vegas and ran over the tunes we were to record. We all went to Los Angeles and recorded them. It was done for Daybreak; they treated us graciously. No pressure. That could have been the most relaxed session I ever had with Basie—even though it was my first—because we had a chance to look at the music. All of the sessions after that were sight-read; we ran right through them.

B.F. Do the arrangers attend the sessions?

J.W. Sammy Nestico attended and conducted all of the sessions he wrote for us.

B.F. What was the role of Norman Granz?

J.W. Norman likes jazz music in the raw. He has never really expressed love for a big band. He and Basie were friends. He respected Basie's band, but he enjoyed the jam session recordings best. That's why he began the JATP recordings.[5] He likes musicians just to blow. He wanted to take Basie on the road without the band, but Basie would not consent to it. Norman was a promoter on many of the European tours, and he owned Pablo records, which recorded Basie.

B.F. At a studio session, would Granz be there? Did he exercise artistic control?

J.W. Yes, he was there. He prefers the blues, and the Basie band was the first band to play the blues, which not many people know. When Basie's band came from Kansas City to New York, all the bands were playing thirty-two–bar tunes. Basie brought a big band to New York that played the blues. Naturally Basie was always close to the blues, and Norman wanted the band to play the blues. Finally we did some things: we recorded an album with Eddie "Cleanhead" Vinson and Joe Turner, *Kansas City Shout*. We had just returned from Japan when we did that album; it must have been around 1980. It was a loose blues session. Basie, and Basie only, was in control.

Occasionally at a country club, Basie would have the band sit out, and he and Freddie Green would play the blues. I grew to admire him greatly as a pianist. He was always so modest and unassuming that he would convince you that he wasn't a good pianist.

One time, we were going to a concert at Purdue University in Lafayette. It was a big rush, and we didn't have time to check our things into the hotel in Chicago. We had only a few hours to rest. We asked that the equipment stay on the bus, and that the same bus pick us up and take us to the concert. The dispatcher sent the bus—which had all the large instruments and uniforms—to Detroit. The university provided some drums. We played the whole concert without music. There was a tune that had a little descending baritone line, and I forgot my part because there was no music. At a flash, I caught Basie's eye, and he realized that something was wrong. He picked it up and played the baritone part note for note with his left hand. Little things like that kept happening. He was a masterful leader.

B.F. Does the band get tired of playing "April in Paris," "Li'l Darlin'," and the other standards in the Basie book?

J.W. Yes, but there are fewer and fewer people who remember the originals.

B.F. Are you still playing "Shiny Stockings"?

J.W. Yes. We play nine or ten of Frank Foster's arrangements, including "Autumn Leaves."

B.F. Let me mention a few names to you. Joe Williams.

J.W. Joe Williams. My brother, Joe. What can I say about Joe? In Japan, I told Joe—we were standing in an airport—that if he isn't the world's greatest singer, there's none greater. He's so versatile, so articulate, so intelligent, so gifted musically that it amazes you; he can go from blues to a ballad to a jazz tune. He's a great musician. There's a great videotape, on a Japanese laser disc, of the band with Thad Jones directing, with Nancy Wilson and Joe Williams.

B.F. How is Nancy Wilson with the band?

J.W. Good. So are Sarah Vaughan, Ella Fitzgerald, Tony Bennett, and Frank Sinatra.

B.F. How is Sinatra to work with?

J.W. Good.

B.F. He has a reputation of being a stern taskmaster, of being a perfectionist.

J.W. He knows what he wants.

B.F. Do I remember correctly that after Sonny Payne left Basie, Basie recorded with Sinatra, but Sinatra requested that Payne rejoin the band for those sessions?

J.W. I don't know, but he did go with Sinatra after he left Basie.

B.F. How's working with Tony Bennett?

J.W. Great. Tony, too, is a perfectionist. He's a bug about microphones, about the balance. He carries his own sound man, his nephew, Tom.[6]

B.F. He has great spirit.

J.W. He is an American singer. He is America. I like his singing; I like our chats.

B.F. Does he ever talk art with you?

J.W. Yes. In St. Louis recently, we opened the concert, and he presented me with a little gift during intermission. He had sketched me while we were playing, and he inscribed it, "To John, My Buddy, Benedetto." It shows a side view of me playing, with Basie on piano and Freddie Green on guitar. Just the three of us.

B.F. Sarah Vaughan has recorded with Basie. How is working with her?

J.W. She overwhelms you with that great voice. She doesn't sing with just any big band in personal appearances; it must be Basie's band?

B.F. Does she use her own pianist?

J.W. Yes. She carries her own trio. They all do.

B.F. Are you still playing Ernie Wilkins arrangements?

J.W. Yes. How do you play with Basie and not play Ernie Wilkins arrangements? They are classic.

B.F. Has he written anything recently for the band.

J.W. No. He's now in Copenhagen. I saw him there with his Almost Big Band. He has some great Danish musicians, and he's a great saxophonist. His brother, Jimmy, has a band in Detroit. Jimmy and Ernie joined the Basie band about the same time. Clark Terry recommended them.

B.F. When you have a night off, do you go out and listen to music?

J.W. Sometimes, but we're so tired that we tend not to go out.

B.F. Are there any bands you would go out to see?

J.W. I try to listen discriminately. Certain cities give me more incentive to listen than do others. The most exciting evening I've had recently was in Europe. We kept bumping into Miles Davis in Europe, and he invited us to his concert in Brussels. We were off that night. I am not the same for two years after hearing Miles. He was first when I first heard him, he's been great all the way through, and to this day he's still giving lessons. He's a very intelligent man; he realizes how visual music has become, whether we like it or not. There's always something exciting going on with him, musically and visually.

In Brussels, Miles was sketching something. I asked him if he's an artist. He said that he tries, but I just learned that he, like Tony Bennett, is an artist. I followed him musically through *Get Up with It*. He does a tune "He Loved Him Madly," which is for Duke Ellington. Dave Liebman plays flute. The most amazing thing about it is that it incorporates the music of the earth: sometimes it sounds Asian, sometimes African, sometimes American. It is all encompassing. It is a beautiful blend of acoustic and electronic. At his concert I was amazed that they could play loud without blasting.

B.F. You mention the visual aspect of music. It's ritualistic.

J.W. Kind of getting back to mother Africa. Everything evolves into what it's come from. Basie's band has been fairly dignified; we sit still and play. Frank Foster, our leader now, has a good blend of comedy, although he's no comedian. Basie was more or less dignified, although he'd occasionally tell a joke or two. Thad Jones was dignified.

B.F. Anything else you'd like to say?

J.W. I'm a recreative musician who has been blessed to play with some great creative musicians. My role is recreative. Tony Bennett once told me that if you want to do something really different in life, just be yourself.

Columbia, S.C., 4 September 1987

Notes

1. "Bird" is Charlie Parker.

2. For financial reasons Count Basie toured with a septet, not a big band, in 1950 and 1951.

3. A straw boss manages a band for its leader and is usually a musician, a member of the band.

4. A head arrangement is kept in musicians' minds and is not written down.

5. Williams refers to Jazz at the Philharmonic, jam session concerts organized by Norman Granz.

6. Williams refers to Tom Chiappa, son of Tony Bennett's sister, Mary Benedetto Chiappa.

Left to right: Tommy Benford, Wild Bill Davison, and Joe Sullivan. Date, place, and photographer unknown. From the collection of Dorothy Benford

Left to right: unknown woman, Jack Howe (standing), Rosy McHargue, Jimmy McPartland, Gilmore Black, Bud Freeman, and Orm Downes (head only). Home of Squirrel Ashcraft, Evanston, Ill., in the mid-1930s. Photographer unknown. From the collection of Jack Howe

Jabbo Smith. Photograph by Nancy Miller Elliott. Date and place unknown. From the collection of Lorraine Gordon

The Buddy Johnson band featuring South Carolinians Ella Johnson, Buddy Johnson, and Arthur Prysock (here misspelled Brysock), 1947. Place and photographer unknown. From the collection of Jean Prysock

Freddie Green, Count Basie, and Johnny Williams (seated, right). Sketched by Tony Bennett in St. Louis. Date unknown. Used with the permission of Tony Bennett and Johnny Williams

Nappy Brown at Wit's End, Columbia, S.C., February 1994. From the collection of the photographer, Tut Underwood

Webster Young, mid-1990s. Place and photographer unknown. From the collection of Gretchen Young and Dorian Young

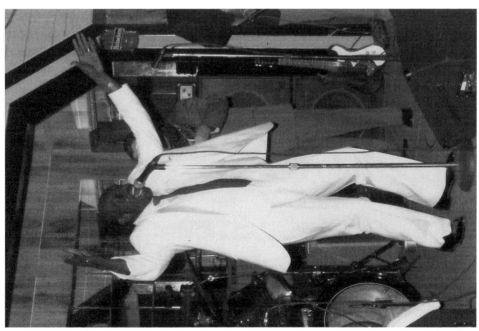

Drink Small (upper left, in jacket) with the class of 1953, Dennis High School, Bishopville, S.C. Photographer unknown. From the collection of Drink Small

Etta Jones and Houston Person. Date, place, and photographer unknown. Used with the permission of HighNote Records

Johnny Helms (right) with Red Rodney. Main Street Jazz Festival, Columbia, S.C., 1980s. Photographer unknown. From the collection of Johnny Helms

Ron Free. Date, place, and photographer unknown. From the collection of Ron Free

Left to right: Billy Eckstine, Frank Foster (leader of the Count Basie band, back to camera), Dizzy Gillespie (trumpet), Johnny Williams (seated, far right), and Duffy Jackson (drums) in 1989. Place and photographer unknown. From the collection of Johnny Williams

Chris Potter (left) with Jimmy Heath, probably at the Main Street Jazz Festival, Columbia, S.C., 1980s. Photographer unknown. From the collection of Ellen Potter

DICK GOODWIN

22 January 1941–

B.F. You are one of the most versatile musicians in South Carolina. Where did it all begin? Did you have a musical family? What was the spark?

D.G. I grew up first in Cape Girardeau, Missouri, on the Mississippi River, and my family moved back and forth between there and El Paso. I was lucky that Cape Girardeau is a really musical town. It's a French name for a German town. There were three services at the Lutheran church every Sunday. The first two were in German, and most of my friends' names were Grossheider.

My first gig was when I was about four. I sang "Some Sunday Morning I'll Walk Down the Aisle" with the municipal band that played concerts in the park in a little gazebo every summer out by the courthouse. I really panicked my folks, as I understand it, because I didn't really bother to learn all the words, which was perhaps the result of my early fascination with Ella Fitzgerald. After the gig, the guy came by my house and brought me a check for a dollar. "This is duck soup," I thought. "I don't even have to learn the words and can make a living at this." So, I think that was the way it was cast. My father was a bass player, and had played clarinet and sax before that.

B.F. Professionally?

D.G. No, although he worked his way through school doing that. When he was in college, the Grand Ole Opry was in Columbia, Missouri, and Nashville on alternate weeks. He was the bass player on that. It was part time.

B.F. Part of the house band, essentially.

D.G. He was playing brass bass, but string bass suddenly became popular. He went to his two older brothers and father and got enough money to buy a string bass so he could keep the job. I still have it.

B.F. Do you use his instrument?

D.G. Yes, it is the same one that he bought when he was in college. Both of my uncles played. One of them was a fine pianist, and the other was a fiddle player—a

Dick Goodwin. Photograph by Robert Corwin of Corwin/Photo-Arts, Philadelphia, summer 1999.
From the collection of Dick Goodwin

violinist—and both cousins on that side of the family are fine musicians. One of them, Fred Goodwin, was the dean of humanities at Southeast Missouri State Teachers College—which is now Southeast Missouri State University—in Cape Girardeau. He continued playing trombone and still plays bass now.

My other cousin is the one with the really great aural skills. I think she can hear the grass grow and know what the pitches are. She was a high school choral teacher and did a lot of community theater, and still does. So yes, it's a musical family. We would sit around and listen to what was hot, like Gerry Mulligan and Chet Baker.

B.F. So this was the early or middle 1950s?

D.G. Yes. I remember the big excitement for my cousin, not so much for my father, was that Stan Kenton had a summer replacement show, and, boy, we watched that religiously. The major shows would take off for the summer, and they would have a summer replacement. I remember Rosemary Clooney had one about that same time, and the house vocal group was the Hi-Lo's. So it was a musical atmosphere for me, and I never thought about doing anything else. When I moved to El Paso, I was fortunate enough to be in the high school band with some good players—a trombone player and a cellist—who would become professional musicians.

B.F. Were you then playing trumpet?

D.G. Yes, I was playing trumpet. I was very fortunate. Both band directors—the one in Cape Girardeau and the one in El Paso—encouraged me to write for the school band and the orchestra. I think the major influence for me was the Sauter-Finegan band, which fascinated me. And I got to hear them when I was in junior high school, and I couldn't believe what they were able to do: all the sounds out of that many guys. They had five saxes, but they doubled on every conceivable woodwind. I mean, a guy would pick up a tenor recorder and play three notes, then grab the bass clarinet, and then an English horn. The woodwinds that they were grabbing from looked like a forest.

B.F. They were on the road? They came through there?

D.G. They came through Cape Girardeau and played a concert in one hall. Then, they picked up and moved to the gymnasium to play a dance.

B.F. When you say you were writing early, do you mean you were composing? Arranging? Both?

D.G. Mostly arranging. I even tried to take down a couple of the Sauter-Finegan things, which my high school band played. I dread to look at how inaccurately I took dictation. This is complicated music. But I tried, and I learned so much from doing it.

One of my band directors had a stack of scores for big band by a local arranger who went on to write some stuff for television. The director gave me the scores to study, and I figured out how this guy worked. He had a couple of quirks. He did a couple of things that weren't standard in the industry, but I did them like he did for a long time until I learned the difference. I was just very, very fortunate to do that.

B.F. So your family was educated and they were educators, and many of them were musical. You had a nurturing environment growing up when it came to music.

D.G. Yes, although my parents weren't educators. My cousin turned out to be. My cousin Jeanne Goodwin Brown and I are the first professional musicians of the group, but they all played. My father did some gigs with Carmen Cavallero. He played in the El Paso Symphony and in a society dance band there called the Society Five.

B.F. A jazz band?

D.G. No. It would be the equivalent of a party band now, or a society orchestra. It had an odd combination: trumpet, piano, bass, accordion, and guitar. So no drums, but four rhythm, and they could all play. Not long ago, I found a recording of the group that we made in our living room, and I made copies for my sisters and children. Then, I set out to try to find the surviving guys in the band. The accordion player is still alive, and I was able to chat with him.

B.F. Did you move from Missouri to Texas and then back to Missouri?

D.G. And then back to Texas.

B.F. What did your father do?

D.G. In Missouri, he worked with his older brother at a car dealership. He was the service manager for a Lincoln/Mercury dealer. In Texas, he worked for an uncle on my mother's side of the family in garment manufacturing and managed a factory there. He ended up staying with that, eventually going to New York but also working in factories in Mexico and North Carolina.

B.F. Between age four when you had your first paying performance and, say, around 1954 when you heard Mulligan and Baker, did you study music in school? Did you have music lessons?

D.G. I didn't have any private lessons. I didn't study privately, period. It was just through the public schools. I was in the band—maybe fourth grade—and chose trumpet, which was a silly thing to do. It's an ungrateful piece of metal, and I'm still fighting with it. I played trumpet and string bass in the school orchestra, but my main passion was writing. I put together a dance band when I was in junior high school and wrote all the music. We rehearsed in the living room, and we played a few gigs I found. It lasted for two or three months. I kept a record of my earnings: six dollars for this job and that job, and so forth.

B.F. Did you have formal training in writing? You mentioned the charts.

D.G. No, I didn't. It was all practical experience. Then, in junior high I checked out of the public library Russell Garcia's *The Professional Arranger-Composer*, which I still think is a fine book.

B.F. So you're largely self-taught both in playing and writing.

D.G. Yes, until college. When I got out of high school, I went into the Coast Guard and ended up being the band director on one of the bases. The band played for recruit ceremonies, and so forth. I was fearless. I was seventeen, and the band director got thrown in the brig for being AWOL. He was a fine instrument repairman and did woodwind repair for some of the guys in the Philadelphia Orchestra. If the oboe player called and said, "My A-flat key's hanging up," he'd fix it. Anyway, he took off and was caught. The military seems to take those things seriously. When you're signed in on the base, you're supposed to be there. So I had already started writing for the Coast Guard band, even though I was a recruit. I'd been in the service for six weeks, or maybe less than that.

B.F. Were you drafted?

D.G. No. In 1958 there was a mandatory draft, so you had to do your duty now or later. Your chances of slipping through were nil. So I went in. I was also married that young, and it seemed like the right thing to do. I ended up taking over the band because I was there writing. They made the position a permanent one, so I auditioned for it and got it. The exam they gave was right up my alley. It had to do with music theory and orchestration. I knew what instruments are in what order, their transpositions, and this sort of thing, which I had been clawing my way through since I was in junior high school.

B.F. Where were you stationed?

D.G. Cape May, New Jersey.

B.F. Did you travel? Stay on the base?

D.G. I was right there the whole time. That's where I went for recruit training, and I ended up staying because I ended up conducting the band while I was still a recruit.

B.F. There must have been a lot of music around you. It wasn't all that far to New York or Philadelphia. Did you have time to go off and hear music, even though you were married?

D.G. Yes. I heard some really significant things in Philadelphia at the Academy of Music. One was Robert Shaw doing the Bach B-minor Mass and *Ceremony of Carols*, by Britten. Boy, that was an education, hearing that live, watching Shaw conduct. What he did was very minimal. He was mainly standing up there giving backbeats, which gave the orchestra a vitality that you don't often hear, or that I hadn't heard before live. So that's a significant one. Also, I went to Jazz at the Philharmonic concerts in Philadelphia in the same hall. I heard Dave Brubeck with Joe Morello, and I guess just about everybody.

B.F. Who are some of the trumpet players you heard? There had to be some with Jazz at the Philharmonic.

D.G. Maynard Ferguson's band was new at the time, too, and I would hear it—and Stan Kenton's band, or Basie at the Steel Pier in Atlantic City, which was even closer. I got to hear Miles Davis in a nightclub in Atlantic City. John Coltrane was with him, and Jimmy Cobb was on drums. We pulled into the parking lot—four of us jammed into a little Austin-Healey—to hear Miles at a club, and there was hardly anybody in there. When we got into the parking lot, there was a long, white Ferrari. We'd not seen anything like that at close range, so we said to the parking lot attendant, "My gosh, whose is that?" And he said, "Well, that belongs to Miles." And then he said, "But for me, I think I'd rather have a Cadillac any day."

B.F. Let's stay with jazz for a moment. You mentioned hearing the Mulligan group with Chet Baker in the '50s. Is that what really piqued your interest in jazz? Or can you identify how it began?

D. G. There's a Shorty Rogers recording with André Previn, one of the first LPs I bought.

B.F. *Collaboration.*

D.G. That was the other big influence on my writing beside Sauter-Finegan. Shorty Rogers and André Previn each wrote three originals on the changes of three standards that the other guy picked. It was kind of a neat setup. But there were other influences. I never got to hear the Hi-Lo's live, but they were one. The Four Freshmen I heard when they came through Cape Girardeau and again when I was in the service.

But the first thing that got me about Sauter-Finegan was the orchestration. And the groups I heard had fantastic soloists, so that became a passion. While I was in the service, my father was living in New York. He had just moved there. I went to the Apollo to see Cannonball Adderley and Nancy Wilson, along with Red Foxx and Oscar Brown, Jr., who I thought was a terrific performer. Just the visuals that went with it were really fantastic, and the show closed with Oscar Peterson.

Red Foxx was telling integration jokes and pointed to my father and me and said, "Oh, when I see friends of mine in the audience, I like to have them stand up." And I knew he was just gonna lay the punch line on us in the middle of Harlem—the only two white guys there except for Joe Zawinul, who was Cannonball's piano player. He said, "No. Come on, stand up." And the guy next to me stood up. Red Foxx said, "Ladies and gentlemen, Horace Silver." And so it was good hearing such music in the area during four years in the Coast Guard.

B.F. Are there trumpeters who inspired you?

D.G. Bobby Hackett might have had the most influence on the way I play, with the possible exception of Clark Terry. I mean, Clark Terry has the sweetest trumpet sound. He can play a whole note, and you know who it is. That's not an easy thing on a brass instrument. I had a Duke Ellington recording that had Clark Terry on it. I just couldn't believe that he could burn with such intensity and then turn around and play something sensual, putting a tear in it. And so I think he's a major influence.

B.F. How about Bobby Hackett, who played the cornet?

D.G. There was nothing out of place. When I got out of the service, I went to the University of Texas as a theory/composition major. When I was an undergraduate, there was no jazz band, although there was a famous one at North Texas. Some of the guys put together a big band just for kicks and played in the student union because we were not allowed to play jazz in the music building. Times have changed.

B.F. Because it was undignified, or not serious?

D.G. Yes. But the dean was on sabbatical for a year, and the guy whose job it was to put together the brochure for the department mentioned in it that there was a jazz band. Well, there really wasn't. The band didn't have anything to do with the music department. But because he knew some of his helpers were playing in a band, he mentioned it in the brochure. Students went to the acting dean and said, "Where's the jazz band? It's not here, and you said it is." So they felt obligated legally to put it in the catalogue. Who would conduct the band? I was still an undergraduate, but they came to me and said, "If we assign you a faculty guy that can sign the grade sheets, will you lead the band?" So I started the jazz program there.

In Austin, there's a guy I still work for who loves every kind of music. His name's Rod Kennedy. He had a commercial classical FM station, so you can see how much he loved music and not money. He had an antique racing car collection and a big house on the hill, but he gradually lost those things. He put on a fundraiser for the radio station. The music was eclectic: a string orchestra, a Bach Brandenburg Concerto, and Frank DeVol, the composer/arranger Hollywood guy who had done themes like *My Three Sons*. He came with charts, so we had a big band, plus the strings. Fran

Warren was the singer, and Bobby Hackett was there. Frank DeVol liked Bobby Hackett, and I'd gotten to play with him one time earlier through Rod.

As I said, Rod likes everything (he even had Earl Scruggs on that same program) and thinks that audiences should be discerning enough to appreciate anything that's good. Period. The genre doesn't matter. I went to pick up Bobby Hackett, who was sitting out on the street on his cornet case. A little bitty guy, but neat as pin. So he's sitting there, on Congress Street in downtown Austin, just below the capitol. While maneuvering to pick him up, I thought, "Here are all these people walking by, and there's not one soul that hasn't heard him play; and they have no earthly idea who he is." He was on all those easy-listening albums Jackie Gleason did, and he's the one that has the trumpet solo that everybody still plays on Glenn Miller's "String of Pearls."

So we got to the concert, and Rod, the promoter, said, "I want Bobby to play 'String of Pearls' with the band." Bobby said, "Okay." Bobby was really quiet, and a nice guy. But when he stepped up to the microphone, he said, "I must tell you. I was the guitar player on Glenn Miller's band, but I had two short solos I would play on cornet occasionally. One of them was 'String of Pearls.' One night, Glenn came over and said, 'Do you remember what you played tonight on "String of Pearls"?' And I said, 'Well, yes, it's just a simple little chordal outline exercise.' Glenn Miller said, 'Well, I want you to play it that way every night.' I knew my days on that band were numbered. There went half the reason that I hung around on the band—to have those little short spurts of solo space."

And so Bobby, when we got to the solo, played the same solo, but upside down.[1] I said, "Man, it was identifiable, but it was upside down. That's really clever." I play the jazz chair a lot in big bands, and so, sure enough, two or three years later we were playing "String of Pearls." I thought I'd play it upside down. I fumbled; I crashed and burned. It's not as easy as Bobby Hackett makes it sound. So that's Bobby Hackett.

B.F. Did any of the players from the Texas band make a living from music or establish a name in it?

D.G. Yes, most of them, actually. I left in 1973 to come to the University of South Carolina. By that time, the guys were serious. One of the guys was in the trumpet section on Natalie Cole's *Unforgettable* album. Another guy was her assistant conductor for a while. One of the guys was playing Broadway shows. I've kind of kept track of them, and most all the guys in the band by the time I left have stayed professional players. I had a reunion about ten years after the fact at one of Rod's festivals, a folk festival. He thought there should be a big band.

I brought a chart that we had worked really hard on when they were in the band. It was sax soli on Jerome Richardson's "Groove Merchant." It was a knuckle-buster thing, and I said, "Well, let's run it through, and we'll come back and run the soli a couple times." They just breezed through it. Nobody had played it in ten years. As I was trying to decide whether we needed to go back and touch it at all, one of the guys said, "You know, we're not any better than we were, but we can cover it an awful lot better."

B.F. I assume you moved to Austin with your family.

D.G. Yes. I was able to do my undergraduate degree in about three years because I was able to skip some of the theory courses.

B.F. Then you stayed on for a master's and a Ph.D.

D.G. Yes. By the time I got out of school, I was directing the jazz band. They asked me to do a master's, and I did. At that time, faculties were more mobile than they are now, so some of the guys I went to study with were gone; but because the ones that were coming in were guys I wanted to study with, I stayed. They offered me a permanent faculty position when I finished the degree.

B.F. Was there a jazz department by that time—or a jazz faculty?

D.G. I was pretty much the jazz faculty. There were a couple of allies that I tapped for help, but pretty much I ran the program. That was just part of my assignment. I was teaching composition and theory. So I taught sixteenth-century counterpoint and jazz improvisation. One of my students there was Doug Graham. He took composition from me.

B.F. So he followed you to South Carolina?

D.G. He followed Bill Moody. Bill and I came from Texas at the same time. He was the concert band director at Texas when I was there, and we didn't see eye to eye on anything. He thought that music education majors should be required to play in the jazz band for a semester. By this time, I had three jazz bands going, so I really resisted. I said, "No. I have everybody signing up because they want to do it. You make it a requirement and I'm dead." It was really funny. But he asked me to apply for an opening at South Carolina when he was taking over the chairmanship of its music department.

B.F. Didn't Jim Hall also come from Texas?

D.G. He was teaching in San Marcos, which was about thirty-five miles down the road from Austin. I was playing gigs with him, and he toured with my quintet in Latin America. So when the percussion teaching job opened here, I asked him to apply for it, which he did. I'm eternally grateful for that. Terry Trentham, the bass player in my group, played trombone in the U.T. jazz band and was my graduate assistant at one point. Jim Mings, a fine guitarist, was also in that band.

B.F. So, really, Texas is the basis of our program.

D.G. There are a number from there, like Charlie Elliott and Ken Pouncey, who was assistant band director here and then took a high school job. Oddly enough, they pay more. No, it's not odd. It's a hard-hat area out there. I have to give schoolteachers all the credit in the world.

B.F. Where did John Emche come from?

D.G. John came from Towson State, which had a good jazz program. I think he did his master's in Ohio. We auditioned a handful of folk, and he was the obvious winner of the piano position.

B.F. You mentioned the Latin America tour. Is that your only tour abroad?

D.G. No. I did about a dozen in Latin America.

B.F. All when you were at Texas?

D.G. When I was at Texas, but also after I moved here.

B.F. How does something like that happen? There are hundreds of jazz bands. Did you apply?

D.G. No, I never applied. When I was at Texas, I was contacted by some outfit in Monterey, Mexico, that wanted to know if we could bring the jazz band down. They had worked out a deal with Mexicana Airlines and would put us up. I think they had us confused with North Texas, but it was okay. We went.

I was living in university housing, in the university slums for married students. The guy living next door to me was working on his doctorate in physics, and I was finishing up my music doctorate. Back home after finishing his degree, he was in charge of the physics department of the University of Honduras. He called me: "We're trying to build a new building. I have five tickets on SAHSA, the Honduran airline, out of New Orleans. Could you guys come down? We'll put you up for a few days, and you can play a benefit concert." And that's why I have a quintet. I had done two or three things in Mexico with different-sized groups—the big band, a septet one time—from the same connections.

What happened in Mexico is that there was a guy that heard us and worked for USIS in the State Department.[2] He realized that it was going over well and thought we should do more of that, and he should take some credit. So he booked it.

The same kind of thing happened in Honduras. We were taking pictures with the mayor of Tegucigalpa and the president of the university, and there's a smiling guy standing next to me in the picture. I asked, "Who are you?" He was John Griffiths. When I asked, "Why are you here?," he said, "It's going well, isn't it?" Another State Department guy. I said, "You must have counterparts in other parts of Latin America. Why don't you set me up something for next summer, and I'll take a group?" So he said, "Sure, no problem." And so we used the USIS communication system to iden-tify a local sponsor.

We ended up playing all over Latin America over a dozen years, and we might be sponsored by the Red Cross of El Salvador or the Women's Auxiliary of the Long-shoremen in Lima, Peru, where we did a trade fair. The Latin American information service guys, who all knew each other, said about us, "These guys are easy to work with and they show up; people like the music, and everybody smiles. It's a good thing."

Our being there didn't really cost the government anything. Basically we played a benefit concert for some people, and they usually got the transportation worked out as an in-kind donation. All our tours worked out that way, though each year was a different routine. At one time or another, we played all the Andean countries, around to Venezuela, and all the Central American countries. We would go out for six weeks at a time. We played a concert or had international travel every day. It was a pretty grueling thing.

This touring lasted about twelve years. It expanded some. We played Haiti. We did a tour with the quintet in Germany. That was fun and kind of a different setup. The German tourist bureau was trying to sell tickets to America, so they got an American show to go around Germany in order to pique people's interest and sell more plane tickets. It was kind of a neat show. My quintet opened it, and we backed some of the acts, which included a singer and a magic act by Lance Burton. Occasionally he'll do one of those television spectaculars. I see his name now and then. There was a cowboy act with stunt men who broke chairs over each other's heads, threw rubber chickens, and shotguns. The Germans seemed to like that a lot.

It was a three-week tour. I think we played fourteen cities in Germany. It isn't exactly like a vacation. (I did a show in Russia and produced a guy's album in Norway, but in January or February. So it wasn't perfect.) Anyway, on this same tour in Germany, there was a Hawaiian group. There was a four-piece band, five hula girls, and two male dancers. They were quite wonderful.

It was an odd entourage on this bus going around. The Hawaiian guys stayed in costume. They were body-builder types who passed out macadamia nuts in the bus. When we would pull up somewhere and start to unload, these guys would hop off the bus and have things set up before we could put on our layers of coats and scarves. They were just delightful. This probably doesn't have a whole lot to do with the history of jazz other than to illustrate that jazz has let me see things and be places that I never would have gone on my own, and from a different angle.

We were in a restaurant with this group of people, and the Hawaiian bass player was doing an impression of Peter Sellers doing an impression of Inspector Clouseau for one of the cowboys whose legal name was Frank Outlaw, from Arizona. We were in a Chinese restaurant in Braunschweig, Germany. So here is a Polynesian guy doing an impression of an English guy doing an impression of a French guy for this cowboy from Arizona—and the picture of all these flowered shirts and looking out the window at piles of snow in a Chinese restaurant. . . . What's wrong with this picture? Everything is wrong with it.

B.F. But a great event, and a great memory.

D.G. Yes.

B.F. You got to the University of South Carolina in 1973. What did you teach? Theory and composition?

D.G. Yes. I also directed the symphony orchestra for five or six years.

B.F. Did you teach jazz courses?

D.G. No, I didn't, though I had been doing that in Texas. They brought me here to start a doctoral program in composition. They were not interested in me as a jazz person.

B.F. Was there a jazz program when you arrived?

D.G. There was a jazz band that the percussion teacher Jack Bircher directed. Pretty soon, we hired John Emche, and he brought it up quite a ways. He had a really optimistic view of being able to teach people to sound right, so consequently it worked most of the time. Unlike him, when I sometimes heard what he was working with in the earlier years, I thought about that poster that shows a pig with a Band-Aid and says, "Never try to teach a pig to sing. It frustrates you and annoys the pig." I thought about that, but John was just absolutely determined, as I was with the jazz program at Texas. Some of the guys that were in the jazz program there came here to finish their degrees.

B.F. Who succeeded John?

D.G. John Serry was here for a couple of years, and then I guess Bert Ligon came next. So there haven't been that many guys at the helm.

B.F. Was Roger Pemberton one of them? Or was he strictly an artist in residence?

D.G. He was artist in residence, but he directed the big band.

B.F. When John Emche and his successors established the program, would they teach a course like the history of jazz? Or improvisation skills? What does such a program entail?

D.G. They would do a jazz history course and a jazz theory course, which is kind of parallel to improvisation. Improvisation to me is kind of theory on your feet. Actually I did start a studio-arranging course here, and we're still doing it, or something similar to it. I also taught some jazz arranging.

B.F. There's a fairly thriving jazz scene out of the music school.

D.G. Yes, and a number of the good guys have stayed here, so there are some good players in town now. That makes a difference, so there's a strong local scene.

B.F. Have you had a group—a quintet, or whatever the configuration—ever since you arrived? I assume that Doug Graham's arrival was important.

D.G. I've had one pretty much the whole time. Right about the time that I got here, the bassist Jimmy Ferguson was an undergraduate. I guess he booked us at the Coal Company, which became Greenstreets, on Monday or Tuesday nights. I was sort of the leader of that quintet, and gradually the group turned over.

When we hired Doug Graham on the faculty to essentially teach legit clarinet, I said, "You're in my quintet." He said, "I took your improv course at Texas but haven't improvised since." And I said, "It's not a problem. You play first, so you won't have to follow anybody, and then the other guys will play after you." Well, that was good for a couple months and then. . . . Now, he's hard to follow.

This was the time when Chris Potter was in middle school, then high school. He would sit in on a regular basis. The scene kind of moved to Pug's where Johnny Helms had a group. Chris Potter often played there, and I subbed sometimes and sat in. I can't bebop at the speed of Mr. Helms, but it was always good for me to put my technique in perspective.

B.F. What was the role of the music department in Chris Potter's development? Didn't Doug mentor him?

D.G. Doug taught him a little bit. I think Bryson Borgstedt did. Bryson was in school at the time and then went to the West Point band. Now, he is retired and has moved back into town. We're happy to have him back.

I got a call from Chris's middle school music teacher asking, "What do I do?" I said, "Well, keep handing him instruments that he's never seen before. You know, so he doesn't get bored and quit the program." Chris is absolutely a gentleman and was at the age of twelve. Although he had to know how special his gifts were compared to everybody else's, he still played in the high school marching band and in the USC jazz band. I ran into him a couple years ago in New York at a jazz conference, and he mentioned that I had given him his first paying job. What a unique opportunity to see something like that happen.

There can't be many of those guys that are so natural that young. When he was thirteen and fourteen, he sounded like he'd been on the road with Basie for thirty years. Many young players have all kinds of technical facility, but there was a depth beyond that with Chris. There was nothing that hung him up technically at all. I mean, we could kick off one of the dreaded tunes like "Cherokee" at a blazing speed, and none of us could actually play a solo so we'd stop and let him play four choruses a cappella, just by himself. We knew exactly where he was, and there was not a hitch, no fumbling—and it goes through every lousy key in the spectrum. He just had it.

One of the guys asked him, "How did you happen to choose to play the saxophone?" He answered by saying, "That's the closest thing to what I was hearing." And of course his career has been quite remarkable, though he's not so likely to be a household name outside the jazz world because he's pretty uncompromising. He's really doing what he thinks is artistically correct, and I really applaud him for doing it. I mean, my band plays "In the Mood" because we're trying to get the job next time. We do beach tunes, or whatever. But Chris in his small group has been developing a contemporary sound that's just remarkable.

B.F. He plays piano occasionally. He takes up miscellaneous instruments.

D.G. Yes. Hand him a bassoon. That'll stop him—for a week. He plays guitar. I don't know that I've heard him record on any of the other things besides woodwinds, but he does flute, bass clarinet, and so forth. I used him as a jingle singer when he was in high school. He's just great. How often does one of those guys come along? Once every fifty years, and he happened to land in our town. It's just a wonderful, wonderful pleasure.

B.F. I heard someone once say it's providential that his initials are C.P.

D.G. Yes, Charlie Parker.

B.F. It must be tremendously rewarding to people like you, Doug, and other professionals to have helped Chris along the way.

D.G. I told Chris not too long ago that I was a little disappointed that he doesn't play either of my licks. He seems to be more inventive. I can hear my licks coming two bars before I get there, as can the guys in my group.

B.F. You've mentioned your quintet a number of times, but you're involved in a big-band project at the moment, I believe.

D.G. The quintet is guitar, bass, drums, and woodwind player, who is almost always Doug. I play keyboard and trumpet. My big band is the same five guys, plus two other trumpets and three trombones. I've had pretty much the same personnel in that band for twenty years, and they're guys who have stayed on top of their games. They're still trying to be the best they can be by putting themselves in pressure situations like the Philharmonic.

It seemed that I really should get a CD of it for us to have on the shelf. We're working on it now. I don't know if there's any commercial gain to be had, but it's sure worth my time and effort and money to get it down. So I have recorded sixteen tunes. Some of them are my originals. Our guitarist, Dwight Spencer, wrote one that I had scored for the big band. Terry Trentham does quite a bit of writing for the big band, so there are three or four of his charts on the CD. Those are the only ones I have to pay royalties on. The rest are either originals or in the public domain.

B.F. But what about recording? You recorded in the 1970s, but hasn't there been a hiatus since then?

D.G. I do have a CD of the quintet from three or four years ago.

B.F. Why record so infrequently? You have a nice group that's been around a long time and plays good tunes. It seems as though a new musician comes on the scene, and the next day there's a CD out. With you, there might be a problem with distribution, but you have your own studio. It seems a perfect match.

D.G. Now, you put your finger on it. It is a perfect match. I have a studio—rather, I'm a partner in a studio—and the cobbler's children go without shoes. I have a recording studio with no album. I get involved in other things and keep putting it off.

One problem is not knowing what to record. When I was doing the Latin American tours, I realized pretty early that jazz is a term that has a really broad definition. We would play a concert, and I would have somebody come up to me devastated because they thought we'd play like Louis Armstrong. They thought it was going to be traditional jazz, dixieland jazz. Somebody else would come up assuming that we would have played Brubeck because that's who they thought jazz was, or Chick Corea.

So I began programming a wide variety of styles. Also, if we did all bebop, it would sound exactly the same to some of them: one texture, one style. Unless listeners have a discerning ear and some experience in that particular style or genre, it's going to sound like wallpaper. I mean, if we listen to Indian music, there are a lot of important subtleties that we don't catch. We hear a drone and somebody noodling.

I thought the fair thing to do would be to make the pieces sound as different as I could from piece to piece. If somebody came really hoping for bebop, we would have played a couple of bebop tunes. We also would have played a Latin tune, a couple of straight-ahead swing things, a traditional thing, or maybe even something earlier, like a rag. This approach seems to work. If the audience is pretty much of the same age group, I'll pitch a majority of the things to them. Still, they may not really be jazz fans, so I feel like they'll get more out of it if I make the sounds different.

B.F. I've heard you play at the senior center, where you feature old-time tunes. The people respond very positively.

D.G. That's the mission of the Carolina Jazz Society. They do traditional jazz—that's the audience—and they really don't do anything else. If somebody comes in and plays something else, they tend to apologize for it. It doesn't matter how good it is. I mean, if a singer sits in who doesn't really deliver like 1920, the members will say it's good music, but it isn't ours.

But at community concerts with my group, I really do a lot of different things. For a CD, I don't know if I should do what I do on concerts, or if I should do what I think jazz is. That took three or four years to sort out. And then, we were getting better in the studio. We were getting a better drum sound and doing a better job at this, that, and the other thing, so I'd say, "Well, if we just wait a year, we'll sound right." I decided that we'll never sound right and that I'll never be in good enough shape on my horn to do it. Maybe we should go ahead and do one.

B.F. What is your involvement with the studio? Do you do jingles? I assume it's not only your own music that you record there.

D.G. We really do whatever is out there. I think we thought when we first started that there would be jingles to do as well as groups that wanted to record. We have a great concert-grand piano in there, so we have people come in to do legit albums: fiddle and piano, voice and piano, or audition tapes with a professional sound.

John Epps, my partner, really runs it. We do an awful lot of scripts for industrial presentations, a lot of local ads, this week's special, and so forth. That's really what kind of keeps it afloat. We have done a handful of documentary music backgrounds and industrial-film backgrounds. Those come and go. It seems like we only have those with the same deadline—two due at the same time—and then nothing for a year.

B.F. It's G.E.M., isn't it? Is that for Goodwin-Epps Music?

D.G. Yes, it is. And actually there was a third partner, the guy who sent us to Germany, Richard McMahan. I still thank him for that. He had a small interest in the studio and we bought him out awhile ago. We knew that we were going to do that when we started it.

B.F. Who is Gordon Goodwin?

D.G. That's a terrific story. Somebody told me about Gordon Goodwin twenty-five or thirty years ago. For the sake of clarification, my name is Gordon Richard Goodwin. My father's name was Gordon, so I went by Dick.

When I went to college, Clifton Williams, my first composition teacher, said, "Dick Goodwin will never do. Do you have any other names?" And I said, "Well, my first name's Gordon," to which he replied, "It's not as catchy as Kent Kennan," who was another composition teacher there, "but it's a better bet. So use that on all your legit stuff." So I used and still use Gordon for my symphonic writing.

When I heard about the other Gordon Goodwin, I sent him a one-page résumé and a hand written note that said, "I'm real. Are you?" Ten years later, I got back a one-page résumé and a handwritten note from the other Gordon Goodwin, who lives in L.A. or Thousand Oaks. It said, "Yeah, just out here in California trying to eke out a living doing music."

He's a very talented writer, and he's really gotten on the radar in the last few years. He has a big band that is just magnificent. Excellent players. It's maybe the cleanest big band and in some ways the most exciting big band I've heard in my life. He's quite good. Three or four years ago I was having a piece done by a school group in Chicago. The publishers put it on the show, and Gordon Goodwin's band was there the same day. I sat in the front row. One of my former students, president of an international jazz group, said, "Come on, I have good seats." After the concert I introduced myself to Gordon.

Judy Green, an outfit in L.A. that prints music for composers, had us confused, as did ASCAP, so our published music is a mess.[3] The next morning, we ran into each other and chatted some more. Now, I've run into him every year. At least once when I was in L.A., he took me to a studio where they were mixing a DVD of the big band, which was terrific. So we've really gotten to be pretty good buddies. The last time we were in New York, he asked Winifred, my wife, "Could he be Dick for these four days, and I'll be Gordon?"

B.F. But in your own musical life, your jazz activities are by Dick Goodwin and your more formal ones are by Gordon Goodwin.

D.G. I've tried to unscramble it. About ten years ago, I started using Gordon for most stuff, with Dick in parentheses. When I started using Dick in parentheses instead of my Gordon Goodwin legit name, I was trying to keep the hats not so separate anymore. I had been really very careful to use one name for one kind of music and the other for another. The styles didn't intersect: my legit style is really abstract and academic. At some point, I thought it was okay for them to begin to intersect a little bit. I don't know that the legit writing gets into the jazz pieces so much, but I have accepted some jazz influences into my legit writing.

B.F. I would guess that the legit and jazz overlap, intersect, in your composition *Jabbo*, which I have not heard. It has flute, cello, and oboe, but pays homage to the most famous jazz player to come out of the Jenkins Orphanage in Charleston, which produced a lot of good jazz musicians. What inspired that composition?

D.G. A lot of folk may not know that Cat Anderson, Ellington's screech trumpeter, also came from the orphanage.[4] Jabbo Smith was just a footnote in most of the jazz books. I knew that he had a lot of technique and that he was considered to be Louis Armstrong's main rival. I think Jabbo didn't show up for a lot for gigs, maybe, and he wasn't always as charismatic as Louis Armstrong. He didn't have a record company that was clever and aggressive, so he kind of disappeared.

In the meantime, I had a commission to do a legit piece for Piccolo Spoleto for the combination of flute, oboe, and cello. I knew the players, and they're really wonderful. When I asked what they wanted, they said, "If we can have something with a low-country connection, it would be great." I thought that since Jabbo grew up in the Jenkins Orphanage, and I was really impressed with a recording of his I had just heard, I just fantasized what it might have been for a boy to grow up in the orphanage and eventually get out of there.

B.F. Did you try to capture a mood in the composition?

D.G. I did. *Jabbo* has a poignant opening about how a kid might have landed at the orphanage. Then, I thought about the school band rehearsals, when they were playing scales and eventually putting them together. I used a hymn tune that they may have played, like "Just a Closer Walk with Thee." The instruments finally come together, quit practicing, and play a jazzy version of it. Unless you're listening for it, I'm not sure you're going to hear it. The last movement reflects his becoming a star in a way, but remaining unknown, so it's kind of a downside to a great artistic success.

B.F. Would you call it program music?

D.G. Yes, I think so. The titles of the movements indicate what's there.

B.F. You've done things other than jazz and strictly legit music. You've written innumerable half-time performances for the USC band to play at football games. How does this figure into your life?

D.G. That was one of the ways Bill Moody got an extra faculty slot at USC: hiring an arranger to teach some theory in the music school. So that was part of my assignment when I came, and I did it for some twenty years. I've got three or four file cabinets full of marching-band arranging projects.

B.F. When big-name performers come through town, you often back them. I saw you doing Cab Calloway twenty years ago. Recently Aretha Franklin, I think. Didn't you do Ray Charles three or four years ago? And Louis Bellson? How does it happen? Does their front man call the local booker and ask about locals who can do the job?

D.G. I don't know that there's a good pipeline. I think they may call the venue and ask who they can get. I've been known as a contractor. The guys I hire show up and can read music and put the show together quickly. I've kind of become known as the guy in this area that does that.

B.F. As I recall, Ray Charles at the Three Rivers Festival did primarily ballads, not rocking tunes. I assume someone from his camp sent you the charts, and you ran them down with your musicians. Then, the concert. Is that it?

D.G. No. There's one rehearsal. They pass out the music, and you run through the show. He usually brings a conductor.

B.F. Do you mean rehearsal with the star himself, like Ray Charles?

D.G. No. The star rarely comes to the rehearsal. Sometimes they'll show up for a minute or two to make sure it's going to work or to do a sound check. With the Three Rivers Festival, there was no sound check we could do because the rehearsal was inside while something else was going on outside. The good guys usually bring their rhythm section, or at least part of it, usually a conductor, and sometimes a lead trumpet player or a lead sax player. They tell me specifically what else to get.

B.F. So you really don't interact much with the stars on a personal basis.

D.G. No. I get to know their conductors.

B.F. Who are some of them?

D.G. It doesn't happen much anymore. In the age of synthesizers, a group can travel with a drummer and two or three keyboard players and maybe something else and get a full sound; and they have the technology to pre-record part of it and have some live guys.

Over the years, we've been quite lucky to have played a lot of really neat shows. One of the nicest folks to work with—and this was years ago—was Carol Burnett. We got to play for Jimmy Durante back in the old days. A lot of the Motown kind of acts, such as the Spinners. Sandy Duncan had a nice show with a nice little group. We did that fairly recently. We even used to do the circus a lot. That was a killer chop thing: three shows on Saturday, and nonstop playing for two hours. Everybody just dreaded it and joked about the circus wiping us out.

B.F. Do you have long-term projects? Or is it more or less ad hoc, whatever comes along you take?

D.G. I think the only long-term project I have is to figure out some way to catalogue the music that I've written over these decades. I have a basement with stacks of stuff. I have catalogued thirteen pieces, and I write every day. I don't know whether I'll ever catch up.

I've been lucky. Since retiring from USC, I've had a string of commissions that have been fun to do: mostly symphonic, but some church anniversaries, and so forth. I have one that's coming up for Shandon United Methodist Church that's really fun. They gave me an interesting text; it's flute, clarinet, harp, and chorus. I look forward to different things, and so far I've been lucky.

Columbia, S.C., 20 June 2006

Notes

1. Playing upside down means inverting the music. Where Hackett's famous solo goes up, the upside-down version goes down; where the original goes down, the upside-down version goes up.

2. The United States Information Service (or Agency) was dedicated to public diplomacy.

3. ASCAP licenses members' creations and distributes royalties.

4. By "screech trumpeter" Goodwin means that Anderson is famous for playing high notes.

GARY ERWIN

10 October 1953–

B.F. You are a native of Chicago. What was it like growing up in the Windy City?

G.E. It was wonderful. Living in the Midwest was great. Of course, you could say a few things about the weather, but we won't go into that. Very hot summers and incredibly cold and snowy winters, but Chicago's a wonderful town and I was privileged to grow up in a large, middle-class family there.

I was born in 1953 and was exposed to music at an early age because my mom was a piano player of sorts. She had a repertoire of mostly ragtime and standards, and we all had music lessons as kids. That was a vital time for music in general in this country because it was the end of the classic blues era, the middle of the rhythm-and-blues era, and the beginning of the soul era. Jazz, bossa nova, and the British Invasion were all about to happen during the late 1950s and early 1960s.

B.F. How old were you when you became aware of music?

G.E. We had a great record collection. I have a sister who is ten years older than me. She was into Elvis and Fabian and Frankie Avalon and Dion and the Belmonts. She liked all those kinds of groups, and we had jazz records in our house. I'm not sure how they got there, but we had quite a good jazz collection. When I was a kid, on weekends my dad used to take us to the city parks or other attractions where I remember there being live music—blues, rock, and soul music.

B.F. How old were you then?

G.E. Seven or eight years old around 1960. Later on, when I was a little bit older, my brothers smuggled me into some of the clubs—the bars and the coffeehouses that flourished in Chicago in the mid and late 1960s. The drinking age wasn't a big issue at that time. I was able to see a lot of guys, as well, so I was pretty impressed at an early age by the music around me. The blues are very much the sound track of Chicago.

B.F. As a college student in the late 1950s, at the Gate of Horn I heard Josh White, one of the South Carolina blues performers.

Gary Erwin. Photograph by Don Taylor. Date and place unknown. From the collection of Gary Erwin

G.E. Right—a famous folk club. I remember places like Mother Blues, the Plugged Nickel, Mr. Kelly's, and Alice's Revisited. When the North Side scene started happening, there was a big renaissance for blues because the guys who had been playing on the South and West Sides finally had another market within the city itself. And the North Side was a little bit more affluent, so they ended up exposing their music to a whole new group of people.

B.F. When you heard this music live or even on record as a youth, was there something about it that really grabbed you?

G.E. The blues really got to me because it was very passionate, very honest, and, of course, energetic. The directness of it really hit me. It was somebody standing up there, more or less baring their soul; and as a kid, as a teenager especially, that was very important to me. When you're a teenager, you start to see the superficiality of a lot of what is associated with what you view as authority. And I loved the fact that there were people ostensibly on the fringe of society who were standing up and telling their story in a bare bones, direct, soul-baring kind of way. I loved the personalities in the blues. Some of the guys I first fell in love with were people like Lightnin' Hopkins and Sonny Boy Williamson, artists who were poets who put music to their lyrics and really told their stories.[1] I really loved that part of it.

B.F. Since you heard so much live music, were you able to meet any of these musicians when you were young?

G.E. No, because on the weekend outings with my dad, there would be a little bandstand set up with a blues band playing. We would just take a little picnic or sit on the grass and listen to the music, but it was years before I realized what an impression it had on me. At the time, there was no concept of meeting the artists. They were just up there entertaining the audience on a Sunday afternoon. Thank God it was that kind of music.

B.F. When did you start buying records?

G.E. When I was about twelve, the first LP I bought was *Lightnin' Hopkins Sings the Blues* on United. After that, I got Sonny Boy Williamson's *Down and Out Blues* on Checker. Then, I started adding a lot more to my collection by actively buying blues records. I left home when I was seventeen to begin college, and I took my blues collection with me. I never returned to Chicago except for a period of less than a year after my mom passed away. When I was living in Boston—which was my adopted home later on—I was able to see a lot of the great blues guys because Boston was a prime stopping point on their tours.

B.F. Were you able to share your blues enthusiasm with friends?

G.E. Yes. When I was in high school, we had a blues band called Little Frodo Blues Explosion, which consisted of me on acoustic guitar and vocals, Jay Sebastian on harmonica, and Dan DeLorenzo on stand-up bass. We played basically country blues at school, coffeehouses, and little festivals. I went to a Catholic high school run by Jesuits, the intelligentsia of the Catholic Church, so we had a really progressive school education—a lot of politics and a lot of arts. We had a lot of opportunities to play music, and we played the blues.

B.F. Were you professional? Did you get paid?

G.E. Usually not. The first professional gig I did was at the age of ten. I played drums at a high school dance and got paid. I don't even remember what I got paid— probably ten dollars. Of course, that is big money when you're ten years old.

B.F. What was your musical training?

G.E. In middle-class America in the late 1950s and early 1960s, it was customary, if you could afford it, to give your kids music lessons. All five children in my family took music lessons. I took a year of drums when I was ten and really liked it. Even to this day I love rhythm, percussion. The drum lessons gave me a little formal education, but I started fooling around with the piano at home because we had a piano in the basement. I started to learn a little bit about theory, the relationship between notes and the nature of harmony: what stringing three notes together in a certain way will sound like. I ended up teaching myself piano and some guitar by just fooling around.

So the only formal education I had was on drums when I was ten. And the funny thing is that my two sisters took lessons for a while but gave them up, like kids will do. My two brothers were quite accomplished: Rick on guitar, and then Don went from accordion to piano. They were both very good jazz players who played through maybe their first year of college and then gave it up. The only one that stayed with the music was me, and I was the one that had the least education. I guess I had a love of it. The fact is, I was personally moved by some of the musicians I had heard.

B.F. Where did you go to college?

G.E. I didn't do real well in high school. The first two years, I kept pretty good grades; but during the second two years my grades took a nosedive, except for my Spanish. I took Spanish for four years, and I got like straight A's all the way through. It just came super naturally to me.

After high school, you either enter the workforce or go to college. When it came time to look at colleges, I considered the University of Illinois, which would be like going to USC here in South Carolina. I found out about the University of the Americas—Universidad de las Americas—in Cholula, Puebla, Mexico, which was cheaper than the University of Illinois. It was exotic, and I felt drawn to it, so I applied and was accepted. I arrived in Mexico on September 30, 1971. That ended up being a life-changing experience.

B.F. Did you take your blues records with you?

G.E. I took a little stack of records with me—blues and rock. I carried them tied up with a rope, which is not a very good way to care for your records. I also took a portable typewriter because all through high school I wrote a lot of poetry. I actually wrote poetry every day. It was a daily ritual, just like some people exercise. Writing poetry every day was one of the reasons I took up the piano and the guitar: so I could commit my poetry to song and put a melody to it.

But I embarked on a year of school for what I thought was going to be four years and an undergraduate degree. I stayed in the classroom only one semester. There were too many distractions. For the rest of the year, I lived with my girlfriend, a gorgeous girl from Texas, and traveled around Mexico, seeing the country from top to bottom. It was a great year, though I wish I had stayed all four years if for no other reason than to stay in Mexico.

B.F. Didn't you have an archaeological interest?

G.E. Yes. I still have the book *Ancient America* from the Time-Life book series. Ancient America was basically Aztec, Maya, Inca, and even North American indigenous people—native people—and when I laid my eyes on the artwork, it just spoke to me. I became very interested in the archaeology, principally of Middle America, which is from the Rio Grande down through most of Central America. I was very interested in the archaeology of the Maya, the Aztec, the Zapoteca, the Olmeca, and I became, as a teenager, an armchair archaeologist.

I read a lot. I basically exhausted the public library. I read all the books I could get my hands on. So I went to Mexico to pursue a degree in anthropology with a specialization in archaeology. Cholula, Puebla—where the University of the Americas is—was in Middle America, pre-Cortés. It would be analogous to Jerusalem, in that it's always been a holy city. It's a really rich archaeological area. One of the largest pyramids in the world is at Cholula. It's actually larger than the pyramid of Cheops in Egypt, and there's archaeological richness everywhere. So the school is perfectly centered there for a degree in archaeology, and that's what I started to study. The academics just didn't agree with me at all. I pursued my devotion to the study of archaeology, but on my own. To this day I'm still very much interested in archaeology.

B.F. Did you go on digs when you were down there? Did you go to archaeological sites?

G.E. I just went to archaeological sites—from the central highlands like Tenochtitlan, Tula, and Cholula, down into the central valleys near Oaxaca, down into the Mayan area, and then to the Yucatan.

B.F. How old were you at the end of this year?

G.E. I was eighteen.

B.F. At the end of the year, what did you do, and why did you do it?

G.E. I was writing a lot of songs. In Cholula, I had a little band that didn't have a name. I had an acoustic guitar player, Frank Corkrum, from Walla Walla, Washington; Raiford Rogers, from Michigan, played flutes and recorders. I played piano. We played at all the little concerts and things around campus and even some coffeehouses inside the town. I was writing a lot of music and taking my music really seriously. I didn't want to go back to Chicago; it was too big.

I decided to go to another city, but one that might be a little more manageable: Boston. So I went there in 1972 and tried my hand in the music field because Boston always has had a very healthy music scene. The first thing I had to do was find a place to live. I got a room in a group house in North Cambridge. There were three of us boys and two girls. At the age of eighteen, I was the youngest; the oldest was a guy who was thirty-one. Although we each had our own room, it was kind of a commune. We shared meals and that kind of thing. I advertised for musicians and put together a band. We rehearsed in the basement of the house. We named the band Boris, after the drummer's cat.

B.F. You had to subsist. Did you have a day job?

G.E. I got a job. I put on the best clothes I had, which weren't so great; I cleaned myself up and went from store to store downtown. I ended up getting a job at the Old Corner Bookstore, which had recently turned into a Doubleday store. It was originally Ticknor and Fields, where Ralph Waldo Emerson and all those guys used to hang out. I got a job in there as a clerk, the youngest in the store. There were some people who had been working there for decades, and I loved books, so it was a perfect place. I really enjoyed it. I stayed there for a few months.

Then I had other jobs, like washing dishes at the Peter Piper restaurant sixty hours a week. It was right behind Jordan Marsh—right behind Filene's department store. Then, I worked as a day laborer for Manpower, where you go to the office every morning and get a gig. That ranged from filing x rays in a doctor's office to being a houseman in the Ritz-Carlton Hotel—vacuuming the elevators, setting up dining rooms, and so forth.

You do what you have to do to survive. I worked a lot of day jobs while still trying to play music at night. I was still writing a lot of tunes and my band, Boris, played my originals. We didn't work all that much. If we had one or two gigs a month, we were really lucky. But we rehearsed all the time. I played Fender Rhodes piano and sang. We had drums, electric bass, and a guy who played saxophone, flutes, recorders, and whistles. We had a real good time with it.

B.F. Did you develop a following at all?

G.E. No, not at all. We played wherever we could. We played for free in coffee-houses, at a park, at a halfway house, at a couple of clubs. We opened for some big names.

B.F. So you were doing what you wanted to do, which was playing music, and your day job allowed you to do it.

G.E. Exactly.

B.F. Did you ultimately succeed musically in Boston? What happened?

G.E. No, not really. I was there for two stints, but left for good in 1983. The whole time I was there, I had a day job.

B.F. You got into the shipping business. How did that happen?

G.E. One morning in 1973, I went through the phone book, trying to find a place where I could use my Spanish because I wanted to keep it in shape. I found a small Cuban-American company. It was actually run by a family, Suarez. The business was exporting shoe components, principally to Central America and the Caribbean Islands. So I went down there and got a job as a shipping/receiving clerk in the ware-house. I did all the shipping and receiving and exporting and packaging for them. As a result, I ended up coming in touch with the shipping business, and that was the first of about thirteen years of working in the shipping field. That's actually how I came to Charleston originally—in the shipping business.

B.F. While you were working in shipping, what was happening with your music?

G.E. Playing at night, either rehearsing or occasionally gigging, if we were lucky.

B.F. What led to your departure from Boston? Did you just finish with that scene and decide to move on?

G.E. I was tired of living in Boston; but what really precipitated that was being laid off from a job at Logan Airport in April of 1983. I was a member of a three-person sales department for a freight forwarder, and they dissolved the department. The three of us were let go. So I told the woman who was my wife at the time, Lauren Van Buiten, that I'd use this as an opportunity to move us down south, because I'd really wanted to move south for a long time. Since about 1975–1976, I'd been looking at places like Miami and New Orleans: Miami, because I liked the heat and Spanish; New Orleans, for the heat and the music.

After I got laid off from the job, I hit the road. I bought a back-to-back Amtrak train ticket. At that time, Amtrak had the All Aboard America pass, where they break up the lower forty-eight states into three sections: Eastern, Central, and Western. I bought a two-part ticket, for Eastern and Central, and basically rode the train for a month, going from Boston down to Washington, D.C., D.C. to Charleston, Charles-ton to Savannah. I took a bus from Savannah to Atlanta because at the time there was no train line connecting them. I got back on the train and went from Atlanta to New Orleans and on to Houston, San Antonio, El Paso. Then, I took a bus to Albuquerque, where I rented a car and went to Santa Fe.

So this whole time I was keeping a journal, taking photographs, dropping off résumés, and trying to decide where I would like to live. After a month, I came back, processed all the information, and decided that Savannah, Georgia, was my first choice. I loved Savannah. It just so happened that I came through Charleston and Savannah right at the peak of the flower bloom in the middle of April, so it was hallucinogenic. I ended up getting a job in Charleston, so in June of 1983 we moved there.

B.F. What was that job? Was it with shipping?

G.E. Yes. I was hired as the export manager for Maersk Line, and I stayed with them for four years. I ended up taking over the inward-freight department, so I was the import manager. I stayed with them from 1983 to 1987, but during that time my multifaceted music thing started to come into bloom.

Boston is great town for radio, with all the college stations, public radio, and the so-called underground FM stations. I moved to Charleston and found a radio wasteland. There was no blues on the radio at all, so in summer of 1984 I visited Marcia Byars-Warnock, the station manager at WSCI, a public radio station on the *Yorktown* at Patriot's Point. When I asked if she would consider having a blues show on the radio, she said, "Well, why not? We're open to anything. What do you mean? Give me a demo." So I made a demo of my voice and the type of music I was interested in. She said, "Well, that sounds pretty good. Let's wait and see if anything opens up." In a few months, a slot opened up—midnight on Friday nights. I started *Blues in the Night* on WSCI on December 7, 1984.

B.F. Did you do it live?

G.E. I did it live for quite a long time until I started working a lot—playing music a lot. Then, I had to tape it and have somebody else run the tape. But *Blues in the Night* stayed on the air for seventeen years. It was very enjoyable. I built up a really large audience.

I was interested in a lot of other types of music, so I ran other program ideas by the station, which was kind enough to accept them. I created another show called *South to Louisiana*, which was all Cajun, zydeco, New Orleans rhythm and blues, swamp pop, et cetera. It ran for approximately fifteen years. Then I started another show called *Erwin Music*, which was an eclectic mix: world music. It started off with two or three hours on Sunday afternoon and ran for probably twelve years. I also had a Latin show at the time called *La Noche Latina*. It lasted for six years, from about 1996 to 2001. South Carolina ETV Radio dropped all four shows in 2001, but since 2004 I've done a blues program, *Blues on the Bridge*, on WCOO-FM, Charleston. I also did a show called *Blue Monday* on the legendary Breeze Radio Network from 1996 to 1999. A lot of folks remember that station . . . fondly.

B.F. There was no blues scene when you arrived in Charleston, but there was an audience for your blues show. I assume that the show helped create the Charleston blues scene.

G.E. Yes. When I came to Charleston, there were some blues acts that would come through town and play at Myskyns Tavern on Market Street. There was also Francis Willard's and a place on Fulton Street called Fulton House, which was later called the Brick. Myskyns would occasionally have somebody like Johnny Copeland or

Clarence "Gatemouth" Brown or Matt "Guitar" Murphy. That was about all that was happening.

Two years after beginning my radio program, I decided to try my hand at bringing live blues to Charleston. Some of the local club owners said, "You're crazy to do it. You're gonna lose your shirt." I decided to get some pretty deep stuff, so I booked R. L. Burnside, who at the time was fairly unknown except to a blues purist like myself and people like me. He was a Northern Mississippi acoustic blues player who had only had some field recordings that were recorded by George Mitchell in the late '60s and later issued by Arhoolie Records. He was traveling around in the car of John Nerenberg, his harmonica player out of New Orleans. I booked the two of them for a concert at the Footlight Players Theatre—then called the Queen Street Playhouse—for a gig in May of 1986. I was still working my day job.

I made up a bunch of cheap posters. During my lunch hour, I'd run downtown and put up as many as I could. I'd do it again the next day. I promoted it myself and sold about three hundred seats for five bucks apiece. So I was able to accomplish what I was told I couldn't do. At the concert, I distributed a questionnaire that asked if the audience would be interested in having more concerts and possibly forming a blues society. I hosted a meeting at which a few friends and I talked about what we could do. One of them, Randy Crowe, and I decided that we would start a monthly blues jam and create a place where people could enjoy themselves and gather around the blues.

In early fall 1986, we approached Scott and Ruth Fales, who ran Pinckney Café and Espresso on Pinckney Street, and asked if they'd be open to something like that. They said, "Yes." We started a monthly blues jam at the Pinckney Café, where it stayed for a year or two. Then, we had one or two jams at the King Street Eden and one or two more at the old AC's on King Street. The jams ended up at Cumberland's on Cumberland Street, where they lasted for about eight years. So we had a monthly blues jam for about twelve years, and it really brought a lot of people together.

B.F. I assume that once word spread about the jams, blues musicians, or aspiring blues musicians, gravitated toward them and had sessions. Is that basically it?

G.E. We had a jam the first Saturday of every month. We had a core band that was typically guitar, bass, drums, and me on piano. We had a sign-up sheet, and I was master of ceremonies. People would sign up and sign up, and I would get them up in order of arrival: first come, first served. While some could be musicians on their nights off, any decent musician wouldn't have a Saturday night off; mostly it was part-time musicians, woodshedders, or wanna-bes, or people who just wanted to play a couple of songs on the guitar with us and bring all their friends and family.[2] So it was a blast.

B.F. For how long did those Saturday-night sessions last?

G.E. We went from 1986 to about 1998, and the last place we had them was at the original Cumberland's. The Lowcountry Blues Society came from that R. L. Burnside concert at Footlight Players Theatre. I did a lot of other concerts there—really deep, historic blues people—and gradually started putting shows into clubs. I started the

Lowcountry Blues Bash in 1991, and that's the ten-day festival that happens every February in Charleston. In 2007, we'll have our seventeenth annual festival.

B.F. When does the musician Shrimp City Slim enter the picture?

G.E. The name of the core group was the Blues Socialites. An offshoot of it was called the Battery Boys. It was the group that in May of 1989 went to Colombia, South America, on a ten-day tour under the auspices of Partners of the Americas.[3] When we returned, we changed some of the personnel and changed the name to Blue Light Special. Blue Light Special lasted until about 1992, when I started doing a lot of European work, traveling, and tour managing. I traveled with, managed, and played with some of the old-time blues guys from this part of the world like Neal "Big Daddy" Pattman, Big Boy Henry, Drink Small, and Chicago Bob Nelson. At this time, I took on the name Shrimp City Slim, which I've used for fourteen years now.

B.F. So all of this—the jams, the travel, Shrimp City Slim—started from people saying, "No, Gary, you can't do it. You won't succeed at this."

G.E. Charleston's a great town. Back then, it was a great town to come to because there really wasn't anything happening—no competition for anything—and it's still that way, to a degree. I mean, there's not much here. So if you want to do something and if you have some drive and energy and a little bit of stubbornness, you can make it happen. All you have to do is find your niche and go for it.

B.F. You had—and have—your finger on so many things relating to blues. Didn't you once have a record shop?

G.E. Yes.

B.F. In it, did you focus on the blues? Or was it all kinds of music?

G.E. In 1987 I decided to quit my straight job and go into music full time. My center of activity was a record store, Erwin Music, I opened at 52 Wentworth Street in October 1987. It had six hundred square feet of space. I had mostly blues, reggae, world music, a little bit of jazz, and as much rock as I needed to pay the bills. It lasted for nine years. In late 1996, I sold it to Clay Scales, who now runs 52.5 Records in a new location.

B.F. How did the blues and what might be called alternative music sell? Was there a market for it?

G.E. Not at first. I had to create a market. I turned a lot of people on to music. Our slogan was, "The music you didn't know you had to have." So people who wanted the Rolling Stones and Bob Dylan would have to listen to musicians like Muddy Waters and Bessie Smith, whose music would be playing. The customers liked this music and often bought it.

B.F. Did people hang out there?

G.E. It became an amazing place because at any given time—lunchtime was busy—there would be dreadlocked kids from the 'hood mixing with lawyers mixing with musicians mixing with truckers. Everybody was in there buying music. It was a great place for people to meet. There are several married couples who, every time they see me, remind me that they met in my shop.

B.F. You mentioned that you were a promoter when you went to Europe.

G.E. I was more of an agent/tour manager, because I made contacts in Europe for old-time blues people. I would organize things and take over somebody like Big Boy Henry. We would do three weeks in the U.K. and Ireland, or whatever. I did that from 1990 to 1999. After that, I started taking my own band over, though we haven't toured Europe since 2003. I'm thinking that next year, 2007, might be a really good year for us.

B.F. When did your group become established?

G.E. My first blues record down here was made under the name Blue Light Special. In 1989 we did a cassette called *Live in Colombia*, as in Colombia, South America, and 1992 was the first CD, *Gone with the Wind*. That was also by Blue Light Special. Since then, everything has been by Shrimp City Slim.

B.F. Now, you have your own record label, Erwin Music.

G.E. That's right. Its first release was a 1988 cassette by Drink Small called *Blues Doctor: Live & Outrageous!* It is a bunch of recordings culled from three different performances in Charleston, 1986–1988. And that cassette, which was a short-run cassette that promptly went out of print, was nominated for a W. C. Handy Award as the Best Traditional Blues release of 1988. It was recently reissued as a CD because Drink and I finally got our heads back together on it, and also because we got a small grant to do it from the Cultural Council of Lexington and Richland Counties.

B.F. So what, exactly, is Erwin Music?

G.E. Everything I was putting out under that name. The name of the store, beginning 1987, was Erwin Music. The label, beginning in 1988, was Erwin Music. The radio show that began around 1988–1989 was *Erwin Music*. I just put everything under the same name. I thought that made sense, business-wise.

B.F. You're a self-taught pianist. Do you practice?

G.E. No, not really, because we play so much. It's like "earn while you learn." The same with the band. We rehearse very rarely. When we have a special gig, like if we have to do a really tight set, we'll have a brief rehearsal; but the rest of the time we're working, so we don't practice. I guess my personal practice time is essentially part of the songwriting process.

B.F. You take yourself very seriously as a musician, don't you?

G.E. Yes. The songwriting aspect is something I've always been heavily into since I was a teenager, and that's what I love the most. I've also learned the value of entertainment. We're out there entertaining the people, so we try to put on a show. I talk to the people; I play for them. I've been fortunate. Maybe I should take credit for having great musicians because I run a pretty tight ship. I try to run the band as a business. So I have really quality, level-headed people playing for me. We have CDs that will stand the test of time. We have seven albums out already, and while you can always make improvements on anything you do, I'm pretty proud of what I've done. I call our music "lowcountry blues and original songs." I'm beginning to think that history might say that the lowcountry blues movement began when Blue Light Special, led by Shrimp City Slim, came on the scene.

B.F. Do you consider yourself, in part, a talent scout?

G.E. Yes, though to a lesser degree now than before.

B.F. How did Wanda Johnson come onto the scene?

G.E. Wanda Johnson is a perfect example of an artist I love to work with. She's a wonderful singer, very grounded, and she writes some of her own material. She can also sing my tunes. She brings them to life. She's interested in making a career out of it. I would love to find more people like her, but there aren't a whole lot of people out there like her.

B.F. How did you get together?

G.E. When I had my record store—and this would happen fairly often—one of my customers would come in and say, "I was just in Atlanta, where I heard a great group. You gotta bring them to Charleston. You'd love them." I'd ask, "What's the name?," and write it down. I had a file.

An artist I know, the painter Rhett Thurman, was at a conference or camp in Anderson, South Carolina, where she heard Wanda Johnson in a club. She wrote Wanda's name and phone number on a cocktail napkin and brought it to me at the store, where I put it in my file and forgot about it. A couple of years later, Rob Schwinn, a friend who had the Boardwalk and Occasionally Blues clubs in Greenville, started raving about someone named Wanda Johnson. I remembered the name on the cocktail napkin. At that point in 1998, I had a six-piece band with two women singers, and I booked a tour to France. One of the singers and I had a parting of ways, so I needed another woman singer. I called her: "Hi. My name is Gary Erwin. I have a band down here with some gigs lined up. Would you like to come down and spend the weekend with us and do a couple shows?" So she came down and fit in perfectly. She got along with everybody and sang like a bird. At the end of the second gig, I asked, "Wanda, what do you say? Do you want to go with us to France?" Of course, she looked surprised, but she said, "Yes. Sure." I told her the deal, and she went with us. That was in 1999, and we went back to France in 2001, and to Italy in 2003.

We've released two albums with Wanda: *Call Me Miss Wanda* in 2003 and *Natural Resource* in 2006. Two days ago, we got back from the Fifteenth Annual Pocono Blues Festival in Pennsylvania, where she just wowed them. That's one of the biggest blues festivals in the U.S., and she just knocked them out. I think it's going to lead to some other good opportunities. I'm still doing my Shrimp City Slim thing, but I'm also really tangled up with Wanda Johnson musically.

B.F. Is she a regular member of your group?

G.E. No. She lives in Anderson, and we're in Charleston. We have four hours between us, which is too bad. She still has a day job. If she were down here with me, she could probably quit her day job; but distance is a problem. Still, we work together a lot. She's forty-two years old and just has powerful talent.

For the latest CD, I wrote nine of the tunes; she wrote five. She's also a songwriter, and I have a great band. Silent Eddie Phillips, on guitar, has been with me for twenty years, off and on; Jerome Griffin, on bass, has been with me since 1994, off and on;

LaMont Garner I met when he was sixteen and playing in a gospel group. He plays drums. It's a killer band. All five of us sing. We have harmonies and really diverse material. So it's something I'm really pleased with so far, and I think it's got great potential.

B.F. Are you Wanda's agent? If her career really took off, would you go with her?

G.E. I will do the very best I can with a new talent like Wanda, and I will go with her as far as I can take her. But if Clive Davis or somebody comes along and wants to lift her up many rungs above where we are, I'd love to come along; but if I don't, I'd say, "God bless you, and good luck."

There's no possessiveness at all. We're doing very much from-the-heart music—from her heart and from ours and from mine. It's really personal music. It's not commercial. I think that if a big-time mainstream producer grabbed her, he might try to make her into something she isn't. The best thing you can do for artists is just let them be who they are because the type of music we're in—roots music—is all about honesty and simplicity. I mean, that's the blues. You can't gloss it up.

B.F. Do you think she aspires to greatness, for lack of a better word?

G.E. I really can't say. I mean, everybody would like to be handed a million dollars. What happens when somebody hands you a million dollars? What is greatness? I'd say we were in touch with greatness the other night in Pocono because we had about five hundred people in front of us who were just going completely gaga at what we were doing. We might have changed some people's lives. So that's greatness, the greatness of the moment. Where any of this is going for any of us, I don't know.

B.F. How do you distribute your music? How do you sell it?

G.E. Almost all these releases come out to be sold off the bandstand by working artists. I have three or four releases on the label that are excellent by deceased artists, so there's limited marketability for them. None of them ever achieved the stature of, say, a B. B. King, where there's always going to be post-mortem sales. So most of what we do is off the bandstand or off the Internet, which of course has revolutionized everything.

B.F. If somebody wanted a recording by Drink Small, for example, and discovered one on Erwin Music, could it be ordered from you on-line with a credit card? Is this how it works?

G.E. No. We don't have it where you can buy it off our site, but we tell you where you can get it. And you can go to Drink's site and learn about his other recordings. For example, I mention all his out-of-print stuff on our site, so a collector can scramble around and find his old singles or the stuff by the Spiritualaires, et cetera. The Internet now has big stores like Amazon and CD Baby, which are basically on-line supermarkets. They've really done a lot for independent artists.

B.F. So someone wanting Drink's Erwin Music release could get it from Amazon?

G.E. Yes, Amazon.com.

B.F. How do businesses such as Amazon get the hard copies? Do you send copies that they keep on hand and send out when people buy them?

G.E. In Amazon's case, yes. They actually have them on the shelf. They keep a portion of the money. It's just like my selling wholesale to Papa Jazz in Columbia: I sell them to him for X, and he sells them for Y. The only thing missing in Internet sales is the tactile experience, touching the thing before purchase. We all love the old days of going through bins of vinyl. That was orgasmic: "Lightnin' Slim? You gotta be kidding. Oh, I gotta get this."

B.F. You're a performer, a booker, a promoter, and a record company executive; you once owned a record store and have had numerous radio programs. Are there other facets to your career? I assume you see yourself as an activist, a promoter of the music you grew to love when you were a child in Chicago

G.E. I'm still a huge fan. I look for the experience of discovery. I'm always amazed at being knocked out by somebody new. Just when I think I've seen and heard it all and become jaded, I'll come across a fresh performer and feel like a kid again. That's the beauty of it. It's the eternal search for that element of discovery, and that's what I try to do in my festival presentations. I bring talent to Charleston or Camden or Greenwood or the other towns—talent that nobody's ever heard of but who's very good, somebody who needs to be heard. They just unleash their talent on the unsuspecting masses. And to see the looks on people's faces and hear their words upon discovering this music is very gratifying.

B.F. Since you know everybody associated with the blues in South Carolina and are probably responsible for a good number of performers being what they are musically, have you heard stories about the old-time South Carolina blues musicians like Baby Tate?

G.E. No. I've met some guys who knew Reverend Gary Davis, but those were people who knew him from New York, from the folk era, because Davis had a lot of students. Freddy Vanderford, in Buffalo, South Carolina, knew Peg Leg Sam, but I've never met anybody who knew Baby Tate or Pink Anderson, though Pink's son, Little Pink, is still out there.

I view all those ancestral-type people of the South Carolina blues scene as part of our heritage, our history. A lot of those guys, like Josh White, have been gone for so long that few living people actually saw them. You talk to somebody like Drink Small, and he'll talk about some of the old-time, unknown players that used to drift in and out of his life when he was younger, but those historic figures who recorded are just part of history.

B.F. So there was not really a blues scene in a place like Bishopville, where Drink grew up. I thought a small town like that at that time might have had music on the corner or on the front porch.

G.E. Drink was born in 1933, so when he was a teenager in the late 1940s, people like Blind Boy Fuller would have been gone. But the blues was still in fashion. You have to remember that in the early 1960s when soul music and then the British Invasion came on the scene, that was basically the death knell for the blues. There was some urban blues in pockets of the big cities, and there were a few old-time country blues players in this part of the world; but they were definitely just remnants.

B.F. How'd you like the movie *The Blues Brothers*?

G.E. Funny. Trashy, but funny. One of the coolest scenes is at the Maxwell Street Market with Big Walter Horton on harmonica and John Lee Hooker. I think it's Pine-top Perkins on piano and possibly Willie "Big Eyes" Smith on drums. They're all just jamming. It's great, as is the other stuff like Matt "Guitar" Murphy and Aretha Franklin in the diner. A lot of people don't realize how much history a guy like Matt "Guitar" Murphy has. When he was young, he played with Sonny Boy Williamson and Junior Parker, and then he toured Europe with Memphis Slim and Sonny Boy Williamson. He and his band used to play at Myskyns in Charleston. They were kind of a funky, rocky band. It was the Blues Brothers band that really put him on the map and a jingle in his pocket. He and his brother, Floyd Murphy, are on a lot of legendary Memphis recordings from the early 1950s.

North Charleston, S.C., 1 August 2006

Notes

1. Here and elsewhere Erwin refers to Aleck "Rice" Miller, also known as Sonny Boy Williamson II (1899–1965).

2. In blues and jazz, "to woodshed" means to practice.

3. Partners of the Americas is a cultural exchange program.

BARRY WALKER

14 April 1961–

B.F. You are the proprietor of Mac's on Main, which is a haven for blues musicians in Columbia. You, yourself, are a blues musician.

B.W. Yes.

B.F. Your own group plays here occasionally.

B.W. Fatback and the Groove Band.[1]

B.F. What's your background? How did you get involved with the blues?

B.W. I grew up in Norwalk, Connecticut, which is about thirty miles from Manhattan. I was exposed to a lot of great musicians who played in Manhattan but lived in Westchester. When I was a little boy, I wanted to be a musician but never had an opportunity to go to a club or restaurant where I could practice performing in front of an audience.

In the South, there were opportunities to play at lots of places—juke joints—where young kids could sneak in the back door and play with the band. If they were good enough, they got paid; if not, they at least got to play. At Mac's on Main, I tried to create a venue where the young musicians can cut their teeth on a professional stage in front of a live audience and see if they have what it takes to become a blues or jazz musician.

B.F. So you provide the opportunity that you did not have as a child.

B.W. Exactly. It's a venue where the young players don't have to feel like they're going into a bar and risk getting shot or into a pool hall and getting cut up. They're going into a nice establishment, a restaurant, where anybody can come, if you're six years old or sixty. We serve full meals here, but at the same time we offer a full bar and a band stage.

B.F. Let's return to your childhood. How did you develop an interest in music?

B.W. I listened to B. B. King before I knew who he was, and Ray Charles. My mom would buy 45 r.p.m. records by the likes of Bobby "Blue" Bland and play them on our phonograph. I tried to play my guitar with them. I was just a young kid who didn't

Barry Walker. Courtesy of the South Caroliniana Library, University of South Carolina

have formal training until I got to high school. There, I learned how to read music and play instruments.

B.F. So before high school you just taught yourself and picked away.

B.W. I strummed and played records, making believe I was a big star. By that time, Jimi Hendrix was very popular. He was alive and performing, and I tried to imitate him. I idolized him, and others.

B.F. So it was primarily from records you learned the blues.

B.W. Yes, because I never had a place to perform and see live performances in Norwalk. We didn't have a place like Mac's on Main to go to.

B.F. But there were musicians in that area.

B.W. Yes, there were.

B.F. Horace Silver is from there, though he's older than you.

B.W. He lives in Westchester County. That's what I'm saying: all the musicians performed in New York but lived out in the suburbs, in the county, in Westchester County, in Connecticut. That area is small and tight. It's real together.

B.F. Was there a music scene when you were young in Norwalk? Even if you couldn't get into clubs, did you have pals you'd gig with?

B.W. We had garage bands as kids. We drove our mothers crazy because we made noise all day Saturday. Some of the garage bands got to the point where they actually played gigs. They got that good.

B.F. Were you in them?

B.W. I was trying to get in them. I never had an opportunity to really develop that blues talent like I should have by performing, by getting a band together at a young age. I was only like ten, eleven, twelve, or thirteen years old. As I went through high school and graduated, then went to college and graduated, I never really put my instrument away. I always kept it. I discovered the blues again in my early thirties.

B.F. So you started out teaching yourself how to play to records—B. B. King, Ray Charles, Jimi Hendrix—and then started real lessons in high school.

B.W. In high school, I had formal lessons and learned how to read music and play.

B.F. And this was still guitar?

B.W. Yes.

B.F. Were they teaching you legit guitar?

B.W. Yes, legit guitar: blues and jazz. As a matter of fact, I was in the jazz band. That's how I learned to read music, understand chords, and read charts. The high school jazz band didn't play gigs. We played in the school auditorium. That was it; that was all I had. There wasn't a place where I could learn how to solo or comp.

You have to come to Mac's on Main to see what I'm talking about. On jam nights, a guy can come here and hit a couple of notes and make a song out of them. It's totally improv.[2] Nothing is written down; there's no formal structure. When musicians play, it's just totally off the top of their heads and out of their hearts. And so that's what you need to have when you want to become a creator: to be able to comp, be able to perform improv. That's what Mac's on Main does. It gives people an opportunity to play.

B.F. You said that as an adult you came back to music, which implies there was a period when you weren't involved with it.

B.W. It was a period of about fifteen years.

B.F. College years?

B.W. Yes. There were about five years of college, and about ten years after college when I didn't play with anybody. I didn't sell my instrument or anything. I still had my guitars, amps, and stuff. All were just mothballing, just sitting there. I picked up the guitar again when I came back to South Carolina. I was rusty because I hadn't played in awhile, but I didn't lose all the things I had learned—the basis, the foundation. I still could play a little, so I started going out to jam sessions—the open jams, the juke-joint jam sessions, like at Decisions back in the early '90s where you could sit in with the band for a couple of songs. I found out that I still had it. I did that for a year or two and then got a band together. That's where Fatback and the Groove Band came from. That was in my early thirties, about ten or fifteen years ago.

B.F. What about college years, when you put music aside? Where did you go to college? What was your major?

B.W. I went to the University of Connecticut and majored in mathematics. During my years there, I didn't play.

B.F. Then, I assume you got a job.

B.W. Yes, as a computer programmer—a nerd—and I programmed people's computers for twenty years, from Connecticut all the way down to Blythewood, South Carolina, where I ended up. In the late '90s, I realized that I'd never become president of this company, so I decided to do what I really wanted to do in life: play guitar, drink beer, and eat food, in that order. So that's what I've done. We opened Mac's on Main in 1999.

B.F. When you worked in the computer business from Connecticut to South Carolina, did you often move your residence? Or was this big area your territory from a single home base?

B.W. I physically moved from Connecticut. I got married in 1983 and lived in Atlanta for a while. We lived in Maryland and Connecticut. So we moved our residence around, discovering different areas of the country.

B.F. You mentioned not having places to play music when you were growing up in Connecticut, yet you said that children in the South had places. How did you know about the South? Do you have southern roots?

B.W. When I came here, we had open jam sessions that we didn't have up North.

B.F. But did you ever get to this area as a child?

B.W. No. I was up North, but knew this is where juke joints came from.

B.F. So you didn't really know this area until you got here through your job?

B.W. Right.

B.F. And when you got to central South Carolina, did you just decide that this is the place for you to put down roots?

B.W. Yes.

B.F. Why did this area appeal to you?

B.W. The weather, first of all. The weather is great: you can be in your shorts almost eleven months of the year. The people are very friendly. And there is something called southern hospitality. It's genuine, and there is a lot of it. It doesn't matter if you're black or white, green or yellow.

Most southerners eat fatback and collard greens, and that's what I offer at Mac's on Main. They eat the same food that I cook and that I've been preparing for years for my family. The restaurant is just an extension of my family. So I have a bigger family now.

B.F. Because of your job you lived in Blythewood. Do you still live there?

B.W. No. I live in Irmo now.

B.F. So you decided, with your family, to establish your life here, to junk the other career?

B.W. I junked the computer career because it wasn't making me happy. I opened Mac's on Main.

B.F. Do you consider yourself primarily a restauranteur? A guitarist?

B.W. I cook food for a living. I play guitar for relaxation. I drink beer because I like it.

B.F. Did you have training in food?

B.W. No. My mama taught me how to cook. I've never been to a culinary school in my life; but I just cook like I cook at home, and that's the appeal of the Mac's on Main menu. This is like Sunday brunch at your grandma's, but we do it every day. If you look at our menu, we have macaroni and cheese, green beans, corn on the cob, rice and gravy, fried chicken. Today, we have barbecue ribs, hushpuppies, world-famous peach cobbler, and banana pudding. These are the things my mama used to cook for a big Sunday dinner.

B.F. It's a pretty big leap from the corporate world to a restaurant and music.

B.W. There's a leap of faith and a transition period. You can't be half pregnant. Either you are or you aren't. You can't go into business halfway. You can't say, "Well, I'll work part time at a restaurant while continuing my day job." You can't do it. You have to make a commitment to either do it or don't.

And so I made that commitment to cut the corporate world and to go after the other. I was trained in corporate for twenty years. I know how corporate works. I took what I learned from corporate and applied it to my own business, which is the Mac's on Main dynasty, if you will. I mean, Mac's on Main is much bigger than the four walls you see here. We're not just a restaurant. We have catering. We have the peach cobbler that we sell in groceries. We sell spices. We have cookbooks. We have a television show. We have a number of things outside of the four walls that generate revenue for the company.

B.F. Is the television show about food? Music? Both?

B.W. Both. The television show is *Chef Fatback's Cooking Blues*. It's syndicated, and right now it's on *Bob Redfern's Outdoor Magazine*. We have a two-minute segment each week. I had a thirty-minute show that was on the Fox market last year, for thirty minutes on Sundays. We had twenty minutes of cooking and ten minutes of a blues band. We did it for thirteen weeks, the whole season. We do so much outside of the restaurant that brings people to it.

B.F. I can see that your corporate experience helped you. Someone like me just walks in here and sees what he sees. But that's not all there is to Mac's on Main.

B.W. It's part of it. You can go into another city or to any convenience store in South Carolina and buy the peach cobbler scratch-off game with Chef Fatback's mug on it. These lottery tickets advertise the peach cobbler that we sell in the restaurant and groceries.

B.F. Do you mean that someone can go into a gas station and buy a Fatback peach cobbler lottery ticket that is part of the education lottery in South Carolina?

B.W. Exactly. The lottery asked if I would be a pitchman for their peach cobbler lottery product. Of course, I accepted the invitation. Don't I want to have statewide exposure for nothing? In fact, they paid me to do it. So that's exactly what we did. We leveraged that free marketing to promote the restaurant and to promote Chef Fatback. That and my two-minute *Bob Redfern's Outdoor Magazine* show give me statewide exposure. People are getting to know about my peach cobbler and the products we sell at Piggly Wiggly.

B.F. Do groceries sell the cobbler frozen?

B.W. It's frozen. You can buy it directly from Piggly Wiggly. We ship about and 108 cases to them on a weekly basis. We do that going out the back door while stuff is coming in the front door. So the business is growing.

B.F. When you gave up the corporate life and decided to commit to food and music, were you first in this building?

B.W. Yes, right here at 1710 Main Street.

B.F. How did you select this location?

B.W. I saw a Chinese restaurant here that was for sale, and I thought it was just the business, but it was the whole building. I decided to buy the building and turn the upstairs into law offices because it's right across from the courthouse. Lawyers would rent the offices, and I would run the business downstairs—and that's exactly what I did. I have four lawyers upstairs now who pay rent to me or the corporation. They're happy because they're right across the street from the courthouse, and I'm happy because I've got tenants paying rent every month. Because of the courthouse, I've got a ready-made crowd of folks that are hungry and got to get a quick lunch, so that's enhanced what the buffet is all about. It's quick, and you can pay one price and have at it.

B.F. It seems perfect.

B.W. If you've got a long time, you can hurt me; but if you don't have much time, you can get in and out.

B.F. One of the features at Mac's on Main is the blues jams.

B.W. The open mic is on Wednesday and Thursday nights. On Wednesdays, anything goes. We have any kind of music. If you play rock, jazz, opera, or whatever, we let you do it on Wednesday nights. We gear Thursday nights more toward the blues, which means I'd rather not have an operatic singer come in then. Thursdays are for the blues. We have a blues bass player who keeps it that way.

B.F. What time does the music begin?

B.W. Eight o'clock at night until midnight. Eight o'clock is good for the kids. As a matter of fact, I've got this young kid that comes in. He's thirteen years old, and his dad, who plays drums, brings him every week. They sit there and wait their turn, and the kid plays blues guitar, backed by his dad. They love it.

B.F. During open mic, are you in the kitchen? Or are you out there playing?

B.W. I have people working in the kitchen, but I'm back and forth.

B.F. But do you play sometimes?

B.W. Yes.

B.F. Have you recorded?

B.W. Yes. We have three CDs out right now: *Fatback and the Groove Band*, *The Next Best Thing*, and *Anthology*. *Anthology* is a collection of everything I've ever recorded, and it accompanies our unique *Mac's on Main Cookbook*. When you select a dish— let's say you're cooking a Mac's on Main macaroni-and-cheese recipe—there's a selection on the CD that goes with that recipe. If you don't have the two—the CD and the cookbook—it won't come out right. That's part of marketing the restaurant. We try to get people to try different things.

B.F. Do you have a recording contract? Or are these self-made recordings?

B.W. These are self-made recordings. They are all my original songs. There are a couple of cover songs, but I don't have to worry about royalty rights because they're in the public domain.

B.F. What about distribution?

B.W. I can sell records out of my suitcase or here at the restaurant and get the money directly rather than going through a big clearinghouse recording company. They pay ten cents a record, but I can get the whole nine dollars a record by selling them myself.

B.F. Do you and your group play gigs outside of Mac's on Main?

B.W. We do, though we're very selective. All of our equipment is up on stage, so if we play a gig outside of Mac's on Main, it's a special event—a wedding reception or something like that—and they pay us very well to do it.

B.F. How many musicians are in the group?

B.W. Four guys in my group, plus me: piano, saxophone, bass, and drums, with me playing guitar.

B.F. Has your personnel been constant over the years?

B.W. That's the funny part about this business. When we started out, we wanted to keep the same guys; but I found that in the music business it's not necessarily going to happen. People move on, their tastes change, their direction may change, and you have to be able to adapt. That's one of the things that you learn cutting your teeth. You need to be able to play with anybody. So my personnel has changed over the last nine years. The fact is, the band is still Fatback and the Groove Band.

B.F. I assume the members of your band, whoever they happen to be, have day jobs, that playing is just something they love doing.

B.W. Exactly. They're not as fortunate as I am to be able to do this for life. Most of the guys work in different fields doing the nine-to-five thing, so they come here to relax, have fun, and make a little money playing on Fridays and Saturdays.

B.F. Have any of them recorded as sidemen with notable musicians?

B.W. Willie Griffin, a young saxophone player, has recorded with Skipp Pearson, Drink Small, and others.

B.F. What happens at Mac's on Main on weekends?

B.W. On the weekends, we tend not to do an open jam. We want the rehearsed bands coming in on Friday and Saturday nights.

B.F. So you have paying customers?

B.W. Exactly. So we don't want the open mic. We want touring bands, quality rehearsed bands—professionals.

B.F. How do you book these groups? I've read that B. B. King and Ray Charles were here.

B.W. Yes. They all popped in, but not necessarily to play. They all had food here or came in. At this point, we've been in business for eight years, so we're on the circuit. We're known as a music venue. Groups stop in when they're going through Columbia and at least get a meal or some of the world-famous peach cobbler. But we're on the circuit now, so I've got people calling me on a regular basis to book gigs. If some of the national and regional touring bands get a gig in Charleston or Charlotte, they'll call me and say, "Hey, can I play for you on Friday?" If it works out, we book them.

We've been able to get some quality folks. Alberta Adams is a very big blues name out of Chicago. We normally couldn't afford her. She's like two thousand dollars a night for her and her band. But because she had a gig in Hilton Head on Saturday, she asked if she could play here on Friday. And we gave her and her band four or five hot meals, hotel rooms, and five or six hundred dollars. She's happy. She got gas money, good meals, and a nice place to stay in exchange for playing a gig for us. We got a national recording artist right here on the stage in an intimate setting.

B.F. How'd she draw?

B.W. We sold out. We were charging ten dollars a head, and we sold out two days before her show.

B.F. How many customers can you accommodate?

B.W. A hundred. So we are very happy with lucky gigs like that. But we do regional bands, too—young guys just starting out and traveling on the circuit. They put us on their call list.

B.F. What happens if there's a weekend several weeks out with no booking?

B.W. That's when Fatback and the Groove Band kicks in.

B.F. So you and your group cover the empty dates?

B.W. Yes. That's the beauty of it: not only am I the cook, I'm a musician with a band. And if the band decides it doesn't want to show up, that's not a problem. I can put together a band in a couple of hours. At Mac's on Main, we are not hostage as far as music is concerned. We're not hostage to the musicians, the bands, because I'm a performing musician. I can always put some guys together and put a band up there if I have to. Normally I like to get the rehearsed bands, but we're not hostage to them.

B.F. So if it's Friday morning and the group for that night cancels, it's no problem?

B.W. No problem at all. There'll be a band up there. It may not be that band, but there'll be a band up there.

B.F. You mentioned the early influence of B. B. King. What other musicians influenced your playing?

B.W. Jeff Beck comes to mind. He is a very good guitar player. He did a lot of jazz stuff, like "Goodbye Porkpie Hat" and Cole Porter tunes. He could play anything. I learned how to play a lot of his stuff in high school when I was learning how to read music.

All the major cities in the country have a Main Street, a downtown, garage bands, and young musicians who come out to experience the art of performance. The cities should have a Mac's on Main to provide good food, a good environment, and a stage for these young musicians to cut their teeth and learn how to play. I can see us having a chain of these things across the Southeast or across the country.

B.F. Is there a pool of blues or jazz talent in Columbia, people who come here for your open jams?

B.W. We have a regular pool of young guys that are learning how to play, and they come and cut their teeth. Let me give you an example: William Boyd. He graduated from South Carolina State in Orangeburg. He's now studying for a master's or Ph.D. in music at the University of Tennessee with a big-name saxophonist. William Boyd is going to be the next big-name saxophone player. He can play anything, any instrument. He got his start right here, and that's the kind of thing we want to promote.

B.F. Does he play the blues?

B.W. Jazz and blues.

B.F. There are a couple of young, very good jazz musicians from Columbia: Ron Westray, the trombone player, and Chris Potter, the saxophonist. Has either of them sat in here?

B.W. They've come in and they've played, but they didn't get their starts here. We want to be a factory for those kinds of guys.

B.F. Have you been here long enough for any of the youngsters who began here to develop into professional musicians?

B.W. Not yet. Give me another ten years and I will have a crop that graduated, gone on, and come back.

B.F. You provide a great service to the musical community. You lament that Connecticut offered nothing like this, but you established this venue in Columbia.

B.W. Yes. It's exactly what I want.

B.F. And it seems perfect. You own the building, you're not at the whim of irresponsible touring musicians, and so forth.

B.W. Right. Exactly.

B.F. And the people who come to enjoy the music have to eat.

B.W. And my world-famous peach cobbler is sold in groceries.

B.F. And the lottery ticket. But you also wear another hat, that of politician.

B.W. Yes. That's my service back to the community. The Columbia-Irmo crowd has been very good in embracing me, letting me into the community, and embracing Mac's on Main. One of the things that I do is give back to the community through public service. I ran for city council in Irmo and won. So now I'm a councilman in my free time.

B.F. How long a term is that?

B.W. Four years. My term is over in 2009. I hope to make a difference in my community, Irmo. I'd love to see more musicians come out of Irmo and more venues to pop up there; but at the same time, I want to be involved in the decision making of how the town is going to grow.

B.F. When you campaigned for that position, did you have a platform? Did you emphasize one thing or another?

B.W. Yes. I first ran as "a fresh new voice." That was my motto. I won by two hundred votes the first time out. When I ran for reelection last September, my motto was "common sense matters," because a lot of times in politics, we have folks making these irrational decisions on things that affect my life directly. In other words, they will raise taxes to support a bus system, which I don't use, which may be the right thing to do at the time, but at the same time it's an irrational decision because you can levy taxes by other means—through business licenses, as opposed to directly taxing me, Joe Blow, consumer. You know what I'm saying?

To make a long story short, I felt there was a need for a commonsense voice on the Irmo council. I'm a businessman, an entrepreneur, and I know, when a law is about to pass, how it's going to affect me as a small businessman. I ask council to think about it for a minute, to slow down and think about it. So we did.

B.F. So you were elected and reelected?

B.W. Yes. The second time, I won by almost four hundred votes over the closest guy to me. My constituents must have liked my message.

B.F. Do you see yourself in politics from here on out?

B.W. No. I have three teenagers in high school, so they'll be out before I finish my term. Unless there's some compelling reason to run again, my contribution back to Irmo will be over in four years. But I can't really say if I'll keep on or stop.

B.F. Do you regret having left the corporate world?

B.W. Not at all. I'm working harder now than ever. I mean, I'm here at ten, eleven o'clock in the morning, and I leave at ten or eleven o'clock at night. But I'm here talking to you now and having a wine, so if that's considered work, it's work. I can live with that. I really enjoy my time and experience here.

B.F. I assume your wife is supportive. You obviously spend a lot of time here.

B.W. Yes. It's a family business. My wife, son, and a daughter work here. I have another daughter who's in the marching band. She got out of working because she's in the high school marching band.

B.F. Do you cook during the day?

B.W. I trained a whole staff of kitchen folks to follow my recipes to the T. So once they've been trained, I let them handle the cooking during the day. At night, I have another staff that I've trained to cook exactly the way I've showed them.

B.F. So you don't cook anymore?

B.W. No. I'm more a supervisor, an executive chef. I do more supervising and planning of meals and testing of new recipes than actually knocking it out. I'm like a director. This is a big play, and I'm the director of the kitchen. I say, "Okay, I need a steak and a crème brûlée, please. I need a Wellington rare. I need a shrimp and grits, please." And then these people execute it for me and bring it out. It's to my satisfaction because they followed my recipe. And then the people enjoy the food.

I hope I'm building an empire. That's what I think I am. After I'm long gone and my children are here at this business, if they continue on, this is always going to be known as a spot where young musicians can cut their teeth. That's what I want it to be known for, especially on Wednesday and Thursday nights, because I never had that opportunity when I was growing up. If I provide it, the young musicians that move on and become professional guys, the ones that go away to college and get gigs, will remember, "Well, I played at Mac's on that jam night, and that's where I got discovered." They'll come back to me and say, "Hey, I remember you, Fatback, from twenty years ago."

 Mac is my

B.F. Why do you call it Mac's on Main?

B.W. Mac is my wife's nickname, her pet name. Some people call their wives Honey, Sweetie, or Kitty. I call mine Mac.

B.F. You named it after her. That's pretty smart.

B.W. Yes, it helps a lot.

B.F. Is there anything you'd like to add?

B.W. I hope people understand that in any kind of business, you have to have the support of the community. You have to have folks coming out. I hope they will at least try my product in the store. If they like my peach cobbler, I hope they'll come down to the restaurant and experience the live part of what we do here. Or if they see me on a television show, they'll see a technique I've done that they've never thought about and come and try the food here. So it's a frontal assault on your psyche to want to come here. I hope people will say, "Hey, I need to go down there and try that restaurant," or "I need to go to the store and look for that peach cobbler."

B.F. You said you were a math major. Did you take any business courses?

B.W. No. I learned from the best, Larry Wilson at PMSC.[3] He taught me how to market a business. I did a ten-year stint at PMSC. This guy created a software package that he sold to insurance companies around the world, but it didn't work. But I thought him a genius for getting a multimillion-dollar corporation off the ground. As the software package developed, eventually it got to the point where it was functional. But he had an idea, and he ran with it. That's what I learned from him. It's all about getting people in the restaurant trying out your product. You can be the best chef in the world, but if nobody knows about you—if you don't get bodies in there trying out your food—you'll be out of business.

B.F. Did you learn from just observing Wilson? Or did he actively help you?

B.W. From observation, though I took professional development classes at PMSC, where I learned to market and about the corporate approach and the corporate philosophy.

B.F. Your food feeds the music, and music feeds the food. It seems perfect.

B.W. Right.

Columbia, S.C., 9 August 2006

Notes

1. "Fatback" is Barry Walker.

2. "To comp" means to play chords or figures in support of a soloist; "improv" means improvise.

3. G. Larry Wilson founded and was chief executive officer of Policy Management Systems Corporation in Blythewood, S.C.

RON WESTRAY

13 June 1970–

B.F. What was the beginning of your interest in music?

R.W. I started very early with piano lessons because my mother was conscientious enough to incorporate piano lessons into my life and my sister's life. The first song I remember hearing as a kid and understanding was a popular song on the radio called "Disco Duck." I used to run around the house singing it all the time. That was my first connection to holding a tune and being attracted to a song. Around that same time, I started taking piano lessons with Winifred Goodwin.

B.F. My children, Abigail and Rebecca, studied with her also. Yes, she's terrific.

R.W. Yes. That lasted for about three years until Winkie kicked me out because I wouldn't use the left hand. But I continued on my own, tinkering at the piano, learning by ear.

B.F. How old were you then?

R.W. I was about five or six. So by age eight, I was not taking piano lessons anymore. The next real interaction I had with music was general music education in school with rhythm sticks and autoharps.

B.F. Where did you go to grade school?

R.W. I was born in Columbia but went to school in Pelion through the third grade because my mother taught there. We commuted every day. Beginning with the fourth grade, I attended Greenview Elementary in Columbia. I didn't study any music that year, but in the fifth grade I picked up the viola. For the sixth grade, I went to Fairwold Middle School, which later became W. G. Sanders, and that's where I was placed on the trombone by my teacher, Al McClain, the longtime band director at Sanders. He was a very, very important figure in putting me on the right track in terms of ultimately becoming a jazz musician.

Dizzy Gillespie and I have opposite stories. I understand from a documentary that Dizzy started out actually wanting to play trombone, but ended up playing trumpet

Ron Westray. Photograph by Keith Major. Date and place unknown. From the collection of Ron Westray

because of instrument availability. Imagine coming out of fifth grade having messed around with the viola and tinkering with the piano. I was the guy in fifth grade who, before classes started in the morning, would be in the cafeteria, and everybody would want me to play some little one-finger something I knew. By sixth grade, the whole idea was to get a wind instrument.

Everybody was signing up for trumpet and saxophone, and I signed up for trumpet. Having the last name Westray, I got last dibs. By the time they got to me, there were no more trumpets, but there was a trombone. Al McClain made me stand up. He said, "You're tall. Look at those arms. I have a trombone. Here. You're a trombone player." That was it. I excelled on the trombone immediately. It sounds arrogant, but I really don't remember an awkward stage on the instrument.

B.F. So you were a natural at it.

R.W. I would say so. I just remember starting on the instrument and excelling. I was the section leader immediately. The same thing happened when I was a freshman in high school. I was the guy who came in and kicked the older students off their posts. And the same thing happened when I went to college.

B.F. Was Al McClain a trombone specialist?

R.W. He was a trumpet player, but, being a band director, he dabbled on all the instruments because he had to know a little bit about them all. He would just make sure I was doing the right things: that I was not puffing out my cheeks, that I was maintaining a good tone, that my sight-reading was improving. He wouldn't let me cut any corners, and he presented me with challenges.

He was one of the first people to incorporate jazz into what I was doing: the theme from *New York, New York,* "As Time Goes By"—melodies we played as a part of assembly programs. I started getting an ear for jazz, but I still didn't have a clue about it. This was around 1980, when I was about ten. From those piano lessons with Winkie Goodwin for a few years to working on my own to getting in touch with just the tonal spectrum of the trombone, I was getting my ears in shape, though I didn't realize it. Then, I just took off on the trombone.

The marching band was also a huge part of my formative stage because even in the sixth grade, when I started the trombone, we had one, the Fairwold Tigers marching band. It was an honor to make the band. I think I started in it a year after I started playing the instrument, so by seventh grade I was in the band. The Fairwold Tigers band wanted to be like the Keenan High School Raiders band, which wanted to be like the South Carolina State Bulldogs band—and this was my progression. The marching-band environment served as a series of building blocks in my command of the instrument.

B.F. I assume this was still before jazz.

R.W. Yes, this was still before jazz, before my enlightenment.

B.F. Did Al McClain or any other teachers recommend that you listen to trombone players? Or did you listen to them on your own?

R.W. Al McClain was important in directing me. He was from Pittsburgh, where my grandfather, Joe Westray, was a huge figure on the Pittsburgh jazz scene. So Al McClain knew Joe Westray. When I ended up in his classroom down here in South Carolina, he was like, "Westray? Man, I know your granddad." He kind of took me under his wing because he had been in bands with Joe and knew Joe's influence in Pittsburgh.

B.F. What instrument did your grandfather play?

R.W. He was an organist and vocalist. He was one of the first people to transcribe Wild Bill Davis's stuff. He had his own groups doing covers of Wild Bill and other early organ trios. But to get to your question about listening to trombonists, Al McClain suggested I listen to Harold Betters, from Pittsburgh. He's not really a well-known player like J. J. Johnson. Al gave me a Harold Betters album, so Betters was one of the first people I heard on the trombone in a jazz setting.

Every now and then, McClain would sit down at the piano with me and demonstrate harmony, though I didn't really start understanding it until my middle years in high school. He introduced me to tunes like Miles Davis's "Four" and "On Green Dolphin Street." I remember being exposed to these things before really understanding them.

B.F. That's pretty hip stuff.

R.W. Yes. McClain was one of those guys who started out wanting to be a great jazz trumpet player but ended up being a school band director. It's an age-old story. He really had a hip conception, and even in dealing with the kids, he was a jazzhead. He would talk really straight up about what you were doing: "Oh, man, you're jivin' around. You're not serious. You're not serious, man. Cut the small talk."

He was a little gruff, but he wanted you to learn. He was a great teacher. I'm talking so much about Al McClain because he was very important to me. He put the trombone in my hands. He drove me to Dallas Music in Columbia to pick out my first trombone. When I left middle school, I went to Keenan High School, where my teacher was Willie Lyles, my next big influence. He's still the band director there.

I came to Lyles as a freshman with a high recommendation from Al, who said, "He's got it. This is your man right here. Take care of him." Lyles just took me under his wing. I was one of the only kids he would let play his own trombone. That was like my letting a student play my horn now. Lyles gave me my finishing, from a formative standpoint, but music was still geared around the marching band: learning to be a good performer and solid player. At this time, around 1984–1985, I still hadn't evolved to the point where I thought about becoming a jazz musician.

B.F. Were you listening to jazz by that time?

R.W. I'd heard some things, but there's a point where I turned a very drastic curve. One day Willie Lyles called me into his office. He said, "Hey, man, I want you to check some of this stuff out." It was *The Smithsonian Collection of Classic Jazz* on LP. "Take this home. I want you to start listening to it." I did. Until then, I really hadn't heard jazz, even though my grandfather and father were musicians. In the 1970s, my father had a funk band.

B.F. What's your father's name?

R.W. He is also Ron Westray.

B.F. What did he play?

R.W. He was a lead guitarist and vocalist. He's one of these guys who wanted to be the next Sly Stone.

B.F. So music was a part of your home life.

R.W. Right, though I was hearing popular music. Some people grow up with parents who are jazzheads and hear pure jazz from the time they're young, but that's not my story. I heard music at home because my mother loves music. I really turned the corner around age fifteen when I heard Duke Ellington's "East St. Louis Toodle-Oo." There's a spooky quality to it, with Bubber Miley's growling "wah, wah, wah, wah." "East St. Louis Toodle-Oo" just kind of froze me. I said, "That's it. That's the way I want to play. I want to do *that*." After hearing it once, I played it over.

The next thing on the collection that caught my attention was Coleman Hawkins's 1939 "Body and Soul." It convinced me. I was like, "Okay, this is the music I want to play. That's it, right there; that sound." I went to the Keenan High School library, where I found a book on jazz history. One of the first transcriptions in the book was of Coleman Hawkins's "Body and Soul." At home, I'd play the recording and look at the transcription. When I started trying to play Hawkins's solo on the trombone, I found out how much work I had to do. That was my enlightenment period, around 1985.

B.F. Were there other kids in the band who also liked jazz?

R.W. No. I was alone. No one else was following that course. For the rest of my time in high school, I was the only one who was going in that direction. From that point on, I was pretty much a big fish, in the context of jazz.

B.F. Like Chris Potter.

R.W. Just like Chris. The same thing. About a year or so from the time of my enlightenment in high school, I was in the regional band; and Chris, three years or so younger than me, was leading it. And I said, "Wow." He had a jump on everybody, really. Chris had that jump, and it was inspiring, actually, because Chris was like a role model. Even when he was younger, he was so talented. It gave me something to aspire to.

So Chris and I were in the regional band together, even though he was out front. I still wasn't an improviser; I wasn't a bona fide improviser, like Chris. I was still trying to figure out things—just kind of getting the basic building blocks in place. I worked on it constantly.

B.F. Did your teachers help you? Or did you just figure it out on your own?

R.W. My teachers helped. Willie Lyles helped. He played a variety of instruments, too, even though trombone was his main instrument. He was a keyboard player, and he would take me on gigs with him. Lyles would put me in a gig situation while I was trying to get my concept together. So he would put me out front and make me play.

He also told me who to listen to. As McClain turned me on to Harold Betters, Lyles pointed me in the direction of Fred Wesley. He wanted to make sure I could get in the groove and put that trombone in the vernacular, a funk realm that Wesley's known for. I immediately absorbed Wesley's style. So by age fifteen or sixteen, I was imitating Fred Wesley.

B.F. Did you listen to him when he was with James Brown? Is that the context?

R.W. This is the stuff I was imitating because I just needed something to latch on to. I hadn't gotten to J. J. Johnson and all those guys. After I learned three or four solos of Fred Wesley, my interest in him waned. Willie Lyles then gave my Urbie Green's *The Fox* on CTI. I realized there was more for me to do. I just fell in love with Urbie's sound, so I went through a phase of trying to sound smooth like Urbie.

I was still a kid; I didn't really have chops, but I knew from listening to Urbie that there was a level of improvisation that I needed to achieve. I knew there was another level of proficiency or another level of expression that I had to unravel. I kind of came at it backwards because I heard Urbie and I heard Bill Watrous before I heard J. J. I was basically graduating high school and getting ready to go to South Carolina State College when I heard Bill Watrous. Even though I was becoming a jazzhead, I was still Mr. Marching Band; so my whole thing was being a section leader in the marching band in order to get a scholarship to State for the Marching 101. I was still the guy who, on the side, was going for a jazz career.

B.F. Earlier, you mentioned that Fairwold Middle School led to Keenan High School and that Keenan led to S.C. State. In deciding on S.C. State, did you just naturally follow that track, that channel? Or did you consider other schools?

R.W. Pretty much, it was the channel of the marching band tradition. The Fairwold Tigers wanted to be the Keenan Raiders and the Keenan Raiders wanted to be the South Carolina State Bulldogs. If you got accepted at State on a marching band scholarship, you succeeded. I did, so I didn't really look in a whole lot of other directions. I just wanted to go to State and be in the band on a marching band scholarship. I also knew I was going to be a music major.

So I left high school—where I was the most talented, won all the talent shows, and was Mr. Keenan—and went off to college. I started in 1988. By this time, I was really serious about the marching band because I was attracted to it.

I started practicing a lot in terms of transcriptions, in terms of actually learning jazz solos, in terms of sitting down at the piano and trying to unravel harmony. South Carolina State also had a jazz ensemble, and I made it as a freshman. That's where I met Alvin Fulton, my next band director. He's from Cleveland, and he really understood the jazz repertoire. He was not a jazz performer, but he led the South Carolina State jazz band with consummate style—a consummate understanding of jazz history—and that's where I got a better understanding of the history of jazz repertoire. We would be playing charts like Horace Silver's "Filthy McNasty." We did a lot of Basie stuff, and that was my introduction to big band jazz. We didn't have that in high school.

B.F. So you mainly played charts?

R.W. Yes, but we had to solo. That's where my interest in becoming a better soloist really began. That's what really got me to buckle down in terms of trying to create a vernacular like I was hearing in other things I noticed in jazz history. It was a long, slow process. I remember playing a modal solo on "So What."[1] My sophomore year, 1989, was really big in terms of getting another level of chops. I can remember them really starting to come together, and I was really starting to command the instrument. So by 1991, I was a bona fide soloist. I could hold my own on the blues and modal tunes. I had good ears, and I could deal with the rudiments of changes.[2] I had enough chops.

As you can see, I was studying many aspects of music. When I started South Carolina State, they didn't have a jazz program; so all we studied was the classical repertoire and classical technique. My trombone teacher, Tim Hinton, is a classical musician. So everything I studied was classical, which was the case through grad school. So my chops were really improving rapidly because of that experience. On the side, I was studying jazz on my own and learning from other musicians in the area. Skipp Pearson, Johnny Williams, and other guys were around when I was there at State; and because they knew I was talented, they took me under their wings. Skipp invited me on gigs.

B.F. Wasn't Johnny on the road with Basie then?

R.W. He would come in and out, but he was very supportive when he was around. Skipp, though, was around all the time. He was very important to me when I was at State. Being on gigs with him—just blowing—gave me valuable experience. Because of my training at State and my jazz playing, by the time I left school, I was known as an equally good classical and jazz trombonist.

B.F. Were you the star of the jazz band?

R.W. Yes.

B.F. Did any of your band colleagues become professional musicians?

R.W. Not those in the college band, though John Blackwell, a funk drummer from Keenan High School, attained success. He now plays with Prince.

By 1991, I was playing a classical repertoire and was in the jazz band. That's the year I met Wynton Marsalis. So whatever my level of talent and whatever level of proficiency I had attained on the trombone, I caught Wynton's ear in February 1991 when he came to Greenstreets in Columbia on, I think, a Thursday night. I drove there with my trombone in the trunk of the car. Wynton had a septet. That's when I met Wynton and Wycliffe Gordon and Eric Reed and Reginald Veal and all these great musicians.

Everybody knew Wynton Marsalis. He was such a good role model. You'd say, "Man, this guy's clean cut. He talks well. Listen to him play the trumpet." I was a junior in college, the big fish on campus in terms of playing; but I was limited to that small environment. During intermission after Wynton's first set, I introduced myself to him: "Mr. Marsalis, it's a pleasure to meet you. I'm Ron Westray, a jazz trombonist." He was like, "Oh, yeah?" I said, "Yes." He said, "Well, where's your horn?" I said, "It's in the car." He said, "Go get it." From that moment, my life changed; it was never the same. All the work I had done was preparation for this moment. I was about to enter into the big leagues.

B.F. How'd you do sitting in that night?

R.W. I did great. Everything was in place. Wynton invited me to play on the second set, and I did. When he introduced me, I received good applause because I was a hometown boy. The first thing we played was "Billie's Bounce." I remember Wynton standing off to the side, grimacing like he will when something's going well.

Then, they pulled the rug out from under my feet. They called one of Wynton's original tunes, "The Majesty of the Blues," which is in the Phrygian mode.[3] I had never heard this mode. I was used to playing the blues, or maybe something in E-minor. So they basically pushed me out on "The Majesty of the Blues." They just said,

"Yeah, go ahead, man." I remember trying to use my ears and construct a melody, and they were impressed with the way I dealt with Wynton's original music. Wynton asked my age, and he was amazed when I told him "twenty."

After the concert, I hung out with Wycliffe Gordon, a fraternity brother in Kappa Kappa Psi.[4] He's from Augusta, Georgia, and went to Florida A&M, though he left there to go on the road with Wynton. This was the first time we met. Oddly enough, he had heard of me even though I was still in school. Of course, I had heard of him because he had already recorded. We instantly bonded.

Being with him, Wynton, and the band that night was like being on cloud nine. It was the biggest moment of my career. Indescribable. Meeting a luminary like Wynton, having him compliment me, and hanging out with them all night: wonderful. The next day I returned to campus. Word had already spread that I had played with Wynton. A week later, Marcus Roberts came to Greenstreets. He'd recently left Wynton to form his own band. The evening I played with Wynton, he told me that he'd tell Roberts about me and that he wanted me to meet and play with J Master.[5] The next Thursday, I returned to Greenstreets. I walked up to the stage and said, "Hey, Marcus, how you doing? I'm Ron Westray." He said, "Oh, yeah. Wynton called me about you." As happened a week earlier, I came out for the second set and played a couple of numbers with Marcus.

B.F. What size group did he have?

R.W. He was playing solo piano. We played a couple of duets together and some standards. I went back to school and settled down from my musical highs. About a month later, I called my mom, asking her if I could bring some laundry home over the weekend. She said, "Okay." She was nonchalant; it was just a typical telephone conversation. Toward the end of it, she said, "Oh, by the way, Marcus Roberts called today. He's sending you airline tickets. He wants you to join his band in Florida." And I just went through the roof.

B.F. Was it just for one date?

R.W. It was for a week of rehearsals and a couple of performances in Tallahassee, where he was based.

B.F. But you were in school. You had to go to class.

R.W. I was still in school. I told my professors, "I'm gone. I'm outta here for a week." That was the start of my touring career. It—my junior year—would also be my last year in the marching band, which had been my love to that point. But Wynton and Marcus steered me in such a direction that I lost interest in the marching band and decided to get things together to become a great jazz trombonist. I needed to concentrate on my development. The marching band was fun, but I needed to leave it in order to get into the jazz environment.

My quitting the marching band was big news: "Ron's not in the marching band this year?" What I saw as a developing jazz career canceled out all other interests except my classical trombone playing. If I could master the instrument in a European classical sense, master the classical repertoire, and master the range of my instrument,

I knew it would enhance what I was trying to learn on the side, jazz. So those became my focuses.

Marcus laid out a lot of harmony and theory for me. Although I had developed a certain amount on my own, I never studied it—theory—with a teacher, not even Al McClain, not Willie Lyles. These guys pointed me in the right direction and showed me basic things I needed to do, but I never had a teacher say, "Okay, this is this and this is that, and this sound creates that sound, and until you master . . ."

So that's where Marcus Roberts comes into my development. When I flew down to Tallahassee to rehearse with his band, he wanted to hear where I was musically, so he basically gave me a proficiency exam. At the end of it, he said, "Okay, this is what you need to do. You gotta learn this. You gotta learn that. You gotta learn four qualities of chords. You gotta learn your seventh chords. You gotta learn your Phrygian scale. You gotta learn all your modes." He laid out all this stuff for me, and I went after it voraciously. I just went after that information, and that's the point where I really started. I was focused, and still am. It began with Marcus Roberts in 1991.

B.F. So you worked on it during your senior year?

R.W. I worked on it through my junior and senior years, and just kept getting better and better. I met Marcus in February, joined him and his band in March, and made my first recording with Marcus in June 1991, when I was twenty-one. We did the recording in New Orleans.

Before the session, he sent me a recording of Lawrence Brown playing "Creole Blues." He said, "Hey, Westray. I'm going in the studio in June, and I think you can do this. I want you to learn this Lawrence Brown tune. We're gonna fly you down to New Orleans. I want you to record it with me as a duet on my album." I spent about three weeks just shedding on nothing but Lawrence Brown's "Creole Blues."[6] I made my first recording with Marcus Roberts at age twenty-one, and things just kept going from that. During my senior year, 1992, three or four times I went out with Marcus for a week or two.

B.F. Was it hard for you to focus on your classes?

R.W. No, because the classes I was enrolled in were basic: music theory, music history, and so forth—plus private instruction with my trombone teacher.

B.F. So the classes you took during your senior year fed into what you were doing.

R.W. Yes. I was living a life of music, essentially, with an emphasis on jazz. I was practicing a lot. I was trying to get up all this stuff Marcus had shown me. He's my mentor because he's the one who laid out conceptually what I needed. He's the one who said, "You've got to go back. First, you gotta go back and listen to the early trombonists. Don't be stuck on bebop right now. Go back and learn the earlier styles. Go back and get some blues in your playing."

B.F. Did he mean players like Jimmy Harrison and Jack Teagarden?

R.W. Jimmy Harrison and Jack Teagarden, exactly, and also Dickie Wells and Vic Dickenson. He wanted me to get some blues in my playing before progressing to J. J. Johnson. It was very important for me to learn Lawrence Brown's style, so Marcus took me way back to the beginning, and I worked myself forward through J.J. and Curtis Fuller with a whole new appreciation of history. Marcus is also the one who set me straight about improvisation. Being a pianist, he would never let me cut corners. I would sit there, playing with him. He'd say, "Oh no, no, no, Bro'. You're not playing the harmony."

B.F. So he taught you.

R.W. Yes, he taught me. He taught me how to approach the chord and how to play the blues. He also showed me how to create a character with what you're playing and how to play two different characters. He'd say, "Okay, I want you to play something really high and crazy, and then I want you to go down real low and play something gutbucket."[7]

He'd always give me these analogies and metaphors of how something should sound. He's the one who got me into the metaphor of sound, like, "Okay, Bro', I want you to sound like a cat who's struggling with his old lady, but at the same time knows a pile about classical music." He'd just give me these crazy metaphors. He'd say, "I want you to go ahead and try that."

And so he got me into incorporating a visual aspect of the character of sound and creating a mood when I'm playing, and not just playing technical information. He's the one who got me into descriptive sound. So he's my mentor. Otherwise, I'm primarily self-taught, other than the people who gave me the basic building blocks. After Marcus helped me with the details, it became a matter of just doing homework.

B.F. But the dynamics of the story you're telling suggest that you will get your degree from South Carolina State. Is this what happened?

R.W. In a sense, it is. After finishing at State in 1992, a couple things happened. As a sophomore or junior, on the advice of my advisor I submitted an application to a school out in Illinois. He said, "This form came through. Why don't you send it in and see what happens? You might be able to get a graduate assistantship when you finish up here." So that was one egg in the nest. The other was that because I had recorded with Marcus, I had had a little exposure on the scene.

There was a little buzz about me in New York by the time I finished at State. George Wein's Festival Productions contacted me. And Wynton had recommended me for the group called Jazz Futures. You had Jazz Futures I with Roy Hargrove, and then Jazz Futures II, which was me, Nicholas Payton, Brian Blade, Peter Martin, Herb Harris, and Chris Thomas. So I came out of South Carolina State in May, and in June I was on my first tour of Europe with Jazz Futures for Festival Productions.

That summer in Europe, I met everybody who would be my colleagues in the professional, performing jazz world. We did the North Sea Jazz Festival and festivals in Nice and Vienna—all the major festivals.[8] But we didn't get a record contract at the end of that tour. As a result, at the end of that tour, I didn't have any gigs. Marcus wasn't working, and I wasn't in Wynton's band yet.

Because of my credentials—professional experience, recording with Marcus, on the road with a professional group—the people at Eastern Illinois University had kept up with me. They offered me a graduate assistantship. They said, "We need a jazz grad assistant, and we want you to be it." At the end of summer 1992, I had no gigs and wasn't ready to go to New York, so I accepted the assistantship. I headed on out to Illinois to pursue a master's degree. That's when I studied with Allan Horney, a classical instructor and my next influence.

In the fall of 1992, I went out there on full tuition plus a stipend as grad assistant and started working toward that degree. During the second semester of my first year at Eastern Illinois, in 1993, Wynton's management agency asked me to join Wynton's band. Even though I was the jazz grad assistant, I was not studying jazz. I was studying classical—twentieth-century harmony, analysis of music, sixteenth-century counterpoint, and so forth—because Allan Horney was a classical instructor. I saw this as an asset. I never felt the need to study jazz formally because I had already gotten the core information from Marcus. I knew that if I could just continue perfecting my classical chops and knocking out the master's degree, I could be a jazz composer, where classical and jazz are brought together.

Anyway, Wynton was doing *Jazz: Six Syncopated Movements* with Peter Martins and the New York City Ballet, which he had been commissioned to write. Wynton Marsalis Enterprises asked me to fly to New Orleans for rehearsals over the Christmas holidays, so I did. When I returned to campus, I had a new credential: I had just joined Wynton's band. All these great things that were happening—being in Wynton's band, being a grad student—inspired me to work harder at everything. I had a grand vision of what I could become.

B.F. How did you juggle schoolwork and performing with Wynton?

R.W. It was just a matter of working extra hard. Ultimately I had a little rift with Al Horney—we had a good relationship and were friends—because I needed to be away for two weeks here and there, and sometimes my absence occurred when important things on campus were happening. So things got a little hairy at times. I was serious about my studies, but I wasn't going to let anything get in the way of playing with Wynton.

Ultimately it all worked out. Toward the end of my graduate career, I maintained full tuition benefits but had to drop the stipend because I was not there enough to qualify for it, even though I was completing all my coursework and I was there 85 percent to 90 percent of the time. The rest of the time I had to really negotiate; I had to let some things go. I finished my degree by working on my thesis while on the road with Wynton's Lincoln Center Jazz Orchestra.

B.F. What was your thesis?

R.W. I did a detailed harmonic analysis of the five pieces I did for my recital. When I got back to campus a couple of months before graduation, the master's thesis was sitting on my teacher's desk with a lot of red ink on it. So I spent the rest of that semester before graduation cleaning up my thesis. I came through with flying colors and left Eastern Illinois in 1994 with a master's degree in classical trombone. I returned to South Carolina, where not much was happening. I didn't have a lot of gigs, but I went out with Marcus now and then. I talked casually with Wynton by telephone. Once, when I asked him what was happening, he said, "I'm forming a big band."

B.F. That's the Lincoln Center Jazz Orchestra.

R.W. Yes. The Lincoln Center Jazz Orchestra was formed around 1990 and was comprised basically of alumni of Duke Ellington's band. It wasn't a touring organization.

B.F. Who were some of the musicians?

R.W. Joe Temperley, Norris Turney, Bill Easley, Jerry Dodgion—older guys that maybe had some influence with Ellington or had been on the New York scene a long time. So it was, for lack of a better term, an old band. The first Lincoln Center Jazz Orchestra was the old cats, and the new one was going to be young. This blew up into a big mess in 1991, when I was still at State, around the time I met Wynton. When we talked on the telephone about his forming a new band, he was talking about the LCJO as we know it today, which is a pretty young group, a majority of young guys. That group had to make the transition from the old guard to the new.

After I finished my master's degree and returned to South Carolina, mainly I was just writing and shedding. I haven't really talked about composition, but it was aligned with my development. I started writing really early. At some point, I needed composition to complement what I was doing on the horn, so I was writing a lot. I was working on a lot of my early tunes and still studying harmony, stuff Marcus had shown me, and things I had gleaned from other players on the scene in 1994.

So the year after grad school was kind of a gathering up, but I was basically just back in Columbia, figuring out what the next move was going to be. But Wynton had called me in 1993 to join his band, and that was my first semester of grad school. A year later, I went on tour with the new Lincoln Center Jazz Orchestra. With that, I was officially a part of the scene. When I joined the Lincoln Center Jazz Orchestra in 1994, Britt Woodman was on first trombone and Art Baron was on second, so I played third. That was the section. But the orchestra was still in transition because Wynton needed it to be younger, and that ended up being a big political debacle in New York because a lot of older guys sued Lincoln Center for age discrimination because the transition was so swift. Basically Wynton just brought in a bunch of young guys to start the new orchestra.

B.F. Could you feel tension in the section?

R.W. Not really.

B.F. Did you get along with Woodman?

R.W. Oh, man, Woodman was such a sweetheart.

B.F. Yes, but he was an older guy.

R.W. Yes, he was one of the guys Wynton was transitioning out, but Woodman and I never felt tension between us. We just knew what was going on and knew we had to hold on to this opportunity. The next year, 1995, I decided to open the Wooden Flute.

B.F. It was a club on Main Street in Columbia.

R.W. I think it was my Joe Westray DNA kicking in because my grandfather was an entrepreneur as well as a musician. He created clubs. I think I was just feeling some of that legacy and wanted to do something in my hometown. I also wanted a musical outlet because the Lincoln Center Jazz Orchestra was not working like we would be ultimately, although I played with it a couple of times that year. In Columbia, I had a band because I was there the majority of the time. On all that down time between gigs with Wynton, I wanted to do stuff here. My quartet had Tommy Gill, Quentin Baxter, Herman Burney, and myself.

B.F. Are they South Carolinians?

R.W. Tommy Gill and Quentin Baxter are from Charleston. Herman Burney is from North Carolina. The whole idea behind the Wooden Flute was just to have another outlet for jazz in South Carolina. I wanted to provide a place to play for whatever jazz community existed here, and I wanted to bring in acts. My band would be the house band, because I needed a place to run this quartet and finish honing my skills on the stage. So I basically created the Wooden Flute as a performance center for myself, for the local musicians, and for outside acts.

That year, 1995, some Broadway show came through Charleston and offered musicians consistent work, so my two main musicians, Tommy Gill and Quentin Baxter, signed up for the Broadway work, which kept them from being in the house band at the Wooden Flute.

Then, I really got into booking, and I actually started managing Marcus Roberts, who taught me how to be a road manager. He toured as a solo pianist and considered me trustworthy and a good guide. He's blind. So I would go out on the road with Marcus, manage, count the heads, talk to the club owners, and get the money at the end of the night. I did that to make money in between other things that were happening.

B.F. Did you still live in Columbia?

R.W. Yes. But those business aspects of music set me in the direction of running a jazz club. I knew how clubs run, so I knew I could run one myself. Using my contacts, I just started booking. My grand opening was the Marcus Roberts trio. Then, I had local events.

The next big concert was Wynton's, also in 1995. After that, the Henry Butler trio and then the Eric Reed trio. Carl Allen played there. I only booked about five major acts that year, and then I had to let it go because I didn't want to go bankrupt at age twenty-four. Running a jazz club was no joke. I was paying a huge tab to have this space to book downtown, and it went well. It was great. The musicians would come to town and we had a great time, but it was something I had to let go of. Plus, it was time to hit the road.

B.F. Not having alcohol made for a nice atmosphere. Was not having it part of the financial problem?

R.W. Yes, but we didn't pursue alcohol licensing because we were on a different kind of timeline. Not having alcohol probably cut the business in half. Wynton's huge concert for me basically bailed me out.

B.F. Didn't he give several shows in one night?

R.W. That's right. Three shows. We turned the house three times.

B.F. His solo on a themeless "Cherokee" during the second set was phenomenal.

R.W. That's his signature.

B.F. It was like Charlie Parker doing "Ko-Ko" on the same chord changes.

R.W. Yes, exactly.

B.F. So that was a tremendous evening. Another thing I liked about it was Wynton's mingling with the audience behind the club between sets. He was very approachable, very pleasant.

R.W. Yes, he's a people person. He's a taskmaster with a serious vision, but he's definitely a people person. He's the kind of person you can walk up to and have a great conversation with, even though he's a luminary.

B.F. Why did you name the club the Wooden Flute?

R.W. The Wooden Flute came from a kind of mystical experience I had in the yard one day. It was raining lightly. A sound was traveling through the air, some kind of ancient sound. I was standing on the edge of my carport when it began misting. The sun was still out. The sound I heard reminded me of a wooden flute.

I already had a lease on the building and needed a name for the jazz club. It seemed like the sound I heard had been traveling for two thousand years. It sounded like a panpipe. I identified it as a wooden flute, so that's why I named the club the Wooden Flute. Over a decade later, I ran into a recording of a wren called the musician wren. I now believe that was the sound I heard that day back in 1995.

The club was open in 1995 and 1996, and in '96 I returned to the road with Marcus Roberts. I was also his music transcriber. He had a big commission from Lincoln Center during the latter part of '94 for *Romance, Swing, and the Blues*. He dictated all that music onto cassette tapes. I had a big carton of like twenty cassette tapes of the whole suite, and that's when I started transcribing.

I created the handwritten score. I still have it out in the shed. So I was his right-hand man. Any time he put together a band, he'd come to me to ask what was happening with the music. The musicians came to me to find out what the score says. So I became known as an arranger with Marcus, and that reputation reached Wynton's organization.

Then, Marcus had another project, the music of George Gershwin. I did the rough analysis for Concerto in F so Marcus could put it into Braille. There was also time for *Rhapsody in Blue* and a big-band version of James P. Johnson's "Yamekraw." I was involved in the arranging of these pieces. We took that music on the road in '96.

Also that year, Wycliffe Gordon and I got together as composers and trombonists, bonded, and did *Bone Structure* for Atlantic Records. No matter where I am, people all over the world—Russia, mainland China—talk to me about that CD. We put a lot of effort into it, but we didn't realize that it was going to be such a landmark. I joined Wynton and the LCJO in 1997, the year he won the Pulitzer Prize for *Blood on the Fields*. We toured with it for something like two months.

B.F. Isn't that close to three hours? It's long.

R.W. Yes, it's a jazz oratorio. Then, during spring of 1997 we did the music of Count Basie in New York. Jon Faddis and Nicholas Payton were in the band. LCJO was still kind of getting wound up to be an aggressive touring machine, and 1997 is the year I moved to New York. Sherman Irby, who was in the band, took me up to

Harlem to show me an apartment he had. Moving to Harlem put me right there in New York with Lincoln Center. I could afford to be in New York because the LCJO was working a lot.

The New York scene was very fertile. I got a couple of independent gigs and did some festival work. I wrote a piece for the Early Music Ensemble of New York and premiered it as part of a summer jazz festival. On the side, I played in Jason Lindner's band at Small's, a club in the Village where young musicians would hang every night: you'd go in there at ten o'clock at night and come out of there at six o'clock in the morning. We still had that kind of essence going on in terms of the jazz club tradition. Jason encouraged everybody to write, and I submitted a couple of charts for the band.

The first year I was in New York, though, I got by on the talent I had in place. I was aggressive in trying to create a full career, though my main work was with the Lincoln Center Jazz Orchestra. It started touring so much that by 1998, we were playing about ninety gigs a year. Ultimately we'd have maybe a hundred.

My first arrangement for Wynton was of Charles Mingus's "Goodbye Porkpie Hat" in 1998. The context wasn't totally pleasant because it involved one of the first big arguments I had with another cat. We were in rehearsal in Aspen, Colorado, and me and another musician I won't name got into it over a harmonic preference, over music. We had an audience there, and it was one of the first times people said, "Well, Westray's coming into his own now. He's standing up for himself." It was one of those times when my personality kind of blossomed. I was no longer just a sideman; I was like someone who had something to say.

So at rehearsal, Wynton brought in an inferior lead sheet of "Goodbye Porkpie Hat" and said, "Well, guys, I want us to play 'Goodbye Porkpie Hat.'"[9] He handed everybody the lead sheet. I knew Mingus's music a little bit by that time, so I told the pianist that a chord he played was wrong. I offered another one. He was offended, and we exchanged words.

At the end of the rehearsal, Wynton called me off to the side and said, "Westray, can you arrange this ['Goodbye Porkpie Hat'] for us, Bro'?" From what I'd done with Marcus, he knew I was an arranger. I said, "Yes." I agreed to bring it in the next day. I was so angry at what had happened that I went straight to my room and wrote my first arrangement for Wynton's band. Everybody loved it. People still talk about it because it has so much emotion in it because of my anger at the time. In 1999 Wynton commissioned me to write three pieces for his Swing Dance Tour.

B.F. By "write," do you mean compose?

R.W. Compose and arrange. We actually played for dance crowds around the country. I did "You Are Out of Sight," a hip, swinging tune; "Maybe Later," another swing tune; and "Mr. Personality." We kept touring, and by 2001 I was becoming known as one of the main soloists. Since Wycliffe Gordon had left the band, I was leader of a young trombone section, which soon included Andre Heyward and Vincent Gardner. Players coming in were kind of like my prodigies, and I recommended them to Wynton, who always came to me for recommendations.

In Europe around 2001, Wynton and I talked about the upcoming season. He asked if I wanted to do anything for it. He said, "Well, Bro', if we give you a concert, what would you want to do?" And I said, "I'd like to continue with the Mingus music." When he asked if I'd like to do it during the 2002 season, I said, "Yes. I can do it."

He told me that he'd book three nights of Mingus music for February 2002. From a CD, I did raw transcriptions of ten of Mingus's not-so-well-known compositions and some of the bigger pieces, and then made my arrangements from the transcriptions. This was a big, big moment for me because I was the only orchestra member to have the stage. At that point, I was the only orchestra member to be booked at Lincoln Center as musical director while still in the orchestra. The music of Charles Mingus was my show.

B.F. By that time, had you been with the Mingus Big Band?

R.W. No. The Mingus Big Band didn't come until the end of this phase of my career in New York.

B.F. What accounts for your fascination with Mingus's music? But then, how could one not be fascinated with it?

R.W. I had been fascinated with Mingus in grad school in 1994 because I was digging on *Tijuana Moods*, one of my favorite records. It has Clarence Shaw on trumpet. I had been digging on that a long time. Little did I know, back in 1994–1995, that I would be transcribing and arranging that suite.

So I transcribed all of *Tijuana Moods* and blew it up into an arrangement for Wynton's band. That was the first part of what I did for the program. For the second, I did the two parts of *Black Saint and the Sinner Lady*. I also arranged "Don't Be Afraid, the Clown's Afraid Too," as well as "Better Git It in Your Soul" and "Meditations on Integration." Sue Mingus would not end up calling me to join the Mingus Big Band until 2005, my last year in New York.[10] I wish I had gotten the call earlier because I was a student of Mingus's music

B.F. Chris Potter was with that band a little before you, wasn't he?

R.W. Yes. Chris was in it when he first got to New York. He's on some of the band's early recordings.

B.F. After your Mingus arrangements for Wynton, I assume you had more and more writing responsibilities

R.W. Right. I was arranging.

B.F. At the same time, you were the main trombone soloist.

R.W. Right. I was one of the primary arrangers and trombone soloists. So, aside from the programs I was writing—my own commissions—I was arranging all kinds of other music. I arranged music for a concert with Odada, a group of African musicians. I arranged stuff for flamenco musicians. I arranged a couple of Ornette Coleman's compositions. So I was a primary arranger. There were only three of us arranging to a degree that could affect the band: Wynton, Ted Nash, and me. Arranging was very important to me.

B.F. Which of Ornette's tunes did you arrange?

R.W. "Lonely Woman" and "Humpty Dumpty."

B.F. Did you have a hand in arranging Paul Whiteman's music?

R.W. We did his standing arrangements, though I thought we should have done new ones. But I had worked very hard to earn the post of arranger in Wynton's band. I had proven myself as arranger by working hard and having good musical conceptions.

Wynton always asked me to arrange music from other cultures. So I'd get a lead sheet of Brazilian music—like "Noites Cariocas" or "Boedo"—and I'd turn it into a swing number. The same with the African music. Wynton would always give me credit. But he was into the systems that dictated other cultures' music, whereas I was into translating the music of other cultures into the jazz idiom.

When we went on tour during the summer of 2002, the book I took with me was Cervantes's *Don Quixote*, which had just been named one of the top five novels of all time. A friend told me to check it out. I had a copy of the old Harvard Classics edition translated by Thomas Shelton, but I bought a copy of the Oxford edition to take on tour.[11]

We were literally on the road, driving across Europe. I was on the bus, a couple of seats behind Wynton, laughing and chuckling at Cervantes. I was falling in love with Cervantes. I'm like, "This guy is brilliant." Every now and again, I would say to Wynton, "Just read this. Read this story of the barber, Mambrino's helmet. See how absurd this character is." After several days of my asking him to read it, Wynton asked if I thought I could write some music for the band based on this story. I said I'd have to read the book again in order to do it. He said, "If you think it's something you want to do, we can program it for the opening season in the new hall in 2005.[12]

So in mid-2002 I started the most in-depth study of my whole career: creating an outline and ultimately a score for *Don Quixote*. I worked on it for a little over two and a half years. I read four editions of the novel—Harvard Classics, Oxford, the Grossman translation, and one other I don't remember—because I wanted to create a flawless outline.[13]

The first year I read and worked on an outline. The next year-and-a-half I spent setting music to the outline. I worked on it all the way up to the premiere. I finished it in Alaska while on the road with the Mingus band. I sent the score in digitally in time for the premiere. I titled my work *Chivalrous Misdemeanors*. It premiered May of 2005 in two parts. It was just huge. It was really the highlight of my career to that point. A performance was recorded, but it has not been released.

B.F. Didn't Strauss interpret Cervantes?

R.W. Strauss wrote a *Don Quixote*, and so did Telemann and a couple of other composers; but mine is the first jazz *Don Quixote*.

B.F. Did you listen to them?

R.W. I listened to Strauss's especially because that's the most popular one. I studied it from a standpoint of theme—theme and variation. Strauss showed us how to create a great theme and how to have that theme come back, so I learned a lot about structure. What really influenced me, though, was Stravinsky's *Soldier's Tale* [*L'Histoire du soldat*] because of its narration. My composition came out as a mammoth piece, and I'm very proud of it.

B.F. How long a performance is it?

R.W. It's two hours. Each part is one hour. It's so highly condensed that it's a complete experience. It got great reviews. It made the *New Yorker*.[14]

B.F. How many performances were there?

R.W. There were three nights, May 5 to 7. From mid-2002 until the premiere, I was very busy—reading four editions of the novel, creating an outline, putting music to the outline. Also, in late 2004 I joined the Mingus band. Every Tuesday night, we played at the Iridium in New York. Around the end of the year, we went on tour; and we toured again in April 2005, right before the premiere. I worked on the music the whole time I was on tour with them.

The University of Texas called me in February 2005. Nathaniel Brickens is an old associate from 1994, when I was studying for my master's degree. He's a classical trombonist who helped me prepare for my graduate recital. He's now at the University of Texas. Texas created a new position of instructor of jazz trombone, to begin in 2005. Between my tours with the Mingus band and while I was still working on the score to *Don Quixote*, he called me in New York.

This is a guy I hadn't seen or talked to since 1994, but he had my name in his head that whole time and knew I was active in the field. He asked if I was ready to leave New York. I told him that I wasn't. Then, he told me about the Texas position and said that he told people there that he'd call me about it. I told him that I'd be interested in learning the details. He said that he'd have Jeff Hellmer call me. He's a pianist and director of the UT jazz program. Jeff called and offered to fly me down for an interview, to meet the executive committee, and do a master class. So in February, I did.

When I returned to New York, I soon went on tour with the Mingus band, and *Don Quixote* premiered. Jeff Hellmer flew out to see *Don Quixote* because they were thinking about hiring me. About a month later, I was offered the job. I had to decide between being a sideman and arranger in New York and starting a jazz trombone studio at the University of Texas. In the summer of 2005, I decided to head on down to Austin.

B.F. Is this a tenure-track position?

R.W. Yes.

B.F. What does being an academic do to you as far as being on the scene is concerned?

R.W. I hope to bring the credentials that I've already established together with a new set of credentials as an educator. I want to bring all the history that I have in New York to my desktop at UT. I want to be like a lot of educators—like Donald Byrd and Jimmy Heath—who bring the creative and academic worlds together. It's going to take a minute to restructure, but I hope to combine the best of both worlds. I want to do a great job as an educator. I want to create a serious trombone studio and be able to link it up with what I've already done. I want to keep recording and arranging from my new base of operations.

Being at UT gives me a base, which a sideman doesn't really have. Even if you're a great soloist, the day of the major-label jazz record company is kind of done. Either an independent label will pick you up, or you have to create your own record. So all things considered, I think it would be best for me to have a base of operations where I can create a new foundation in education. That's what I'm prepared for because I thought I'd knock out my degrees, put them in my back pocket, get some real experience, and then come on back into education.

And that's exactly how my career is panning out. I spent eight years in New York and chalked up a lot of experience. I have a reputation as a soloist and a composer/arranger. Now, I'm trying to pass on my understanding of music to my students. I'm doing what I really didn't get: jazz instruction. So I'm giving back, in a sense, what I didn't get. Many people helped me, and I had influences, but people didn't really teach me the rudiments, from start to finish, of what jazz is about: how to command the instrument, how to play, how to improvise.

B.F. Would you teach a course about the history of jazz?

R.W. Yes.

B.F. I assume your academic assignment is for nine months.

R.W. Exactly.

B.F. So in the summer, if you want to record, tour, or whatever, you can.

R.W. Yes. And they encourage me to be active. In fact, they brought me in on the understanding that I won't stop my performing career. This year, I was very careful not to abuse that because I actually needed to be there to figure out how things are done. This is a brand new setting for me: coming from the road, which has no parameters, to a university, which has lots of parameters. This year was really light for me in terms of gigs. I went back to New York to play only two or three times during this whole year. Still, if I need to be away for half a semester, I could, as long as I organize it properly. That's the great thing about this new gig at UT.

B.F. Academic jobs are hard to get, yet they came after you.

R.W. Yes. I was sitting on my futon in New York when they called. They had two candidates, Delfeayo Marsalis (Wynton's younger brother) and me. He went down for the interview process months before I did and flopped. Then, they called me. I was the right man for the job. I understood the conception of education. I understood what they wanted to accomplish. I didn't go in asking how much they needed me to be there.

B.F. If you didn't gig very much during this last academic year, did you practice to keep up your lip?

R.W. Yes. Now, I'm more conscientious about practicing because being on the road naturally keeps you in shape. My chops feel good. And I'm able to play in Austin, which has a fertile music scene. There's a bona fide jazz club, the Elephant Room. I've been booked there a few times this year. I've been playing in the local big bands. It's been a huge transition coming from the status of my previous career to the university setting, to the local scene, to just being a part of an average local big band again. It's been a huge mental adjustment.

B.F. Since it has a scene and since you were a booker for a while, do you book groups into Austin?

R.W. The people who do that in Austin have been doing it for a while. Between education, keeping my chops up, continuing to shed, and developing as a composer/arranger, I don't have time to do a Wooden Flute in Austin. Plus, I like being on the performing end, by which I mean getting booked. Eventually I will form a big band. The next big thing for me in Austin will be the second premiere of *Chivalrous Misdemeanors*. I hope to run it through the university grants system. I submitted it for the Pulitzer Prize this year and hoped to win, but didn't.

B.F. I asked about booking because of all your contacts.

R.W. Yes. In terms of being that link between the scene in New York and things happening in Austin, I hope I can be of some service; but in terms of full-out booking, no.

B.F. If you succeed in getting a grant for the second premiere, would you need to edit the original score?

R.W. Not much editing needs to be done. There are a couple of things I want to do differently, but not much. It's pretty much self-contained.

When most jazz musicians get a large commission, they think in terms of a symphonic orchestra. My goal was to make the jazz band as we know it sound like a different animal. I wanted it to sound full, like an orchestra. I wanted it to do a lot of things a symphonic orchestra can do. I wrote to have a jazz band play in its purest form, in a really broad way; therefore, it doesn't need a symphonic orchestra to make the piece sound any bigger. The instrumentation is five saxes, three trombones, four trumpets, and rhythm section. My whole idea was to expand the jazz band and make it sound like something else.

B.F. Do you allow for improvisation?

R.W. There's a lot of improvisation. There are twenty-three movements based on different subject matter. There's a narrator; there are two vocalists, one female and one male. The female vocalist is in the role of Dulcinea, and the male vocalist is Don Quixote, the narrator, so it's a really complete and compact experience.

I am, though, in the process of editing a lot of other compositions from my time in New York because all my compositions and arrangements will be channeled down through the university system. The university will preserve my work. So within the university system, I not only get to pass along my musical concepts to students, but I actually get to preserve my work through publishing and by having these pieces played by the college musicians. This is totally different from having professionals play it, but it allows the students to experience that material. So it's good being at UT. I'm settling down, trying to establish myself and my music within that system.

B.F. Do you have any more big-time composition projects?

R.W. I don't have anything on the table. I'm in an editing phase with my pre-existing stuff, with the goal of getting it published. I want to get a grant to have *Chivalrous*

Misdemeanors recorded and released, and I'm looking forward to its second premiere. The transition to UT from the professional world has been huge, but everybody's treated me really well. Nobody's tried to tie me down. They give me as much freedom as I need. It's up to me to create an academic career.

Columbia, S.C., 26 June 2006

Notes

1. Modal jazz, of which "So What" is a prime example, is based on scale patterns that are more varied than the traditional major and minor scales.

2. Westray refers to chord changes.

3. Phrygian is a mode of the major scale that is exotic in sound and is often heard in flamenco music.

4. Kappa Kappa Psi is the national honorary band fraternity.

5. "J Master" is Marcus Roberts.

6. "Shedding" is short for woodshedding, which means practicing.

7. "Gutbucket" means earthy.

8. The North Sea Jazz Festival was held in The Hague, The Netherlands, from 1976 until 2005. Since then Rotterdam has hosted it.

9. A lead sheet is a musical score containing only the melody, chord symbols, and lyrics, if any.

10. Sue Mingus is the widow of Charles Mingus.

11. The 1998 Oxford University Press edition of *Don Quixote* is translated by Charles Jarvis and edited by E. C. Riley.

12. The opening season for the Frederick P. Rose Hall (New York) was 2004–5.

13. Ecco Press published Edith Grossman's translation of *Don Quixote* in 2003.

14. The *New Yorker* announces the forthcoming concerts of 5–7 May, though not by name, in the issue of 9 May 2005: 13. A color caricature of Westray, with the caption "Ron Westray leads a tribute to 'Don Quixote,' at Jazz at Lincoln Center," appears on page 12. The magazine did not review the concerts.

CHRIS POTTER

1 January 1971–

B.F. I was first aware of you during your years at Dreher High School in Columbia, but you had a musical story before then. Did you go to Hand Middle School?

C.P. Yes. I went to Rosewood Elementary, and then I went to Hand Middle School. I started playing the saxophone when I was in the fifth grade at Rosewood. I had always played different instruments by ear. Whenever there was a piano around, I would try to figure out how to play it. The same with a guitar.

But when I was around ten or eleven, I decided that I really wanted to play the saxophone. I think I had listened to some of my parents' records. They had some Miles Davis records with John Coltrane, some Dave Brubeck records that I really loved for the sound of Paul Desmond, and some Eddie Harris records. I just checked out a few different things and decided that I really wanted to play the saxophone.

B.F. Did your parents listen to much music? Did they play music around the house?

C.P. Yes, but my interest in music probably developed from raiding their record collection. There was music on the radio, but the major thing was discovering what was on all these records. I was just always attracted to music. Before that, when I was seven or eight, I discovered the Beatles, and my parents also had records by Chicago, Buddy Guy, Otis Rush, and others.

B.F. All the blues.

C.P. Right. That was kind of the first thing that really got me into music, and I guess it went from there into jazz, just from their record collection.

B.F. To me that seems a natural evolution, to go to jazz.

C.P. Yes.

B.F. But I think most people would probably not then have considered it a natural evolution because your generation, and other generations, generally gravitated toward rock.

Chris Potter. Columbia, S.C., 30 December 2005. Photograph by Benjamin Franklin V

C.P. I was the only kid around my age I knew who was into it at all. I was definitely off by myself in that little world. Something about the music just really grabbed me: the idea of improvisation and the spontaneous expression of whatever's going on at the moment, as well as the rigorous things you have to learn. There was just something about the sound of it that really spoke to me. I, myself, wonder what I had to relate it to as a ten-year-old growing up in Columbia, South Carolina, hearing no jazz around me; but there was just something about it that immediately clicked, and I went, "Wow, yeah, that's what I want to do."

B.F. Of those three saxophonists you mentioned—Paul Desmond, Coltrane, and Eddie Harris—I think most people, I included, would say, "Well, I can understand Desmond, who is so lyrical and beautiful." I don't know if at ten you were interested in beauty or facility or what.

C.P. Yes. He was the one who first really grabbed me in that way, for those exact reasons. His playing is not simple, but it's very lyrical and just sounds really good.

B.F. But then, Coltrane is not exactly Desmond. With Miles, in the middle and late '50s, he was pretty far out for the time, though he'd later go much further out. He also has a hard tone—not that he's not lyrical—but he's more aggressive than Desmond. Yet he appealed to you, too.

C.P. I think so. It was a little bit later that I really got into him heavily. I remember some of my reaction to his playing at the time, which was that I didn't quite understand it. In my opinion, he was really searching at that time. Now, I can appreciate it; I understand that he was looking for a certain thing.

I was listening to Miles's *Workin'* and *Steamin'* and was, if anything, more attracted to Miles, like the way he plays "It Never Entered My Mind." Unbelievable. But there's just a feeling you get from all those musicians, whether you think about the notes they're using or their tone. You can hear who they were as people, even if you're not quite ready to understand what they're doing. Coltrane sounded like a very sweet person looking for something. That was my impression at the time.

B.F. Then, there's the third saxophonist you mentioned as having listened to, Eddie Harris. The usual take on him is that he was something of a middleweight, as opposed to the heavyweights Desmond and Coltrane. He was known for recording the theme from *Exodus*, for example, that was popular at the time. I think Harris is more substantial than most people seem to think.

C.P. I think so, too. I mean, the fact that he had some commercial success perhaps didn't help him in some ways, and maybe his actions didn't really help him. I don't know because I never met him. I've heard a lot of stories, though. He sounds like he was quite a character. At gigs with local rhythm sections, if he didn't like them, he would just play solo piano. Apparently he could sing just like Billie Holiday. He would do stand-up comedy, just tell jokes.

B.F. What did your grade-school music teacher do with you, a student with uncommon and advanced musical taste?

C.P. I was extremely fortunate. I have no idea where she is, but there was my regular music teacher at Rosewood, Miss Hall. I don't remember her first name — I would have never called her by her first name — but she was so helpful.[1] I remember learning how to play "Take Five" by ear, and she figured out how to play the piano part. I learned how to play "Sweet Georgia Brown." She would stay after school with me and figure out how to play the piano parts and I would improvise over them. I mean, it was one of those really rare, great situations where someone who's in a position to encourage a young person made an extra effort. And there were a lot of people around like that, too. When I began taking saxophone lessons, it was Bryson Borgstedt. He was in the U.S. Military Academy Band for a long time.

B.F. I believe he played in groups at the University of South Carolina.

C.P. A long time ago, right. He was a graduate student at that time. He could see right away that I was really interested in it, so he took the time to show me what harmony was, what a chord progression was. He explained how people improvise. He hooked me up with John Emche, who was teaching here at the University of South Carolina, and from there . . .

B.F. This was still when you were in grade school?

C.P. Yes: ten, eleven, twelve. For a while, I was just taking lessons with Emche. We would just talk about music and play tunes.

B.F. Were you still a student of his when he died? He died young.

C.P. Yes. I don't remember if I was still taking lessons every week, but we played a lot. We used to do a lot of gigs together and things like that. So I was definitely around a lot at that time.

B.F. You had this kind of professional encouragement, from your teacher at Rosewood to the people at USC. What about your parents' role in all this? I assume they encouraged you from the beginning.

C.P. Very much. I never once had that classic "you want to do what?" It wasn't like that at all. I think they saw it was something I enjoyed doing, so they encouraged me. I don't even remember deciding to be a professional musician; it never seemed like a decision that needed to be made. It was just what I did. I was starting to work and make money—playing weddings—when I was fifteen or so. It was just kind of a natural thing.

B.F. After Miss Hall at Rosewood, was there a music teacher at Hand who carried on the tradition?

C.P. Yes. Mary Lou Warth, who, I believe, is now Mary Lou Schweikert. By that time, once there was kind of a school band situation, most of my jazz—my actual learning how to play the saxophone better and working on how to play jazz—was done outside the school situation. I was a member of the school band, but I was just doing that music there while working on my other music.

B.F. I'm interested in that because the first time I saw you was in the music room at Dreher High School. I was there to pick up my daughter Rebecca, and I heard the band practicing; naturally I looked in the band room. It struck me as a typical high school band. Yet there you were—by then a good musician—seated in the front row with your legs crossed, sending off flowing phrases. I was impressed that you were going through the discipline of the band program when you were so obviously advanced.

C.P. Yes. I think it was more a social thing for me at that point. It wasn't really about learning how to play music on a higher level when I was in the high school band. I was there to hang out with my friends, in addition to being able to play.

B.F. You took lessons and schooling seriously. I believe your parents are educators and that from them you probably absorbed the belief that education is important. After high school, you could have become a full-time professional musician, but didn't.

C.P. Yes. As soon as I finished high school, I moved to New York to attend the New School. So I went there for a year and then to the Manhattan School of Music. I was focused on how to become a professional musician in New York. But it was really important, I think, to go to college with a crowd of similarly minded young people who wanted to play jazz. That was my first real experience with people my age that were also interested in it.

B.F. Who were some of them?

C.P. At the New School were Larry Goldings, Peter Bernstein, and Brad Mehldau. I think Roy Hargrove was technically a student, though I don't know how often he was there. A whole bunch of really amazing musicians. John Popper, who's the lead singer and harmonica player with Blues Traveler, was also at the New School at that time.

B.F. Why did you change schools?

C.P. A lot of it boiled down to scholarship money. I got a lot more from Manhattan, and it was just up the street, so I could stay in New York.

B.F. Did you finish your schooling there?

C.P. I did. I got my undergrad degree. There were some dicey moments because I was already starting to work. I was playing in Red Rodney's band. I guess I joined that band maybe three months after I moved to town, so I was trying to balance it all.

B.F. Let's pick up on Red Rodney. He's an important figure in your life. I believe you met him at the Main Street Jazz Festival here in Columbia.

C.P. Yes, that's where I first met Red. He said to give him a call when I moved to New York. I think the Main Street Festival was in the spring, so I met him right before I was going to graduate high school and move to New York. So that was excellent timing. But yes, playing with real musicians who came down from New York and various places was very important.

B.F. I think it is fair to say that Red Rodney was purely, or almost purely, a bebop player. Those were his roots, and he continued playing bop. You've gone beyond it.

C.P. Well, you feel like you want to make music that's reflective of how you live and the culture that you live in. That's what bebop was. That reflected a certain time and place, and they were striking out on their own, doing something that their elders didn't approve of, et cetera. Seems like the real way to follow that tradition is to look for something new that somehow expresses the way life feels to you.

That's what an artist's job is, I think. If you listen to Charlie Parker, you can just hear that. It sounds so new now. If you listen to his music now, it still has some of that shock of being something that no one had done before, a new way of looking at the world. So that's what we're all looking for.

B.F. Red Rodney, though, took you from being a local to a national musician.

C.P. Yes, and beginning to tour around Europe. That was my first introduction to the life of a traveling jazz musician, and just what is involved. Also, there are not many of those guys left from that generation. I'm probably one of the last people in my age group to play with Red and a few of those guys. I didn't have a chance to play with them much, but I had a chance to play with some of them, even the swing guys. I did a little bit of work where I ended up meeting these people, like Sweets Edison and Ray Brown, and having a chance to play with them.

B.F. How about Jay McShann?

C.P. I never met him. A saxophone player I know in Indianapolis used to work with him a lot, so I got stories. There's definitely an element of folklore and handing things down from one generation to the next that's very attractive to me about the jazz tradition.

I'm trying to think of some examples from my own life. The other week was Jim Hall's seventy-fifth birthday at the Village Vanguard. Joe Lovano, I, and a few other people came down to sit in. We were all hanging out afterwards, and Jim was telling stories about driving from Philadelphia to New York with Sonny Rollins and Ben Webster. When someone put a recording of Ben Webster's over the sound system, we were all silent for about five minutes just listening to it. It was really moving, and it was something that really affected Jim. It was an important event in his life, and he's telling these stories.

B.F. Did he ever play with Ben Webster?

C.P. He played with him a fair amount, I think. I actually just bought a CD with both of them on it, which I had never seen.

B.F. What is it?

C.P. *Live at the Renaissance*, with Jimmy Rowles and Frank Butler, I think. I haven't had a chance to listen to it yet.

B.F. Did Jim Hall ever talk about Eric Dolphy?

C.P. I know his name has come up. I toured a little bit with Jim and definitely various people's names have come up. I don't really remember.

B.F. I ask that, though, because I think you play the bass clarinet, don't you?

C.P. A little bit.

B.F. When I think of bass clarinet, I think of Dolphy: "God Bless the Child," for example.

C.P. He had such a language on that instrument; he really was able to find his own thing. It's a really ridiculously hard instrument, I find. I can only play ballads on it. I usually restrict myself to not having to play too fast.

B.F. He played "God Bless the Child," which I guess is a ballad, even though he made it rococo. I don't know why, but there are two instruments that appeal to me for just their natural sounds. The bass clarinet is one.

C.P. I can see that.

B.F. And the cello is the other. There's just something mellow about them. Is there anything about the sound that attracts you to the bass clarinet? Or is it just another reed instrument?

C.P. There's obviously a special thing about the bass clarinet. It's always appealed to me, too. The fact that the low range has a certain sonority, and then high range can actually be a whole other thing. It has different tone qualities. I think of it as having almost three separate registers. It can get like the screaming Albert system kind of thing way up high, but then a low, almost bullfrog kind of thing down low.[2] It's a great instrument.

B.F. Not to belabor Dolphy, but it's funny about these connections: you know Jim Hall, who knows . . .

C.P. Yes, that's what I've discovered the jazz scene is like. There are connections everywhere.

B.F. You mentioned traveling to Europe with Red when you were not yet twenty. Did he look after you?

C.P. Yes. I wish I had the . . . I don't know how to explain it. He was a character. He was no longer using any kind of drugs, but I think the experience of being a junkie and just growing up kind of lower middle class, or maybe lower than that even. . . . He was always scheming, always trying to pull something over on someone; and he had a million stories about all the crimes he committed.

B.F. There was prison time for impersonating a general.

C.P. Yes, impersonating the general, which I heard several times, with slight differences each time. And just watching him: he would try to get on the plane first by faking a limp so the pretty girls would fawn over him. He would turn back to me and smile. These kinds of things.

B.F. But was he protective of you?

C.P. I think he was. He went way out of his way to mention me in interviews and to help me out. I guess he saw something, and whatever his own motives were for anything, it was always hard to separate. But yes, I think he was looking out for me and wanted me to do well.

B.F. He was *the* hit at the Main Street Jazz Festival. He's the one who had to be there. He was so effervescent and so inclusive.

C.P. And he was playing so well.

B.F. He was, after having lost his teeth.

C.P. Yes; oh, yeah.

B.F. I've often wondered how somebody like you gets noticed by a foreign recording company, like Criss Cross in Denmark. Was it because you were touring with Red?

C.P. I guess so. He kind of kept his ears open as to what was going on in New York. After I started recording, he asked if there was someone he should know about, if there was someone new in town. So, I think he wanted to be in the position similar to that of Alfred Lion at Blue Note, because when Joe Henderson and all those guys were recording for Blue Note, they weren't huge stars at all. You show up, and you make a record in a day, and there it is. Some of those records turn out really well.

B.F. But I assume Criss Cross contacted you.

C.P. Yes, probably because of my work with Red. That's about all I had done professionally, except various little gigs around New York.

B.F. People in the know know of Criss Cross.

C.P. Right.

B.F. But everybody knows of Verve, which is, I believe, your current contract or where you have recorded recently. It's big time. How did you become afflliated with Verve?

C.P. I'm trying to remember. In the interim, I did maybe two records for Criss Cross, then I did a series for Concord. I met them through playing on one of Marian McPartland's records, and then the Verve thing came about because of Jason Olaine, a West Coast fan of mine. I don't know where he first heard me; but when he became an A&R man at Verve, he somehow pushed through a contract with me.[3] Whatever machinations went on in back room I'd rather not know about.

B.F. Were they still Verve U.S.A. then?

C.P. I was signed to Verve U.S. I did one recording directly for them, *Gratitude*. Jason helped with it, and he helped produce the next one, too. But there was a whole thing that went down. They basically got rid of almost all of their jazz roster. They didn't want anything that wouldn't sell a fair amount. I was supposed to record in about a month, but they said that although they wouldn't do it, they would pay for it, which I didn't really appreciate very much. In the meantime, I had gotten to know the guys in France, Verve France. Fortunately they wanted to record me, so now I'm signed with French Verve, and they've been completely great. I hope they're able to continue doing it.

There's been such upheaval in the recording industry because of all the competition from independent labels, things over the Internet, people burning their own CDs, and so forth. Major companies are less and less willing to take risk; it's not the way it used to be. It's even more that way in the pop world, I think. Someone like Joni Mitchell would probably have a really hard time doing what she did in this kind of climate; she'd probably be more of an independent.

So fortunately the guys at Verve France have been really great, and I hope that their supply of money doesn't run out. Verve was originally like Criss Cross is now. They all kind of started out that way: Blue Note, Verve, independent labels that represented someone's dream. Then, they get sold to a large company, and all of a sudden they're part of a huge corporation that is eventually owned by an even bigger corporation that's owned by . . . ultimately, someone says, "Hey, we need to watch the bottom line here." The way it often ends up is that they don't take chances anymore. This is okay because it leaves more to the independents. Maybe with the Internet, the playing field is leveled a little bit.

B.F. Somebody like Charles Mingus, for example, in the early '50s started his own label, Debut.

C.P. Right. A lot more people are doing that now, I think. Ones that are more well known are in a good position because they can have their own label, so they finance their own projects and can get them distributed by a large distributor. I think this is what Herbie Hancock is doing; it's what Dave Holland is doing, as are some other people, such as Ornette Coleman.

B.F. Is Ornette recording these days?

C.P. He hasn't put anything out for a while. I don't really know what he's been up to because the last ones that came out were a couple perhaps four or five years ago. I think that's maybe the last thing, but he was able to get it out through Verve, although it is on his label. If my records go out of print, there's nothing I can do unless I want to buy the tapes from the company, which they're going to charge me a lot of money for.

B.F. So in France you're released on Verve France, and in this country, in the United States, on Sunnyside.

C.P. It gets licensed to Sunnyside because Verve U.S. isn't all that friendly with Verve France.

B.F. But Verve U.S. continues.

C.P. Yes.

B.F. Is Sunnyside a subsidiary of Verve? Or is it independent?

C.P. It's an independent company.

B.F. So they license?

C.P. They license a few different things, yes, and then they also record their own music. I don't really know all that much about exactly who's on the label.

B.F. But you mentioned Concord, between Criss Cross and Verve. As Red was your guide or your entrée into the big time, Marian McPartland was your guide into Concord.

C.P. Yes. I've worked with her a few times over the years. Concord heard me playing with her and expressed interest in signing me. I knew of them as a conservative label in their musical tastes, and I knew I didn't want to do that. I figured I didn't have anything to lose, so I said, "Okay, I'd be happy to record, but I have to have complete say over what music goes on it and who's on it," all that kind of thing. I just expected them to say, "Sorry, no." And they said, "Yes."

B.F. Is "they" Carl Jefferson?[4]

C.P. It was Carl at that time, yes. So he agreed, and I don't know what he thought of the records; but I appreciated that they kept their word.

B.F. Did you meet Marian here in Columbia?

C.P. Yes, I did. This is where I first met her because her radio show was produced here. I'm trying to remember how it's all connected.

B.F. When she began the series *Piano Jazz*, she came to Columbia to record it.

C.P. Right.

B.F. And she would play here occasionally. I think Ambrose Hampton would have her to his home sometimes. She appeared at Main Street Jazz, and maybe at a couple of other venues, but do you recall how you first met?

C.P. I recall it being more of a private party that maybe had to do with the radio. Someone invited me to show up with my horn. I don't remember what the specifics were, but I do remember being at this kind of party and playing some duo with her when I was maybe fifteen.

B.F. She is just such a great ambassador for jazz and such a lovely person.

C.P. She really is; yes, absolutely. I've been on her radio show, too, and I see how she does it. She's so good. They have the two pianos in the studio. There were a couple of things where I played piano with her, and then I think Scott Colley showed up, and we played some stuff with me playing saxophone and him playing bass. Really nice.

B.F. So basically you've had, as a leader, three affiliations: Criss Cross, Concord, and Verve.

C.P. Which is where I am now. More and more, I'm trying to establish my own thing as a leader, being able to work more. I made some albums, but I hadn't really gone on tour or played a whole lot of gigs as a leader until my first Verve record came out, which I think was in 2000. It's definitely not the easiest thing to do if you don't have huge label support, if you're doing it by relying on word of mouth. It still feels like I'm trying to push a boulder up a hill, but I've seen the example of a lot of musicians I really respect who've done the same thing.

I work with Dave Holland, who has been a leader now for thirty-something years, and he really took off only in the past six or seven years. It's been interesting for me to see it because I've been in his quintet now for eight or nine years, and I've seen the level of gigs get bigger and bigger to where now it's mostly concert halls; it's not nearly as many clubs. The money is better. It's interesting to see that progress, because it's the same musicians but somehow it catches on if you just keep persevering. It's the only thing you can do.

B.F. To illustrate your point: in the 1970s, I saw him in Columbia in a duet performance with Sam Rivers. They played at the Golden Spur in the Russell House to perhaps a hundred people.

C.P. And that's just what you go through. I think anyone spending time as a musician in the jazz business sees how it all works. You just realize that everyone's in the same boat, and you can't give up. You have to believe in what you're doing, and to a certain extent you have to put some blinders on. A lot of voices will say, "What are you, nuts?" You just can't afford to listen to them.

B.F. You've played with a lot of impressive leaders. You've been in the Mingus Big Band, for example. How did that come about?

C.P. I don't quite remember. I think somebody recommended me to Sue Mingus when somebody couldn't show up.[5] I don't remember exactly when that was, but I was a regular member of the band for a few years. That's what led to the Steely Dan thing, too. Walter Becker came to hear the Mingus Big Band, and things developed from that. Then, on the recommendation of somebody else, I started playing with Paul Motian. It seemed that after a certain point I just ended up getting called for various things, and I wasn't quite as scuffling or worried as I had been before.

B.F. Did you ever hear Mingus live?

C.P. No.

B.F. I heard him several times. I just love Mingus' music, and especially its texture. There is so much going on, like when George Adams and Don Pullen were there. That is some powerful music.

C.P. Yes. I get the impression that he was not always the easiest guy to get along with, and Sue kept that spirit with the big band by having in it people who had known Mingus and some who had worked with him. It often led to fights between members of the band. When you hear all the anger, that's for real, too. It's just an expression of a certain way of life.

B.F. You make the point that Mingus was mercurial.

C.P. And that comes out in the music. That's part of the beauty.

B.F. It appeals to me, too. What was the mood in the Mingus Big Band? Was it loose, as were Mingus's own groups?

C.P. Yes. It wasn't about real tight ensemble playing. The spirit of it was more important than the playing of every note.

B.F. Did the band use charts?

C.P. Yes, but it's hard to explain. Somehow when it all got put together, it had that kind of sound created by a bunch of guys who are not necessarily getting along— maybe this guy's drunk and this guy's something else. Whatever was going on worked in that particular way.

B.F. You mentioned Mingus as a springboard for your getting to Steely Dan. How long were you with them?

C.P. I toured with them off and on for about two years.

B.F. Was that your steady gig?

C.P. I think there were three or four six-week tours that weren't back-to-back, so I was doing other things. I always admired their music. They're huge jazz fans and are very serious about trying to make their music as good as possible. I remember someone asking Donald Fagen what he tries to do musically. He said that from the beginning he's tried to make records as good as the Duke Ellington records he grew up loving, and that he's still trying. So that's kind of where they're coming from.

B.F. How did life on the road with Steely Dan differ from touring with a jazz group?

C.P. It differs a lot. You get to the hotel and somebody's already brought your suitcase into your room. It's also a little antiseptic because you don't really meet anyone. I realized that you feel a lot more human connection playing in a club with 150 people than playing at Madison Square Garden with 30,000 people. It just becomes a sea; it's not on the human scale anymore. It's just a different feeling that's hard to explain.

B.F. Are there roadies whose job it is to keep the fans at a distance?

C.P. Oh, yes. They don't just let people backstage. So usually, whatever hopes you might have had of the whole rock-and-roll scene, you don't really see that much of it. It seemed like it was just us every day, with the same catering, after a performance saying that we guess we should just go to bed.

B.F. You have been with other significant musicians like James Moody, who goes way back into the 1940s. You mentioned Jim Hall. Another is Joanne Brackeen. Your solo on the album *Pink Elephant Magic* was nominated for a Grammy. How did you link up with her?

C.P. Again, I don't quite recall. I just remember getting a phone call to do a record date. I think that might have been the only time I've played with her. I don't recall playing gigs, although I might have played a couple. She just called me to do that date, and we rehearsed. Her writing is challenging. She's like one chord on top of another chord on top of another chord. Like, wow; what is that? I don't know what that means, and I've been to music school. I just used my ears.

B.F. Did you hang out with her?

C.P. I remember going down to her apartment to look at the music, and I've seen her every now and then.

B.F. You were a finalist in the Monk competition.

C.P. A long time ago.

B.F. That must have been pretty heady experience. Weren't you and Joshua Redman and Eric Alexander the three saxophonists at the end?

C.P. I think I tied for third with Tim Warfield. It had its good and bad parts, which we don't need to go into.

B.F. But you won the Danish Jazzpar Award.

C.P. Which came out of left field. That was very nice. It coincided with my first record, when I started touring Europe as a leader.

B.F. The Jazzpar Award, although not very well known in the United States, is a big deal. It's given for musical accomplishment, but what are the criteria?

C.P. I don't know. It's not something that you can apply for or anything. They just give it every year to whatever musician they see as worthy of more recognition.

B.F. I believe that it generally goes to established, mature musicians. Aren't you the youngest recipient?

C.P. Yes. It was completely a shock, completely out of the blue. It helped me gain a little more confidence, like maybe I should be doing my own thing more. Maybe I should really follow that.

B.F. I believe there's a significant monetary award.

C.P. Yes, it was a fair amount of money.

B.F. Is there a ceremony? Do you receive the award in Denmark?

C.P. Yes. There was a concert with Danish and American musicians performing music I wrote specifically for that occasion. I think the prime minister gave me the award. It was nice. It came at a nice time.

B.F. While the Jazzpar Award was a real highlight, there's something potentially negative, and that is your hearing problem.

C.P. I developed Ménière's disease when I was around twenty-six, about eight or nine years ago. I guess I had been losing some hearing in my left ear, but I didn't really notice it. I noticed that I was asking people what they said more frequently than usual.

B.F. Has it affected your playing?

C.P. Not in any significant way. Initially I freaked out for about a year and was also having a lot of dizzy spells, which also was awful. Knowing that I was losing hearing in one ear, and then also not being sure from one day to the next if I would be able to stand up when it was time to go to the airport to get to the next gig—this was all hard.

B.F. What do the doctors say about your other ear? If one ear is diseased, is the other one susceptible to it?

C.P. It's usually fine; the disease usually just happens in one ear. It was obviously a really hard experience just not knowing what was going to happen and hoping that it didn't happen in my other ear. The doctors say that if it's going to appear in both ears, it usually happens around the same time. So the more time goes by where nothing happens to my good ear, the more out of the woods I am.

B.F. But when you're playing, you need to interact with your fellow musicians.

C.P. I tend to make sure that I set up so I can hear everyone. However, having the disease can be helpful because if I'm playing with a really loud drummer who sets up to my left, he can bash away, and I can still hear everything else that is going on, which I might not be able to do if I had hearing in both ears. It has little advantages in weird ways, such as being able to sleep in loud situations.

B.F. Do you wear a plug in your good ear to protect it when you play?

C.P. Not usually. It's like when you have a cold—you just hear your own voice and everything else sounds kind of quiet. That's kind of the effect of having an earplug while you're actually playing. Now, if it's a really loud situation and I can't get away, I'll take a solo, and I'll get out of the way so I'm not in the middle of it. So it's actually a fairly short amount of time that I'm being subjected to really loud sounds. But if I can't move away from it, then I'll use some kind of an ear plug when I'm not actually playing.

B.F. Has the vertigo subsided over time?

C.P. Yes. I haven't had that for a good seven or eight years.

B.F. Other than not hearing in one ear, the condition seems to have stabilized.

C.P. It's stabilized and has, if anything, made me more determined. I guess when something like that happens, you begin thinking about it all, about mortality, that kind of thing. Man, this is it; I have to just completely go for it because it doesn't last forever.

B.F. On the album of dedications you recorded for Verve, you dedicate the tunes to saxophonists who have been meaningful to you. Two are Coleman Hawkins and Lester Young. They are so different. What do you hear in them?

C.P. Beauty, different kinds of beauty. That's a big challenge, I think, for a young jazz musician today. There's so much music that's been made, there's so much to digest, that to really get into Coleman Hawkins's way of playing the saxophone requires a lot of study. But then to really get the whole thing, you have to do that with so much music. There's so much beautiful music to check out that's beautiful in different ways, that's constructed in a slightly different way.

Listening to Lester Young, Ornette Coleman—these are huge worlds. Weather Report. These are all kinds of music that are part of me now, and even if it's wildly different, you ultimately get an overview and ask, "Why does this work? What are the parameters that he's dealing with? How is he constructing his music and making it beautiful in that way?" Then there's this other person whose music is also beautiful. What is he doing differently? What choices are he making that affect this and that? It's just like Picasso and Rembrandt: which is more beautiful? Maybe at certain times you feel like seeing one more than the other.

B.F. Do you find that people of your generation—musicians, serious musicians, especially saxophonists—know Hawkins and Young, that they've done their homework and know the tradition?

C.P. Oh, yes. It's one thing to have listened to it, but it's another thing to really digest it. I still go through it. I've really spent a lot of time copying all these guys. When I first was listening to Charlie Parker, I wanted to sound just like him. I asked, "How is he doing that?" I want to do it just like that. The same with many of my heroes—trying to actually phrase like they do, getting the sound in your head.

It's one thing to be familiar with it, and it's another thing to have really checked it out in a way that you can kind of do it yourself. And out of all this is how you find your individual voice, I think. We all want to find our individual voice. I think the only real way to do it is to check out everything you can and learn how it's done, then just play normally, and it will come.

B.F. Would you say you have a primary influence?

C.P. I wouldn't know. There are definitely people that are more important to me than others, and there are people that are more important at certain times, such as someone I might be listening to a lot. It's not necessarily a saxophone player, and it's not necessarily jazz. Stravinsky has been a huge influence on a lot of jazz musicians. You might not even hear it, because the situation is so different, but there's a certain esthetic thing about it.

B.F. Those dedications go from Young and Hawkins up to Ornette, the most recent. Do you know Ornette?

C.P. I met him when I first moved to New York, but I wasn't that familiar with his music. I actually went up to his studio, and we just talked for a couple hours, which I wish I could do again. I haven't seen him in a long time. He's an interesting character, too. He has a different way of expressing himself; he talks in riddles. He just thinks in a different way.

B.F. I don't quite understand what he means by "harmolody."[6]

C.P. I don't think anyone does. It's not quite scientific. It doesn't ever seem quite clear. I've asked a lot of people who have worked with Ornette, "What is he talking about?," and everyone has a different answer. I think it's more just a sound in his head than a codified set of rules.

B.F. It works.

C.P. It works. It sounds good. His ears are so good, and you can hear the influences in his playing so strongly: the folk-blues melody thing is so strong, no matter how out it gets. That's what ties it together. He just has such a beautiful sense of melody, I think. And I remember him saying that he was attracted to the saxophone because you can make it sound like a human voice. He said you can really make it sing in a way it's hard to do on some other instruments.

B.F. You mentioned the folksy, bluesy quality. Another saxophonist and clarinetist with those qualities is Jimmy Giuffre. Do you ever listen to him?

C.P. Yes. I've worked a lot with Steve Swallow, too, who worked with him, so we talked a lot about Jimmy.

B.F. To me, Giuffre is a minor major figure.

C.P. Yes. He's not as well known as he should be. His position in jazz history seems to be as an inspirer of other people who perhaps got more famous than he.

B.F. He's probably most famous for having composed "Four Brothers."

C.P. Which is so different from most of his music.

B.F. You're one of an impressive generation of saxophonists. As I listen to that generation, you and James Carter most appeal to me. Do you know Carter?

C.P. Sure.

B.F. Do you hang out at all?

C.P. Yes, I see him from time to time. I've played with him on a few occasions, such as at the Montreal Jazz Festival. He really knows a ton about the saxophone. You'll often find him hanging out at saxophone shops, no matter what town he's in. He collects them; he has a lot of them. He knows a ton about them. He's just way into it.

B.F. To me, he's an impressive player.

C.P. Yes.

B.F. Do you know Joshua Redman? Do all you guys know each other?

C.P. Sure. It's a fairly small world, really. Yeah, sure. I see him every now and then. I like him. He's great.

B.F. One group we haven't talked about is the one at USC, as well as other musicians who played with you early in your career in Columbia. You studied with Doug Graham, didn't you?

C.P. I studied with Doug Graham after Bryson left. He's a fantastic classical clarinet player, really great—one of the best I've ever heard. And he's also just a really fantastic teacher. He's just a really, really amazing guy.

B.F. Do you stay in touch with him?

C.P. I see him every now and then. It's pretty irregular, but every now and then we end up hanging out.

B.F. I saw you play one time at the Koger Center with Terry Rosen.

C.P. I ended up working a lot with him. There was always the Tuesday night group at Pug's, which was Johnny Helms and Terry Rosen and various people for a while —Andy Watson when he lived in town, Frank Duvall, and others. There were a whole bunch of gigs with Teddy Linder. And then, Wednesday nights I played with Jim Mings, usually Teddy, and for a long time it was a bassist named John Schwabe.

So the group on Tuesday night was bebop: Clifford Brown, Max Roach, early Art Blakey, Bird tunes, old standards.[7] Then on Wednesdays with Mings and those guys, we'd do an old standard, then play free for a while, then play a Rolling Stones tune, and then come back. It was really great to have those performance opportunities, to have a chance to play in front of people. I mean, you can practice by yourself, and you just don't learn the same things that you learn when you're playing in front of an audience. Even if they're not paying attention, it's just a whole different thing. You learn a whole different set of skills when performing.

B.F. Then I heard you one night at Hunter Gatherer, sitting in with Skipp Pearson. It was pretty much blues, as I recall.

C.P. Right. With Skipp, there are all these kids coming out to play. It's like a line of saxophone players.

B.F. Do you mean that they're from Columbia?

C.P. Most of them are, or from nearby towns. Whatever Skipp is doing, all these kids show up with horns and sit in on various instruments. They're talented. They're obviously checking out the history of music and trying to learn to play jazz. It's very encouraging.

B.F. Do you mean that they have been students of Skipp's?

C.P. I think most of them have been. I didn't get a chance to really talk to anyone in great detail because music was going on.

B.F. I admire somebody like Skipp, who is essentially a local musician. He's never made it on the national scene; perhaps he never tried to make it. But he plays well, inspires, and keeps the flame burning. Hurrah for him.

C.P. Absolutely. That's what creates a scene: people who really care about it and try to make things happen in their town. It's something I see over and over again. Someone in a town will say, "Man, I am such a big fan. I would love to have these guys come to town." They raise money and do whatever they have to do to make these things happen, and we show up. It seems that jazz relies on grassroots stuff like that. And someone like Skipp creates a scene that has some life to it. That's really what the music needs.

B.F. About money: for years I have heard jazz musicians say the money does not come from recordings. Does it in your case?

C.P. No, usually not. I mean, you make some for doing the record date, but no. Most of it is going out and playing live.

B.F. So you really don't see many royalties from recordings.

C.P. I get royalties from music I have written. I have gotten more and more into composing. A lot of the projects I have coming up, which haven't been recorded yet, are larger group things that I've written. I do see money from that. If you write most of the music on a CD, there are royalties from the sales of the record, which is negotiated into your recording contract. There are also publishing royalties if you write the tune and it goes through your music-publishing company.

Now, a lot of times record companies will insist that it goes through their music publishing company so they get the money, but I've fortunately been able to negotiate. I don't have to do that because my manager and various people have helped in negotiating. So I actually see not a huge amount, but maybe a few thousand a year from music I've written. It's not royalties on the record. You just don't ever expect to see that. But at least it's something.

B.F. I asked that same question of Houston Person, who gave essentially the same answer as you: that there's next to nothing in the recordings, but they offer exposure.

C.P. That's what a recording is for, in a way. Now, we look at it like we're so glad we have these documents of all of these groups playing; but for them, most of the benefit is to get the word out so they can play gigs.

B.F. Since you mentioned composing and Stravinsky, can you ever see yourself doing something classical?

C.P. I would love a chance to write for orchestra. There's a project—a kind of chamber ensemble—I premiered at the Jazz Standard this year: me, bass, drums, nylon-string guitar, flute, clarinet, bassoon, violin, viola, cello.[8] I just always wanted to write for a group like that, a mixture of strings and woodwinds, and a mixture of improvisation and written things.

B.F. Were you pleased with it, the way it came off?

C.P. Yes. I really want to get that recorded because I think I learned a lot about how to use writing, how to think in more of a compositional way even in a smaller group setting. So writing is something I want to explore more and more. That lost money because it's a larger group. You just have to expect it. But in the long run, I think it's something worth pursuing because it's music I really want to get heard. I feel like it turned out well, and I hope I can share it with everyone.

B.F. But I assume that more immediately your goal is to keep your group together, tour, play with Dave Holland, and so forth.

C.P. Yes. It's a balancing act. It ends up meaning that I'm gone a lot because I am doing my own thing and Dave's thing and various other things as they come up, so I end up being out of town maybe a little more than I would be otherwise.

B.F. How often do you get to Columbia?

C.P. Usually just during the holidays. It would be nice to come here more, but it's always like, "Oh, God; I just got off the road and I have to leave again."

Columbia, S.C., 30 December 2005

Notes

1. Potter refers to Gwen Hall.
2. Albert is a fingering system favored by early jazz clarinetists.
3. A&R stands for artists and repertoire.
4. Carl Jefferson founded and operated Concord Jazz Records.
5. Sue Mingus is the widow of Charles Mingus.
6. By "harmolodic" Ornette Coleman means something like fusing harmony and melody through collective improvisation.
7. "Bird" is Charlie Parker.
8. Jazz Standard is a New York club.

DISCOGRAPHY

This discography details the recording sessions mentioned or alluded to in the interviews. The information comes from records and record covers, CDs and inserts, with details about jazz recordings augmented by information from Tom Lord's *The Jazz Discography* (West Vancouver, B.C., Canada: Lord Music Reference, 1992–2001), 26 volumes. For sessions recorded after the publication of volume 26, I used Lord's continuation of the discography on CD-ROM, version 7.0. I arranged the sessions for each musician chronologically. The sequence of information within entries is as follows:

name of the leader (if different from the interviewee; if there are coleaders, I use only the one indicated by a Lord letter)
album title (if originally released as a vinyl album or CD)
personnel and instrumentation
place and date of recording, name of company that first released the music (in parentheses), identifying letters and numbers Lord gives to sessions (those from the CD-ROM are preceded by an asterisk)
selections recorded

All sessions lacking Lord letters and numbers are not included in Lord's discography. Within sessions I do not identify selections on which some of the musicians do not appear. I do not correct tune titles or make uniform their various spellings.

Abbreviations

accor	accordion	drm-cg	conga drum	sax	saxophone
arr	arranger	drm-st	drum set	sax-al	alto saxophone
bj	banjo	eng-hrn	English horn	sax-bs	bass saxophone
bs-el	electric bass	fl	flute	sax-bt	baritone saxophone
cel	celeste	flug	flugelhorn		
cl	clarinet	gtr	guitar	sax-cm	c-melody saxophone
cl-bs	bass clarinet	gtr-el	electric guitar		
cond	conductor	hrmca	harmonica	sax-sp	soprano saxophone
crnt	cornet	key	keyboards		
db	double bass	mello	mellophonium	sax-tn	tenor saxophone
dir	director	org	organ	synt	synthesizer
drm	drums	perc	percussion	tamb	tambourine
drm-bg	bongo drum	pno	piano	tba	tuba
		pno-el	electric piano	tpt	trumpet

trb	trombone	vibr	vibraphone
trb-bs	bass trombone	vln	violin
trb-v	valve trombone	voc	vocals

Tommy Benford

(Benford plays drums on all selections.)

Charlie Skeete
Leonard Davis, Tommy Hodges (tpt);
  Tommy Jones (trb); Gene Johnson (cl,
  sax-alt, sax-bs); Clifton Glover (cl, sax-alt,
  sax-ten); Charlie Skeete (pno); Joe Jones
  (db); Bill Brown (tba)
New York, 8 June 1926 (Edison), S7092
  "Tampeekoe"
  "Deep Henderson"

Jelly Roll Morton
Ward Pinkett (trp); Geechie Fields (trb);
  Omer Simeon (cl); Jelly Roll Morton
  (pno, voc); Lee Blair (bj); Bill Benford
  (tba)
New York, 11 June 1928 (Victor), M10611
  "Georgia Swing"
  "Kansas City Stomp"
  "Shoe Shiner's Drag" ("London Blues")
  "Boogaboo"
  "Shreveport" (2 takes)
  "Mournful Serenade"
  "Honey Babe"
  "Sidewalk Blues"

Jelly Roll Morton
Ward Pinkett, Bubber Miley (trp); Wilbur
  de Paris (trb); Lorenzo Tio (cl); Jelly Roll
  Morton (pno); unknown (bj); Bernard
  Addison (gtr); Bill Benford (tba)
New York, 19 March 1930 (Victor), M10620
  "Little Lawrence"
  "Harmony Blues"

Jelly Roll Morton
Personnel as on previous session, but with
  either Ernie Bullock or Jerry Blake (cl,
  cl-bs) replacing Tio.
New York, 20 March 1930 (Victor), M10621
  "Fussy Mabel"
  "Ponchartrain"

Bubber Miley
Bubber Miley, Ward Pinkett, unknown
  (trp); Wilbur de Paris (trb); Hilton Jeffer-
  son, unknown (cl, sax-al); Happy Cald-
  well (sax-tn); Earl Frazier (pno, cel);
  Bernard Addison, unknown (gtr); Bill
  Benford (tba); Frank Marvin (voc)
New York, 16 May 1930 (Victor), M6689
  "I Lost My Gal from Memphis"
  "Without You, Emaline"

Bubber Miley
Personnel as on previous session, but with
  Buster Bailey (cl, sax-al) and unknown
  (db) added, George Bias (voc) replacing
  Marvin, and Bill Benford out.
New York, 3 July 1930 (Victor), M6690
  "Black Maria"
  "Chinnin' and Chattin' with May"

Jelly Roll Morton
Ward Pinkett (trp); Geechie Fields (trb);
  Albert Nicholas (cl); Jelly Roll Morton
  (pno); Howard Hill (gtr); Pete Briggs
  (tba)
New York, 14 July 1930 (Victor, HJCA,
  Raretone), M10623
  "Low Gravy"
  "Strokin' Away" (2 takes)
  "Blue Blood Blues" (2 takes)
  "Mushmouth Shuffle"

Bubber Miley
Bubber Miley, unknown (trp); Charlie
  Irvis (trb), unknown (trb); Buster Bailey,
  Hilton Jefferson (cl, sax-al); Earl Frazier
  (pno); unknown (db); Edith Wilson (voc)
New York, 11 September 1930 (Victor, but
  unissued), M6691
  "Loving You the Way I Do"
  "The Penalty of Love"

Bubber Miley
Personnel as on previous session.

New York, 17 September 1930 (Victor),
    M6692
    "Loving You the Way I Do"
    "The Penalty of Love"

Coleman Hawkins
Benny Carter (trp, sax-al, arr); André Ekyan
    (sax-al); Alix Combelle (sax-tn, cl); Cole-
    man Hawkins (sax-tn); Stephane Grap-
    pelli (pno); Django Reinhardt (gtr);
    Eugene d'Hellemmes (db)
Paris, 28 April 1937 (Victor, HMV), H2977
    "Honeysuckle Rose"
    "Crazy Rhythm"
    "Out of Nowhere"
    "Sweet Georgia Brown"

Eddie South
Eddie South (vln); David Martin (pno);
    Isadore Langlois (gtr); Paul Cordonnier
    (db); Glee Club (voc)
Hilversum, Holland, 13 March 1938
    (Brunswick), S9559
    "Honeysuckle Rose"
    "On the Sunny Side of the Street"
    "Black Gypsy"
    Unknown title
    "Fiddleditty"

Bill Coleman
Bill Coleman (trp); Edgar Currance (cl,
    sax-tn); John Mitchell (gtr); Wilson Myers
    (db, voc)
Paris, 28 September 1938 (Swing), C4353
    "Way Down Yonder in New Orleans"
    "Sister Kate"

Willie Lewis
Louis Bacon, Henry Mason (trp); Billy
    Burns (trb); Willie Lewis (sax-al, voc);
    Ernst Hollerhagen (cl, sax-al); Johnny
    Russell (cl, sax-tn); Denis Chapelet (sax-
    tn); Alfred Siegrist (pno); Peter Angst
    (gtr); June Cole (db, voc)
Zurich, 19 June 1941 (Elite-Special), L3917
    "What Will I Do?"
    "Happy Feet"
    "Baby, Ain't You Satisfied?"

"Ti-pi-tin"
"Roses of Picardy" (plus 1
    unissued take)
"Les Bateliers de la Volga"
"Lover Come Back to Me"
"Swinging at 'Chez Florence'"
"I Ain't Got Nobody"
"Bacon's Blues"

Willie Lewis
Johnny Russell (sax-tn); Alfred Siegrist
    (accor); Heyo Scholl (gtr); June Cole (db)
Zurich, 19 June 1941 (Elite-Special), L3918
    "Lady Be Good"
    "Chinatown"

Willie Lewis
Louis Bacon, Henry Mason (trp); Billy
    Burns (trb); Willie Lewis (sax-al, voc);
    Ernst Hollerhagen (cl, sax-al); Johnny
    Russell (cl, sax-tn); Denis Chapelet (sax-
    tn); Alfred Siegrist (pno); Peter Angst
    (gtr); June Cole (db, voc)
Zurich, 27 June 1941 (Elite-Special), L3919
    "Christmas Night in Harlem"
    "Ol' Man River"
    "Christopher Columbus"
    "I've Found a New Baby"
    "After You've Gone"
    "Body and Soul"

Willie Lewis
Henry Mason (trp); Johnny Russell (sax-tn);
    Alfred Siegrist (pno); Peter Angst (gtr);
    June Cole (db); Florence Mason (voc)
Zurich, 27 June 1941 (Elite-Special), L3920
    "Margie"
    "Some of These Days"
    "Blue Skies"
    "My Blue Heaven"
    "Avalon"
    "You Can't Stop Me"

Bob Wilber
Henry Goodwin (trp); Jimmy Archey (trb);
    Bob Wilber (sax-sp, cl); Dick Wellstood
    (pno); Pops Foster (db)
New York, 28 April 1949 (Circle), W5366

"Sweet Georgia Brown"
"The Mooche"
"Coal Black Shine"
"Limehouse Blues"
"Zig Zag"
"When the Saints Go Marching In"

Bob Greene
The World of Jelly Roll Morton
Ernie Carson (crnt); Eph Resnick (trb);
  Herb Hall (cl); Bob Greene (pno); Alan
  Cary (gtr); Milt Hinton (db)
New York, c. 1974 (RCA), G5123
  "Mr. Jelly Lord"
  "Someday Sweetheart"
  "Wolverine Blues"
  "Buddy Bolden's Stomp"
  "Steamboat Stomp"
  "Sweet Substitute"
  "Kansas City Stomps"
  "Big Lip Blues"
  "Grandpa's Spells"
  "Winin' Boy Blues"

Bob Greene
Bob Greene's World of Jelly Roll Morton
Ernie Carson (crnt), Bob Conners (trb);
  Herb Hall (cl); Bob Greene (pno); Marty
  Grosz (gtr, bj); John Williams (db)
Hatfield, England, May 1982 (Ghb)
  "My Little Girl"
  "Steamboat Stomp"
  "Just a Closer Walk with Thee"
  "Down in Honky Tonk Town"
  "Jelly Roll Blues"
  "Mr. Jelly Lord"
  "My Gal Sal"
  "Buddy Bolden Blues"
  "You Tell Me Your Dreams"
  "Black Bottom Stomp"
  "Smoke House Blues"
  "The Chant"
  "Winin' Boy Blues"
  "Grandpa's Spells"
  "London Blues" (2 takes)
  "Milenberg Joys"
  "Cannonball Blues"
  "Kansas City Stomps"
  "Til We Meet Again"

Nappy Brown

(With the possible exception of the first session, Brown sings on all selections.)

Jubilators (Selah Jubilee Singers)
Raymond Barnes, Allen Bunn, David
  McNeil, Eugene Mumford, Hadie Rowe,
  Thermon Ruth
New York, October 1950 (Jubilee)
  "Why Not Today?"
  "Down Here I've Done My Best"
  "Sorrow Valley"
  "Since Mother's Gone"

(The only source I can find for this session
does not mention Brown. Soon after the session, the group recorded "Lemon Squeezer,"
which—given the title of Brown's "Lemon
Squeezin' Daddy," written before leaving
for New York—suggests Brown's possible
involvement in the October session. Brown
turned twenty-one that month. See Marv
Goldberg, "The Larks": http://home.att.net/
~marvy42/Larks/larks.html. Goldberg indicates that the group was a sextet and identifies the singers listed here. He also notes that
the lead singers on "Why Not Today?" are
Bunn and Rowe. In the interview, Brown
states that he sings lead on this song.)

The Heavenly Lights
Unknown personnel.
New York, 1954 (Savoy, Regent)
  "Freedom after Awhile"
  "Jesus Said It"
  "Come over Here"
  "Vacation in Heaven"
  "Lord, I'm in Your Hands"

Sam Taylor, Budd Johnson (sax-tn); Maurice Simon (sax-bt); Howard Biggs (pno,
  arr); Mickey Baker (gtr); Abie Baker (db);
  Dave Bailey (drm)
New York, 1 February 1955 (Savoy)
  "Just a Little Love"
  "It's Really You"
  "Don't Be Angry"
  "It's All Yours"

Budd Johnson, Al Sears (sax-tn); George
  Berg (sax-bt); Howard Biggs (pno, arr);
  Everett Barksdale (gtr); Milt Hinton (db);
  Connie Kay (drm)
New York, 8 June 1955 (Savoy)
    "There'll Come a Day"
    "Well, Well, Well, Baby-La"
    "Piddly Patter Patter"
    "Land I Love"

Buster Cooper (trb); Hilton Jefferson (sax-
  al); Budd Johnson (sax-tn); Kelly Owens
  (pno); Skeeter Best (gtr); Leonard Gaskin
  (db); Bobby Donaldson (drm)
New York, 1 October 1957 (Savoy)
    "The Right Time"
    "If You Need Some Lovin'"
    "Because I Love You"
    "Oh, You Don't Know"

Thanks for Nothing
Unknown personnel.
Unknown place and date (c. 1969)
  (Elephant V)
    "So Fine"
    "I Gotta Go"
    "I Done Got over It"
    "I Found It"
    "If I Had My Life to Live Over"
    "The Night Time Is the Right Time"
    "Thanks for Nothing"
    "Forgive Me, Girl"
    "Long Time"

Bell Jubilee Singers
Unknown personnel.
Place and date unknown, though possibly
  recorded in the early 1970s (Jewel)
    "Do You Know the Man from Galilee"

Brother Napoleon Brown and the
  Southern Sisters
When I Get Inside
Willie P. Maxwell, James Maxwell, Margaret
  L. Davis, Charlie Mae Ashby (voc); Mar-
  ian C. Feldon (pno, voc)
Place and date unknown, though the album
  was released in 1977 (Savoy)

    "You Gonna Need a Friend"
    "Let's Go Around the Wall"
    "This May Be My Last Time"
    "When I Get Inside"
    "God Has Been So Good to Me"
    "He Will Provide"
    "Until I Die"
    "It's in My Mind"

I Done Got Over
Willie Cook (trp); Fredrik John (trb); Jan
  Lööf (sax-tn); Per "Slim" Notini (pno,
  arr); Knut Reiersrud (gtr, arr); Bertil Pet-
  tersson (db); Karsten Loly (drm)
Blackeberg, Sweden, 26 February 1983
  (Stockholm Records), *B14120–7
    "That Man"

I Done Got Over
Personnel as on previous session.
Oslo, Norway, 7 March 1983 (Stockholm
  Records), *B14121–7
    "I Done Got Over"
    "Who?"
    "Baby, Let Me Lay It on You"
    "If You Need Some Lovin'"
    "The Land I Love"

I Done Got Over
Personnel as on previous session.
Kristiansand, Norway, 8 March 1983 (Stock-
  holm Records), *B14122–7
    "Well, Well, Well, Baby-La"

I Done Got Over
Personnel as on previous session.
Jönköping, Sweden, 10 March 1983 (Stock-
  holm Records), *B14123–7
    "It's Been a Long Time Coming"
    "Down in the Alley"
    "Going Down Slow"
    "Baby-Cry-Cry-Cry-Baby"

Tore Up
The Heartfixers: Tinsley Ellis (gtr); Wayne
  Burdette (db); Michael McCauley (drm);
  plus Andy Hagan, George Rollins (trp);
  Billy McPherson (sax-tn); Skip Lane

(sax-bt); Scott Alexander (pno); Oliver
Wells (org); Albey Scholl (hrmca); Yon-
rico Scott (drm-cg)
Atlanta, 1984 (Landslide)
    "Who"
    "You Can Make It if You Try"
    "Heartbreak"
    "Lemon Squeezin' Daddy"
    "Jack the Rabbit"
    "Hidden Charms"
    "Losing Hand"
    "Tonight I'll Be Staying Here with You"
    "Hard Luck Blues"
    "Tore up over You"
    "Ain't My Cross to Bear"

Something Gonna Jump out the Bushes!
Kaz Kazanoff (sax-al, sax-tn, sax-bt, arr);
  Mr. Excello, Saxy Boy (sax-tn); Matt
  McCabe (pno); Ron Levy (org, perc);
  Anson Funderburgh, Eugene "High Rise"
  Ross, Ronnie Earl (gtr); Earl King (gtr,
  pno, tamb); Rhandy Simmons (db); Marc
  Wilson (drm); Larry Wallace (perc)
Dallas, April 1987 (Black Top)
    "Have Mercy, Mercy Baby!"
    "Dirty Work"
    "I'm with You All the Way"
    "Something Gonna Jump out the
      Bushes!"
    "You Mean More to Me Than Gold"
    "Flamingo"
    "My Jug and I"
    "Life's Ups and Downs"
    "Your Love Is Real"
    "You Were a Long Time Coming"
    "Nothing Takes the Place of You"
    "I'm Walking out on You"

Gary Erwin (Shrimp City Slim)

(Erwin plays piano or keyboards on all
selections.)

Blue Light Special
Live in Colombia
David Coulter (sax); Silent Eddie Phillips
  (gtr, db); Nik Pappas (gtr, db, voc); Jay
  Niver (drm); Gary Erwin (voc)
Bogota, Colombia, May 1989 (Erwin Music)

    "Just a Little Bit"
    "Cry to Me"
    "Sea Monkey Shuffle"
    "How Blue Can You Get"
    "Just Your Fool"
    "Sitting on Top of the World"
    "Blue Monday"
    "Three Hundred Pounds of Joy"
    "Flip Flop & Fly"

Blue Light Special
Gone with the Wind
Juke Joint Johnny (hrmca, voc); Silent Eddie
  Phillips (gtr); Shrimp City Slim (wash-
  board, voc); Jerry Hiers (db); Jay Niver
  (drm)
Charlotte, N.C., 16–17 March 1992 (Erwin
  Music)
    "Fool for You"
    "Ain't No Future in This Town"
    "Get Ready (To Fall in Love)"
    "In My Sights"
    "The Saddle"
    "Gone with the Wind"
    "God Is Calling"
    "Amazing Grace"
    "Rockin' in My Baby's Arms"
    "Wedding Band Blues"
    "Don't Tell Me (Not to Tell You I Really
      Love You)"
    "Tommy's House"

Blue Light Special
Gone with the Wind
Personnel as on previous session, but with
  Jerome Griffin (db, voc) for Hiers and
  Dudley Birch (drm, voc) for Niver.
Charleston, S.C., 13 May 1995 (Erwin
  Music)
    "Phosphate Woman"
    "Sticky Fingers"

Wanda Johnson
Call Me Miss Wanda
Chuck Morris (hrmca, voc); Silent Eddie
  Phillips (gtr); Shrimp City Slim (voc,
  gtr); John Etheridge (drm, voc); Cup
  Brothers (handclaps); Wanda Johnson
  (voc)

Johns Island, S.C., 24–28 August 2003
   (Erwin Music)
     "Can You Handle This?"
     "The River"
     "Always"
     "If I Rise in the Morning"
     "I Need You"
     "Finally Home"
     "I Apologize"
     "Airport Road"
     "Bad Case of the Blues"
     "I'm Through with You"
     "Switch Me Over"
     "Breakin' Out"

Wanda Johnson
Natural Resource
Mike Kincaid (sax-tn, sax-bt); Silent Eddie
   Phillips, Shrimp City Slim (gtr, voc);
   Jerome Griffin (db, voc); LaMont Garner
   (drm, voc); Wanda Johnson (voc)
Johns Island, S.C., 13–16 January 2006
   (Erwin Music)
     "Natural Resource"
     "Hot Potato"
     "Heading North"
     "Drop in the Bucket"
     "Lovely on the Water"
     "It's Good"
     "Mama's Recipe"
     "Blue Ain't Nothin' but a Color"
     "It's So Nice to Have Someone"
     "Just Tell Me"
     "Bath Water"
     "Time to Get over You"
     "Enjoy the Ride"
     "Behind a Cloud"

Ron Free

(Free plays drums on all selections.)

Chris Connor
Chris Connor Sings the George Gershwin
   Almanac of Song
Herbie Mann (fl); Ralph Sharon (pno, cel,
   arr); Barry Galbraith (gtr); Oscar Petti-
   ford (db); Chris Connor (voc)
New York, 7 February 1957 (Atlantic),
   C5361

     "I've Got Beginner's Luck"
     "Slap That Bass"
     "For You, For Me, For Evermore"
     "Love Is Sweeping the Country"

Sal Salvador
A Tribute to the Greats
Eddie Costa (pno, vibr); Sal Salvador (gtr);
   Sonny Dallas (db); George Roumanis
   (arr)
New York, 3–5 June 1957 (Bethlehem), S374
     "Artistry in Rhythm"
     "Cool Eyes"
     "Four Brothers"
     "In Your Own Sweet Way"
     "Manteca"
     "Prelude to a Kiss"
     "Ruby My Dear"
     "Solo for Guitar"
     "Taps Miller"
     "Walkin' Shoes"
     "Yardbird Suite"

Mose Allison
Ramblin' with Mose
Mose Allison (pno, voc); Addison Farmer
   (db)
Hackensack, N.J., 18 April 1958 (Prestige),
   A1779
     "Saritha"
     "Stranger in Paradise"
     "Ingenue"
     "You Belong to Me"
     "Old Man John"
     "Ramble"
     "The Minstrels"
     "I've Got a Right to Cry"
     "Ol' Devil Moon"
     "Kissin' Bug"

Mose Allison
Creek Bank
Personnel as on previous session.
Hackensack, N.J., 15 August 1958 (Prestige),
   A1780
     "Creek Bank"
     "Moon and Cypress"
     "Mule"
     "Dinner on the Ground"

"Prelude to a Kiss"
"If I Didn't Care"
"Cabin in the Sky"
"If You Live"
"The Seventh Son"
"Yardbird Suite"

Mose Allison
Autumn Song
Personnel as on previous session.
Hackensack, N.J., 13 February 1959
  (Prestige), A1781
    "Spires"
    "Promenade"
    "It's Crazy"
    "Autumn Song"
    "The Devil in the Cane Field"
    "Strange"
    "That's All Right"
    "Do Nothin' till You Hear from Me"
    "Eyesight to the Blind"
    "Groovin' High"

Lee Konitz
Lee Konitz Meets Jimmy Giuffre
Lee Konitz, Hal McKusick (sax-al); Warne
  Marsh, Ted Brown (sax-tn); Jimmy Giuf-
  fre (sax-bt, arr); Bill Evans (pno); Buddy
  Clark (db)
New York, 12–13 May 1959 (Verve), K3496
    "Moonlight in Vermont"
    "The Song Is You"
    "Somp'm outa' Nothin'"
    "Uncharted"
    "Someone to Watch over Me"
    "Palo Alto"
    "When Your Lover Has Gone"
    "Cork 'n' Bib"
    "Darn That Dream"

Dizzy Gillespie

(Gillespie plays trumpet on all selections.)

Teddy Hill
Shad Collins (trp); Bill Dillard (trp, voc);
  Dickie Wells (trb); Russell Procope (cl,
  sax-al); Howard Johnson (sax-al); Teddy
  Hill, Robert Carroll (sax-tn); Sam Allen

(pno); John Smith (gtr); Richard Full-
  bright (db); Bill Beason (drm)
New York, 17 May 1937 (Bluebird), H5781
    "San Anton'"
    "I'm Happy, Darling, Dancing
      with You"
    "Yours and Mine"
    "I'm Feeling Like a Million"
    "King Porter Stomp"
    "Blue Rhythm Fantasy"

Cab Calloway
Mario Bauza, Lammar Wright (trp); Claude
  Jones, Keg Johnson, DePriest Wheeler
  (trb); Jerry Blake, Andrew Brown (cl, sax-
  al); Chu Berry, Walter Thomas (sax-tn);
  Benny Payne (pno); Danny Barker (gtr);
  Milt Hinton (db); Cozy Cole (db); Cab
  Calloway (voc)
New York, 30 August 1939 (Vocalion,
  Meritt), C571
    "For the Last Time I Cried over You"
    "Twee-Twee-Tweet"
    "Pluckin' the Bass" (2 takes)
    "I Ain't Getting' Nowhere Fast"

(From 30 August 1939 through 10 September 1941, Gillespie recorded eighteen sessions with Calloway. I include only the first
of them. For full details, see Lord C571,
C573–83, C585–90.)

After Hours
Unknown (trp); Don Byas, Chu Berry (sax-
  tn); unknown (pno); Nick Fenton (db);
  Kenny Clarke (drm)
New York, May 1941 (Musidisc, Esoteric),
  G1635
    "Stardust"

After Hours
Kenny Kersey (pno); Nick Fenton (db);
  Kenny Clarke (drm)
New York, May 1941 (Musidisc, Esoteric),
  G1636
    "Stardust"
    "Kerouac"

(Sessions G1635–36, recorded at Minton's Playhouse in Harlem, have no leader. Some sources list Gillespie as playing on "Up on Teddy's Hill," recorded at Minton's Playhouse in May 1941 [C2955], with personnel probably drawn from Joe Guy, Hot Lips Page [trp], Don Byas, Kermit Scott [sax-tn]; Thelonious Monk [pno]; Charlie Christian [gtr]; Nick Fenton [db]; Kenny Clarke or Harold "Doc" West [drm].)

Sarah Vaughan
Aaron Sachs (cl); Georgie Auld (sax-tn); Leonard Feather, Dizzy Gillespie (pno); Chuck Wayne (gtr); Jack Lesberg (db); Morey Feld (drm); Sarah Vaughan (voc)
New York, 31 December 1944 (Continental, Remington), V882
   "Signing Off"
   "Interlude"
   "No Smoke Blues" (2 takes)
   "East of the Sun"

Slim Gaillard
Charlie Parker (sax-al); Jack McVea (sax-tn); Dodo Marmarosa (pno); Slim Gaillard (gtr, pno, voc); Bam Brown (db, voc); Zutty Singleton (drm)
Hollywood, probably 29 December 1945 (Pol Special, BelTone, Halo, Alamac), G82
   "Dizzy Boogie" (2 takes)
   "Flat Foot Floogie" (2 takes)
   "Popity Pop"
   "Slim's Jam"

Charlie Parker (sax-al); Lucky Thompson (sax-tn); Milt Jackson (vibr); Al Haig (pno); Ray Brown (db); Stan Levey (drm); Dizzy Gillespie (voc)
Los Angeles, 24 January 1946 (MeexaDiscox), G1643
   "Salt Peanuts"

Personnel as on previous session, but with Jackson out, George Handy (pno) replacing Haig, and Arv Garrison (gtr) added.

Glendale, Calif., 5 February 1946 (Dial), G1644
   "Diggin' Diz"

Don Byas (sax-tn); Milt Jackson (vibr); Al Haig (pno); Bill DeArango (gtr); Ray Brown (db); J. C. Heard (drm)
New York, 22 February 1946 (Victor), G1646
   "52nd Street Theme" (2 takes)
   "Night in Tunisia" (2 takes, 1 incomplete)
   "Ol' Man Rebop"
   "Anthropology" (2 takes)

Dave Burns, Elmon Wright, Matthew McKay, Ray Orr (trp); Taswell Baird, Bill Shepherd (trb); John Brown, Howard Johnson (sax-al); James Moody, Joe Gayles (sax-tn); Cecil Payne (sax-bt); John Lewis (pno, arr); Milt Jackson (vibr); John Collins (gtr); Ray Brown (db); Joe Harris (drm,); Dizzy Gillespie, Kenny Hagood (voc)
New York, 22 August 1947 (Victor), G1657
   "Ow!"
   "Oop-Pop-a-Da"
   "Two Bass Hit"
   "Stay on It"

Dave Burns, Elmon Wright, Benny Bailey, Lammar Wright (trp); Bill Shepherd, Ted Kelly (trb); John Brown, Howard Johnson (sax-al); Joe Gayles, Big Nick Nicholas (sax-tn); Cecil Payne (sax-bt); John Lewis (pno); Al McKibbon (db); Kenny Clarke (drm); Chano Pozo (drm-bg, drm-cg, voc); Dizzy Gillespie, Kenny Hagood (voc); Tadd Dameron, George Russell, Gil Fuller, Linton Garner (arr)
New York, 22 December 1947 (Victor), G1664
   "Algo Bueno" ("Woody'n You")
   "Cool Breeze"
   "Cubana Be"
   "Cubana Bop"

Personnel as on previous session.
New York, 30 December 1947 (Victor),
   G1665
      "Manteca"
      "Good Bait"
      "Ool-Ya-Koo"
      "Minor Walk"

Willie Cook, Dave Burns, Elmon Wright
   (trp); Andy Duryea, Sam Hurt, Jesse Tarrant (trb); John Brown, Ernie Henry (sax-
   al); Joe Gayles, Budd Johnson (sax-tn);
   Cecil Payne (sax-bt); James Foreman
   (pno, cel); Al McKibbon (db); Teddy
   Stewart (drm); Sabu Martinez (drm-bg,
   voc); Joe Harris (drm-cg); Dizzy Gillespie
   (voc); Gerald Wilson (arr)
New York, 29 December 1948 (Victor),
   G1675
      "Guarachi Guaro"
      "Duff Capers"
      "Lover Come Back to Me"
      "I'm Be Boppin' Too" (2 takes)

Benny Harris, Willie Cook (trp); Andy
   Duryea, Sam Hurt, Jesse Tarrant (trb);
   John Brown, Ernie Henry (sax-al); Joe
   Gayles, Bill Evans (Yusef Lateef) (sax-tn);
   Al Gibson (sax-bt); James Foreman (pno,
   cel); Al McKibbon (db); Teddy Stewart
   (drm); Vince Guerra (drm-cg); Johnny
   Hartman (voc); Budd Johnson, Gil Fuller,
   Dizzy Gillespie, Jimmy Mundy (arr)
New York, 14 April 1949 (Victor), G1678
      "Swedish Suite"
      "St. Louis Blues"
      "I Should Care"
      "That Old Black Magic"

Personnel as on previous session, but with
   Joe Carroll and Dizzy Gillespie (voc)
   added.
Possibly Chicago, 6 May 1949 (Victor, RCA
   Bluebird), G1679
      "Katy"
      "Jump Did-Le Ba"
      "You Go to My Head"

Benny Harris, Elmon Wright, Willie Cook
   (trp); Andy Duryea, Charles Greenlee, J. J.
   Johnson (trb); John Brown, Ernie Henry
   (sax-al); Joe Gayles, Bill Evans (Yusef
   Lateef) (sax-tn); Al Gibson (sax-bt);
   James Foreman (pno, cel); Al McKibbon
   (db); Teddy Stewart (drm); Joe Carroll,
   Dizzy Gillespie, Johnny Hartman (voc);
   George Handy (arr)
New York, 6 July 1949 (Victor), G1683
      "Hey Pete, Let's Eat Mo' Meat!"
      "Jumpin' with Symphony Sid"
      "If Love Is Trouble"
      "In the Land of Oo-Bla-Dee"

John Coltrane (sax-al, sax-tn); Milt Jackson
   (vibr, pno); Kenny Burrell (gtr); Percy
   Heath (db); Kansas Fields (drm); Calypso
   Boys (drm-cg, maracas); Fred Strong
   (voc)
Detroit, 1 March 1951 (Dee Gee), G1695
      "Love Me"
      "We Love to Boogie"
      "Tin Tin Deo"
      "Birk's Works"

J. J. Johnson (trb); Budd Johnson (sax-tn);
   Milt Jackson (vibr, pno); Dizzy Gillespie
   (pno); Percy Heath (db); Art Blakey
   (drm); Joe Carroll, Melvin Moore (voc)
New York, 16 April 1951 (Dee Gee), G1697
      "Lady Be Good"
      "Love Me Pretty Baby"
      "The Champ"

Bill Graham (sax-bt); Milt Jackson (pno);
   Percy Heath (db); Al Jones (drm); Joe
   Carroll, Dizzy Gillespie, Melvin Moore
   (voc)
New York, 16 August 1951 (Dee Gee, Savoy),
   G1699
      "I'm in a Mess"
      "School Days"
      "Swing Low Sweet Cadillac"
      "Bopsie's Blues" (2 takes)
      "I Couldn't Beat the Rap"

Bill Graham (sax-bt); Stuff Smith (vln); Milt Jackson (pno, voc); Percy Heath (db); Al Jones (drm); unknown (perc); Joe Carroll, Dizzy Gillespie (voc)
New York, 25 October 1951 (Dee Gee, Savoy), G1700
    "Caravan" (2 takes)
    "Nobody Knows the Trouble I've Seen"
    "The Bluest Blues"
    "On the Sunny Side of the Street"
    "Stardust"
    "Time on My Hands"

Bill Graham (sax-bt); Wynton Kelly (pno); Bernie Griggs (db); Al Jones (drm); Joe Carroll, Dizzy Gillespie (voc)
New York, 18 July 1952 (Dee Gee), G1709
    "Blue Skies"
    "Umbrella Man"
    "Pop's Confessin'"
    "Oo-Shoo-Be-Doo-Bee"
    "They Can't Take That Away from Me"

Dick Goodwin

(Except as noted, Goodwin plays trumpet on all selections.)

Dick Goodwin Jazz Quintet
Dick Goodwin (db, voc, arr, miscellaneous instruments); Paul Ostermayer (saxes, fl); Jim Mings (gtr); David Sloan (db); Jim Hall (drm, perc)
Martinez, Ga., July 1978 (no label)
    "The Old Wine Bottle"
    "Harshly, As in a Morning Freight Train"
    "Little Liza Jane"
    "April 30th"
    "When He Gets Sweaty His Glasses Slide Down His Nose Blues"
    "The Sheik of Araby"
    "Ja-Da"
    "Lickety Split"
    "Xalapa"
    "The American Patrol March"
    "Ann Street"

USC Faculty Jazz Quintet
Palomar Transport to the Silver Saddle
Doug Graham (sax-al, cl); John Emche (pno); Bob Burns (db); Jim Hall (drm)
Columbia, S.C., 7, 19 November 1980 (University of South Carolina Recordings)
    "Sarah's Song"
    "Pony Show"
    "Funk Fite"

(Goodwin does not play on other selections from this album.)

Studio Time
Doug Graham (saxes, cl); Dick Goodwin (key); Dwight Spencer (gtr); Terry Trentham (bs-el); Jim Hall (drm)
Columbia, S.C., 2001 (South Carolina Commercial Music Productions), *G4431–7
    "I've Found a New Baby"
    "The Provincial Correspondent (to the Wall Street Journal)"
    "Shiny Stockings" (Goodwin on keyboards only)
    "Just a Closer Walk"
    "Miss Information"
    "Waltz for a Princess" (Goodwin on keyboards only)
    "Tangerine"
    "Jobim's Closet"
    "Sugar Blues"
    "Lovely in Leather"
    "Young Brother"
    "China Boy"
    "I'll Be Seeing You" (Goodwin plays keyboards only.)

Studio Time 2
Charlie Polk, Dave Allison (trp, flug); Bruce Clark, Ashley Fleshman (trb); Ed Craft (trb-bs); Kevin Jones (trb, sax-tn); Doug Graham (sax-al, cl); Dick Goodwin (key, voc); Dwight Spencer (gtr); Terry Trentham (bs-el); Jim Hall (drm); Kristi Kirk Hood, John Wilkinson (voc)
Columbia, S.C., 2006 (South Carolina Commercial Music Productions)
    "The Sheik of Araby"

"100 in the Shade"
"When You're Smiling"
"Shannon's Song"
"It's All Right with Me"
"The Very Thought of You"
"Little Liza Jane"
"The Improbable Love Life of Acapulco
  Goldstein"
"Since I Fell for You"
"I Heard It through the Grapevine"
"Lady on the Mountain"
"Crash Jr."
"Come Rain or Come Shine"
"Diz"
"Saint James Infirmary"
"Ory's Creole Trombone"

Johnny Helms

(Helms plays trumpet on all selections.)

Perdido: Columbia Art Museum
Clark Terry (trp); Bucky Pizzarelli (gtr)
Columbia, S.C., 28 April 1974 (private
  recording)
  "Perdido"
  "I Can't Get Started"
  "Now's the Time"

Jack Howe

(Howe's recordings are difficult to document. Lord includes slightly more than half
of them. The fullest, most reliable source
of information other than the recordings
themselves is Howe's *Friends with Pleasure:
A History of the Sons of Bix* [privately distributed by Howe, n.d.], though it is not
always clear. Whenever a discrepancy exists
between Howe and Lord, I use Howe's
information. Although Howe mentions or
alludes to the following sessions, I include
so many of them—all the More Informal
Sessions dates on which he plays and of
which I am aware, for example—because so
little is known about them. Because I have
not heard all these recordings, I do not
know if Howe appears on every selection.)

Princeton Triangle Jazz Band (also known as
  the Equinox Orchestra)
Bill Priestley (crnt, gtr); Brainerd Kremer
  (cl, sax-al); Philip Nash, Jack Howe (sax-
  tn); Squirrel Ashcraft (accor); DeFord
  Swann (pno); Doug MacNamara (db);
  Palmer Lathrop (tba, db); Bob Bole (drm)
New York, 31 March 1928 (Columbia),
  P6215
  "You Know Who"
  "Everybody and You"
  "China Boy"
  "That's a Plenty"

Squirrel Ashcraft
Jimmy McPartland, Paul Mares (trp);
  Bobby Hackett (crnt); Bill Priestley (crnt,
  gtr); Bud Wilson (trb); Rosy McHargue,
  Joe Rushton, Jack Howe (cl); Squirrel
  Ashcraft, Jack Gardner, Roy Bargy, Floyd
  Bean (pno); George Barnes, Howard
  Kennedy (gtr); Orm Downes, Hank Isaacs
  (drm); Johnny Mercer (voc)
Various locations(?), 1930s (More Informal
  Sessions)
  "Jazz Me Blues"
  "What Is This Thing Called Love?"
  "I Cried for You"
  "Whistle While You Work"
  "Blue Skies"
  "Glory Cloud"
  "China Boy"
  "Lord, I Give You My Children"
  "Darkness on the Delta"
  "I Know That You Know"
  "Rock-a-Bye Baby"
  "Gum"
  "Till We Meet Again"

Squirrel Ashcraft
Bill Priestley (crnt); Bud Wilson (trb);
  Joe Rushton, Jack Howe (cl); Squirrel
  Ashcraft (pno); Howard Kennedy (gtr)
Chicago, 1947 (Paramount, Private Issue),
  A4057
  "Sunday"
  "Muskrat Ramble"
  "I Only Want a Buddy"

"Riverboat Shuffle"
"That's a Plenty" (2 takes)
"Manhattan"
"Jazz Me Blues"
"What's the Use"
"Farewell Blues"
"Embraceable You"
"Me and the Ghost Upstairs"
"Susie"
"You Took Advantage of Me"
"Everybody and You"
"Poor Butterfly"
"Bourre"
"I Found a New Baby"
"Out of Nowhere"
"My Baby's Lovin' Arms"

Squirrel Ashcraft
Jimmy McPartland (crnt); Bill Priestley
    (crnt, gtr); Bud Wilson (trb); Jack Howe
    (cl); Spencer Clark (sax-bs); Squirrel
    Ashcraft, Jack Gardner, Marian McPart-
    land (pno); Hoyt Smith (drm)
Chicago, July 1950 (Paramount)
    "That's a Plenty"
    "Manhattan"
    "Jazz Me Blues"
    "What's the Use"
    "Farewell Blues"
    "Embraceable You"
    "Me & the Ghost Upstairs"
    "You Took Advantage of Me"
    "Suzie"
    "Everybody and You"
    "Poor Butterfly"
    "Bouree"
    "I Found a New Baby"
    "Out of Nowhere"
    "My Honey's Loving Arms"

Squirrel Ashcraft
Doc Evans (crnt); Bill Priestley (crnt, gtr);
    Bud Wilson (trb); Jack Howe (cl); Spencer
    Clark (sax-bs); Squirrel Ashcraft, Jack
    Gardner (pno); Howard Kennedy (gtr)
Chicago, 2–4 July 1951 (Paramount), A4058
    "Bill's Guitar"
    "Squeeze Me"

"Talk of the Town"
"Fidgety Feet"
"Baby Won't You Please Come Home"
"Riverboat Shuffle"
"Clarinet Marmalade"

Squirrel Ashcraft
The 3rd Squirrel
Bill Priestley (crnt, gtr); George Kenyon (tpt,
    crnt, mello); Bud Wilson, Tommy Dorsey
    (trb); Jack Howe (cl); Spencer Clark (sax-
    bs); Jarvis Fernsworth, Jack Gardner
    (pno); Squirrel Ashcraft (pno, voc);
    Howard Kennedy, Doc Schliesman (gtr);
    Phil Atwood (db); Duke Morris (drm)
Chicago, 4 July 1952 (Paramount), A4059
    "TD's DT's"
    "Baby Please!"
    "Coquette"

(Howe does not play on other selections
from this session.)

Squirrel Ashcraft
The 4th Festival
Eston Spurrier (crnt); George Kenyon (crnt,
    mello); Bill Priestley (crnt, gtr); Bud Wil-
    son (trb); Jack Howe (cl); Avery Sherry
    (sax-al); Spencer Clark (sax-bs); Squirrel
    Ashcraft, Phil Nash (pno); Howard
    Kennedy (gtr); Phil Atwood (db); Freddie
    Wacker (drm)
Chicago, 3–5 July 1953 (Paramount), A4060
    "Emmaline"
    "Farewell Blues"
    "Blue Room"
    "Da Da Strain"
    "Shiek"

(Howe does not play on other selections
from these sessions.)

Sons of Bix
Unknown album title
Max Kaminsky (tpt); Tom Pletcher (crnt);
    Bud Wilson (trb); Ron Hockett (cl); Jack
    Howe (sax-tn); Spencer Clark (sax-bs);
    Squirrel Ashcraft, Marsh Sprague (pno);

Bill Priestley (gtr); Doug James (drm)
Princeton, N.J., 1975 (More Informal
   Sessions)
   "The Sheik"
   "Japanese Sandman"
   "East of the Sun"
   "Jazz Me Blues"
   "Three Blind Mice"
   "Only Want a Buddy"
   "Suzie"
   "Riverboat Shuffle"
   "Singing the Blues"

Unknown album title
Tom Pletcher (crnt); Bud Wilson (trb); Ron
   Hockett (cl); Jack Howe (sax-tn); Spencer
   Clark (sax-bs); Squirrel Ashcraft (pno);
   Bill Priestley (gtr); Cliff Leeman (drm)
Princeton, N.J., 1976 (More Informal
   Sessions)
   "China Boy"
   "Poor Butterfly"
   "Strutting with Some Barbecue"
   "Tea for Two"
   "I Can't Believe"
   "Fidgety Feet"
   "Japanese Sandman"
   "After You've Gone"

Sons of Bix
Unknown album title
Tom Pletcher (crnt); Bud Wilson (trb); Ron
   Hockett (cl); Jack Howe (sax-tn); Spencer
   Clark (sax-bs); Squirrel Ashcraft, Mike
   Katz (pno); Bill Priestley (gtr); Bob Hag-
   gart (db); Tom Martin (drm)
Princeton, N.J., 1977 (More Informal
   Sessions)
   "Margie"
   "Song of the Wanderer"
   "My Gal Sal"
   "There'll Be Some Changes Made"
   "Blue Skies"
   "You Took Advantage of Me"
   "Way Down Yonder in New Orleans"
   "Clementine"
   "I Found a New Baby"

Maxine Sullivan
We Just Couldn't Say Goodbye
Ernie Carson (crnt); Jack Howe (sax-tn);
   Spencer Clark (sax-bt); Art Hodes (pno,
   arr); Johnny Haynes (db); Tom Martin
   (drm); Maxine Sullivan (voc)
Columbia, S.C., 6 February 1978 (Audio-
   phile), S13038
   "We Just Couldn't Say Goodbye"
   "Someday Sweetheart"
   "Exactly Like You"
   "That Old Feeling"
   "Miss Otis Regrets"
   "I'm Gonna Sit Right Down and Write
      Myself a Letter"
   "I Gotta Right to Sing the Blues"
   "He's Funny That Way"
   "St. Louis Blues"
   "Between the Devil and the Deep
      Blue Sea"
   "Legalize My Name"
   "You Were Meant for Me"

Sons of Bix
Unknown album title
Tom Pletcher (crnt); Ron Hockett (cl); Jack
   Howe (sax-tn); Spencer Clark (sax-bs);
   Squirrel Ashcraft, Mike Katz (pno); Bill
   Priestley (gtr); Bob Haggart (db); Doug
   James (drm)
Princeton, N.J., 1978 (More Informal
   Sessions)
   "Goody, Goody"
   "Blue Room"
   "S'Wonderful"
   "My Honey's Lovin' Arms"
   "Ain't Misbehavin'"
   "Just a Closer Walk with Thee"
   "Cherry"
   "It Had to Be You"
   "Someday You'll Be Sorry"
   "Oh, Baby"

Sons of Bix
Princeton Bix Festival 1979
Jackson Howe (tpt); Tom Pletcher (crnt);
   Bud Wilson (trb); Ron Hockett (cl); Jack
   Howe (sax-tn); Spencer Clark (sax-bs);

Squirrel Ashcraft, Mike Katz (pno); Bill Priestley (gtr); Bob Haggart (db); Doug James (drm)

Princeton, N.J., 7–8 June 1979 (More Informal Sessions), S9394

"At the Jazz Band Ball"
"At Sundown"
"Wolverine Blues"
"I'll Be a Friend with Pleasure"
"Nobody's Sweetheart"
"Swing That Music"
"Ja-Da"
"Farewell Blues"

Sons of Bix
Princeton Bix Festival 1980
Jackson Howe (tpt); Tom Pletcher, Dave Jellema (crnt); Bud Wilson (trb); Ron Hockett (cl); Jack Howe (sax-tn); Spencer Clark (sax-bs); Squirrel Ashcraft, Mike Katz (pno); Bill Priestley (gtr); Bob Haggart (db); Doug James (drm); Maxine Sullivan (voc)

Princeton, N.J., 6–7 June 1980 (More Informal Sessions), F1010, S9396

"'S Wonderful"
"Sunday"
"Just One of Those Things"
"I Could Write a Book"
"We Just Couldn't Say Goodbye"
"Back Home Again in Indiana"
"Singing the Blues"
"Coquette"
"I Never Knew"

Bob Haggart
Bob Haggart Makes a Sentimental Journey
Tom Pletcher (crnt); Joe Robertson (trb); Tom Gwaltney (cl); Jack Howe (sax-tn); Spencer Clark (sax-bs); Dill Jones (pno); Bob Haggart (db); Tom Martin (drm)

New York, November 1980 (Jazzology), H244

"Sentimental Journey"
"Mandy, Make up Your Mind"
"It's the Talk of the Town"
"I Can't Believe That You're in Love with Me"

"Exactly Like You"
"'Deed I Do"
"Someday Sweetheart"
"Beale Street Blues"
"Deep Down South"
"Sheik of Araby"

Bob Haggart
Carolina in the Morning
Tom Pletcher (crnt); Mike Katz (trb-v); Ron Hockett, Bill Rappaport (cl); Jack Howe (sax-tn); Spencer Clark (sax-bs); Dill Jones (pno); Bob Haggart (db); Tom Martin (drm)

New York, April 1981 (Jazzology), H245

"On a Slow Boat to China"
"It Happened in Monterrey"
"I Never Knew"
"Carolina in the Morning"
"Way Down Yonder in New Orleans"
"Oh! Baby"
"June Night"
"Mississippi Mud"
"Louisiana"
"Song of the Wanderer"

Sons of Bix
1981 Princeton Bix Festival
Tom Pletcher, Dave Jellema (crnt); Mike Katz (trb); Tom Gwaltney (cl); Ron Hockett (cl, sax-cm); Jack Howe (sax-tn); Spencer Clark (sax-bs); Dill Jones (pno); Bill Priestley (gtr); Bob Haggart (db); Doug James (drm)

Princeton, N.J., 4–6 June 1981 (More Informal Sessions), S9397

"Everybody Loves My Baby"
"What's New?"
"I'll Be a Friend with Pleasure"
"Lady Be Good"
"Mandy"
"Mack the Knife"
"Moonglow"

Sons of Bix
Unknown album title
Tom Pletcher (crnt); Joe Robertson (trb); Tom Gwaltney (cl); Jack Howe (sax-tn);

Spencer Clark (sax-bs); Dill Jones (pno);
    Bob Haggart (db); Tom Martin (drm)
Pinehurst, N.C., early 1980s (More Informal
    Sessions)
        "Sentimental Journey"
        "Mandy"
        "I Can't Believe"
        "'Deed I Do"
        "Exactly Like You"
        "Someday Sweetheart"
        "Beale Street Blues"
        "Deep Down South"
        "The Sheik"

Sons of Bix
Unknown album title
Tom Pletcher (crnt); Mike Katz (trb); Tom
    Gwaltney, Bill Rappaport (cl); Jack Howe
    (sax-tn); Spencer Clark (sax-bs); Dill Jones
    (pno); Bob Haggart (db); Tom Martin
    (drm)
Pinehurst, N.C., early or mid 1980s (More
    Informal Sessions)
        "Slow Boat to China"
        "It Happened in Monterey"
        "Way Down Yonder in New Orleans"
        "I Never Knew"
        "Oh, Baby"
        "Carolina in the Morning"
        "June Night"
        "Mississippi Mud"
        "Louisiana"
        "Song of the Wanderer"

Bob Haggart
A Portrait of Bix
Tom Pletcher (crnt); Ron Hockett (cl, sax-
    cm); Jack Howe (sax-tn); Spencer Clark
    (sax-bs); Mike Katz (pno); Bob Haggart
    (db); Doug James (drm)
Atlanta, March 1986 (Jazzology), H246
        "In a Mist" (intro)
        "Dardanella"
        "Peg o' My Heart"
        "Clementine"
        "Blue River"
        "There'll Come a Time"
        "I Need Some Pettin'"
        "Louise"

        "Davenport Blues"
        "You Took Advantage of Me"
        "Somebody Stole My Gal"
        "In a Mist" (coda)

Etta Jones

(Jones sings on all selections.)

Joe Thomas (tpt); Barney Bigard (cl);
    Georgie Auld (sax-al, sax-tn); Leonard
    Feather (pno); Chuck Wayne (gtr); Billy
    Taylor (db); Stan Levey (drm)
New York, 29 December 1944 (Black &
    White), J4523
        "Salty Papa Blues"
        "Evil Gal Blues"
        "Blow Top Blues"
        "Long, Long Journey"

Floyd "Horsecollar" Williams
Jesse Drakes (tpt); Joe Evans, Floyd "Horsec-
    ollar" Williams (sax-al); Johnny Hartzfield
    (sax-tn); Duke Jordan (pno); Gene Ramey
    (db); J. C. Heard (drm)
New York, January or February 1945
    (Chicago), W6194
        "You Ain't Nothin,' Baby"

(Jones does not sing on other selections from
this session.)

Pete Johnson
Hot Lips Page (tpt); Clyde Bernhardt (trb);
    Don Stovall (sax-al); Budd Johnson (sax-
    tn); Pete Johnson (pno); Jimmy Shirley
    (gtr); Abe Bolar (db); Jack Parker (drm)
New York, 2 January 1946 (National, Savoy),
    J4177
        "I May Be Wonderful"
        "Man Wanted"

(Jones does not sing on other selections from
this session.)

George Treadwell (tpt); Richard Harris
    (trb); Budd Johnson (sax-tn); Jimmy
    Jones (pno); Al McKibbon (db); J. C.
    Heard (drm)
New York, 11 June 1946 (Victor), J4525

"Blues to End All Blues"
"Among My Souvenirs"
"Mean to Me"
"Osculate Me, Daddy"

Joe Newman (tpt); Richard Harris (trb);
  George Nicholas, Pete Clarke (sax-tn);
  Jimmy Jones (pno); John Collins (gtr);
  Al McKibbon (db); J. C. Heard (drm)
New York, 11 March 1947 (Victor), J4526
  "My Sleepy Head"
  "I Sold My Heart to the Junkman"
  "The Richest Guy in the Graveyard"
  "Ain't No Hurry, Baby"

Budd Johnson (sax-tn); Luther Henderson
  (pno); Herman Mitchell (gtr); Herman
  Alpert (db); Denzil Best (drm)
New York, 8 October 1947 (Victor), J4527
  "What Ev'ry Woman Knows"
  "Overwork Blues"
  "Misery Is a Thing Called Moe"
  "This Is a Fine Time"

Earl Hines
Jonah Jones (tpt); Benny Green (trb); Aaron
  Sachs (cl, sax-tn); Earl Hines (pno);
  Tommy Potter (db); Osie Johnson (drm)
New York, 15 December 1952 (D'Oro,
  Crown), H5877–78
  "One Night in Trinidad"
  "Stop"

(Jones does not sing on other selections
from this session.)

Jerome Richardson (sax-tn, fl); Don Abney
  (pno); Bill Jennings (gtr); Tommy Potter
  (db); Bobby Donaldson (drm)
New York, 18 April 1957 (King), J4528
  "People Will Say We're in Love"
  "When I Fall in Love"
  "S'posin'"
  "Mountain Greenery"

Personnel as on previous session, but with
  Skeeter Best (gtr) replacing Jennings.
New York, 20 April 1957 (King), J4529
  "Don't Worry 'bout Me"

"White Cliffs of Dover"
"Sweethearts on Parade"
"You Call It Madness"
"I Thought about You"
"Since I Fell for You"
"I'm Gonna Lock My Heart and Throw
  Away the Key"

Don't Go to Strangers
Frank Wess (sax-tn, fl); Richard Wyands
  (pno); Skeeter Best (gtr); George Duvivier
  (db); Roy Haynes (drm)
Englewood Cliffs, N.J., 21 June 1960 (Pres-
  tige), J4530
  "On the Street Where You Live"
  "Something to Remember You By"
  "Bye Bye Blackbird"
  "Where or When"
  "All the Way"
  "Yes Sir, That's My Baby"
  "Don't Go to Strangers"
  "I Love Paris"
  "Fine and Mellow"
  "If I Had You"

(Jones had fourteen sessions for Prestige
from 21 June 1960 through 12 February
1963. I include only the first of them, which
includes "Don't Go to Strangers." For full
details, see Lord J4530–43.)

Ms. Jones to You
Houston Person (sax-tn); Walter Davis
  (pno); Jimmy Ponder (gtr); Buster
  Williams (db); Grady Tate (drm); Larry
  Killian (drm-cg, perc)
New York, 1 July 1976 (Muse), J4546
  "I'm Gonna Lock My Heart and Throw
    Away the Key"
  "Gone Again"
  "Second Time Around"
  "If That's the Way You Feel"
  "Exactly Like You"
  "I'm All for You"
  "You'd Better Love Me"

(From 1976 until, probably, 1993, Jones
released twelve Muse albums as leader. I
include only the first of them. For details

about almost all of them, see Lord
J4546–50, J4552–54, J4556–59.)

Horace Ott

(Because Ott's writing for "popular" musicians and groups is generally well known,
I detail only his involvement with leaders
included in Lord's discography. Except as
noted, Ott arranged all selections listed
here.)

Doris Troy
Horace Ott (pno); Napoleon "Snags" Allen
    (gtr); Barney Richmond (db); Bruno Carr
    (drm); Doris Troy (voc)
New York, 5 March 1963 (Atlantic), T5595
    "Just One Look"

(I cannot determine if Ott arranged another
selection from this session.)

Solomon Burke
Irv Markowitz, Robert Scott (tpt); Ben
    Smith, Sam Taylor (sax-tn); Haywood
    Henry (sax-bt); Artie Butler (pno); Billy
    Butler, George Barnes, Bob Bushnell (gtr);
    Russ Saunders (bs-el); Bobby Donaldson
    (drm); Solomon Burke (voc)
New York, 16 August 1963 (Atlantic), B9575
    "You're Too Good for Me"

(I cannot determine if Ott arranged other
selections from this session. Lord states that
Gary Sherman arranged all the selections.)

Nina Simone
Broadway Blues Ballads
Horace Ott (dir); Nina Simone (voc); other
    personnel unknown
Unknown location, 1964 (Philips), S6517
    "Don't Let Me Be Misunderstood"
    "Don't Take All Night"
    "Our Love"
    "Why Keep on Breaking My Heart"

Nina Simone
Nuff Said!
Nina Simone (voc, pno); unknown (gtr);
    Gene Taylor (db); unknown (drm)

New York, 7 April 1968 (RCA), S6538
    "Do What You Gotta Do"

(I cannot determine if Ott arranged other
selections from this session.)

Jimmy McGriff
Electric Funk
Blue Mitchell (tpt); Stanley Turrentine (sax-
    tn); Jimmy McGriff (org); Horace Ott
    (pno-el, dir); unknown (bs-el), unknown
    (drm)
Englewood Cliffs, N.J., September 1969
    (Blue Note, Solid State), M4134
    "Back on the Track"
    "Chris Cross"
    "Miss Poopie"
    "The Bird Wave"
    "Spear for Moon Dog" (pt 1)
    "Spear for Moon Dog" (pt 2)
    "Tight Times"
    "Spinning Wheel"
    "Funk Junk"

Joe Williams
Worth Waiting For
Horace Ott (cond); Joe Williams (voc);
    unknown large orchestra
Los Angeles, 5–6, 8 May 1970 (Blue Note),
    W6404–6
    "Baby"
    "Here's That Rainy Day"
    "Something"
    "Bridges"
    "I'd Be a Fool Right Now"
    "I Hold no Grudge"
    "Lush Life"
    "Little Girl"
    "Didn't We"
    "Oh, Darling"
    "Can't Take My Eyes off You"
    "You Send Me"

Houston Person
Houston Express
Ernie Royal, Thad Jones, Money Johnson
    (tpt); Jack Jeffers, Garnett Brown (trb);
    Harold Vick (sax-tn, fl); Houston Person
    (sax-tn); Babe Clark (sax-bt); Jimmy

Watson (org); Paul Griffin (pno, pno-el); Billy Butler (gtr); Gerry Jemmott (bs-el); Bernard Purdie (drm); Buddy Caldwell (drm-cg); Horace Ott (cond)
Englewood Cliffs, N.J., 8 April 1971 (Prestige), P2751
  "Young, Gifted and Black"
  "Houston Express"
  "Lift Every Voice"
  "Enjoy"

Bobbi Humphrey
Dig This!
Bobbi Humphrey (fl); George Marge (oboe, eng-hrn); Harry Whitaker (pno-el); Paul Griffin (pno-el, clavinet); William Fontaine, David Spinozza (gtr); Ron Carter (db); Wilbur Bascomb, Jr. (bs-el); Alphonse Mouzon (drm, bell tree, arr); Warren Smith (perc); Paul Winter, Paul Gershman, Irving Spice, Seymour Berman (vln); Julian Barber (viola); Seymour Barab (cello); Gene Bianco (harp)
New York, 20–21 July 1972 (Blue Note), H8600
  "Lonely Town, Lonely Street"
  "I Love Every Little Thing about You"
  "Nubian Lady"

(Ott did not arrange other selections from this session.)

Lou Donaldson
Sassy Soul Strut
Thad Jones (tpt); Garnett Brown (trb); Lou Donaldson (sax-al); Seldon Powell (fl, sax-tn); Buddy Lucas (hrmca); Horace Ott (pno-el, cond); Paul Griffin (pno-el, pno, org); David Spinozza, John Tropea, Hugh McCracken (gtr-el); Wilbur Bascomb (db); Bernard Purdie (drm); Omar Clay, Jack Jennings (perc)
New York, 17–18 April 1973 (Blue Note), D3837–38
  "Sanford and Son Theme"
  "This Is Happiness"
  "Inner Space"
  "Pillow Talk"
  "Sassy Soul Strut"

  "Good Morning, Heartache"
  "City, Country, City"

Richard "Groove" Holmes
Night Glider
Garnett Brown (trb); Seldon Powell (sax-tn); Richard "Groove" Holmes (org); Horace Ott (pno-el); Lloyd Davis (gtr); Paul Martinez (db); Bernard Purdie (drm); Kwasi Jayourba (drm-bg, drm-cg)
New York, c. 1973 (Groove Merchant), H7105
  "Night Glider"
  "Flyjack"
  "It's Going to Take Some Time"
  "Pure Cane Sugar"
  "Go Away, Little Girl"
  "One Mint Julep"
  "Young and Foolish"

(I cannot determine if Ott arranged all selections from this session.)

Lou Donaldson
Sweet Lou
Danny Moore, Joe Shepley, Ernie Royal (tpt); Garnett Brown (trb); Lou Donaldson (sax-al); Seldon Powell, Arthur Clark (sax-tn, fl); Buddy Lucas (hrmca); Horace Ott (key, synt, cond); Paul Griffin (clavinet); Cornell Dupree, David Spinozza, Hugh McCracken (gtr); Wilbur Bascomb (bs-el); Bernard Purdie, Jimmy Young (drm); unknown (drm-cg), unknown (vibr), unknown (perc); Barbara Massey, Hilda Harris, Eileen Gilbert, Carl Williams, Jr., William Sample, Bill Davis, Eric Figueroa (voc)
New York, 14, 19, 21 March 1974 (Blue Note), D3839–41
  "Hip Trip"
  "If You Can't Handle It, Give It to Me"
  "Love Eyes"
  "Peepin'"
  "Sugar Foot"
  "Herman's Mambo"
  "Lost Love"
  "You're Welcome, Stop on By"

Dakota Staton
Madame Foo Foo
Richard "Groove" Holmes (org); Horace Ott
    (pno-el); Cornell Dupree (gtr); Paul Mar-
    tinez (db); Bernard Purdie (drm); Kwasi
    Jayourba (drm-cg)
New York, July 1974 (Groove Merchant),
    S11127
        "Let It Be Me"
        "Congratulations to Someone"
        "Let Me off Uptown"
        "A House Is not a Home"
        "Blues for Tasty"
        "Losin' Battle"
        "Deep in a Dream"
        "Confessin' the Blues"
        "Candy"
        "Moonglow"

(I cannot determine if Ott arranged all
selections from this session.)

Houston Person
Harmony
Jon Faddis (tpt); Houston Person (sax-tn);
    Babe Clark (sax-bt, fl); Paul Griffin (key);
    Horace Ott (key, cond); John Tropea,
    Jerry Friedman (gtr); Wilbur Bascomb
    (db); Lawrence Killian, George Devens,
    Master Henry Gibson (perc)
New York, March 1977 (Mercury), P2768
        "Harmony, Perfect Harmony"
        "Do It While You Can"
        "I Write the Songs"
        "I No Get Eye for Back"
        "Love Is All We Need"

Houston Person
The Gospel Soul of Houston Person
Houston Person (sax-tn); Ogletree
    Brothers, Atlanta Philharmonic
    Chorale, Verolyn Hardwick, Morris
    Bankston (voc)
Atlanta, c. 1978 (Savoy), P2771
        "Enjoy"

(I cannot determine if Ott arranged other
selections from this session.)

Arthur Prysock
Here's to Good Friends
Evan Solot, Rocco Bene (tpt, flug); Roger
    Delillo, Bob Moore (trb); Richard Gen-
    ovese (trb-bs); Michael Pedicin, Jr. (sax-al,
    sax-bt); Carlton "Cotton" Kent (key);
    Ronnie James (gtr); Vince Fay (db); Grant
    MacAvoy (drm); Larry B. Washington
    (drm-cg); Don Reynaldo
Philadelphia and New York, c. 1978 (Old
    Town / MCA)
        "Midnight Blue"
        "Here's to Good Friends"
        "Sad Eyes"
        "The Love I Need"
        "All I Can Do Is Cry"
        "Sad"
        "Spunky"
        "Funny How Time Slips Away"
        "Baby, I'm-a Want You"

Houston Person
Suspicions
Virgil Jones (tpt); Houston Person (sax-tn);
    Ernie Hayes, Sonny Phillips, Horace Ott
    (key); Jack Cavari, Melvin Sparks Hassan
    (gtr); Wilbur Bascomb (db); Idris
    Muhammad (drm); Ralph Dorsey (perc)
Englewood Cliffs, N.J., 24 April 1980
    (Muse), P2772
        "Suspicions"
        "Pieces"
        "Let's Love Again"

(Ott did not arrange other selections from
this session.)

Houston Person
Heavy Juice
Houston Person (sax-tn); Jon Logan (org);
    David Braham (pno-el, synt); Melvin
    Sparks (gtr); Wilbur Bascomb (db);
    Bernard Purdie, Billy James (drm); Ralph
    Dorsey (perc)
Englewood Cliffs, N.J., 24 June 1982 (Muse),
    P2774
        "Theme from Loveboat"
        "Let the Feeling Flow"

(Ott did not arrange other selections from this session.)

Houston Person

(Person plays tenor saxophone on all selections.)

Johnny "Hammond" Smith
Mr. Wonderful
Sonny Williams (tpt); Johnny "Hammond" Smith (org); Eddie McFadden (gtr); Leo Stevens (drm)
New York, 1963 (Riverside), S8117
    "Blues for De-De"
    "Mr. Wonderful"
    "Cyra"
    "Lambert's Lodge"
    "Love Letters"
    "Blues on a Sunday"
    "Departure"
    "Opus 2"

(Person recorded at least eleven sessions with Smith from 1963 through 21 September 1970. I include only the first of them. For full details see Lord S8120, S8122–24, S8126–29, S8132–33.)

Sonny Phillips
Sure 'Nuff
Virgil Jones (tpt); Sonny Phillips (org); Joe Jones (gtr); Bob Bushnell (bs-el); Bernard Purdie (drm)
Englewood Cliffs, N.J., 20 October 1969 (Prestige), P3739
    "Sure 'Nuff, Sure 'Nuff"
    "Mobile to Chicago"
    "Be Yourself"
    "The Other Blues"
    "Oleo"
    "Two Different Worlds"

Gene Ammons
The Boss Is Back
Gene Ammons, Prince James (sax-tn); Junior Mance (pno); Buster Williams (db); Frankie Jones (drm)
Englewood Cliffs, N.J., 10 November 1969 (Prestige), A2337

    "The Jungle Boss"

(Person does not play on other selections from this session.)

Horace Silver
That Healin' Feelin'
Randy Brecker (tpt, flug); Horace Silver (pno-el); Jimmy Lewis (db); Idris Muhammad (drm); Jackie Verdel, Gail Nelson (voc)
Englewood Cliffs, N.J., 18 June 1970 (Blue Note), S6293
    "Permit Me to Introduce You to Yourself"
    "Wipe Away the Evil"
    "Nobody Knows"
    "There's Much to Be Done"

Bernard Purdie
Shaft
Gerry Thomas, Danny Moore (tpt); Willy Bridges (sax-tn); Neal Creque (pno-el); Billy Nichols, Lloyd Davis (gtr); Gordon Edwards (bs-el); Bernard Purdie (drm)); Norman Pride (drm-cg)
Englewood Cliffs, N.J., 11 October 1971 (Prestige). P6597
    "Shaft"

(Person does not play on other selections from this session.)

Tiny Grimes
Profoundly Blue
Harold Mabern (pno); Tiny Grimes (gtr, voc); Jimmy Lewis (bs-el); Freddie Waits (drm); Gene Golden (drm-cg)
New York, 6 March 1973 (Muse), G5448
    "Blue Midnight"
    "Backslider"
    "Tiny's Exercise"
    "Profoundly Blue"
    "Matilda"
    "Cookin' at the Cookery"

The Real Thing
Marcus Belgrave, Donald Townes (tpt); Eli Fountain (sax-al); Wild Bill Moore

(sax-tn); Jack McDuff, Sonny Phillips, Jimmy Watson (org); Robert Lowe, Grant Green (gtr); James Jamerson (bs-el); Hank Brown, Idris Muhammad (drm); Bobby Caldwell (drm-cg); Etta Jones, Spanky Wilson (voc) (collective personnel)
Detroit, 14–15 March 1973 (Eastbound), P2756–62
 "You Are the Sunshine of My Life"
 "Where is the Love?"
 "Tain't Nobody's Business If I Do"
 "Don't Go to Strangers"
 "Since I Fell for You"
 "Easy Walker"
 "Angel Eyes"
 "Until It's Time for You to Go"
 "Crazy Legs"
 "Could It Be I'm Falling in Love"
 "Pain"
 "Kittitian Carnival"

Stolen Sweets
Sonny Phillips (org); Jimmy Ponder (gtr); Frankie Jones (drm); Buddy Caldwell (drm-cg)
New York, 29 April 1976 (Muse), P2765
 "If Ever I Would Leave You"
 "At Last"
 "Stolen Sweets"
 "Skylark"
 "T-Bone Steak"

Pure Pleasure
Cecil Bridgewater (tpt); Paul Griffin (key); Bruce Nazarian (synt, gtr); Bob Babbitt (db); Alan Schwartzberg (drm); Lawrence Killian (drm-cg); Patti Austin (voc); Jimmy Roach (arr, cond); unknown strings and voices
New York, 14–17 June 1976 (Mercury), P2767
 "Pure Pleasure"
 "Déjà vu"
 "Dancing Feet"
 "Soul Serenade"
 "Inseparable"
 "You'll Never Find Another Love"

Harmony
Jon Faddis (tpt); Babe Clark (sax-bt, fl); Paul Griffin (key); Horace Ott (key, arr, cond); John Tropea, Jerry Friedman (gtr); Wilbur Bascomb (db); Lawrence Killian, George Devens, Master Henry Gibson (perc)
New York, March 1977 (Mercury), P2768
 "Harmony, Perfect Harmony"
 "Do It While You Can"
 "I Write the Songs"
 "I No Get Eye for Back"
 "Love Is All We Need"

Wild Flower
Bill Hardman (tpt); Sonny Phillips (org); Jimmy Ponder (gtr); Idris Muhammad (drm); Larry Killian (drm-cg, perc)
Englewood Cliffs, N.J., 12 September 1977 (Muse), P2769
 "Preachin' and Teachin'"
 "Dameron"
 "Wild Flower"
 "Ain't Misbehavin'"
 "My Romance"

Ran Blake
Suffield Gothic
Ran Blake (pno)
New York, 28–29 September 1983 (Soul Note), B5230
 "Curtis"
 "Vanguard"
 "Indian Winter"
 "Midnight Local to Tate Country"

(Person does not play on other selections from this session.)

Chris Potter

Presenting Chris Potter
John Swana (tpt, flug); Chris Potter (sax-sp, sax-al, sax-tn); Kevin Hays (pno); Christian McBride (db); Lewis Nash (drm)
New York, 29 December 1992 (Criss Cross), P5284
 "Juggernaut"
 "Uneasy Dreams"

"The Tail That Wags the Dog"
"Reflections"
"So Far"
"Solar"
"Cindy's Story"
"General Rodney"

Fujitsu-Concord 25th Jazz Festival Silver Anniversary Set
Chris Potter (sax-tn); Marian McPartland (pno); Bill Douglass (db); Omar Clay (drm)
Concord, Calif., 30–31 July 1993 (Concord), P5285
    "Gone with the Wind"
    "My Foolish Heart"
    "I'll Remember April"

(Potter does not play on other selections from these sessions.)

Sundiata
Chris Potter (sax-sp, sax-al, sax-tn); Kevin Hays (pno); Doug Weiss (db); Al Foster (drm)
New York, 13 December 1993 (Chris Cross), P5286
    "Fear of Flying"
    "Hibiscus"
    "Airegin"
    "New Lullaby"
    "Sundiata"
    "Body and Soul"
    "Leap of Faith"
    "C. P.'s Blues"

Concentric Circles
Chris Potter (sax-sp, sax-al, sax-tn, fl, cl-bs); Kenny Werner (pno); John Hart (gtr); Scott Colley (db); Bill Stewart (drm)
New York, 17, 20 December 1993 (Concord), P5287
    "El Morocco"
    "Klee"
    "Blues in Concentric Circles"
    "Dusk"
    "Lonely Moon"
    "You and the Night and the Music"

"Mortal Coils"
"In a Sentimental Mood"
"Aurora"

Pure
Chris Potter (sax-sp, sax-al, sax-tn, fl, cl-bs); Larry Goldings (pno, org); John Hart (gtr); Larry Grenadier (db); Al Foster (drm)
New York, 14–15 June 1994 (Concord), P5288
    "Salome's Dance"
    "Checking Out"
    "Resonance"
    "Bad Guys"
    "Boogie Stop Shuffle"
    "Second Thoughts"
    "That's What I Said"
    "Fool on the Hill"
    "Bonnie Rose"
    "Easy to Love"
    "The Distant Present"
    "Every Time We Say Goodbye"

Chris Potter / Kenny Werner
Chris Potter (sax-sp, sax-tn, cl-bs); Kenny Werner (pno)
Berkeley, Calif., 9 October 1994 (Concord), P5289
    "Hibiscus"
    "Boulevard of Broken Time"
    "Istanbul"
    "Sail Away"
    "Tala"
    "September Song"
    "The New Left"
    "Epistrophy"
    "Hey Reggie"
    "Giant Steps"

Moving In
Chris Potter (sax-sp, sax-tn, cl-bs); Brad Mehldau (pno); Larry Grenadier (db); Billy Hart (drm)
New York, 6–7 February 1996 (Concord), P5291
    "Nero's Fiddle"
    "Book of Kells"

"Moving In"
"A Kiss to Build a Dream On"
"Rhubarb"
"South for the Winter"
"The Forest"
"Pelog"
"Chorale"
"Old Faithful"

Unspoken
Chris Potter (sax-sp, sax-tn); John Scofield
  (gtr); Dave Holland (db); Jack DeJohnette
  (drm)
West Shokan, N.Y., 21–23 May 1997
  (Concord)
    "Wistful"
    "Seven Eleven"
    "Hieroglyph"
    "Amsterdam Blues"
    "Et Tu, Bruté?"
    "Unspoken"
    "No Cigar"
    "Time Zone"
    "New Vision"

Vertigo
Chris Potter (sax-sp, sax-tn, cl-bs); Joe
  Lovano (sax-tn); Kurt Rosenwinkel (gtr);
  Scott Colley (db); Billy Drummond
  (drm)
New York, 9–10 April 1998 (Concord)
    "Shiva"
    "Vertigo"
    "Long Walk, Short Pier"
    "Act III, Scene I"
    "Fishy"
    "This Will Be"
    "Almost Home"
    "Modeen's Mood"
    "Wake Up"

Joanne Brackeen
Pink Elephant Magic
Nicholas Payton (tpt); Chris Potter (sax-sp);
  Joanne Brackeen (pno); John Patitucci
  (db); Horacio Hernandez (drm); Jamey
  Haddad (perc)
New York, June or August 1998 (Arkadia),
  *B11226–7, *B11228–7, *B11231–7

"Pink Elephant Magic"
"Beethoven Meets the Millennium
   in Spain"
"In Vogue"
"Cram 'n Exam"

(Potter does not play on other selections
from these sessions.)

Gratitude
Chris Potter (sax-sp, sax-al, sax-tn, cl-bs, fl);
  Kevin Hays (pno); Scott Colley (db);
  Brian Blade (drm)
New York, 27–28 September 2000 (Verve)
    "The Source"
    "Shadow"
    "Sun King"
    "High Noon"
    "Eurydice"
    "The Mind's Eye" (intro)
    "The Mind's Eye"
    "Gratitude"
    "The Visitor"
    "Body and Soul"
    "Star Eyes"
    "Vox Humana"
    "What's New"

Traveling Mercies
Chris Potter (sax, cl-bs, fl, org, voc, sam-
  ples); Adam Rogers, John Scofield (gtr);
  Scott Colley (db); Bill Stewart (drm)
New York, 27–29 January 2002 (Verve)
    "Megalopolis"
    "Snake Oil"
    "Invisible Man"
    "Washed Ashore"
    "Children Go"
    "Any Moment Now"
    "Migrations"
    "Azalea"
    "Highway One"
    "Just As I Am"

Lift: Live at the Village Vanguard
Chris Potter (sax-tn); Kevin Hays (pno);
  Scott Colley (db); Bill Stewart (drm)
New York, 13–14 December 2002 (Sunny-
  side), *P5603–7

"7.5"
"What You Wish"
"Stella by Starlight"
"Lift"
"Okinawa"
"Boogie Stop Shuffle" (saxophone
   intro)
"Boogie Stop Shuffle"

Underground
Chris Potter (sax-tn); Craig Taborn (pno);
   Wayne Krantz, Adam Rogers (gtr); Nate
   Smith (drm)
Brooklyn, N.Y., January 2005 (Sunnyside)
   "Next Best Western"
   "Morning Bell"
   "Nudnik"
   "Lotus Blossom"
   "Big Top"
   "The Wheel"
   "Celestial Nomad"
   "Underground"
   "Yesterday"

Arthur Prysock

(Except as noted, Prysock sings on all selections.)

Buddy Johnson
Gus Aiken, Lewis Dupree (Dupree Bolton),
   Henry Glover, Willis Nelson, Herbert
   Turner (tpt); Bernard Archer, Leonard
   Briggs, Gordon Thomas (trb); Joe
   O'Laughlin, Maxwell Lucas (sax-al);
   Frank Henderson, Jimmy Stanford (sax-
   tn); Teddy Conyers (sax-bt); Buddy John-
   son (pno, arr); Leon Spann (db); George
   Jenkins (drm)
New York, 4 October 1944 (Decca), J3502
   "They All Say I'm the Biggest Fool"

(Prysock does not sing on other selections
from this session. He had eighteen recording
sessions with Buddy Johnson from 4 October 1944 through 24 January 1952. I include
only the first. For full details, see Lord
J3502–19.)

Coast to Coast
Herb Gordy (arr); other personnel
   unknown
Unknown location, c. 1962 (Old Town),
   P6407, P6409
   "Love Look Away"
   "Blue Velvet"
   "You Are Too Beautiful"
   "I Left My Heart in San Francisco"
   "What Kind of Fool Am I"
   "Fly Me to the Moon"
   "You'll Never Know"
   "I'll Follow You"
   "April Showers"
   "What's New"
   "They All Say I'm the Biggest Fool"

Count Basie
Count Basie / Arthur Prysock
Probable personnel: Al Aarons, Sonny Cohn,
   Wallace Davenport, Phil Guilbeau (tpt);
   Grover Mitchell, Henderson Chambers,
   Bill Hughes, Al Grey (trb); Marshal Royal
   (sax-al, cl); Bobby Plater (sax-al, fl); Eric
   Dixon (sax-tn, fl); Eddie "Lockjaw" Davis
   (sax-tn); Charlie Fowlkes (sax-bt); Count
   Basie (pno); Freddie Green (gtr); Norman
   Keenan (db); Rufus Jones (drm); Frank
   Foster, Billy Byers, Mort Gerson (arr)
New York, 13–14 December 1965 (Verve),
   B2516
   "I Worry 'bout You"
   "What Will I Tell My Heart"
   "I'm Lost"
   "Come Rain or Come Shine"

Count Basie
Count Basie / Arthur Prysock
Personnel as on previous session, but with
   Grady Tate (drm) replacing Jones; Henry
   Coker (trb) and Dick Hyman (org, arr)
   added.
New York, 20–21 December 1965 (Verve),
   B2517
   "I Could Have Told You"
   "Ain't No Use"
   "I Could Write a Book"
   "Gone Again"

"Come on Home"
"Don't Go to Strangers"
"I'm Gonna Sit Right Down and Write
   Myself a Letter"

This Is My Beloved
Arthur Prysock, recitation; other personnel
   unknown
Los Angeles, 16 December 1968 (Verve),
   P6433
   "I Need Your Love"
   "Your Eyes"
   "Your Words"
   "Your Body Makes Eyes at Me"
   "Come Love Me"
   "I Was Very Tired and Lonely"
   "You Did not Come"
   "I Stood Long Where You Left Me"
   "Each Season Every Year"
   "Eleven Years"
   "Remembering How We Could Be
      Warm Together"
   "Sleeping . . . So Still, So Still"
   "I Shall Wish for You"

Here's to Good Friends
Evan Solot, Rocco Bene (tpt, flug); Roger
   Delillo, Bob Moore (trb); Richard Gen-
   ovese (trb-bs); Michael Pedicin, Jr. (sax-al,
   sax-bt); Carlton "Cotton" Kent (key); Ron-
   nie James (gtr); Vince Fay (db); Grant
   MacAvoy (drm); Larry B. Washington
   (drm-cg); Horace Ott (arr); Don Reynaldo
Philadelphia and New York, c. 1978 (Old
   Town / MCA)
   "Midnight Blue"
   "Here's to Good Friends"
   "Sad Eyes"
   "The Love I Need"
   "All I Can Do Is Cry"
   "Sad"
   "Spunky"
   "Funny How Time Slips Away"
   "Baby, I'm-a Want You"

A Rockin' Good Way
Red Prysock (sax-tn); Lloyd Wilson (key);
   Randy Caldwell (gtr); Ralph Hamperian
   (db); Don Williams (drm)

New York, 29–30 July 1985 (Milestone),
   P6449
   "I Want to Thank You, Girl"
   "Bloodshot Eyes"
   "Every Morning Baby"
   "Next Time You See Me"

(Milestone was part of what was then
Fantasy.)

A Rockin' Good Way
Personnel as on previous session, but with
   Betty Joplin (voc) added.
New York, 1–2 August 1985 (Milestone),
   P6450
   "Baby (You've Got What It Takes)"
   "Teach Me Tonight"
   "Passing Strangers"
   "A Rockin' Good Way"

This Guy's in Love with You
Personnel as on previous session, but with
   Jimmy Lewis (db) replacing Hamperian.
New York, August 1986 (Milestone), P6451
   "Rainy Night in Georgia"
   "Bring It on Home to Me"
   "At Last"
   "This Guy's in Love with You"
   "I Wonder Where Our Love Has Gone"
   "Good Rockin' Tonight"
   "Don't Misunderstand"
   "Everything Must Change"
   "Send Me the Pillow That You
      Dream On"

Drink Small

(Small plays guitar on all selections.)

The Spiritual Airs of Columbia, S. C.
Bernard Codwell, Charles Derrick, Joseph
   Hollis, Louis Johnson, Norris Turner (voc)
Columbia, S.C., April 1956 (Vee-Jay)
   "When the Saints Go Marching In"
   "Can't Hide Sinner"

The Spiritualaires of Columbia, S. C.
Personnel as on previous session, but with
   Small (voc) added on "I'm Going on to
   Glory."

Columbia, S.C., August 1956 (Vee-Jay)
  "I'm out on Life's Ocean"
  "I'm Going on to Glory"

The Spiritualaires of Columbia, S. C.
Personnel as on previous session, but with
  Small (voc) out.
Columbia, S.C., 1957 (Vee-Jay)
  "Pressing On"
  "Family Prayer"

Kip Anderson
Columbia, S.C., 1959 (Vee-Jay)
Kip Anderson (pno, voc); Howard Overton
  (drm)
    "I Want to Be the Only One"
    "The Home Fire Is Brighter after
      a While"

Newark, N.J., 20 November 1959 (Sharp)
Drink Small (voc); and others (studio musicians)
    "I Love You Alberta"
    "Cold, Cold Rain"

*I Know My Blues Are Different, Cause I'm the
  One Who Has Them*
Columbia, S.C., 197? (Southland)
Drink Small (voc)
    "Ugly Woman Blues"
    "Worth a Million Dollars"
    "If My Luck Don't Change"
    "Liquor and Women"
    "A Sad Time"
    "You Make Me Feel So Good"
    "One Woman Is Enough for Me"
    "Bow Legged Woman"
    "You Can Call Me Country"
    "Can't Kill Nothing"
    "My Baby Loves Me Right"
    "My Rod"
    "Hangover Blues"
    "Corn Whiskey"

Blues Doctor: Live & Outrageous!
Charleston, S.C., 10 October 1986 (Erwin
  Music)
Doug Allen (db); Larry Palmer (drm);
  Drink Small (voc)
    "Charleston Woman Blues"

Blues Doctor: Live & Outrageous!
Charleston, S.C., 1 June 1987 (Erwin Music)
Drink Small (voc)
    "Swing Low, Sweet Chariot"
    "Glory Hallelujah"
    "I Really Don't Want to Know"
    "The Red Rooster"
    "Thank You, Pretty Baby"
    "Shout"
    "The Twist"
    "Stormy Monday Blues"

Columbia, S.C., June 1987 (Bishopville)
Drink Small (voc)
    "I'm Gonna Shag My Blues Away"
    "I'm in Love with a Grandma"

Blues Doctor: Live & Outrageous!
Charleston, S.C., 21 February 1988 (Erwin
  Music)
Donnie Reid (key); Donald Johnson (drm);
  Drink Small (voc)
    "I Feel Good"
    "I Stand Accused"

The Blues Doctor
Atlanta, 1990 (Ichiban)
James Carter (key, org); Drink Small (voc);
  and others
    "Tittie Man"
    "Little Red Rooster"
    "So Bad"
    "Something in the Milk Ain't Clean"
    "Rub My Belly"
    "Baby Leave Your Panties Home"
    "Stormy Monday Blues"
    "I'm Going to Move to the Outskirts
      of Town"
    "John Henry Ford"

Round Two
Atlanta, 1991 (Ichiban)
Ernie Baker (tpt, arr); Ted Dortch (sax); Jeff
  Baker (hrmca); Buzz Amato (pno); James
  Carter (pno, org); Wayne Goins (gtr);
  Lebron Scott (db); Bryan Cole (drm) Sal
  Padillo (perc); Drink Small (voc)
    "D.U.I."
    "Steal Away"

"Thank You, Pretty Baby"
"Don't Let Nobody Know"
"Widow Woman"
"I'm Tired Now"
"Honky Tonk"
"They Can't Make Me Hate You"
"Bishopville Women"
"Can I Come over Tonight?"

Drink Small Does It All
Columbia, S.C., 2003 (Bishopville)
Drink Small (voc, pno); Mamie Roberts,
   Preston Rivers (voc)
   "I Want to Make Love"
   "You Don't Have to Be Funky"
   "Fish Fryin' Mama"
   "A Woman Is the Sweetest Thing God
      Ever Made"
   "Bingo Lover"
   "Mr. Green Is the Barbecue Man"
   "South Carolina Boogie"
   "You Can't Take the Country out of
      Me"
   "Coon Shine Baby"
   "Plain Old Country Blues"
   "Come on, Let Me Love You"
   "You Got to Love Everybody in the
      World"
   "Glory, Glory"
   "Motherless Child"
   "I'm Gonna Run On"
   "Roll, Jordan, Roll"

Jabbo Smith

(Smith plays cornet or trumpet on all selections.)

Thomas Morris
Thomas Morris (crnt); Geechie Fields (trb);
   Ernest Elliott (cl, sax-tn, sax-bt); Happy
   Caldwell (cl, sax-tn); Mike Jackson (pno,
   voc); Lee Blair (bj); Bill Benford (tba)
New York, 17 August 1926 (OFC, Vic, RCA),
   M10442
   "Georgia on My Mind" (2 takes)
   "Ham Gravy" (2 takes)

Eva Taylor
Charlie Irvis (trb); Clarence Williams (pno);
   unknown (gtr); Eva Taylor (voc)
New York, 10 February 1927 (Okeh), T1044
   "I Wish You Would Love Me Like I'm
      Loving You"
   "If I Could Be with You One Hour
      Tonight"

Duke Ellington
Louis Metcalf (tpt); Joe Nanton (trb); Otto
   Hardwick (cl, sax-al, sax-bt); Rudy Jack-
   son (cl, sax-tn); Harry Carney (cl, sax-al,
   sax-bt); Duke Ellington (pno); Fred Guy
   (bj); Wellman Braud (db); Sonny Greer
   (drm); Adelaide Hall (voc)
New York, 3 November 1927 (Okeh), E949
   "What Can a Poor Fellow Do?"
   "Black and Tan Fantasy" (3 takes)
   "Chicago Stomp Down" (3 takes)

Louisiana Sugar Babes
Garvin Bushell (cl, sax-al, bassoon); James P.
   Johnson (pno); Fats Waller (org)
Camden, N.J., 27 March 1928 (Victor, HMV,
   Bluebird), L5438, where the group is
   named Louisiana Sugar Babies
   "Willow Tree" (3 takes)
   "'Sippi" (3 takes)
   "Thou Swell" (3 takes)
   "Persian Rug" (2 takes)

Omer Simeon (cl, sax-al); Cassino Simpson
   (pno); Ikey Robinson (bj)
Chicago, 29 January 1929 (Brunswick),
   S7902
   "Jazz Battle"

Personnel as on previous session, but with
   Hayes Alvis (tba) and Jabbo Smith (voc)
   added.
Chicago, 22 February 1929 (Brunswick),
   S7903
   "Little Willie Blues"
   "Sleepy Time Blues"

Personnel as on previous session.
Chicago, 23 February 1929 (Brunswick),
   S7904

"Take Your Time"
"Sweet and Low Blues"

Personnel as on previous session.
Chicago, 1 March 1929 (Brunswick), S7905
    "Take Me to the River"
    "Aces of Rhythm"
    "Let's Get Together"
    "Sau Sha Stomp"

Personnel as on previous session, but with
    Earl Frazier (pno) replacing Simpson.
Chicago, 30 March 1929 (Brunswick), S7906
    "Michigander Blues"

Personnel as on previous session.
Chicago, 4 April 1929 (Brunswick), S7907
    "Decatur Street Tutti"
    "Till Times Get Better"

Personnel as on previous session, but with
    Jabbo Smith (trb) and Millard Robbins
    (sax-bs) added.
Chicago, 17 April 1929 (Brunswick), S7908
    "Lina Blues"
    "Weird and Blue"

Personnel as on previous session, but with
    George James (cl, sax-al) replacing
    Simeon and Jabbo Smith (trb) out.
Chicago, 9 June 1929 (Brunswick), S7909
    "Croonin' the Blues"
    "I Got the Stinger"

Personnel as on previous session, but with
    Omer Simeon (sax-tn) added, Lawson
    Buford (tba) replacing Alvis, and Jabbo
    Smith (voc) out.
Chicago, 8 August 1929 (Brunswick), S7910
    "Boston Skuffle"
    "Tanguay Blues"

Personnel as on previous session.
Chicago, 22 August 1929 (Brunswick),
    S7911
    "Band Box Stomp"
    "Moanful Blues"

Hidden Treasure, vols. 1 and 2
Jabbo Smith (tpt, trb, voc); Frank Chace
    (cl); John Dengler (sax-bs); Art Gronwall
    (pno); Marty Grosz (gtr); Bob Saltmarsh
    (drm)
Chicago, 3 June 1961 (Jazz Art), S7013–15
    "Love Me or Leave Me" (2 takes)
    "Sunday" (2 takes)
    "Anything for You"
    "These Foolish Things" (4 takes)
    "Diga Diga Doo"
    "Rosetta" (3 takes)
    "Keepin' out of Mischief" (3 takes)
    "I Found a New Baby"

Hidden Treasure, vols. 1 and 2
Jabbo Smith (tpt, voc), Frank Chace (cl);
    Marty Grosz, Big Mike McKendrick (gtr);
    Whitey Mitchell (db)
Chicago, 15 October 1961 (Jazz Art), S7015
    "When a Woman Loves a Man"
    "I Want a Little Girl"
    "Sweet Georgia Brown" (2 takes)
    "I Can't Believe That You're in Love
        with Me"
    "Squeeze Me"

Barry Walker (Fatback)

(Walker plays guitar on all selections.)

Anthology
Michael Martin (tpt); George Pindar (key);
    Barry Walker (Fatback) (gtr, db, voc);
    Michael Mahoney (db); Kenny Rolle,
    Bryan Harris (drm)
Columbia, S.C., 1991–2004 (no label)
    "Soup De' Jour"
    "If You Don't Love Me"
    "I'd Rather Go Blind"
    "Found Your Man"
    "Everyday Blues"
    "King Bee"
    "G Funk"
    "Mind Travel"
    "Blues Had a Baby"
    "The Next Best Thing"
    "Saint James Infirmary"
    "C.O.D."

"Hey Now"
"Little Girl"
"I Got My Eye on You"
"Drum Interlude"
"G Jam"
"I Tried To"

(*Anthology* includes all the tunes originally released on the CDs *Fatback and the Groove Band* and *The Next Best Thing*.)

Ron Westray

(Westray plays trombone on all selections.)

Marcus Roberts
As Serenity Approaches
New Orleans, June 1991 (Novus), R4363
Marcus Roberts (pno)
    "Creole Blues"

(Westray does not play on other selections from these sessions.)

Marcus Roberts
Portraits in Blue
Scotty Barnhart, E. Dankworth (Wynton Marsalis), Marcus Printup (tpt); Wycliffe Gordon (trb); Mark Shim, Ted Nash, Wessell Anderson, Victor Goines, Walter Blanding, Bill Easley, Vincent Herring, Peter Yellin (reeds); Marcus Roberts (pno); James Chirillo (bj, gtr); Ronald Guerin, Ben Wolfe (db); Jason Marsalis (drm); William Grant Still (orchestration); Robert Sadin (cond)
New York, 2, 4, 7 June 1995 (Sony), R4368
    "Rhapsody in Blue"
    "Yamekraw"

Marcus Roberts
Portraits in Blue
Personnel as on previous session.
New York, 13 July 1995 (Sony), R4369
    "I Got Rhythm" (variations)

Wycliffe Gordon
Bone Structure

Wycliffe Gordon (trb, tba); Marcus Roberts (pno); Reginald Veal (db); Herlin Riley (drm)
New Orleans, January 1996 (Atlantic), *G4705–7
    "Coming Is Going"
    "What?!"
    "Modern Nostalgia"
    "It's Time"
    "Rhythm Cone"
    "Blooz"
    "New Beginnings (Groove Cone)"
    "Esoteric Advent (Turkish Coffee)"
    "Everyday . . ."
    "Way Back When"
    "Mayfest Junction (Cone's Place)"

Lincoln Center Jazz Orchestra
Don't Be Afraid: The Music of Charles Mingus
Lew Soloff, Marcus Printup, Ryan Kisor, Wynton Marsalis (tpt); Andre Heyward (trb, tba); Vincent Gardner (trb); Ted Nash (fl, sax-sp); Victor Goines (cl, cl-bs, sax-tn); Joe Temperley (cl-bs, sax-bt); Wessell Anderson (sax-al); Walter Blanding (sax-tn); Eric Lewis (pno); Carlos Henriquez (db); Herlin Riley (drm); Ron Westray (arr)
New York, 22–28 August 2003 (Palmetto), *L4479.60–7
    "Dizzy Moods"
    "Black Saint and the Sinner Lady" (parts 1 and 2)
    "Meditation on Integration"
    "Tijuana Gift Shop"
    "Los Mariachis"
    "Don't Be Afraid, the Clown's Afraid Too"

Johnny Williams

(Williams plays baritone saxophone on all selections.)

Count Basie
Have a Nice Day
Paul Cohen, Sonny Cohn, George Minger, Waymon Reed (tpt); Al Grey, Bill Hughes,

Melvin Wanzo, Grover Mitchell, John
Watson, Sr. (trb); Bobby Plater, Curtis
Peagler (sax-al); Eddie "Lockjaw" Davis
(sax-tn); Eric Dixon (sax-tn, fl); Count
Basie (pno); Freddie Green (gtr); Norman
Keenan (db); Harold Jones (drm); Sammy
Nestico (arr)
Hollywood, July–August 1971 (Daybreak),
B2561
    "Have a Nice Day"
    "The Plunger"
    "Jamie"
    "It's about Time"
    "This Way"
    "Scott's Place"
    "Doin' Basie's Thing"
    "The Spirit Is Willing"
    "Small Talk"
    "You 'n' Me"
    "Feelin' Free"

Joe Williams
Live in Vegas
Probable personnel: Paul Cohen, Sonny
Cohn, Pete Minger, Waymon Reed (tpt,
flug); Al Grey, Grover Mitchell, Melvin
Wanzo, John Watson (trb); Bill Hughes
(trb-bs); Bobby Plater (sax-al, fl); Curtis
Peagler (sax-al); Eric Dixon (sax-tn, fl);
Eddie "Lockjaw" Davis (sax-tn); Cecil
Payne (sax-bt, fl); Count Basie (pno);
Freddie Green (gtr); Norman Keenan
(db); Harold Jones (drm)
Las Vegas, June or October 1971 (Monad),
W6411
    "Las Vegas" (intro)
    "Everyday"
    "Don't Get around Much Anymore"
    "Please Send Me Someone to Love"
    "Watch What Happens"
    "Smack Dab in the Middle"
    "Monologue"
    "A Time for Love"
    "Nobody Loves You When You're Down
      and Out"
    "When You Gotta Go"
    "Roll 'Em Pete"

Count Basie
Flip, Flop & Fly
Paul Cohen, Sonny Cohn, Pete Minger,
Waymon Reed (tpt); Al Grey, Frank
Hooks, Melvin Wanzo (trb); Bill Hughes
(trb-bs); Bobby Plater (sax-al, fl); Curtis
Peagler (sax-al); Eric Dixon (sax-tn, fl);
Eddie "Lockjaw" Davis, Jimmy Forrest
(sax-tn); Count Basie (pno); Freddie
Green (gtr); Norman Keenan (db);
Harold Jones (drm); Joe Turner (voc)
Paris, 17 April 1972; Frankfurt, 24 April
1972 (Pablo), B2563
    "Hide and Seek"
    "T.V. Momma"
    "Corrinne, Corrinna"
    "Cherry Red"
    "Shake, Rattle & Roll"
    "Since I Fell for You"
    "Flip, Flop & Fly"
    "Every Day I Have the Blues"
    "Good Morning Blues"

Count Basie
Kansas City Shout
Pete Minger, Sonny Cohn, Dale Carley,
David Stahl (tpt); Mitchell "Booty" Wood,
Bill Hughes, Dennis Wilson, Grover
Mitchell, Dennis Rowland (trb); Eddie
"Cleanhead" Vinson (sax-al, voc); Danny
Turner, Bobby Plater (sax-al); Eric Dixon
(sax-tn, fl); Kenny Hing (sax-tn); Count
Basie (pno); Freddie Green (gtr); Cleve-
land Eaton (db); Duffy Jackson (drm); Joe
Turner (voc)
Hollywood, 7 April 1980 (Pablo), B2599
    "Just a Dream on My Mind"
    "Blues for Joe Turner"
    "Blues for Joel"
    "Everyday I Have the Blues"
    "Blues au Four"
    "I Got a Gal That Lives up on a Hill"
    "Cherry Red"
    "Apollo Daze"
    "Standing on the Corner"
    "Stormy Monday"
    "Signifying"

Sarah Vaughan
Send in the Clowns
Sonny Cohn, Bob Summers, Frank Szabo,
 Willie Cook, Dale Carley (tpt); Mitchell
 "Booty" Wood, Bill Hughes, Dennis Wil-
 son, Grover Mitchell (trb); Kenny Hing,
 Danny Turner (sax-al); Eric Dixon, Bobby
 Plater (sax-tn); George Gaffney (pno);
 Freddie Green (gtr); Andy Simpkins (db);
 Harold Jones (drm); Sammy Nestico,
 Allyn Ferguson (arr)
Hollywood, 16–18 February, 16 May 1981
 (Pablo), V1091
  "I Gotta Right to Sing the Blues"
  "Just Friends" (2 takes)
  "Ill Wind"
  "If You Could See Me Now"
  "I Hadn't Anyone 'til You" (2 takes)
  "Send in the Clowns"
  "All the Things You Are"
  "Indian Summer"
  "When Your Lover Has Gone"
  "From This Moment On"

Webster Young

(Except where noted, Young plays trumpet
or cornet on all selections.)

Ray Draper
Ray Draper Quintet
Ray Draper (tba); Jackie McLean (sax-al);
 Mal Waldron (pno); Spanky DeBrest (db);
 Ben Dixon (drm)
Hackensack, N.J., 15 March 1957 (Prestige),
 D4990
  "House of Davis"
  "Terry Ann"
  "You're My Thrill"
  "Pivot"
  "Jackie's Dolly"
  "Mimi's Interlude"

Interplay for Two Trumpets and Two Tenors
Idrees Sulieman (tpt); John Coltrane, Bobby
 Jaspar (sax-tn); Mal Waldron (pno);
 Kenny Burrell (gtr); Paul Chambers (db);
 Art Taylor (drm)
Hackensack, N.J., 22 March 1957 (Prestige),
 I470

  "Anatomy"
  "Interplay"
  "Light Blue"
  "Soul Eyes"

(This session has no leader. Young does not
play on another selection from this session.)

For Lady
Paul Quinichette (sax-tn); Mal Waldron
 (pno); Joe Puma (gtr); Earl May (db); Ed
 Thigpen (drm)
Hackensack, N.J., 14 June 1957 (Prestige),
 Y832
  "The Lady"
  "God Bless the Child"
  "Moanin' Low"
  "Don't Explain"
  "Good Morning, Heartache"
  "Strange Fruit"

Ray Draper and Jackie McLean
Strange Blues
Ray Draper (tba); Jackie McLean (sax-al);
 Jon Mayer (pno); Bill Salter (db); Larry
 Ritchie (drm)
Hackensack, N.J., 12 July 1957 (Prestige),
 D4991, M4603
  "Disciples Love Affair"
  "Millie's Pad"

(Young does not play on another selection
from this session.)

Jackie McLean
Makin' the Changes and *A Long Drink of the
 Blues*
Curtis Fuller (trb); Jackie McLean (sax-al,
 sax-tn); Gil Coggins (pno); Paul Cham-
 bers (db); Louis Hayes (drm)
Hackensack, N.J., 30 August 1957 (New
 Jazz), M4604
  "Jackie's Ghost"
  "What's New"
  "Chasing the Bird"
  "A Long Drink of the Blues" (2 takes)

Jackie McLean
Fat Jazz

Ray Draper (tba); Jackie McLean (sax-al);
  Gil Coggins (pno); George Tucker (db);
  Larry Ritchie (drm)
New York, 27 December 1957 (Jubilee),
  M4605
    "Filide"
    "Millie's Pad"
    "Two Sons"
    "What Good Am I without You"
    "Tune Up"

*Webster Young Plays the Miles Davis Song-
  book*, vol. 3
John Hicks (pno); John Mixon (db); Gene
  Gammage (drm); Webster Young (voc)
St. Louis, 5 August 1961 (VGM), Y833
    "Shirley's Horn"
    "What's New"

*Webster Young Plays the Miles Davis Song-
  book*, vols. 1–3
Freddie Washington (sax-tn); John Chap-
  man (pno); John Mixon (db); Chauncey
  Williams (drm)
St. Louis, 21 August 1961 (VGM), Y834,
  Y836, Y838
    "Whispering"
    "Stablemates"
    "Ray's Idea"
    "Beautiful Love"

"East St. Louis Shoot Out"
"Miles' Theme"

*Webster Young Plays the Miles Davis Song-
  book*, vol. 2
Personnel as on previous session, but with
  Red Anderson (sax-tn) added.
St. Louis, 21 August 1961 (VGM), Y837
    "When Lights Are Low"

*Webster Young Plays the Miles Davis Song-
  book*, vol. 3
Personnel as on previous session, but with
  Jodie Christian (pno) replacing Chap-
  man.
St. Louis, 21 August 1961 (VGM), Y839
    "Oleo"

*Webster Young Plays the Miles Davis Song-
  book*, vol. 1
Personnel as on previous session, but with
  Red Anderson out.
St. Louis, 21 August 1961 (VGM), Y835
    "When I Fall in Love"

*Webster Young Plays the Miles Davis Song-
  book*, vol. 2
Webster Young, unknown (narration)
St. Louis, 24 October 1980 (VGM), Y840
    "A Trumpet Player's Town" (interview)

INDEX

Pages in bold type indicate subject interviews.

ABOUT THE AUTHOR

BENJAMIN FRANKLIN V is Distinguished Professor Emeritus of English at the University of South Carolina. He hosted the program *Jazz in Retrospect* on the South Carolina Educational Radio Network and NPR from 1977 until 1992. Franklin has published numerous books, articles, and reviews about American literature, including *The Other John Adams, 1705–1740.*